CONTEMPORARY PUBLIC SPEAKING
HOW TO CRAFT AND DELIVER A POWERFUL SPEECH
SECOND EDITION

ANDREA D. THORSON-HEVLE
MARK L. STALLER
MICHAEL M. KORCOK

Kendall Hunt
publishing company

Kendall Hunt
publishing company

www.kendallhunt.com
Send all inquiries to:
4050 Westmark Drive
Dubuque, IA 52004-1840

CONTENTS

PREFACE

The purpose of this book is to provide our readers with a clear and comprehensive understanding of the public speaking process. Traditional textbooks are written from one point of view. However, every public speaking instructor has a unique and valuable perspective. Consequently, this textbook incorporates multiple voices, perspectives, and approaches. We believe this contemporary, collaborative endeavor creates more space for the classroom instructor's own voice.

In its original conception this book was written with college class instruction in mind, but it certainly has its usefulness outside of the classroom. Public speaking is a skill and art that has enormous power. People of all ages, places in life, and employment situations can benefit from learning how to craft and deliver a powerful speech.

This textbook covers the traditional areas of public speaking, but it also dives deeper than most other texts, into conversations of language, technology, and verbal support. It is our hope that first-time speakers will find this book provides a clear path to becoming excellent speakers and that experienced speakers will find great growth through reading and understanding the more complex and reflective processes of public speaking.

An important undercurrent of the book is diversity and accommodation. Each instructor who helped create this book currently teaches at Bakersfield College, which is known for its celebrated and large communication program and its great diversity. Our book recognizes the importance of multicultural teaching and diversity in public speaking.

Additionally, textbook prices have, for four decades now, substantially outpaced the broader economy. Neither taxpayers nor our students will pay escalating costs. The textbook business has even been described as a "broken market" as a consequence. Here at Bakersfield College, a substantial part of the student body just can't afford to pay for over-priced texts.

One of the primary motivations in writing this book has been to create an affordable public speaking textbook. The publishers have worked with us to keep the price of the textbook and associated online content well below comparable work. For many of our students, that isn't just a nicety, it might well be the difference between having a textbook for the course or not. We have worked hard to make the text affordable.

The authors who created this book did so out of a deep appreciation for public speaking and a desire to have a useful tool to teach with. Our book is saturated with the deep experience, unique background, and extensive knowledge of its authors. The authors of this text have over 150 years of combined experience teaching the public speaking course.

The primary authors have been involved in competitive, advocacy, and instructional speaking for most of their lives. They have each coached or competed for teams that won national recognition. To us, speech is not just a subject that we teach; it is a skill and art. A carefully crafted and effectively delivered speech has the power to change the world.

The Bakersfield College Communication Department has collaborated with Kendall Hunt publishers to produce a series of affordable, practical communication textbooks for first and second year college students: *Contemporary Public Speaking: How to Craft and Deliver a Powerful*

Speech, Small Group Work in the Real World: A Practical Guide, and *Intercultural Communication: Building Relationships and Skills*. A fourth textbook, *Let's Get Personal: Creating Successful Relationships Through Effective Interpersonal Communication*, will be available in the Fall of 2015.

FOREWORD

PRESIDENT OF BAKERSFIELD COLLEGE
SONYA CHRISTIAN

Bakersfield College started in 1913 when a small and isolated rural community decided to expand access to education by offering college classes. The town had only recently reincorporated in the late 1890s but some of its citizens had a vision of the central valley as a land of opportunity, and they wanted to give their youth a path to the great university of Berkeley.

Just as streams create the path for rivers, this modest beginning has grown into the current Bakersfield College campus, a vibrant community of scholars of all types: budding scientists, skilled workers, musicians, and technicians. Each year, hundreds of students complete their studies and continue on to CSUB, Berkeley, and beyond; each year, hundreds more join a diverse workforce with its roots at Bakersfield College.

The Communications Department is situated on the northern edge of this educational community. One of the largest communication certificate programs and one of the top 20 community college departments in the discipline, the department has won a model teaching award from the Western States Communication Association, and has multiple national titles in forensics and debate.

From this educational wellspring comes the book you have in hand. The three main authors are talented educators and highly decorated forensic coaches, and two equally recognized competitors. They value information being "openly" available and are in the process of submitting this book as an "open educational resource," meaning that it is created in hopes of becoming expressly free for educational use—and the life of education grows where information flows.

I trust that you will enjoy this book, appreciate its origins, learn from the wealth of skill and experience that went into its making, and, as opportunities arise, freely contribute in turn to the Communications community.

INTRODUCING PUBLIC SPEAKING

Mark L. Staller

Learning Objectives

1 Recognize the power and purposes of public speaking

2 Appreciate the ancient and modern influences in the field of public speaking

3 Distinguish public speaking from other forms of discourse

4 Apply ethical principles to public speaking situations

Welcome, first, into the ranks of public speaking students. Practically every college student in every state of our nation has to take (and pass) a course in public speaking in order to fulfill a general education requirement in oral communication. Educators and legislators have decided that speaking in public is an essential life skill that every well-educated person should develop.

Welcome, second, to this public speaking textbook. It has been written by over half a dozen different public speaking instructors who have pooled together their public speaking knowledge and experience for your benefit. Our goal is to provide clear, accessible, useful information about the art of public speaking. If you read this textbook carefully and apply its principles to the speeches you give in your public speaking class, you should have little difficulty fulfilling the course requirements.

However, our hope is that, with the help of your public speaking instructor and this textbook, you will do more than fulfill the requirements of a required college course: we hope that you will become a proficient public speaker who can communicate effectively in any public speaking situation you face, inside or outside the college classroom. In addition, we want to foster in you an admiration of, and respect for, public speaking. We want you to become an enthusiastic, confident public speaker. We also want you to become a perceptive, appreciative audience member when you listen to others speak.

To get you started in your public speaking course, we have divided this introductory chapter into six main sections: 1) The Power and Purposes of Public Speaking, 2) The Foundations of Public Speaking, 3) The Three Rhetorical Appeals, 4) The Transactional Model of Communication, 5) Public Speaking and Other Forms of Communication, and 6) Public Speaking and Ethics. As you read this chapter, you will learn about the basic public speaking concepts and concerns listed here, and you will begin to develop the vocabulary you need to grasp the theory and practice of public speaking.

You will also discover how the following chapters in this textbook can enhance your public speaking knowledge. We reference the other chapters often in this introductory chapter to orient you to this textbook and to let you know what to expect as you read on. We instructors wish you good success as you enter into our discipline!

FIGURE 1.1

Susan B. Anthony is memorialized on the Liberty dollar coin. *Answer Q1*

PART 1: THE POWER AND PURPOSES OF PUBLIC SPEAKING

Public speaking is powerful. It can change the world. One person can use the power of public speaking to influence and transform society. Susan B. Anthony (1820–1906) lectured tirelessly for women's rights in America and Europe throughout the late 1800s; through her efforts and the efforts of other determined women suffragists, women in America were finally granted the right to vote in 1920.

Martin Luther King, Jr. (1929–1968) gave speeches that galvanized and unified complacent black and white moderates to participate in Civil Rights demonstrations for African-Americans in the 1960s. His "I Have a Dream" speech, given on the steps of the Lincoln Memorial in Washington, DC, on August 28, 1963, is now recognized as a defining moment in the Civil Rights movement in America. This speech was a catalyst for the passage of the Civil Rights Acts of 1964 and 1968.

Cesar Chavez (1927–1993), cofounder of the National Farm Workers Association, gave hundreds of speeches to migrant farm workers in the 1960s and 1970s that instilled pride in the Latino community and led to grass roots organizing for higher wages and better working conditions. His slogan, "Si, se puede," ("Yes, it is possible," or "Yes, it can be done") is still inspiring new generations of Mexican-Americans.

Public speaking is an integral and essential part of our political system, our legal system, and our modern media culture. In American politics, public speeches are used to influence the election of candidates, to promote the passage or defeat of public policies, and to increase or decrease public support for political parties and their platforms. Sometimes the outcome of an election is primarily determined by the success or failure of one public speech.

FIGURE 1.2

Martin Luther King, Jr. is memorialized in a stone monument. *Answer Q1*

FIGURE 1.3

Cesar Chavez is memorialized on a United States postage stamp. *Answer Q1*

FIGURE 1.4

Modern media technology makes public speaking more powerful than ever.

In the American legal system, public speeches are used to prosecute criminals, to defend human beings and human rights, and to determine the intent and scope of laws. Sometimes one public speech can alter the course of legal history.

In our modern media culture, public speeches that inform, persuade, and entertain are broadcast over our airwaves and through our digital devices twenty-four hours a day, seven days a week. Public speeches are used in newscasts, infomercials, and variety shows. Public speeches are heard on the radio, watched on the television, and streamed on the Internet. Sometimes a public speech preserved by modern electronic media becomes a cultural treasure, memorializing and representing the values and beliefs of our nation at a particular point in time.

THREE MAJOR TYPES OF PUBLIC SPEECHES

Three common speech types are 1) the speech to inform, 2) the speech to persuade, and 3) the speech to entertain. An informative speech is designed to present information that most audience members do not already know. A persuasive speech is designed to move an audience to action, or to convince audience members to change their minds or shift their positions on controversial issues. A speech to entertain is designed to make an audience laugh or to provide pleasure to audience members through the creative use of language.

You will learn more about informative speaking in Chapter 15 (Speaking to Inform), you will learn more about persuasive speaking in Chapter 16 (Speaking to Persuade), and you will learn more about speaking to entertain in Chapter 17 (Speaking for Special Occasions).

Public speaking is not a "dying art" that is being undermined by modern electronic media. On the contrary, public speaking is more powerful than ever. One public speech originally given to a relatively small audience can now "go viral" and reach millions of additional people.

Public speaking has the power to change the world at large, but it also has the power to change your personal world. You can transform your life by becoming an effective public speaker. Good public speaking skills can help you land a great job or get a coveted promotion at work. Good public speaking skills can help you win a prestigious scholarship or earn a spot on a popular team at school.

FIGURE
1.5 Good speaking skills give you a public voice.

If you lack public speaking skills, some doors of opportunity will be forever closed to you. You will not be able to become a trial lawyer. You will not be able to become a successful salesperson. You will not be able to become a teacher or professor. It will be difficult to become a boss or supervisor or leader of any kind.

You need public speaking skills to give oral reports in class, at club meetings, and at work. You need public speaking skills to fulfill your social obligations at family gatherings, weddings, and funerals. You need public speaking skills to participate in some student government activities. You need public speaking skills to participate in some religious services or observations. You need public speaking skills to advocate at your local city council or school board meeting for issues that matter to you.

You can influence others through your public speaking skills, but other people are also trying to influence you through their speeches. You need instruction in public speaking to become an effective listener and evaluator of the speech messages of others. As you hone your skills in public speaking, you will improve your ability to identify and respond to the persuasive strategies employed by other speakers. Knowledge is power. Public speaking knowledge gives you the power to become both a good speaker and a perceptive listener.

PART 2: THE FOUNDATIONS OF PUBLIC SPEAKING (THE WESTERN RHETORICAL TRADITION AND MODERN COMMUNICATION STUDIES)

We should acknowledge that if you were studying public speaking in another country, you might be focusing on different historical facts and figures; after all, human beings in almost every culture have been fascinated by the power of public speaking. We can trace an interest in eloquence to ancient India, China, Africa, and the pre-European cultures of North and South America. However, you are studying public speaking in modern America, so you are part of the "western" rhetorical tradition with Greco-Roman roots.

The Greek term *rhetor* is equivalent to the Latin term *orator*, so ancient rhetoric was the "art of oratory." In the ancient Greek city-states, if you wanted to carry a lawsuit forward, you would have to represent yourself in court—there was no professional class of lawyers to plead your case. In addition, you might find yourself speaking in front of a jury of five hundred (or even five thousand) fellow citizens. You faced a similar public speaking situation if you wanted to get involved in the politics of your city: every free male in your town was granted a vote in the local political assembly. (Women and slaves were excluded.) If you were a male citizen, you might find yourself addressing several hundred or several thousand people at once—a daunting public speaking challenge.

FIGURE
1.6 Aristotle systematized Greek rhetoric.

FIGURE
1.7 Cicero developed Roman rhetoric.

The pressing need for effective public speaking skills in ancient Greece quickly gave rise to public speaking instructors and textbooks. Corax and his student Tisias are recognized as two of the earliest teachers of forensic (legal) rhetoric in the West, practicing their craft in ancient Sicily as early as 466 BC. Gorgias (483–376 BC) was a popular speechmaker and teacher who made a name (and a living) for himself in Athens by emphasizing an ornate speaking style that generated strong emotions in his audience.

The philosopher Plato (428–348 BC) founded an influential school of philosophy in Athens and wrote several philosophical dialogues which called Gorgias' art of oratory into question. However, across town, Plato's educational rival, Isocrates (436–376 BC), set up a school of oratory that also had a wide influence on the citizens of Athens. (Tip: Do not confuse *Socrates*, Plato's teacher and mentor, with *Isocrates*, Plato's educational rival. Socrates was a private citizen of Athens considered by many to be the founder of western philosophy, whereas Isocrates was a teacher of rhetoric recognized primarily for his instruction in public speaking.)

In ancient Greek and Roman society, the educational competition between philosophers and rhetoricians was eventually won by the rhetoricians: the height of a Greek and Roman education was training in rhetoric. In order to be an effective citizen, in order to succeed in law and politics, a person needed specialized training in public speaking. Plato's student Aristotle (384–322 BC) abandoned Plato's attacks on oratory and wrote *The Rhetoric*, a foundational and very influential public speaking textbook. Two Romans greatly influenced by Aristotle's *Rhetoric* were Cicero (106–43 BC) and Quintilian (35–95 AD). Both men further developed and expanded the study of rhetoric—Cicero in his *De Oratore*, and Quintilian in *The Institutes of Oratory*.

As a student of public speaking in the western rhetorical tradition, you have inherited a host of useful concepts and vocabulary words from the Greeks and Romans. For example, there is a well-established way of describing the speech-making process based upon the Five Canons of Rhetoric. You learned a certain vocabulary from your English writing instructors to describe the essay-writing process, words like pre-writing, brainstorming, rough draft, revision, editing, and final draft.

This vocabulary that describes the writing process has only been developed in the last few decades. However, the vocabulary that your public speaking instructor may use to describe the speech-making process is about two thousand years old. The **Five Canons of Rhetoric** break the speech-making process down into five processes or stages: 1) Invention; 2) Arrangement; 3) Style; 4) Memory; and 5) Delivery.

1 **Invention** is the process of coming up with the ideas for your speech. The chapters in this textbook that will help you work through the invention process are Chapter 3 (Considering Your Audience), Chapter 4 (Choosing Your Speech Topic), Chapter 5 (Researching for Your Speech), and Chapter 6 (Developing Verbal Support).

2 **Arrangement** is the process of placing your ideas in an appropriate order. The chapters in this textbook that focus on the arrangement process are Chapter 7 (Organizing Your Speech) and Chapter 8 (Outlining Your Speech).

3 **Style** is the process of choosing the precise words to express your ideas. Check out Chapter 13 (Using Language Effectively) to learn how to express your ideas in effective words.

4 **Memory** is/was the process of committing your words to memory. Memory is the one canon of rhetoric that has been substantially altered in modern public speaking instruction and practice. Four primary methods of delivery are now recognized: 1) impromptu, 2) manuscript, 3) memorized, and 4) extemporaneous delivery.

Impromptu delivery is "spur of the moment" or "off the cuff" speaking. At most, the speaker uses a "scratch" outline to keep on track, but much of the speech is created on the spot as the speaker speaks.

Manuscript delivery requires the speaker to write the speech out word-for-word and then read from a manuscript word-for-word.

Memorized delivery requires the speaker to write the speech out word-for-word, commit it to memory, and then deliver the speech from memory word-for-word.

Extemporaneous delivery is the method of delivery most often taught by public speaking instructors today because it allows the speaker to prepare and practice the speech ahead of time, but it does not require the speaker to read or memorize the speech word-for-word for delivery. The speech is written out in a detailed, logically structured preparation outline, and then it is transferred to a "key word" delivery outline. During the delivery of the speech, the speaker only glances at the delivery outline when necessary. You can learn more about the strengths and weaknesses of these four primary types of delivery in Chapter 9 (Delivering Your Speech).

5 **Delivery** the fifth and final canon of rhetoric, is the process of presenting your speech to your audience. The chapters in this textbook that will help you deliver your speech effectively are Chapter 2 (Managing Public Speaking Anxiety), Chapter 9 (Delivering Your Speech), Chapter 10 (Making and Using Presentation Aids), and Chapter 11 (Using Technology for Oral Presentations).

The Five Canons of Rhetoric	Definition
Invention	Creating your ideas
Arrangement	Organizing your ideas
Style	Expressing your ideas in words
Memory	Committing your words to memory
Delivery	Presenting your speech to your audience

FIGURE
1.8 The Five Canons of Rhetoric (The Five Steps of the Speech-Making Process).

The five canons of rhetoric have been introduced in this first chapter because they help you get a basic understanding of the speech-making process. The specialized terms invention, arrangement, style, and delivery provide speech instructors and their students a common vocabulary to discuss how to put a speech together.

Another useful foundational concept we introduce in this chapter is the concept of the **Three Rhetorical Appeals**. In *The Rhetoric*, Aristotle noted that there are three primary ways a speaker can persuade an audience: 1) the *ethos* appeal, 2) the *logos* appeal, or 3) the *pathos* appeal. **Ethos** is an appeal to the audience through the projected character of the speaker. **Logos** is a persuasive appeal directed at the understanding or reasoning capacity of the audience. **Pathos** is a persuasive appeal that works by generating emotions in the audience.

A specialized vocabulary is an element of almost any academic subject. Some people may wish to replace the Latin or Greek terms used in the field of rhetoric—terms like *invention* and *ethos*—with modern, "less-confusing" English equivalents. However, these specialized terms have been part of the vocabulary of public speaking teachers and students in the western world for over two thousand years, and they will continue to be used because this jargon is an accurate, shorthand way of referring to important rhetorical concepts.

One more word needs to be said about the specialized vocabulary of modern public speaking: modern public speaking instruction is not only influenced by the two-thousand-year-old western rhetorical tradition, but it is also greatly influenced by the approximately one-hundred-year-old history of the National Communication Association.

This organization traces its roots back to 1914, when the National Association of Academic Teachers of Public Speaking (NAATPS) was founded. Over the years, the name of the organization changed several times: in 1923, the NAATPS became the NATS (National Association of Teachers of Speech). In 1946, the NATS became the SAA (Speech Association of America). In 1970, the SAA became the SCA (Speech Communication Association). Finally, in 1997, the SCA became the NCA (National Communication Association).

One reason for the name changes in the organization was the increasing influence of the social sciences. An organization that was once narrowly focused on public speaking over time took a broader interest in all forms of human communication. This new interest was accompanied by new research methods and programs that focused on the systematic development of scientific terms and theories that could help us better understand all forms of human communication.

Public speaking is now classified by Communication scholars as one type of oral communication among several. Public speaking is usually defined as the monological (one-way) oral

public speaking
Answers @9

communication of one speaker with a large, live audience; **interpersonal communication** is one-on-one communication that occurs between two human beings; **small group communication** is communication that occurs in groups of approximately three to twelve people; **organizational communication** is both communication within an organization and communication between that organization and outside entities; **intercultural communication** is communication between people of substantially different culture groups; and **mass communication** is communication with masses of people through the aid of communication technologies.

Types of Communication	Definition
Public speaking	Monological, one-way verbal discourse
Interpersonal	One-on-one, dyadic discourse
Small group	Discourse between 3 and 12 people
Organizational	Discourse within and without an organization
Intercultural	Discourse between substantially different culture groups
Mass	Discourse mediated by communication technologies

answer Q8

Different types of communication.

FIGURE
1.9

Because Communication scholars have taken a broad interest in all forms of human communication, they have developed a scientific vocabulary that helps us describe any type of communication interaction. After introducing you to the three rhetorical appeals (which is a product of classical rhetoric) in the third section of this chapter, we then introduce you to the Transactional Communication Model (which is a product of the modern social science approach to the study of communication) in the fourth section. You will learn the terminology that lets you describe any human communication in general terms: a communicator *encodes* a *message* and sends it through a communication *channel* to another communicator who *decodes* this message and sends *feedback* to the originator. This modern communication vocabulary, like the vocabulary we can trace back to the Greeks and Romans, is also very useful.

As a modern public speaking student, you are fortunate to belong to a hybrid discipline that owes a debt to both the classical rhetorical tradition and to the modern study of communication. Respect both the old and the new, and you will thrive in your study and practice of public speaking.

PART 3: THE THREE RHETORICAL APPEALS
(AND THE RHETORICAL TRIANGLE)

As we mention in Part 2 of this chapter, the ancient Greek philosopher Aristotle wrote a foundational public speaking text called *The Rhetoric* that sets forth three primary rhetorical appeals: speakers can try to persuade an audience by projecting a positive image of themselves (the *ethos appeal*), or speakers can try to persuade an audience by appealing to their understanding or rea-

Speaker
(Ethos)

Speech
(Logos)

Audience
(Pathos)

1.10 The Rhetorical Triangle.

soning capacity (the *logos appeal*), or speakers can try to persuade an audience by appealing to their emotions (the *pathos appeal*).

An explanation of these three primary rhetorical appeals or modes of persuasion obviously belongs in Chapter 16 (Speaking to Persuade), but we have introduced you to ethos, logos, and pathos in this chapter because these appeals are associated with **the Rhetorical Triangle**. As the diagram here indicates, ethos is closely associated with *the speaker* who gives a speech, logos is closely associated with *the speech* or message given by the speaker, and pathos is closely associated with *the audience* that hears the speech and receives this message.

The rhetorical triangle visually reminds us that public speakers must always keep in mind these three essential elements: the speaker, the speech, and the audience. Let us take a closer look at each of these elements in reverse order.

The Audience: The pathos appeal is most closely associated with the audience. A public speaker may experience many emotions when delivering a speech, but the pathos appeal is concerned with the emotions that a speech stirs in the *audience*. Either a speech moves an audience, or it does not. Other communicators (writers, for example) may sometimes lose sight of their audience, but public speakers rarely do—the audience is right in front of them as they speak, and the audience will have an immediate favorable or unfavorable response to their message. As a public speaker, you need to be audience-centered. You should ask yourself, "What does my audience need in order to understand and receive my message, and what can I do to fulfill these needs?"

You will learn more about pathos appeals in Chapter 13 (Using Language Effectively) and Chapter 16 (Speaking to Persuade), but here is some advice about pathos appeals at the beginning of your public speaking course: do not rely solely on gripping stories or audience-pleasing delivery to make your speeches a success. Remember that pathos is only one of the three primary persuasive appeals. You are getting a college education, in part, to develop your reasoning skills, so do not overlook the importance of the logos appeal. In addition to emotionally powerful delivery techniques, you need to develop skills that will help you effectively research, organize, and support the ideas in your speech.

The Speech: The logos appeal is most closely associated with the speech itself. The speech itself is the vehicle that transports the thoughts and assertions of the speaker to the audience. Audience members can accept or reject the assertions and arguments contained in a speech. If the speech is recorded and transcribed, others can later analyze and evaluate the arguments and logic embedded in the speech text. Be aware that when you speak in public, people will evaluate not only *how* you delivered your words, they will also evaluate your thoughts themselves. Were your thoughts clear and understandable? Were your assertions reasonable? Were your arguments supported with good evidence and reasoning?

If you want to be a well-rounded, complete public speaker, then you must be a good thinker. The words you speak are verbal symbols for the ideas in your mind. If you do not have good ideas in your mind, it will be very difficult to generate words worth sharing. However, well-developed arguments and sound reasoning will give you quality thoughts and words of substance.

Chapter 6 (Developing Verbal Support) will teach you how to fully develop your ideas, and Chapter 14 (Reasoning) will help you make sure that your reasoning is sound.

The Speaker: The ethos appeal is most closely associated with the speaker. Ethos is the *projected* character of the speaker. Your ethos is not whom you actually are—it is the person whom you seem to be. Modern equivalents for the classical term "ethos" are "the public self" or "the presenting self." You need to think about the way you present yourself to your audience. Speakers often strive to come across as honest, sincere, intelligent people. (You wouldn't make much headway with an audience who thought you were a stupid, insincere liar, would you?)

In Chapter 7 (Organizing Your Speech), you will learn that ethos appeals are often placed near the beginning of a speech. After all, "you never get a second chance to make a first impression." Ethos appeals are also important at the beginning of a speech class. The very first day of your class, you started forming impressions of your speech instructor and the other students in the class. Be aware that they are also forming an impression of you.

Your accidental ethos is the part of your ethos you do not easily control—factors such as your sex, age, and prior reputation. Audience members will make assumptions about you because you are a man or a woman. They will make assumptions about you because you are young, middle-aged, or old. They will also make assumptions about you based on any "prior reputation" you may have.

At the beginning of your speech class, endeavor to create a good reputation for yourself. Show up to class on time with your work done. Listen attentively to your instructor and to the other students in the course. Strive to present yourself as an intelligent, organized, engaged student. Your good reputation will make it much easier to get the audience on your side when you stand to deliver your class speeches.

On the other hand, if you often come to class late or unprepared, if you "zone out" and appear to be uninterested or self-absorbed when others are speaking in class, then this bad behavior will create a bad reputation that becomes part of your accidental ethos. No matter how hard you try to present yourself in a positive light in your class speeches, your prior reputation will make giving a successful classroom speech an uphill battle.

As you conclude reading this section, we hope that you now see how relevant the two-thousand-year-old concepts of ethos, logos, and pathos are to your present public speaking efforts. Keep the rhetorical triangle in mind when you prepare your speeches. Your speeches are not just words written out on pieces of papers. Your speeches are communication transactions that can have a profound effect on both you and your audience. You will learn more about the interactive or "transactional" nature of public speaking in the next section.

The Rhetorical Triangle	The Rhetorical Appeals	Description
The Audience	The Pathos Appeal	An appeal to or through the emotions of the audience
The Speech	The Logos Appeal	An appeal to the reasoning capacity of the audience
The Speaker	The Ethos Appeal	An appeal through the projected character of the speaker

The Rhetorical Triangle and the Three Rhetorical Appeals.

FIGURE 1.11

PART 4: THE TRANSACTIONAL COMMUNICATION MODEL

One of the first modern conceptual models of the human communication process was developed by social scientists Claude Shannon and Warren Weaver in the late 1940s. Working for Bell Laboratories, they developed a linear model of human communication in order to analyze and explain some of the essential components of a telephone transmission.

In the 1960s and 1970s, social scientists and communication scholars modified and expanded this early model to describe in a general but precise way the essential elements of any human communication interaction. Rather than presenting human communication as a linear, one-way process, one of the most current models of human communication presents a communication event as a *transaction* between two or more human communicators.

Locate these eight essential elements of communication included in the diagram below:

1. The **communication situation** is the context in which the communication occurs.
2. A **communicator** is someone who either sends or receives a message.
3. **Encoding** is the mental process of transforming ideas and feelings into symbols.
4. A **message** is the content of a communication.
5. A communication **channel** is the medium that carries a message.
6. **Decoding** is the mental process of transforming received symbols back into ideas.
7. **Feedback** is any response that a receiver gives to a message.
8. Communication **noise** is anything that interferes with the transmission of a message.

COMMUNICATION SITUATION

noise

noise

Encodes/decodes
COMMUNICATOR
(sends & receives)

channel (MESSAGE) channel

channel (FEEDBACK) channel

noise

Encodes/decodes
COMMUNICATOR
(sends & receives)

noise

noise

© Kendall Hunt Publishing Company

FIGURE 1.12
The Transactional Model of Communication.

The transactional model of human communication is a conceptual device that helps us think about and describe what occurs in any human communication event. You can also use the transactional model of human communication to better understand what occurs when you stand in front of an audience to deliver a speech. Think about each of the essential communication elements in the context of public speaking.

The Communication Situation: The context in which communication occurs includes factors such as the location, the time, and the people involved. To be an effective public speaker, you must consider your speaking situation. How will the room you are speaking in be set up? When exactly will you be presenting your speech? How much time will you have? Who will be present in the audience? What frame of mind are they likely to be in when you present your speech?

The Communicator(s): In a public speaking situation, you are one of the primary communicators involved in the speech event, but you must also remember that every single audience member is also a communicator that is receiving (or not receiving) your message. You should use speaking strategies and techniques that will engage as many of your co-communicators as possible. For example, you should scan the entire audience and establish eye contact with many audience members. You should also use various arguments and examples that will appeal to the different kinds of people in your audience.

Encoding: The concept of encoding reminds you that there is a lot of mental work and "wordsmithing" involved in preparing a speech. You must develop and organize the ideas for your speech, and then you must choose the word symbols you will use to transmit these ideas. Chapter 13 (Using Language Effectively) includes instruction in types of words you need to avoid, as well as instruction in effective language that can enhance your speech message.

The Message Itself: The content of a human communication carries the encoded thoughts and feelings of the sender. Public speakers need to weed through the thousands of thoughts and emotions that flow through their stream of consciousness, and they need to select the ones that deserve to be encoded and transmitted in a formal speech message. Chapter 4 (Choosing a Speech Topic) will teach you how to select and narrow your speech topic so that you can come up with high-quality speech content.

You need to consider *where* you will be speaking and *to whom* you will be speaking and *how* you will be speaking, but you should not lose sight of *the speech message itself*. Your speech message should be designed to fulfill your speaking purpose, and your focus as a public speaker should be on delivering this message effectively.

Communication Channels: The two sensory communication channels used most often by public speakers are the visual channel and the auditory channel. Your audience *sees* you standing in front of the room, and they *hear* your voice as you speak. To be an effective public speaker, you must make good decisions about how to use these communication channels. Where should you position yourself during your speech to most effectively transmit your visual and auditory signals to your audience? Should you present your speech primarily through the auditory channel, or should you reinforce and enhance your message with visual aids?

Chapter 9 (Delivering Your Speech) will help you think about the visual and aural elements of your delivery. Chapter 10 (Making and Using Presentation Aids) will help you determine whether you should use visual aids in your speech, and, if so, what type of visual aids you should use.

Modern technology has created new communication channels for human communication. As a public speaker, you also need to use these technological channels of communication effectively. Should you speak to your audience "unplugged," or should you amplify your voice through a microphone? Should you mount your visual aids on low-tech poster boards, or should you present your visual aids with high-tech projection equipment? Should you load your presentation on a flash drive, or should you access your presentation through a high-speed Internet connection?

Chapter 11 (Using Technology) will teach you some of the different kinds of technology you can use to prepare and present your speech, and it will give you some of the pros and cons of each type of technology.

Decoding: The concept of *decoding* can sensitize you to the importance of using clear, unambiguous language when you speak in public, especially if your primary goal is to inform your audience. You may know what *you* mean when you use certain words or phrases in a speech, but will your audience members necessarily understand or interpret these words the same way you do? Meanings are not in words—meanings are in minds. When you deliver a speech message, you must be aware that your audience members have minds of their own, and you must make an effort to determine if they are decoding or interpreting your message correctly.

Feedback: Feedback is any verbal or nonverbal response that a receiver gives to a message. Take advantage of any oral or written feedback that your instructor and classmates provide to you after your classroom speeches. You can continuously improve your public speaking skills by using constructive feedback to strengthen any weak areas you may have as a speaker.

For any speech you deliver, pay attention to the immediate feedback your audience gives to you during your speech. This feedback will usually be nonverbal. You can gauge how your audience is responding to your speech message by paying attention to their body positions and facial expressions. For example, if many of your audience members are slouched in their chairs with blank looks on their faces, you probably are not communicating your speech message effectively. You can adjust your speech message or your speech delivery in an attempt to more fully engage your audience.

Noise: Communication noise can be either **external noise** or **internal noise**. External noise is anything outside the communicators that interferes with the transmission of messages. Internal noise is anything inside the communicators that interferes with the transmission of messages. When speaking in public, you want to reduce or eliminate any obvious external noise that might distract your listeners. (For example, you might ask audience members that are talking during your speech to quiet down, or you might remove or cover a distracting poster in the room.)

As a public speaker, you want to be just as concerned about internal noise. You must avoid thinking distracting thoughts in order to keep your mind focused on your speech message. More importantly, you need to use good strategies to gain and maintain the attention of your audience members. Their minds can easily wander if you do not motivate them to listen or if your ideas or words are unclear or uninteresting. Chapter 12 (Critiquing and Listening to Speeches) will teach you more about communication noise and the listening barriers that may exist in your audience.

PART 5: PUBLIC SPEAKING AND OTHER FORMS OF COMMUNICATION

This section compares and contrasts public speaking and other forms of communication. We want to point out the similarities that public speaking has to other forms of communication in order to convince you that you have already developed many communication skills that you can apply to the art of public speaking. However, public speaking also has some unique features of which you need to be aware. As a public speaker, there are some new communication skills for you to learn and some new communication strategies for you to employ.

Let us first compare and contrast giving a speech and writing an essay. Both processes involve brainstorming ideas, developing material, organizing thoughts, and using constructive feedback. If you can write an essay, you have already developed some useful skills you can also use to prepare a speech.

However, delivering a speech is much different than turning in an essay. When you turn in a "final draft" essay for a college writing class, your work is basically done—you have expressed your thoughts in writing, and others can now read these thoughts. However, when you make a detailed speech outline for an extemporaneous speech, you still have a lot of work to do: you still need to create delivery note cards, you need to develop presentation aids, you need to practice delivering your speech using these presentation aids and delivery note cards, and then you need to manage your public speaking anxiety as you deliver your speech in front of a live audience.

Your public speaking class is one of the most challenging and rewarding courses you will take in college because it asks you to draw upon and develop many different skills and abilities. As a public speaker, you must develop skills in creating, researching, developing, and organizing ideas. You must use good critical thinking skills to analyze your audience, to determine your speaking purpose, and to employ effective strategies to accomplish this purpose. You must effectively encode your thoughts and feelings in written, spoken, and visual symbols. You must use both your mind and your body to transmit your speech message through multiple communication channels. You must become adept at reading nonverbal cues. You must be flexible, able to adjust your presentation in response to audience feedback or unforeseen circumstances. You must develop and demonstrate confidence as you speak in front of a live audience.

Fortunately, you have already developed many of the skills and abilities you need for public speaking because you have lots of experience with other forms of oral communication. Other forms of oral communication also require you to consider your audience, tailor a message for your audience, deliver your message verbally and nonverbally, and deal with communication apprehension. You have participated in tens of thousands of one-on-one conversations and small group discussions in the course of your lifetime. Through these other types of oral communication interactions, you have already learned much about communicating verbally and nonverbally with a live audience.

However, public speaking has some unique elements that also differentiate public speaking from other forms of oral communication. Unlike interpersonal or small group communication situations, public speaking situations often involve addressing a fairly large audience. As a public speaker, you have a special opportunity to address and influence many people at once. The larger size of your audience often requires a cer-

Interpersonal communication.

FIGURE 1.13

Small group communication.

FIGURE 1.14

© Faraways, 2013. Used under license from Shutterstock, Inc.

FIGURE
1.15 Public speakers sometimes address very large audiences.

tain level of formality that is not present in informal conversations and discussions. The vocabulary you use when speaking casually with your close friends may not be appropriate for a public speech. The comfortable clothes you wear while knocking about at home may not be appropriate attire for a formal speech occasion. For a formal public speaking situation, you may need to adjust the words you use, and you may need to adjust the way you present yourself to your audience.

Public speaking often involves addressing a large audience, but a large audience is not a necessary requirement. What distinguishes public speaking from most other forms of oral communication is the fact that it involves a monological, one-way verbal performance. A public speech is not a dialogue. In a public speaking situation, you are expected to speak, and your audience is expected to listen. Your speech message is communicated verbally and nonverbally, whereas the audience feedback is primarily nonverbal. If audience members interrupt your speech and speak back to you, they are labeled as "hecklers." You may elicit brief verbal responses from your audience during a speech, but the bulk of your speech will showcase *your* thoughts and words.

The one-way verbal flow of a speech gives it a definite sense of being a "performance." People do not normally clap for you when you speak to them in the give-and-take of a one-on-one conversation or a small group discussion. However, your audience will most likely applaud your speech performance when you have finished your speech. The fact that your speech is a communication performance creates certain expectations in your audience. If you are a featured speaker at some gathering or event, your audience expects you to prepare and practice your speech ahead of time. Your audience also expects your speech to have a point, and they expect you to stick to this point.

The one-way verbal flow of a speech also presents certain unique challenges to you, the public speaker. You must work to gain and maintain the attention of your audience. You must monitor their nonverbal feedback, and you must strive to keep them engaged. Because your audience cannot usually ask you to clarify your ideas or repeat your points during your speech, you also need to provide a clear structure for your speech, and you need to make this structure obvious to your audience. As a public speaker, you need to repeat your ideas more than you might in other forms of discourse, and you must make this necessary repetition interesting. You must preview, explain, and review the main points of your speech without sounding redundant.

After comparing and contrasting public speaking and other forms of communication, you should now realize that even if you are just starting out as a public speaker, you have a lot going for you. You have already developed many communication skills that can be adapted and used for public speaking. However, you should also now realize that there are important concepts and skills unique to public speaking that you can learn with the help of your public speaking instructor and this textbook. You have been speaking since about age two, but you may just now be entering the fraternity of public speakers. Give yourself credit for the many communication skills and abilities you already possess, and apply yourself to learning the specialized skills you will need to become an effective public speaker.

PART 6: PUBLIC SPEAKING AND ETHICS

Consider the following scenarios in a college public speaking classroom:

- Pressured for time, a student finds a speech outline posted online and turns it in as if it was original work.
- A student presents an informative speech titled "Three Easy Ways to Cheat on Your Taxes."
- During a class debate, a student uses abusive language to demean his opponent.
- In order to gain credibility, a student makes up a story about a nonexistent past job.
- During a speech contest, a student circles "first place" on her friend's ballot before hearing any of the other speeches in the speech round.

Ethics help us decide what is right and wrong.

FIGURE 1.16

© marekuliasz, 2013. Used under license from Shutterstock, Inc.

Each of these examples illustrates why public speaking students and instructors need to consider **ethics** and what constitutes ethical communication. Ethics are moral principles that govern our actions: they help us to decide what is right and wrong and what is good and bad behavior. The students in the above examples behaved badly because they violated commonly accepted ethical principles like honesty, respect, and fairness.

Unfortunately, such bad behavior is not limited to college speech classes, and much more than an "F" grade or dismissal from a class is at stake when ethical principles are violated. When ethical principles related to public speaking are ignored or violated in our law courts, our political assemblies, and our business institutions, the very foundations of our society are weakened.

In ancient Greece, the philosopher Plato brought the whole public speaking enterprise into question when he pointed out that speech teachers and their students seemed more interested in what appeared plausible than in what was actually true. He also questioned the validity of democracy by pointing out that a skillful speaker could use the power of words to sway a crowd to vote for a policy that might not actually be in their best interest. The art of public speaking, Plato implied, was a dangerous art that could easily be misused.

In his dialogue *Gorgias*, Plato portrays the rhetorician Gorgias attempting to sidestep his moral responsibility as a public speaking instructor. In Plato's dialogue, Gorgias argues that boxing instructors are not held liable if their students kill others in a boxing match, so public speaking instructors should not be responsible for the way their students use their public speaking skills.

Fortunately, the rhetorical education that developed in ancient Greece and Rome after Plato's time was not the amoral art Plato portrayed in his dialogue. Aristotle, Plato's most famous student, pointed out in *The Rhetoric* that public speakers of good character are more believable and convincing than people of questionable character. The Roman rhetorician Quintilian is famous for his proclamation that an effective speaker is a "good man speaking well." In spite of Plato's concern and criticism, ethical instruction was an important element of a classical rhetorical edu-

FIGURE 1.17 Adolf Hitler used his speaking skills for evil purposes.

cation. In addition to being good speakers, public speaking students were encouraged to be good people.

In the final section of this introductory chapter, we want to reinforce and expand the ethical instruction provided by public speaking instructors of the past. Public speaking is a powerful tool for influencing others, and this power must be recognized and respected. Any craftsperson owning power tools knows that they can cause serious injury, so these tools must be used carefully. With power comes responsibility. Public speakers must also carefully consider their motives and their methods when crafting and delivering their speeches.

Adolf Hitler's Nazi rhetoric is a great example of the terrible results of public speaking separated from sound ethical principles. Hitler was a master at manipulating a crowd. Through the power of his words and his charismatic delivery, he convinced many German people to join him in his attempt to dominate the world and exterminate those he considered weak or unworthy of existence. His public speaking genius was used in the service of a diabolical goal that caused millions of people to suffer and die in misery.

Public speaking is powerful and therefore dangerous, but it can also be used for great good. When Hitler's Nazi forces swept across Europe in World War II and the fall of England seemed imminent, English Prime Minister Winston Churchill gave several brilliant war-time speeches that encouraged the disheartened, shell-shocked English citizens to hold on and never, ever give up. Churchill's speeches were an important part of the allied arsenal that eventually stopped Hitler's advance. World War II was won not just with bombs and bullets, but also with Churchill's good words.

FIGURE 1.18 Winston Churchill rallied the British in WW II through his powerful public speaking.

Clearly, public speaking, like every other human activity, cannot be separated from ethics. Human beings are rational, ethical animals. Rather than instinct, it is our moral principles that guide us in most of our human endeavors. This section on public speaking and ethics has been placed at the end of this introductory chapter to emphasize this point.

We could have written an entire chapter on public speaking and ethics, but we do not want our students to think that they can thumb through an "Ethics" chapter and then dispense with thinking about ethics. Ethical concerns are woven into almost every task related to public speaking, so we have woven ethical instruction throughout the chapters of this textbook.

When you read Chapter 3 (Considering Your Audience), you will learn to differentiate between "skillfully adapting to your audience" and "pandering." When you read Chapter 5 (Researching for Your Speech), you will be taught the appropriate and ethical use of researched evidence, and you will learn how to avoid **plagiarism**, the unacknowledged use of another person's words or ideas. When you read Chapter 6 (Developing Verbal Support), you will learn to avoid the fabrication and distortion of verbal support. When you read Chapter 12 (Critiquing and Listening to Speeches), you will learn the ethical responsibilities you have as a listener to be courteous and attentive, to avoid prejudging the speaker, and to maintain the free and open expression of ideas. When you read Chapter 13 (Using Language Effectively), you will learn to avoid both abusive language (like name-calling) and language that marginalizes other people. When you read Chapter 16 (Speaking to Persuade) and Chapter 14 (Reasoning), you will learn the appropriate and inappropriate uses of the three rhetorical appeals (ethos, logos, and pathos).

At the beginning of this textbook (which you are probably reading toward the beginning of your public speaking course), we would like to offer you a very helpful, very basic ethical principle found in many religious and ethical systems (sometimes referred to as The Golden Rule): *treat other people the way you would like to be treated.*

When you are up in front of the class giving a speech, what kind of listener would you like to have in the audience? Be that kind of listener for your peers: pay attention to each speech, act interested and engaged, and give supportive feedback and helpful criticism when asked.

When you are sitting in class listening to speeches, what kind of speeches do you want to listen to? Prepare those kinds of speeches for your classmates: put good thought into the topics that you select, research and outline your speeches diligently, prepare professional-looking presentation aids, and practice delivering your speech until you can deliver it smoothly and with enthusiasm.

You are responsible for being well-prepared for each of your class speeches. Jenkin Lloyd Jones (a pioneering American minister, educator, and journalist) has been immortalized in public speaking textbooks for this admonition: "A speech is a solemn responsibility. The man who makes a bad thirty-minute speech to two hundred people wastes only half an hour of his own time. But he wastes one hundred hours of the audience's time—more than four days—which should be a hanging offense." You may not be speaking to two hundred people in your speech class, but your peers still deserve your best effort. Do not waste their time.

We will end this section on public speaking and ethics by presenting an official public statement on ethics by the National Communication Association titled "NCA Credo for Ethical Communication." This public statement is located on the official webpage of the NCA, and this national organization of communication researchers and teachers has encouraged the publication and discussion of this credo in college textbooks and classes.

NCA CREDO FOR ETHICAL COMMUNICATION

Questions of right and wrong arise whenever people communicate. Ethical communication is fundamental to responsible thinking, decision making, and the development of relationships and communities within and across contexts, cultures, channels, and media. Moreover, ethical communication enhances human worth and dignity by fostering truthfulness, fairness, responsibility, personal integrity, and respect for self and others. We believe that unethical communication threatens the quality of all communication and consequently the well-being of individuals and the society in which we live. Therefore we, the members of the National Communication Association, endorse and are committed to practicing the following principles of ethical communication:

We advocate truthfulness, accuracy, honesty, and reason as essential to the integrity of communication.

We endorse freedom of expression, diversity of perspective, and tolerance of dissent to achieve the informed and responsible decision making fundamental to a civil society.

We strive to understand and respect other communicators before evaluating and responding to their messages.

We promote access to communication resources and opportunities as necessary to fulfill human potential and contribute to the well-being of families, communities, and society.

We promote communication climates of caring and mutual understanding that respect the unique needs and characteristics of individual communicators.

We condemn communication that degrades individuals and humanity through distortion, intimidation, coercion, and violence, and through the expression of intolerance and hatred.

We are committed to the courageous expression of personal convictions in pursuit of fairness and justice.

We advocate sharing information, opinions, and feelings when facing significant choices while also respecting privacy and confidentiality.

We accept responsibility for the short- and long-term consequences for our own communication and expect the same of others.

Do you agree with the NCA Credo for Ethical Communication? Which statements in this credo are most important? Are there any statements with which you disagree? Are there any statements you do not understand? Are there other principles of ethical communication that should be added to this credo? We encourage you to think about this Credo and to discuss your ethical concerns with others.

SUMMARY

Public speaking is powerful. It can be used to change the world, and it can change your life. The hybrid field of modern public speaking is influenced by both the western rhetorical tradition and modern communication studies. The western rhetorical tradition has bequeathed to us the concept of the three rhetorical appeals (ethos, logos, and pathos) that correlate with the corners of the rhetorical triangle (speaker, speech, and audience). Modern communication scholars have developed for us the transactional model of communication. (Communicators encode and send messages through communication channels that other communicators receive and decode.) This communication model helps us to understand how public speaking is similar to, and different from, other forms of communication. For emphasis, this chapter ended with a discussion of public speaking and ethics. Ethics matter in every area of human activity, and they matter in public speaking.

As your class gets under way, we want to wish you great success on your first speech! If you are nervous about your first speech assignment, keep on reading right into the next chapter. Chapter 2 (Managing Public Speaking Anxiety) will give you many strategies and techniques you can use to reduce and manage your anxiety about speaking in public.

Review Questions

1. Why is public speaking such a powerful form of communication?

2. What are the major purposes of public speaking?

3. What are the ancient and modern influences on the study and practice of public speaking?

4. How is public speaking the same as and different from other forms of discourse?

5. What ethical principles relate most directly to public speaking? How do they relate?

Glossary

Accidental ethos: The part of your ethos you do not easily control—factors such as your sex, age, and prior reputation.

Arrangement: The second canon of rhetoric, and the second stage in the speech-making process. After discovering or inventing your ideas, you must place these ideas in some order or arrangement.

Channel: Any medium that carries a message. The visual and auditory sensory channels are use most often for human communication.

Communication situation: The context in which a communication occurs, including factors such as location, time, and persons involved.

Communicator: Someone who either sends or receives a message.

Decoding: The mental process of transforming received symbols back into ideas.

Delivery: The fifth canon of rhetoric, and the final stage of the speech-making process. After creating a speech, you must finally present your ideas to an audience.

Encoding: The mental process of transforming ideas and feelings into symbols.

Ethics: Moral principles that govern our actions and help us to decide what is right and wrong and what is good and bad behavior.

Ethos appeal: One of the three primary rhetorical appeals. An ethos appeal is an attempt to persuade an audience through the projected character of a speaker.

Extemporaneous delivery: A delivery method in which a speech is prepared ahead of time but delivered without a manuscript. The speaker first prepares a detailed preparation outline, and this outline is then condensed into an abbreviated delivery outline.

External noise: Anything outside communicators that interferes with the transmission of a message.

Feedback: Any response that a receiver gives to a message.

Five canons of rhetoric: The five steps or stages of public speaking recognized in the western rhetorical tradition—invention, arrangement, style, memory, and delivery.

Impromptu delivery: A delivery method in which a speech is created and delivered with little or no preparation time.

Intercultural communication: Communication between people of substantially different culture groups.

Internal noise: Anything inside communicators that interferes with the transmission of messages.

Interpersonal communication: One-on-one communication occurring between two human beings.

Invention: The first canon of rhetoric and the first stage in the speech-making process. You must invent or discover the ideas for your speech.

Logos appeal: One of the three primary rhetorical appeals. A logos appeal is an attempt to persuade an audience through their understanding or reasoning capacity.

Manuscript delivery: A delivery method in which a speech is written out word-for-word and read from a manuscript word-for-word.

Mass communication: Communication with masses of people through the aid of communication technologies.

Memorized delivery: A delivery method in which a speech is written out word-for-word, committed to memory, and then delivered from memory word-for-word.

Memory: The fourth canon of rhetoric, and the fourth stage in the speech-making process. This canon of rhetoric has been modified in the modern world. You may choose to commit the words of a speech to memory, or you may choose another delivery method.

Message: The content of a communication.

National Communication Association: An organization representing communication researchers, scholars, and teachers. The NCA promotes the appreciation of the widespread importance of communication in public and private life.

Noise: Anything that interferes with the transmission of a message.

Organizational communication: Communication within an organization and communication between that organization and outside entities.

Pathos appeal: One of the three primary rhetorical appeals. A pathos appeal is an attempt to persuade an audience by generating emotion.

Plagiarism: Using the words or ideas of others without giving them credit.

Public speaking: Monological oral communication of a speaker with a large, live audience.

Rhetoric: An academic discipline that studies persuasive discourse. In the classical world, rhetoric was synonymous with oratory or public speaking.

Small group communication: Communication among a group of approximately three to twelve people.

Style: The third canon of rhetoric and the third stage in the speech-making process. After you have invented and arranged the ideas for a speech, you must choose the precise words you will use to express these ideas.

The rhetorical triangle: A conceptual device that emphasizes that every communication is an interaction between an author, a communicative text, and an audience.

The three rhetorical appeals: Three primary ways to persuade an audience. The three rhetorical appeals are ethos (the appeal through the projected character of the speaker), pathos (the appeal to or through emotion), and logos (the appeal to reason or understanding).

MANAGING PUBLIC SPEAKING ANXIETY

Mark L. Staller

Learning Objectives

CHAPTER 2

❶ Identify the major causes and symptoms of public speaking anxiety.

❷ Eliminate ineffective habits and behaviors related to public speaking anxiety.

❸ Develop a personal plan for reducing or managing public speaking anxiety before, during, and after your speech.

One day in my junior high school speech class, I had to stand up and draw a random topic for a mandatory three-minute impromptu speech. I have no recollection of the speech topic I drew from the glass fishbowl sitting on the chair in front of the class, but I have a very vivid memory of what happened after I looked at the topic. I turned to face my classmates . . . and my mind went totally blank. My heart started to thump wildly. My hands began to shake. I knew that I was supposed to say something, so I opened my mouth . . . and out came an agonized, totally unexpected, high-pitched giggle.

As I listened to myself giggle, my face flushed with embarrassment. The redness of my face deepened, sweat drenched my body, and I shifted nervously from foot to foot as I struggled valiantly to say something, anything, that made sense. All that came out of my boyish, preteen mouth for the entire three minutes was what I considered to be a mortifying "girly" giggle. After I took my seat, the only words my kind instructor spoke before asking the next student to step up to the fishbowl was, "Mark, I never knew you could giggle so high."

The above story is true. I am a survivor of severe public speaking anxiety. Even as a seventh grader in junior high, I knew that public speaking was an important skill I needed to develop, so I worked hard to prepare and present the rest of my speech assignments the remainder of that school semester. Despite my severe public speaking anxiety during the impromptu exercise, I earned an "A" grade in my speech class. I later joined my high school speech and debate team and continued to push myself to become a better speaker.

For the first ten years of my public speaking career, I was a fairly nervous speaker. As I developed more public speaking competence and confidence, I learned to channel my nervous energy. Today, about thirty-five years later, audience members most often describe me as an energetic and enthusiastic speaker. I seek out opportunities to speak in public, and I even enjoy demonstrating how to give an impromptu speech in my college public speaking courses.

If you have ever experienced public speaking anxiety, you are a member of a vast group of people. At the beginning of my public speaking courses, I often hear students proclaim, "I have put off taking this class as long as possible," and, "This is the last course I need to take to fulfill my graduation requirements." Why have they avoided taking a public speaking class? They are afraid to speak in public.

Public speaking anxiety.

FIGURE 2.1

When asked to list their greatest fears, people often place public speaking at the top of their list—even above the fear of death. When stand-up comedian Jerry Seinfeld learned this fact, he quipped that at a funeral most people would rather be laying in the coffin than standing up front delivering the eulogy. One day I asked the students in my public speaking class why anyone would fear public speaking more than death. A student explained, "I know that I only have to die once. However, once I have survived one stressed-filled speech, the possibility always exists that I will have to speak in public again!"

Q1 answer Public speaking anxiety is so common among the general population, it has been given its own acronym: PSA. Social scientists have identified several different forms of communication apprehension. Some people get anxious in one-on-one interpersonal communication situations. Some people get anxious about communicating in small groups. Anxiety about public speaking, however, is so widespread that many communication scholars and public speaking instructors refer to it as "PSA."

This chapter will help you manage your PSA through the power of ten. You will find some very useful ideas and helpful advice in the following "top ten" lists.

1. Ten statements to gauge your PSA
2. Ten causes of PSA
3. Ten common symptoms of PSA
4. Ten ways *not* to manage PSA
5. Ten ways to reduce PSA before your speech
6. Ten ways to reduce PSA during your speech
7. Ten ways to reduce PSA after your speech
8. Ten exercises to help manage PSA
9. Ten inaccurate thoughts related to PSA
10. Ten positive affirmations to help reduce PSA

Q2 answer

You can skim through these "top ten" lists randomly, but I suggest that you begin by taking the following ten-statement self-test to determine how much time and care you need to take reading this chapter.

PART 1: TEN STATEMENTS TO GAUGE YOUR PSA

For each of the ten statements listed below, indicated whether you strongly disagree (0), disagree (1), agree (2), or strongly agree (3).

1. __3__ I get tense when I see or hear the words "public speaking."

2. __3__ I purposely avoid situations where I may be asked to speak in public.

3. __3__ I feel a sense of dread when I am asked to give a speech.

4. __3__ I usually feel very nervous days or weeks before an assigned speech. _Q3 answer_

5. __3__ I have trouble sleeping the night before a public speaking engagement.

6. __3__ I get panicky right before I am supposed to speak.

7. __3__ I have difficulty delivering my speech because of my anxiety.

8. __3__ I think my symptoms of anxiety are greater than those of most people.

9. __3__ During my speech, I feel a sense of helplessness.

10. __3__ After my speech, I still worry about my speech performance.

Total: __30__

Total your score. This score will help you determine how important this chapter is for you. If you scored:

0–5: You have very little PSA. Read this chapter to understand and empathize with the majority of the population that does experience PSA.

6–15: You have a common, moderate level of PSA. You should be able to effectively manage your PSA using the principles and techniques presented in this chapter.

16–25: You have a substantial level of PSA. Read this chapter through carefully. You need to identify your particular PSA triggers, and then you need to develop and implement a plan to manage your PSA.

26–30: You have a very high level of PSA. This chapter is crucial for you. You should read and thoroughly understand each section. You also need to identify your particular PSA triggers and then develop a plan to manage your PSA. Consider making an appointment with your instructor to share the results of this self-test and to get help developing your PSA management plan.

PART 2: TEN CAUSES OF PSA

Good doctors know that they must do more than just treat the symptoms of an illness. In order to provide an effective cure for a disease, physicians must identify the *causes* of the disease; then they can develop a long-term cure that attacks these root causes. Similarly, if you understand the causes of your PSA, you will be able to do much more than just manage your anxiety symptoms: you may be able to greatly reduce (and even eliminate) some of these symptoms by actually eliminating a lot of your anxiety.

Doctors must diagnose the cause of an illness to treat it effectively.

© Alexander Raths, 2013. Used under license from Shutterstock, Inc.

FIGURE 2.2

Cause Number One: Becoming the center of attention. Practicing a speech at home alone or in an empty room is not the same as walking to the front of the room and having all eyes suddenly focused on you. Some people do not like to be the center of attention, especially if they are introverted or shy. If you are an introvert, becoming the center of attention can be part of the reason you experience PSA. If you are an extrovert, you may actually enjoy being the center of attention, so your PSA is most likely due to other causes.

Cause Number Two: Fear of the unknown. We fear the unknown, and often when speaking in public one "unknown" we have to deal with is the audience. We often do not personally know many of the people sitting in the audience, so we do not know how these audience members will react to our public speaking efforts.

Students who complete a public speaking course often find that their last speech is much easier to give than their first speech of the course. In part, the last speech is easier to give because the students have developed effective public speaking skills; however, the last speech is also much easier to deliver because the students in the class have gotten to know each other and have bonded over the course of their time together. Instead of facing a group of strangers, they stand up and speak one last time to a group of peers they have gotten to know quite well, so their anxiety is greatly decreased.

Another "unknown" faced by public speakers is an unknown outcome—we do not know how the speech will go. Recognizing this uncertainty leads us into our next cause of PSA.

Cause Number Three: Performance anxiety. There is no denying that a formal public speech is a performance: the speaker is "on stage," and the audience members are spectators. After the speech concludes, the audience members usually show their appreciation for the speech performance by applauding. Public speakers, like other performers, have to deal with performance anxiety. Good actors and actresses, athletes, musicians, stand-up comedians, and public speakers are all concerned with performing well.

Performance anxiety is one reason why a moderate level of PSA is appropriate and even necessary. Coaches would probably be concerned if their athletes didn't have any pregame jitters. Concert-goers would feel slighted if musicians didn't get "up" for their performance. Similarly, public speaking instructors are not trying to get their students to eliminate their PSA, but to manage it effectively so they can perform well. A speaker without any PSA is probably going to give a speech that is "flat."

Cause Number Four: Unrealistic Expectations. Some speakers have unrealistic expectations about eliminating PSA. About ten years ago, a middle-aged woman approached me after the first day of her speech class and revealed that she had high levels of PSA. I told her that I would work with her and that she could even get extra practice delivering her speeches during my office hours. She never needed my help. She earned an "A" grade for each of her speeches, and at the end of the semester, her classmates voted her the best all-around speaker of the class.

However, the first sentence of this woman's end-of-term self-evaluation essay was, "I am a failure as a public speaker." As I read further in her self-evaluation, I discovered that she thought excellent public speakers learned to eliminate all symptoms of speech anxiety. Because she still got nervous when she spoke, she considered herself to be a "failure." She was a victim of her own unrealistic expectations.

Some speakers have unrealistic expectations about giving a perfect, flawless performance. Striving for excellence is good, but expecting perfection is unreasonable. Speakers who give themselves no room for error put themselves under tremendous pressure. Their perfectionism leads to a sense of "failing" if anything in their speech is less than perfect.

Some speakers have unrealistic expectations about a fantastic audience response. Speakers should try to engage their audiences, but they need to remember that a public speech, like any form of oral communication, is a *transaction* between the speaker and the audience. Speakers must do their part, but the audience members also must do their part. Sometimes some audience members may not fulfill their responsibilities as audience members. It is unrealistic to think that everyone in the audience will give you a standing ovation, or laugh at all your jokes, or even give you their undivided attention.

Cause Number Five: Fear of failure. Some people mistakenly derive their worth as human beings from the successful performance of tasks. For example, some men think that they prove their worth as "men" by performing sexually. If a man cannot perform sexually, they believe, then he is not much of, or not really, a man. Similarly, some people think that giving a bad speech will make them a bad or worthless person. They believe that if they fail at public speaking, they will literally *be* a failure. Consequently, the mere possibility of a public speaking failure is not worth the great risk involved—they avoid public speaking at all costs to protect their very personhood.

Cause Number Six: Fear of being harshly criticized. Because public speaking is a performance, there is an evaluation component. Public performers are sometimes rewarded with hearty applause, but sometimes their efforts are met by jeers and shouts of "Boo!" and requests to leave the stage.

Having your weaknesses and flaws exposed in front of others can be especially traumatic. For example, some adults have severe math anxiety because they once "bombed out" on a math problem while at the chalkboard in front of their grade school classmates. Other adults experience high anxiety about writing an essay because many years earlier they received an essay covered in red ink from a zealous writing instructor.

Even if people have never received harsh criticism for their public speaking efforts, they may *imagine* that such criticism awaits. They fear that their audience will be bored, or unimpressed, or hostile. They are afraid that their best efforts will be met by yawns, or frowns, or outright ridicule.

Some of my students have discovered that they experience more PSA in their college speech class (with only thirty people in the audience) than they ever experienced while delivering speeches to hundreds or even thousands of people in other public speaking situations outside the classroom. I point out to them that in their speech class people are not only focusing on *what* they say, but also on *how well* they are saying it. Verbal and written feedback is a standard element of most public speaking classes. If you can give a speech in a class where you know you are being evaluated, you should be able to give a speech just about anywhere.

Cause Number Seven: Negative self-talk. Often the negative criticism we fear from our audience actually originates in ourselves. We can be our own worst critic. Psychologists and Communication scholars refer to our intrapersonal communication or internal monologue as "self-talk."

Self-talk can be positive or negative. If, as children, our caregivers or "significant others" harshly criticized us or put us down, we may have developed the habit of negative self-talk. Negative self-talk before a speech can result in a **self-fulfilling prophecy**. Speakers may put themselves down and belittle themselves as they prepare to give their speech. Their negative expectations are then realized in their speech performance.

Very negative self-talk during a speech can even make a person "freeze up." For example, a man in his forties indicated to me that he had high speech anxiety, so I had him practice his speeches ahead of time. He was able to deliver his speeches in my office, but when he stood up in front of the class, he could not get one word to come out of his mouth.

After several weeks of solid effort on his part, I finally recommend that he think about consulting a therapist. When I made this recommendation, he broke out in a big grin and said, "I have been in therapy for seven years!" He shared with me that he had a domineering, critical mother, and whenever he stood up to speak in class, he heard her voice inside his head. This voice would say things like, "Why are you even attempting to speak? Sit down before you make a fool of yourself! No one wants to hear what you have to say."

Negative self-talk can make you "awfulize" both your speech performance and the constructive criticism offered by your instructor and peers. You may tell yourself, "I did a terrible job," and "the audience hated my speech."

Cause Number Eight: Excessive focus on the self. In Chapter 1, you learned about the speaker triangle: a speech is a communication transaction in which a message (1) is passed from a speaker (2) to the audience (3). All three of these elements are important. Speakers must consider themselves, their messages, and their audiences. When speakers place excessive focus on themselves, problems arise. Speakers can focus excessively on how they are coming across to the audience (e.g., "Why did that person in the third row just chuckle? Do I have spit on my lips? Are my pants unzipped?"), or speakers can focus excessively on their symptoms of speech anxiety (e.g., "My, how my hands are shaking!" "I can hardly breathe—I am going to keel over as I am trying to speak.")

Cause Number Nine: Fear of the symptoms of speech anxiety. Surprisingly, many people are not actually afraid of giving a speech. They are afraid of being afraid. They are afraid that they will experience the symptoms of public speaking anxiety. Usually this fear is based on a prior public speaking experience when some strong symptoms of PSA were activated. (It can be very disconcerting when your body does things you are not expecting it to do.) Perhaps during a previous public speaking experience their face turned bright red and the palms of their hands sweat profusely. Perhaps they experienced a very loud, very rapid heartbeat and their legs shook violently. If the experiencing of these past symptoms is viewed and remembered as a "traumatic" event, any onset of similar symptoms of PSA can trigger anxiety in the present.

Unfortunately, people who are afraid of the symptoms of PSA can get caught in a vicious cycle of fear. They are anxious about experiencing the symptoms of PSA. In turn, their anxiety brings about the onset of these symptoms. When they realize that the symptoms of PSA are occurring, their anxiety increases. When their anxiety increases, they experience even more of the symptoms of PSA. When they realize that the symptoms of PSA are increasing, their anxiety greatly increases. When their anxiety greatly increases, the symptoms of PSA are further magnified. And on it goes . . .

Cause Number Ten: Fight or Flight Response. The **fight or flight response** is a biological defense mechanism. When human beings sense they are in a dangerous situation, their body is flooded with adrenaline. This adrenaline gives them an incredible short-term energy boost so they can defend themselves: either they can stand their ground (the fight response) or they can flee to safety (the flight response).

If, for some reason, a person views a public speaking event as a "danger" situation, the fight or flight response will kick in and their body will be flooded with adrenaline and extra energy. Unfortunately, the fight or flight response is not appropriate for a public speaking situation. The speaker should not start punching audience members in the face (the fight response), and if the speaker runs out the nearest exit (the flight response), the speech cannot be delivered. The speaker is forced to stand in front of the audience and deal with the extra adrenaline flooding his or her system.

The flood of adrenaline resulting from the fight or flight response is responsible for almost all the common symptoms of PSA. The sudden release of adrenaline causes your heart to beat quickly, which pumps more blood through your body, which causes you to flush and turn red, which causes you to sweat profusely, etc. The extra energy created by the adrenaline in your system has to dissipate somehow, so your body shakes and twitches as this extra energy is discharged.

FIGURE 2.3 The fight or flight response is triggered by a perceived danger situation.

© Vitezslav Valka, 2013. Used under license from Shutterstock, Inc.

When I learned about the fight or flight response in my high school health class, my PSA decreased by about twenty-five percent. Until I learned about this biological defense mechanism, I thought that my symptoms of public speaking anxiety were abnormal. Once I understood some of the basic physiological processes that were taking place when I experienced PSA, I came to realize that I was a perfectly normal, healthy human being. My body was not betraying me—it was doing precisely what it was supposed to do in a perceived danger situation. If this is the first time you have heard about the fight or flight response, you now have important knowledge that can boost your self-esteem and help you accept the symptoms of PSA. You

TEN CAUSES OF PSA

1. Becoming the center of attention
2. Fear of the unknown
3. Performance anxiety
4. Unrealistic expectations
5. Fear of failure
6. Fear of being harshly criticized
7. Negative self-talk
8. Excessive focus on the self
9. Fear of the symptoms of speech anxiety
10. Fight or flight response

are not defective, weird, or abnormal if you experience anxiety symptoms produced by the fight or flight response.

If you experience public speaking anxiety to any extent, consider the ten causes of PSA reviewed on the previous page and determine which of these causes might be an important source of your public speaking anxiety.

Which of these causes probably have very little to do with your PSA? Which of these causes are at the root of your PSA? Can any of these causes of your PSA be eliminated?

PART 3: TEN COMMON SYMPTOMS OF PSA *Q4 answer*

Although it is crucial to understand and deal with the *causes* of a problem, it is also important to be aware of and deal with the *symptoms* of a problem. When you stand up to speak in public, here are ten common symptoms of PSA that you may experience.

Public speaking anxiety has common symptoms.

© Kentoh, 2013. Used under license from Shutterstock, Inc.

FIGURE 2.4

1. *Q5 answer* Increased heart rate. Your heart may beat more quickly and more loudly. You may feel your heart beating quickly in your chest, or you may feel your pulse pounding in your head.

2. **Blushing or redness.** You may flush red on your face, upper chest, arms, or thighs. In addition to general flushing, you may develop red blotches or a nervous rash.

3. Sweating. Parts of your body may start to sweat. You may feel "hot flashes," and sweat may break out on your forehead, your upper lip, your armpits, or the palms of your hands. This anxiety-sweat may be more odorous and profuse than the sweat that develops from physical exertion.

4. **Urge to urinate.** Just a minute or two before you have to speak, you may suddenly feel the urge to relieve yourself.

5. **Dry mouth.** Dry mouth is also called "cotton mouth" because it feels like you have a big wad of cotton in your mouth and you cannot swallow. The flow of saliva in your mouth may suddenly decrease, and your tongue may feel thick and dry.

6. **Unplanned, unnecessary movement.** Your arms or legs may tremble. Your hands may shake. You may pace around the room. You may begin to fidget with your note cards or twirl your hair or scratch yourself.

7. **Queasiness or nausea.** You may feel "butterflies" in your abdomen, or you may feel like your stomach is doing flip-flops. If this symptom persists, you may feel nauseous or queasy, and you may even have to vomit.

8. **Increased speaking rate.** You may find yourself speaking very quickly. You may discover that a speech that took eight minutes to deliver during a practice run-through only takes four minutes in front of your live audience because your speaking rate doubled.

9. **Verbal clutter or vocalized pauses.** You may find yourself cluttering your speech with "uhs," "ums," and "ya knows." You may unconsciously fill every pause with one of these vocalized filler words or sounds.

10. **Blanking out.** You may find it difficult to remember your speech content. In the middle of a sentence or thought, your mind may go suddenly blank. You may even have difficulty recalling very basic facts about yourself.

The symptoms of PSA listed here are ten of the most common symptoms, but there are other, rarer, symptoms. You may find yourself speaking very slowly. You may break out into hard-to-control laughter or giggling. You may turn pale, and then you may faint.

An important strategy for overcoming the fear of the symptoms of public speaking anxiety is to expect and accept these symptoms. Read over the list of symptoms again, and anticipate which symptoms you are most likely to experience when you give a speech. Which of these symptoms have you experienced in the past? Which of these symptoms do you struggle with now? Can you accept the fact that you may experience these symptoms?

TEN SYMPTOMS OF SPEECH ANXIETY

1. Increased heart rate.
2. Blushing or redness.
3. Sweating.
4. Urge to urinate.
5. Dry mouth.
6. Unplanned, unnecessary movement.
7. Queasiness or nausea.
8. Increased speaking rate.
9. Verbal clutter or vocalized pauses.
10. Blanking out.

Now that we have considered the causes and symptoms of public speaking anxiety, it is time to look at possible solutions. There are effective and ineffective solutions to public speaking anxiety. Let us first dispose of the ineffective responses to PSA.

PART 4: TEN WAYS NOT TO MANAGE PSA

1. **Procrastinate and try to "wing it."** You may be tempted to avoid preparing for your speech so you do not even have to think about it. Do not put off the necessary preparation. "Winging it" is one of the most stressful ways to deliver a speech, and it greatly increases the chances that your speech will have major flaws and weaknesses.

2. **Over-prepare and attempt to memorize your speech.** Memorizing a speech word-for-word is one of the most difficult tasks you can attempt. You are creating more work and more pressure for yourself: not only do you have to deal with the pressure of speaking in public, but you also have to deal with the pressure of remembering your speech word-for-word. Memorized deliv-

FIGURE 2.5 The following habits and behaviors are prohibited.

© 3Dmask, 2013. Used under license from Shutterstock, Inc.

ery also provides no "safety net" if your mind goes blank. You may find yourself stalled in front of your audience with no way of getting your speech back on track.

3. **Write out your entire speech and read it word-for-word.** If you are reading your speech word-for-word in a speech class, you are probably doing exactly what your speech instructor has asked or told you *not* to do. Your instructor does not want you to read your speech word-for-word because of delivery problems and difficulties. If you bury your head in your manuscript, disconnect from your audience, and read through your "script," you may not experience many symptoms of speech anxiety, but that is because you have not really given a speech. Your audience does not expect you to read to them. Your audience expects you to *speak* to them.

4. **Come to class late on your speaking day.** If you are already nervous about giving a speech, why make yourself more nervous by coming to class late? In addition to worrying about your speech, you now have to worry about the bad impression you have made on your instructor and classmates. Rushing into class while other student speeches are in progress puts both you and your audience in a bad state of mind.

5. **Make excuses and bail out of your speech.** Your may find yourself making excuses and rationalizing why you cannot give your speech. Consciously or unconsciously, you may be creating an "out" for yourself—you are having car problems, or you are experiencing relationship difficulties; your back is hurting, or your throat is sore; you need to do some more research, or your visual aids are not quite ready. Do not make excuses. You need to fulfill your obligations as a public speaker. You need to fulfill the requirements of your public speaking class. You need to face your fear and learn to manage your public speaking anxiety effectively.

6. **Self-medicate with drugs or alcohol.** You may take prescribed antianxiety drugs under a doctor's supervision—that is okay. However, it is not okay to self-medicate and treat your PSA with "recreational" drugs and alcohol. You need all of your faculties when presenting a speech in public. You may feel no pain if you speak while "buzzed" or high, but your audience will suffer. Under the influence of drugs and alcohol, you are likely to experience problems with perception, recall, pacing, and enunciation.

7. **Announce your nervousness before, during, and after your speech.** Before your speech, you may be tempted to say things like, "I really don't want to do this," or "let's get this over with." During your speech, you may want to announce, "my hands are really shaking," or "I can't believe how nervous I am." After your speech, you may want to share, "that was nerve-wracking," or "I don't want to have to do that again." Do not make these comments.

   Announcing your nervousness may sometimes gain the sympathy of some audience members, but it also draws attention away from your message and makes the audience focus on and think about your nervousness. Your job as a public speaker is to set your audience at ease and get them to focus on your speech. You need to project a positive ethos: you should present yourself as a confident, competent person who is ready and willing to speak. If you are really nervous, your audience will be able to figure that fact out for themselves.

8. **Apologize for your nervousness.** Apologizing for your nervousness is just another way of announcing your nervousness to your audience. Worse, an apology implies that you have done something wrong. You have done nothing wrong by experiencing the symptoms of PSA. No apology is necessary. Instead of apologizing, you need to mask and effectively manage your PSA symptoms.

9. **Imagine the worst.** You may be tempted to imagine the worst of yourself and your public speaking efforts. You may be tempted to imagine the worst of your audience and their response to your speech. Motivational speaker Zig Ziglar calls such negative thoughts "stinking thinking." Do not stink up your speech efforts with negative thoughts about yourself, your speech, or your audience.

10. **Refuse to acknowledge what you did well.** After your speech is over, you may be tempted to fixate on what you did wrong, rather than on what you did well. For example, you may have done an excellent job working through the invention, arrangement, and style stages of the speech-making process. However, after delivering your speech, instead of giving yourself credit for the hours of work you put into the preparation process, you may beat yourself up for saying "um" too many times.

When you refuse to acknowledge what you did well, you deny any "positives" that could boost your self-esteem. When you refuse to acknowledge your strengths as well as your weaknesses, you rob yourself of any sense of satisfaction or accomplishment for your public speaking efforts.

Read through the ten ways *not* to manage your PSA reviewed here and determine whether you have been guilty of any of these bad behaviors.

To which of these bad behaviors are you most prone? Which of these bad behaviors do you need to avoid?

TEN WAYS *NOT* TO MANAGE PUBLIC SPEAKING ANXIETY

1. Procrastinate and try to "wing it."
2. Over-prepare and attempt to memorize your speech.
3. Write out your entire speech and read it word-for-word.
4. Come to class late on your speaking day.
5. Make excuses and bail out of your speech.
6. Self-medicate with drugs or alcohol.
7. Announce your nervousness before, during, and after your speech.
8. Apologize for your nervousness.
9. Imagine the worst.
10. Refuse to acknowledge what you did well.

Now that you know what *not* to do to manage your PSA, read through the next three sections of this chapter to learn what you can do before, during, and after your speech to effectively manage your public speaking anxiety.

PART 5: TEN WAYS TO REDUCE PSA BEFORE YOUR SPEECH

1. **Retrain your brain. Cognitive restructuring** is the technical term for the process of retraining your brain. Cognitive psychologists train their patients to identify inaccurate, false, unhelpful thoughts and replace them with accurate, true, helpful thoughts.

The related concept of **cognitive conservatism** explains why cognitive restructuring is necessary. Cognitive conservatism is a term that describes an interesting mental phenomenon: once an idea lodges in our minds, it is very difficult for us let go of this idea, even if it is an outdated or incorrect notion. Thought patterns are like grooves in a road. Once we are accustomed to thinking certain thoughts, we tend to follow these thought patterns even if these thoughts do not lead our minds in the best direction.

If you are mired in false, inaccurate thoughts about public speaking or PSA, these inaccurate thoughts may be the source of some of your public speaking fears and negative self-talk. You can engage in cognitive restructuring to break out of these unhealthy thought patterns. Part 8 of this chapter contains a cognitive restructuring exercise, and Part 9 models this exercise by showing you how to identify inaccurate thoughts related to public speaking and PSA and how to correct these inaccurate thoughts with the information you are learning in this chapter.

2. **Envision success.** Practice positive imagery. Sports psychologists have helped athletes dramatically improve their personal bests by asking them to mentally envision the sports performance they want to have *before* the performance actually occurs. For example, a runner may be asked to envision each lap of a race and the exact times to be run for each lap. If the runner trains both physically and *mentally* for the race, a record-breaking performance is much more likely to occur.

Similarly, you can envision the public speech you want to give in order to improve your odds of actually giving such a speech. (Part 8 of this chapter also describes a positive imagery exercise you can do for a public speaking situation.) If you practice positive imagery for your public speeches, you will find what sports psychologists and athletes have also discovered: "What the mind can conceive and believe, it can achieve."

3. **Get to know your audience.** Because we fear the unknown, getting to know your audience eliminates at least one of the "unknown" factors. If you are speaking at an event, ask the event organizers to give you some insight into the type of audience they expect to be at the event. If you are speaking in a speech class, you can administer a formal audience survey or take an informal poll to get to know your classmates and their attitudes and experiences better. Sometimes it may be possible to speak one-on-one with some of your audience members before you give your speech. You can use these one-on-one conversations to begin to establish a relationship with your audience. You can also gain insight into the immediate mood of your audience.

Getting to know your audience can also reduce your anxiety because you know that you are able to meet the needs of your anticipated audience and fulfill your speech purpose. If you can verify that you have correctly anticipated the type of audience at your speaking event, you gain confidence that your speech is on the right track.

4. **Choose an interesting or important topic that you are familiar with.** When you choose an interesting or important topic that you are familiar with, there is less chance that you will "blank out" or not have anything to say. You gain confidence knowing that you "know your stuff," and a genuine passion for your speech topic can make giving your speech a pleasure.

Remember, however, that as a public speaker you need to be audience-centered. You may be interested in and know a lot about a particular topic that matters a great deal to you, but will a majority of your audience members also find this topic interesting or important? By choosing a topic that you are familiar with and that your *audience* will find interesting or important, you are making your public speaking task much easier.

5. **Thoroughly prepare your speech.** Preparing a solid speech manuscript for manuscript delivery or a detailed preparation outline for extemporaneous speaking will help you

FIGURE 2.6 Plenty of preparation promotes positive performance.

work through the "invention," "arrangement," and "style" stages of the speech-making process. You will gain confidence knowing that you have thoroughly developed your ideas, clearly arranged your ideas in an easy-to-follow speech structure, and effectively expressed these ideas in words and sentences that let you move smoothly from point to point.

The work you put into preparing your speech should reduce your "performance" anxiety. Although a solid manuscript or a detailed preparation outline does not guarantee good delivery, it does indicate that you have covered the "content" and "structure" bases and are on your way to hitting a "home-run" speech.

6. **Improve your speech** *before* **you deliver it.** One of the best ways to reduce the fear of negative criticism is to reduce any flaws or weaknesses in your speech. If your speech instructor asks you to develop a preparation outline for a classroom speech, you should share this outline with people who can help you make your speech better—your instructor, tutors, classmates, etc. Give them an easy-to-read outline and ask them to write suggestions for improvement right on your outline.

If you take suggestions for improvement seriously and revise your speech accordingly, you gain confidence knowing that some kinks have been worked out of your speech. However, it doesn't help to get feedback on your preparation outline if you do not make any of the necessary corrections. If you know that your speech has flaws and do nothing to correct these weaknesses, then you deserve some negative criticism.

7. **Practice delivering your speech.** Practice eliminates another "unknown" element of your speech: by practicing your speech delivery, you have some sense of how your speech performance will go. Practice delivering your speech with your delivery outline and your presentation aids. Practice your speech in an environment similar to the actual speech environment. If possible, practice your speech in front of a live audience. Creating a practice situation that is very close to the actual speech situation gives you confidence that you are ready and able to deliver your speech effectively.

You eventually need to reach the point where you practice your speech all the way through, without stopping. Practicing your speech from beginning to end gives you confidence that minor "glitches" will not ruin your delivery. If you are delivering your speech extemporaneously, using only brief key word note cards, allow yourself to have variations in your words. One major benefit of extemporaneous delivery is that there is no pressure to remember your speech word-for-word.

8. **Prepare yourself.** Get a good night's sleep. Eat a nutritious breakfast. If the speech is later in the day, avoid meals that will upset your stomach, and avoid overloading your system with caffeine or sugar. Prepare yourself mentally by reviewing your speech outline and note cards once or twice before your speech. Prepare yourself physically with relaxation exercises and warm-up exercises. (Part 8 of this chapter contains five physical exercises to help you prepare for a public speaking situation.) Preparing yourself mentally and physically can reduce both your PSA and the symptoms of public speaking anxiety.

9. **Prepare your communication environment.** Arrive early and check out the room set-up for your speech. If you can anticipate potential problems in the speaking environment and work to solve these problems, you will gain confidence knowing that you have set the stage for success. Where will the audience be sitting? Where will you be standing? If possible, test all the equipment you will be using, including microphones, timers, and technology for presentation aids. If you are using any technology, remember Murphy's law: anything that can go wrong, will go wrong. Have backup plans in place for common problems that arise in public speaking situations.

10. **Create a supportive speaking environment.** Listen attentively to other speakers, and show your appreciation for their efforts. Participate in any question-and-answer sessions. If you are asked to give feedback to other speakers—either verbally or in writing—begin by emphasizing what the speakers did well, then provide helpful suggestions for improvement. (Chapter 12, Critiquing and Listening to Speeches, will provide more instruction on how to give effective feedback to speakers.) Every effort you make to be a good audience member should pay off when you stand up to speak. You will benefit from the comfortable, supportive speaking environment that you have helped to create.

TEN WAYS TO REDUCE PSA BEFORE YOUR SPEECH

1. Retrain your brain *answer*
2. Envision success.
3. Get to know your audience.
4. Choose an interesting and important topic that you are familiar with.
5. Thoroughly prepare your speech.
6. Improve your speech *before* your deliver it.
7. Practice delivering your speech. *Q8*
8. Prepare yourself.
9. Prepare your communication environment.
10. Create a supportive speaking environment.

PART 6: TEN WAYS TO REDUCE PSA DURING YOUR SPEECH

1. **Expect and accept some symptoms of speech anxiety.** First, anticipate the common symptoms of speech anxiety that you will most likely experience. Second, *give yourself permission* to experience these symptoms. These psychological steps can be taken before you deliver your speech, but you must also accept the symptoms of speech anxiety *during* your speech.

   Remember, many people are not afraid of public speaking—they are afraid of *being afraid* of public speaking and of experiencing the symptoms of PSA. If you give yourself permission to experience these symptoms, then there is nothing to fear when your face flushes, or your heart beats rapidly, or your hands shake.

FIGURE
2.7 Breathing is a crucial tension reliever.

Experiencing the symptoms of public speaking anxiety is no big deal—do not make these symptoms a big deal by dreading their appearance. Most of these symptoms are caused by the "fight or flight" response, a natural biological defense mechanism. Your body is operating properly if you experience the symptoms of PSA. Break the cycle of fear by accepting these symptoms.

This chapter is not titled "*Eliminating* Public Speaking Anxiety." It is titled "*Managing* Public Speaking Anxiety." You need to accept the fact that you will usually experience some symptoms of PSA when you speak in public, and you need to learn to *manage* these symptoms effectively.

2. **Act confident to become confident.** Or, as some of my students say, "Fake it until you make it." In Chapter 1, you learned that your "ethos" is your *projected* image. Even if you do not feel confident, you can act confident. Acting confident (when you do not feel confident) is not unethical. As a speaker, you have the responsibility to put your audience at ease and prepare them to listen to your speech, so it is fitting and proper that you present yourself as a competent, confident speaker.

However, you may only need to *act* confident for a short while. A confident demeanor on the outside can actually create a confident person on the inside. Your mental state affects your physical state, but your physical state can also affect your mental state. For example, if you are happy, your happiness may cause your face to break out into a smile; however, if you put a smile on your face, your smiling face may also help you to *become* happy. Similarly, if you hold your head up proudly, project your voice firmly, and look your audience members squarely in the eye when you speak, these physical actions can actually help you to become confident.

3. **Realize you do not look as nervous as you feel.** Often when my students are told that they looked calm and confident when standing in front of the class, they say something like, "No way! I was shaking like a leaf," or, "Are you kidding? I was a nervous wreck!" What they did not realize was that their audience could not *see* their nervousness. Many of the symptoms of speech anxiety are internal. No one can see that your heart is beating rapidly. No one can see that your mouth is dry. No one can see that your stomach is doing flip flops. No one can see that you are "blanking out."

Furthermore, many of the external symptoms of PSA are not that obvious. You may *feel* like your hands are shaking violently, but your audience may only notice a slight tremor, or they may not notice any trembling at all. You may *feel* like your face has turned beet red, but it may only appear slightly flushed. You may think that your increased speaking rate clearly broadcasts your nervousness, but your audience might think that your rapid speaking rate signals your energy and enthusiasm. Once you realize that you do not look as nervous as you feel, you have another good reason to "bluff" and act confident.

4. **Deliver your introduction effectively.** An effective introduction will increase your confidence. After all, "Well begun is half done." When you deliver an introduction that engages your audience and effectively sets up the speech body, you know that an important speech objective has been reached. An effective introduction also carries you through

what is commonly the period of greatest anxiety for speakers—the first minute or two of the speech. A poor introduction puts more stress on a speaker right when his or her anxiety is fairly high, whereas a good introduction lessens stress and allows a speaker to "settle down" and ease into the body of the speech.

5. **Focus on your message.** "Focus on your message" is a brief way of saying, "Do not think of your speech as a time to be evaluated, but as a time to share your message with your audience." If you focus on being evaluated, you may experience "performance anxiety," and you may fear negative criticism that could arise. Focusing on evaluation can make you think of giving your speech as a "danger" situation.

However, if you think of your speech as a time to share your message with your audience, you can view your speech as an *opportunity*. An opportunity is something to take advantage of and welcome. If you never view your speech as a "danger" situation, the fight or flight response can be avoided. Instead, you can enjoy taking advantage of the opportunity you have been given to share your speech message. Focusing on your message also gives you a reasonable, attainable speech goal: if you get your message across to your audience, then you can consider your speech a success.

6. **Use visual aids effectively.** Visual aids reinforce your verbal message, but they also give you something to do with your hands to help you expend some of your nervous energy. If you do not like being the center of attention, visual aids also take some of the focus off of you.

You must use your visual aids effectively—you cannot "hide" behind them or use them as visual substitutes for your verbal message. However, if you construct a variety of professional-looking visual aids and use them appropriately, you will increase your speaker credibility and decrease your public speaking anxiety. You will also have visual memory cues to aid in your delivery.

7. **Strive for excellence, but don't expect perfection.** Do not make yourself a victim of unrealistic expectations. If you expect your speech to be perfect, your confidence may crumble when any kind of "mistake" happens. Nobody is perfect. Allow yourself to be human, and enjoy giving your speech even with some minor flaws. You may mispronounce a word. You may drop a note card. You may blank out for a moment. No need to apologize or to start your speech over.

Seasoned musicians focus on the overall effect of a musical performance: if they miss a musical note, they continue on without missing a beat. Similarly, you should focus on your overall speech message without getting sidetracked or demoralized by speech "glitches."

Remember, your audience does not know how you intended to deliver your speech. If you do not meet your own expectations, or if you deviate from your speech plan, the audience does not view these unfulfilled expectations or deviations as mistakes. If you maintain your composure and continue on with your speech, your audience will think you are doing exactly what you are supposed to be doing.

Do not place unnecessary stress on yourself by actually expecting yourself to give a flawless performance—just strive to give the best speech you can give, and you should be very pleased with the results.

8. **Be flexible and maintain a sense of humor.** Although you may envision what a successful speech will look like, this envisioned success should not become a mental straitjacket. Your speech does not have to go just the way you planned, and it probably will

not. You cannot control all the variables in a speech situation, especially variables that depend on the actions and attitudes of other people. The event organizer may ask you to shorten your speech. A timekeeper may give you a wrong time signal. The audience may be lethargic after eating a large banquet lunch and sitting for some time.

Take your speech task seriously, but do not take yourself too seriously. Adjust your expectations and actions as needed for the unfolding speech situation. Sometimes you have to make the best of a difficult situation. A good sense of humor can help you deal with difficult people or problems.

9. **Engage your audience.** Although you are expected to speak, your audience also has certain responsibilities in the communication transaction. They should listen attentively. They should provide you with nonverbal feedback. Let them know that you expect them to fulfill these responsibilities through your words and your actions. Ask for their attention, and encourage their nonverbal feedback. You can even ask for brief verbal responses.

Presenting your speech as a communication *interaction* places some of the burden for the success of your speech on your audience. Human beings are altruistic—they like helping other people. If you skillfully send the message that you want your audience's help and involvement, they will respond with enthusiastic applause, and they will show their appreciation and interest. Focus on audience members who are responding to your message and feed off of their positive energy. Enlist their help and support in getting others to focus on your message.

It is a speaking cliché to end a speech by saying, "Thank you for being such a great audience!" However, this cliché acknowledges the important role that the audience plays in a speech performance. Do not think that you are "on your own" when you stand in the front of the room. Realize that every person in the room is entering into your speech with you. Treating your audience members as allies should reduce your PSA and increase your confidence.

10. **Breathe!** Naturally and freely inhale and exhale air as you deliver your speech. Your brain and body need oxygen, especially when you are in a stressful situation. You cannot think clearly and your body cannot function properly if it does not receive the oxygen it needs. When you inhale, you take in oxygen; when you exhale, you expel carbon dioxide. When you exhale, you can also expel a lot of your nervous tension.

TEN WAYS TO REDUCE PSA DURING YOUR SPEECH

1. Expect and accept some symptoms of speech anxiety.
2. Act confident to become confident.
3. Realize you do not look as nervous as you feel.
4. Deliver your introduction effectively.
5. Focus on your message.
6. Use visual aids effectively.
7. Strive for excellence, but don't expect perfection. answer
8. Be flexible and maintain a sense of humor.
9. Engage your audience.
10. Breathe! Q10

When some speakers get nervous, they hold their breath. Without realizing it, they are cutting themselves off from a basic biological necessity. As they hold their breath, they are fighting not only their public speaking anxiety—they are fighting to remain alive!

PART 7: TEN WAYS TO REDUCE PSA AFTER YOUR SPEECH

1. **Make a graceful exit from the speaking stage.** When your speech is over, sincerely acknowledge any applause. Be willing to answer audience questions if required to do so. Gather up your presentation aids and speaking notes and clear the stage. If more speakers are scheduled, quickly return to the role of audience member. When you are no longer the center of attention, you can then relax and do "cool down" exercises if necessary.

2. **Give yourself credit for what you did well.** Review all four stages of the speech-making process—invention, arrangement, style, and delivery —and recognize what you did well in both the preparation and presentation of your speech. Recognizing your strengths as a speaker will boost your self-esteem and give you confidence that you are able to face future speech situations.

Celebrate your speaking success with others.

FIGURE
2.8

3. **Recognize your weaknesses as a speaker.** Apply the concept of "continuous quality improvement" to your public speaking. Become your own best critic. Use realistic, constructive self-criticism to improve your speaking skills, attitudes, and behaviors.

4. **Receive verbal criticism graciously.** Many speech classrooms require a verbal evaluation time after speeches are presented. Do not get into a verbal altercation or argument with the instructor or other student evaluators. Be aware that immediately after your speech you will be pumped full of adrenaline, so it is easy to go into "defense" mode. Do not get defensive. Politely thank the evaluators for their feedback. If you think a comment is way off base, you can approach the evaluator at a later, more appropriate time.

5. **Use written evaluations and critiques to improve your future speeches.** The speech you just gave is completed, but you can use written feedback to reduce your anxiety about future speeches. If several evaluators give you written critiques, look for patterns or repeated comments—pay attention to these.

   You can dismiss questionable comments made by only one evaluator that are not reinforced by others. Realize that evaluating speeches, like giving speeches, is a skill that needs to be learned and improved. Appreciate the detailed written evaluations you receive—these are the most useful evaluations for improving your future efforts.

6. **Do not "awfulize" your speech performance or critiques of your speech.** Do not say your speech was "awful" when it was actually decent. Do not say the symptoms of PSA were "horrible" when you actually managed them fairly well. Do not say the verbal criticism you received was "terrible" when it was actually accurate and useful. Do not form

a false, negative perception of either your speech or your speech critiques. Strive to gain an accurate perception that recognizes both the positive and negative aspects of the speech experience.

7. **Keep a record of your speaking experience.** Keep your speech outline and make a copy or printout of your visual aids. Take notes about what went well, and record the positive feedback you received from either the audience or the event organizers. Save any mementos that could trigger positive memories of the speaking experience. Build up a memory bank full of positive memories about your previous speaking experiences, and you will face future speaking opportunities with enthusiasm.

8. **Reward yourself for your efforts and your performance.** Did you put effort into preparing your speech? Did you succeed in getting your message across? Did you effectively manage your symptoms of speech anxiety? Recognize what you accomplished, and reward yourself. Positive reinforcement works. Plan a "prize" or gift to give to yourself when you have accomplished your speech task. You will then have another positive memory to associate with your speech experience.

9. **Share your speaking success with others.** Have a post-speech celebration with some close friends or family members. Describe and rehearse what went well. You are not just "bragging". you are creating more good memories that can be associated with your speech.

10. **Seek out additional speaking opportunities.** Speaking skills are improved with use. If you continue to improve your speaking *competence*, you will also increase your speaking *confidence*. See if your college offers other communication courses that involve public speaking, and take these additional courses. The best way to overcome any negative public speaking experiences you have had is to create many more positive public speaking experiences.

TEN WAYS TO REDUCE PSA AFTER YOUR SPEECH

1. Make a graceful exit from the speaking stage. *Q12 answer*
2. Give yourself credit for what you did well.
3. Recognize your weaknesses as a speaker.
4. Receive verbal criticism gracefully.
5. Use written evaluations and critiques to improve your future speeches.
6. Do not "awfulize" your speech performance or critiques of your speech.
7. Keep a record of your speech experiences.
8. Reward yourself for your efforts and your performance.
9. Share your speaking success with others.
10. Seek out additional speaking opportunities.

Q11 answer

In the last three sections of this chapter (Part 5, Part 6, and Part 7), I have presented thirty different ways to reduce and manage the symptoms of PSA before, during, and after your speech. You need to identify and apply the solutions that will work best for you. What are the best three ways you can reduce your PSA before your speech? What are the best three ways you can reduce your PSA during your speech? What are the best three ways you can reduce your PSA after your speech?

PART 8: TEN EXERCISES TO HELP MANAGE PSA

When you speak in public, you must prepare both your mind and your body. The first five exercises in this list are mental exercises that will help you get in the right frame of mind for your speech. The last five exercises are physical exercises that will help you prepare your body for your speech performance.

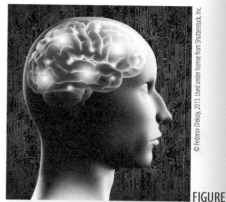

Mental exercises can prepare your mind for public speaking.

FIGURE 2.9

Exercise #1: Cognitive restructuring. To replace false, inaccurate thoughts about public speaking with true accurate thoughts, follow these steps: first, identify times and situations when you experience public speaking anxiety; second, identify the false or inaccurate thoughts you may be thinking when you experience this anxiety; third, mentally eliminate these thoughts and replace them with true, accurate thoughts. Cognitive restructuring is most effective when practiced regularly over a period of time. To start "retraining your brain," take a look at some inaccurate thoughts related to public speaking listed in Part 9 of this chapter.

Exercise #2: Systematic desensitization. If you have severe PSA, you may want to try "systematic desensitization" with the help of a psychologist or therapist. (This therapeutic method is used to manage severe phobias, like the fear of flying.) First, you imagine a relatively low-stress public speaking situation and practice relaxation exercises until you are mentally comfortable imagining that scenario. You then work your way through a series of increasingly stressful public speaking scenarios and practice relaxation exercises on each level until you are able to mentally cope with even the most stressful public speaking situations.

Exercise #3: Positive visualization. Use your mind to help create the speech performance you desire. Imagine the ideal speech from beginning to end. Mentally rehearse how you will stand, how you will look at the audience, how you will speak, etc. Envision your speech in the third person; using your imagination, place yourself in the audience. Watch yourself, the speaker, approach the podium. Watch yourself speak with enthusiasm and confidence. See and hear the audience respond appreciatively when your speech is concluded.

Exercise #4: The worst case scenario. If you find yourself constantly worrying about what might go wrong, perform the "worst case scenario" exercise. Ask yourself, "what is the worst that can happen?" Allow yourself to envision the worst—blanking out, throwing up, dropping all your note cards on the floor—then ask yourself, "can you live with that?" Would your life be over, or would you continue to exist upon this earth? Once you reconcile yourself to your worst case scenario, put it aside and go back to positive visualization.

Exercise #5: Positive affirmations. Positive affirmations take positive visualization in a different direction. Instead of *visualizing* the speech you want to give, you *verbalize* the speaker you want to be. First, identify your areas of personal concern related to public speaking; second, write out what you want to accomplish in these areas; third, write first-person, present-tense, positive affirmations that envision these accomplishments as already realized; finally, recite these affirmations to yourself. Positive affirmations are a specific tool used for cognitive restructuring, so they must be repeated often to become effective. Part 10 of this chapter demonstrates how you can develop positive affirmations for different public speaking concerns.

Exercise #6: Aerobic exercise. Aerobic exercise is important for your general physical well-being. Take care of your body by exercising it regularly. Work out at home or at a gym. Partici-

FIGURE 2.10 Stretches and isometric exercises can help you prepare physically for your speech.

pate in recreational sports. Walk around your neighborhood. Exercising the day before a speech can help you get a restful night's sleep. Exercising the day of your speech can help you release tension and use up some of your extra adrenaline. Aerobic exercise will also give you a natural vitality that you will not have to "fake" for your speech presentation.

Exercise #7: Deep breathing. Deep breathing is an excellent way to promote full relaxation. It is best practiced while laying on the floor on your back. Breathe in slowly through your nose until your diaphragm is fully extended, and then breathe out slowly through your mouth until all the air in your lungs is expelled. If you concentrate on the breathing process, deep breathing can relax both the body and the mind. Here is a deep breathing variation you can do right before you speak: as you sit in your chair, inhale through your nose, and exhale while quietly saying "ahh." Let your body relax as you exhale. You are ready for your speech!

Exercise #8: Stretches. To prepare your body, you can perform stretching exercises before you enter the room in which you will be speaking. (It is not appropriate to do stretches in front of your speaking audience!) Stretch your neck, your shoulders, your arms, wrists, and hands. Stretch your back and your legs. These stretches will release some nervous energy, ensure that your body is ready to perform, and get you in tune with your physical "instrument."

Exercise #9: Vocal warm-ups. To warm up your larynx, vocal folds, tongue, and lips, you can practice vocal warm-ups. Some people practice these warm-ups every day. Perform a "lip trill" by holding your lips loosely together and releasing the air in a steady stream while you say the "b" sound. Perform a tongue trill by placing your tongue behind your upper teeth and pronouncing the "r" sound as you exhale. Stretch your vocal cords by pronouncing the "me" sound on a low pitch, and then gliding up and back down the octave scale. (As with stretches, it is not appropriate to do your vocal warm-ups in front of your audience!)

Exercise #10: Isometric exercises. Isometric exercises can be done right in your chair just before you speak. Systematically tense and relax the different muscle groups of your body—tense your arms, and then relax them, tense your stomach, and then relax it, tense your legs, and then relax them. These isometric exercises can help you use up extra energy, but they can also help

TEN EXERCISES TO REDUCE PSA

1. Cognitive restructuring.
2. Systematic desensitization.
3. Positive visualization.
4. The worst case scenario.
5. Positive affirmations.
6. Aerobic exercise.
7. Deep breathing. ✓
8. Stretches.
9. Vocal warm ups. ✓
10. Isometric exercises.

you to relax, especially if you combine them with deep breathing: breathe in, tense a muscle group for a few seconds, and then relax as you exhale.

Which of the five mental exercises will be most useful for you? Are you willing to try some of these mental exercises to improve your frame of mind for public speaking? Why or why not? Which of the five physical exercises listed here will be most useful for you? Are you willing to perform some of these physical exercises to prepare your body for public speaking? Why or why not?

PART 9: TEN INACCURATE THOUGHTS RELATED TO PSA

If you think false, inaccurate *thoughts* about public speaking, you will have false, inaccurate *perceptions* of public speaking. Unfortunately, your perception is your reality. If you do not question your false, inaccurate thoughts about public speaking and public speaking anxiety, these thoughts will keep you trapped in an anxiety-filled pseudo-reality.

This section helps you flex your mental muscle by presenting ten inaccurate thoughts people think about public speaking and public speaking anxiety. Read each false, inaccurate assumption and then practice "cognitive restructuring" by replacing it with a true, more accurate, more realistic assertion. You can develop your response by using the information provided in this chapter. As you speak the truth about public speaking and PSA, you may be set free from much of your public speaking anxiety.

Flex your mental muscle by questioning false, inaccurate thoughts.

FIGURE 2.11

TEN FALSE ASSUMPTIONS RELATED TO PSA

False Assumption #1:	Very few people experience public speaking anxiety like I do.
False Assumption #2:	If I were a good public speaker, I would eliminate almost all symptoms of public speaking anxiety.
False Assumption #3:	My public speaking anxiety will ruin my speech.
False Assumption #4:	In order to succeed, I must give a perfect speech.
False Assumption #5:	Everyone can see how nervous I am.
False Assumption #6:	My anxiety will increase throughout my speech.
False Assumption #7:	My audience will harshly criticize my speaking efforts.
False Assumption #8:	My worth as a human being is determined by my speech performance.
False Assumption #9:	My audience will be thinking about my speech performance long after my speech has ended.
False Assumption #10:	I am better off avoiding public speaking altogether.

Our thoughts create our attitudes, and our attitudes lead to our actions. If you have been making any of the false assumptions listed above, these inaccurate thoughts may have caused you to become discouraged and engage in negative "self-talk."

The point of cognitive restructuring is to turn this negative internal monologue into an internal *dialogue*. How successful were you at questioning these false, inaccurate assumptions and replacing them with true, more accurate assertions? I will restate each false assumption once more, but this time I will counteract it with the truth:

False Assumption #1: *Very few people experience public speaking anxiety like I do.*

The truth: Very few people do *not* experience public speaking anxiety. When asked to list their greatest fears, people often put public speaking at the top of their list, even ahead of death. Most people experience public speaking anxiety, and a good amount of people have high levels of PSA.

False Assumption #2: *If I were a good public speaker, I would eliminate almost all symptoms of public speaking anxiety.*

The truth: Even excellent speakers deal with symptoms of PSA. Good speakers learn to *manage* their symptoms, not eliminate them. The symptoms of public speaking anxiety are almost always present to some extent for almost all speakers.

False Assumption #3: *My public speaking anxiety will ruin my speech.*

The truth: Speakers without a productive amount of PSA can have "flat" speeches. Properly managed PSA can actually enhance your speaking efforts. You can use the extra nervous energy that results from PSA to your advantage.

False Assumption #4: *In order to succeed, I must give a perfect speech.*

The truth: You can give an excellent speech without being perfect. Most people would consider an excellent speech to be a successful speech. There are also many ways to measure success. One measure of success is that you gave your speech your best effort. Another measure of success is that you communicated your message to your audience—who says the message has to be communicated perfectly?

False Assumption #5: *Everyone can see how nervous I am.*

The truth: You do not look as nervous as you feel. Many of the symptoms of speech anxiety are internal, and many of the external symptoms of speech anxiety are not that noticeable.

False Assumption #6: *My anxiety will increase throughout my speech.*

The truth: Speakers usually report being the most nervous right before their speech and right as their speech begins. Your anxiety will most likely decrease as you get into your speech.

False Assumption #7: *My audience will harshly criticize my speaking efforts.*

The truth: A public speaking audience is made up of a variety of individuals; some may be highly critical, but unless you do something to alienate your audience, most will probably be supportive and encouraging. If you are speaking in a college public speaking class where almost all the audience members also have to give speeches, you can expect a very supportive audience.

False Assumption #8: *My worth as a human being is determined by my speech performance.*

The truth: Your worth as a human being does not come from any particular speech that you give. Even if a speech you gave was an unqualified failure, this single poor performance would not rob you of your human worth or dignity.

False Assumption #9: *My audience will be thinking about my speech performance long after my speech has ended.*

The truth: It is difficult enough to get your audience to pay attention during your speech—why would you think they are going to pay much attention to you or your speech after your speech is over? The truth is, you are not that important to your audience. After your speech is over, your audience members will turn their attention to the next speaker, or to what they are going to eat for their next meal, etc. You can verify this fact by checking your own mental life. How often do you think about the speeches given in your speech class once they are over? No matter how excellent or poor these speeches were, they soon receded from your conscious thoughts.

False Assumption #10: *I am better off avoiding public speaking altogether.*

The truth: You are better off facing your fear of public speaking and learning how to manage your public speaking anxiety. Some of my students who proclaim at the beginning of a class, "I have put off taking a public speaking course as long as possible" say at the end of the same course, "I should have taken this class a long time ago," or "what I learned in this class sure would have helped me in my other college classes."

One of my past students, a firefighter, shared with me how his fear of public speaking caused him to miss out on many promotions at work. Over the years, he had passed up the opportunity to apply for supervisory positions with more pay and benefits because these leadership positions required some public speaking. He had decided that he was better off avoiding public speaking altogether.

After taking my class and learning how to manage his public speaking anxiety, he expressed sincere regret for the opportunities he had let slip by. As a firefighter, he had risked his life many times by running into burning buildings, but he had never faced his fear of public speaking. When he learned that he could speak in public, and that he could do it well, he realized that his long-standing fear of public speaking was unreasonable. Unfortunately, he felt that this "cognitive restructuring" occurred twenty years too late in his career.

If fire fighters can face death, you can face your fear of public speaking.

FIGURE 2.12

© TFoxFoto, 2013. Used under license from Shutterstock, Inc.

Do not let inaccurate thoughts about public speaking or public speaking anxiety hold you back. The ten inaccurate thoughts listed here are only a representative sample—there could be other false, inaccurate assumptions you are making about public speaking and PSA.

PART 10: TEN POSITIVE AFFIRMATIONS TO HELP REDUCE PSA

Positive affirmations have been another very successful tool in the field of cognitive psychology. Psychologists and therapists have helped people with negative self-images and very low self-esteem to transform themselves through the power of positive affirmations.

FIGURE 2.13 Positive affirmations can help you succeed.

By positively affirming themselves, many people have overcome poor self-images and boosted their self-esteem. You can use positive affirmations to transform your negative worries and fears about public speaking into positive visions that will lead you to become the best public speaker you can be.

This section models how to take a negative worry or fear and turn it into a positive affirmation in three simple steps: 1) identify and express in specific words what you are worried about, 2) express this negative worry or fear as a positive desire, and 3) create an affirmation that envisions this positive desire or wish as realized in the present.

For example, suppose you are worried about having a lot of verbal clutter when you speak. First, you would express this fear clearly: "I am afraid I will say 'uh' and 'um' a lot when I speak." Next, change this negative statement into what you want to see happen: "I want to speak smoothly during my speech." Finally, create a positive affirmation that states your positive desire as a present reality: "When speaking in public, I use pauses effectively, and I let my words flow smoothly from my mouth."

Here are ten more model positive affirmations:

1. Negative Fear: I am afraid I will procrastinate and put off preparing my speech.
   Positive Desire: I want to put good effort into my speech so I can be successful.
   Affirmation: **"I prepare and practice my speeches ahead of time."**

2. Negative Fear: I am afraid my audience will find my speech boring or irrelevant.
   Positive Desire: I want my speech topics to be important and interesting.
   Affirmation: **"I discover and develop important speech topics that hold the interest of my audience."**

3. Negative Fear: I am afraid my speech will be disorganized and hard to follow.
   Positive Desire: I want my speech to be easy to follow.
   Affirmation: **"I prepare well-organized speeches, and I make my speech structure clear to my audience."**

4. Negative Fear: I am afraid that my audience will not listen to me.
   Positive Desire: I want my audience to believe that I deserve their attention.
   Affirmation: **"I present myself as a confident, competent speaker."**

5. Negative Fear: I am afraid that I am a boring speaker.
   Positive Desire: I want to be a dynamic, charismatic speaker.
   Affirmation: **"I deliver my speeches with energy and enthusiasm."**

6. Negative Fear: I am afraid I will self-obsess and tune out my audience.
   Positive Desire: I want to make a real connection with my audience.
   Affirmation: **"I pay attention to my audience members, and I strive to engage them in my speech."**

7. Negative Fear: I am afraid my audience will really dislike my speech.
Positive Desire: I want to worry less about possible audience criticisms.
Affirmation: **"I view the speech as a time to share my message, and I keep my mind focused on sharing this message effectively."**

8. Negative Fear: I am afraid I will sabotage myself with my negative thinking.
Positive Desire: I want to think positively about my efforts.
Affirmation: **"Regardless of the outcome, I am proud of the effort I put into preparing and presenting my speeches."**

9. Negative Fear: I am afraid I will freak out if something unexpected happens.
Positive Desire: I want to handle distractions and difficulties well.
Affirmation: **"I am flexible. If problems arise, I adjust my presentation as needed."**

10. Negative Fear: I am afraid I will not be able to handle criticism.
Positive Desire: I want to be able to accept feedback and criticism gracefully.
Affirmation: **"I appreciate constructive criticism, and I use audience feedback to become an even better speaker."**

TEN POSITIVE AFFIRMATIONS

1. "I prepare and practice my speeches ahead of time."
2. "I discover and develop important speech topics that hold the interest of my audience."
3. "I prepare well-organized speeches, and I make my speech structure clear to my audience."
4. "I present myself as a confident, competent speaker."
5. "I deliver my speeches with energy and enthusiasm."
6. "I pay attention to my audience members, and I strive to engage them in my speech."
7. "I view the speech as a time to share my message, and I keep my mind focused on sharing this message effectively."
8. "Regardless of the outcome, I am proud of the effort I put into preparing and presenting my speeches."
9. "I am flexible. If problems arise, I adjust my presentation as needed."
10. "I appreciate constructive criticism, and I use audience feedback to become an even better speaker."

Remember that positive affirmations state what you want, rather than what you do not want—they help bring about change by envisioning the positive attitudes and behaviors you want to create. Remember also that positive affirmations should be stated in the present tense, as though the positive attitudes or behaviors have already come into existence. Do not worry if an affirmation is not "true" when you first speak it—positive affirmations become true over time as your positive vision is realized.

If you are prone to negative thinking, you may find that you want to argue with yourself after stating a positive affirmation. You may say to yourself things like, "yes, but . . .," or, "who are you trying to kid?" Do not argue with yourself. Affirm yourself. If you insist on seeing yourself in a negative light, then you will continue to be influenced by your negative self-fulfilling prophecies. To break the power of negative thinking, allow yourself to believe in a different, better you.

SUMMARY

Public speaking anxiety may be a real problem you face, but after reading this chapter, you can create your own PSA management plan. Review the top ten lists of information provided in this chapter to come up with the best solutions for your PSA:

1. The ten-question self-test will help you determine how much of this chapter you need to digest and apply.
2. The ten causes of public speaking anxiety will help you find the sources of your PSA.
3. The ten common symptoms of PSA will help you expect and accept these symptoms.
4. The ten ways *not* to manage PSA will help you avoid bad behaviors and wasted time and effort.
5. The ten ways to reduce PSA before your speech will help you prepare a speech.
6. The ten ways to reduce PSA during your speech will help you present a speech.
7. The ten ways to reduce PSA after a speech will help you accept feedback and apply this feedback to future speeches.
8. The ten exercises to help manage PSA will help you address both the psychological and physiological elements of PSA.
9. The ten inaccurate thoughts related to PSA will help you retrain your brain and avoid "stinking thinking."
10. The ten positive affirmations to help reduce PSA will help you envision public speaking success.

If you apply the information in this chapter to manage your public speaking anxiety, you should be able to successfully give speeches in public. After delivering the assigned speeches in your public speaking class, you should be able to give many other speeches at work, in your community, and wherever and whenever necessary. You will then be able to compile a special top ten list for yourself: My Top Ten Most Successful Speeches.

Review
Questions

❶ What is your level of public speaking anxiety?

❷ What are some of the major causes of public speaking anxiety?

❸ What are the common major symptoms of public speaking anxiety?

❹ What are some ineffective ways to manage public speaking anxiety?

❺ How can you reduce or manage your public speaking anxiety before, during, and after you speech?

Glossary

Aerobic exercise: Low-intensity physical exercise that stimulates your heart and lungs.

Awfulizing: Remembering, perceiving or imagining events as "awful" or "terrible."

Cognitive conservatism: The tendency to hold on to ideas, even when they are inaccurate or false.

Cognitive restructuring: The mental process of identifying false or inaccurate ideas and replacing them with truer, more accurate ideas.

Communication apprehension: Fear and anxiety related to different human communication situations.

Fight or flight response: A biological defense mechanism activated by a perceived danger situation.

Isometric exercise: Exercise involving the tensing of major muscle groups without the movement of joints.

Performance anxiety: Nervousness and apprehension created by the concern for effective task completion.

Positive affirmation: A statement that posits a desired future outcome in the present tense. Positive affirmations can be used to change the way you think and feel about things.

Positive visualization: Using the power of imagination to envision a desired outcome.

Public speaking anxiety: A very common form of communication apprehension related to the fear of speaking in public.

Self-talk: The internal dialogue that occurs in individual human psyches.

Self-fulfilling prophecy: A thought or statement about a person or event that becomes true by virtue of having been expected or predicted.

Systematic desensitization: A therapeutic method used to overcome fears and phobias. A person is exposed to a perceived danger situation for longer and longer intervals until the perceived danger situation no longer triggers fear or alarm.

CONSIDERING YOUR AUDIENCE

Andrea D. Thorson-Hevle

Learning Objectives

CHAPTER 3

❶ Examine ways to analyze your audience's demographics.

❷ Examine ways to analyze you audience's psychographics.

❸ Determine how to adjust your speech according to audience analysis.

❹ Understand the role of attitudes, beliefs, and values on message understanding.

A good speaker knows to do their research not only on their topic but also on their audience. The first phase in considering your audience begins before you ever arrive to give your speech and even before you write it. Understanding what is expected from you, what your audience needs, what predispositions they may have, and how their various affiliations will impact the success of your speech are all bits of information that will help you adapt to your audience. **Audience adaptation** refers to the speaker adjusting their message for a specific audience based on demographic and psychographic information of their audience as well as their general expectations given the occasion, needs, and setting. The process of audience analysis is meant to unveil as much information as possible about a given audience for the purpose of enhancing communication and message appeals. As soon as you know you are going to be giving a speech there are a series of questions you should know the answers to that will help you understand and thus appeal to the audience:

1. What are the demographics and psychographics of the audience?
2. How can people with disabilities be accommodated?
3. What are the attitudes, beliefs, and values of your audience?
4. What is the occasion?
5. What does the audience need from my speech?
6. What is the speech setting going to be?

Audience analysis helps a speaker construct main points, and supporting material with an audience's traits, affiliations, and characteristics. The foundation of analysis starts with assessing the degree of homogeneous characteristics in a given audience. Homogeneous means the audience shares several similar characteristics, while heterogeneous refers to an audience that holds mostly dissimilar traits. In order to consider your audience you need to conduct a demographic and psychological analysis of your potential audience. Determining the physical characteristics, roles, and norms of your audience is known as demographic analysis. Demographic analysis will in turn permit you to better understand the psychological tendencies (by means of psychographic analysis) of your audience, which will permit you a great understanding of how to approach your audience regarding specific topics.

The aim of analyzing demographic and psychographic information is to discern which characteristics are relevant to your speech intent and goal. Evaluating your audience for their group affiliations will help you cater your message to a specific audience, setting, and occasion. The goal is not to stereotype groups but, rather, recognize characteristics that may affect the way your listeners will interpret your message, listen to your message, and the degree to which they may agree with your message.

CONSIDER DEMOGRAPHICS
DEMOGRAPHICS

Demographics are various sociological categories to which an audience may belong. Examples of demographics include geographic location, age, gender, sex, race, ethnicity, disability, education level, experience level, occupation, socioeconomic status, religion, social groups, and political ideologies.

A speaker may want to consider demographics before a speech and during a speech. Various appeals and language may be more effective depending on the demographics of an audience. Using demographic analysis will also help you get an idea of how your audience may interpret your message.

SEX AND GENDER

When providing examples be careful to use only evidence-based examples when it comes to sex. Avoiding sexist language and sexist assumptions is a must in public speaking. See the chapter on language for specific examples of sexist language to avoid. One sexist example or comment can immediately ruin a speaker's credibility.

Sex refers to whether a person is male, female, or unisex, it takes into consideration sex chromosomes, sex hormones, and internal and external reproductive structures. Gender is the tendency for men or women to exhibit characteristics of masculinity or femininity. We are brought up with a series of expectations based on our sex. Humans tend to conform to expectations they are given,

© Matthias Pahl, 2013. Used under license from Shutterstock, Inc.

It is very important that you understand the difference between sex and gender and the fact that they are not necessarily related in any way.

FIGURE
3.1

but this does not mean this is innately who they are nor does it mean that certain sexes are all a certain way. What it does mean is that we teach men and women that they should act and perform in certain ways. From the toys you played with as children to the clothes you purchase today, you are participating in the construction of your perceived gender.

If you are a woman you may be purchasing items that society has told you is acceptable and attractive for women. Perhaps you buy dresses. Do you buy dresses because you really want to buy dresses, because you were born knowing you were meant to wear a dress? No. you wear dresses because society has bombarded you with images of what it means to be a woman and you have conformed to that model. When people have conformed to an expected gender they usually don't find themselves concerned with the difference between sex and gender and are less likely to see gender as important. Gender characteristics like strength, assertiveness, empathy, and submissiveness are not distinctly linked to a specific sex. Despite common assumptions, human characteristics like strength, aggression, emotional display, and ability to nurture are not linked biologically to certain sexes. Be open to the idea of various genders.

Gender expression for example, refers to the ways people tend to communicate their gender externally. This may come in the form of clothing, jewelry, tattoos, hairstyles and color, and even the sounds of their voice. **Gender identity** on the other hand refers to how a person perceives themselves and how they prefer to refer to themselves. **Gender roles** refer to the various expectations, roles, and behaviors that have been assigned to men and women based on the idea that men should be masculine and women should be feminine.

Gender can be understood on a spectrum of masculinity and femininity with androgyny in the middle. It refers to the idea that masculine and feminine genders think, behave, and understand the world differently. Our culture assigns women to be feminine and men to be masculine, but as I'm sure you have noticed, these distinctions are not altogether accurate. In fact, the idea

Sex Spectrum

Female	Intersex	Male

Gender Spectrum

*"Beyond anatomy, there are multiple domains defining gender. In turn, these domains can be independently characterized across a range of possibilities. Instead of the static, binary model produced through a solely physical understanding of gender, a far more rich texture of biology, gender expression, and gender identity intersect in multidimensional array of possibilities. Quite simply, the **gender spectrum** represents a more nuanced, and ultimately truly authentic model of human gender"* (GenderSpectrum.org, 2014, para. 4).

Femininity	Androgyny	Masculinity

that women should be feminine and men masculine can actually be harmful. Femininity and masculinity are established in the social (one's gender) rather than the biological (one's sex) aspects of people. Androgynous gender is somewhere in between the two other types and is defined as someone who cannot be determined to be clearly feminine or masculine. Although it seems like most people are feminine or masculine, most are actually a combination of feminine traits and masculine traits. The United States has very specific stereotypes for men and women. People tend to conform to one or the other, but that does not mean they are innately born with those traits, nor does it mean they are limited to them. As explained by GenderSpectrum.org, "At birth, it is used to identify individuals as male or female. *Gender* on the other hand is far more complicated. Along with one's physical traits, it is the complex interrelationship between those traits and one's internal sense of self as male, female, both or neither as well as one's outward presentations and behaviors related to that perception" (2014, para 2).

For instance, boys are not born liking blue and hating pink. Similarly, girls are not innately keen on pink. Society, rather, has taught us that certain colors are suited and appropriate for different sexes. In the 1950s blue was actually the color associated with girls and pink was the color for boys. As a speaker, you want to refrain from using gender as a constant guide for your approach to examples and explanations. Similarly, men and women are born nurturers. Girls are not more naturally nurturing than boys, society socializes girls overtime to be nurturing and tends to discourage the natural male nurturing tendencies more. This tendency makes people have expectations and conform, but it is not an accurate reflector of the sexes natural ways of being. It is important to recognize that gender is not related to sex. It is equally important to remind yourself that most people in the world actually exhibit a combination of traits that would land them in the androgyny category more than any other, as such, you should use diverse examples that appeal to an androgynous audience as a general rule.

Masculine	Feminine
Logical	Emotional
Assertive	Nurturing
Stable	Patient
Confident	Affectionate
Independent	Dependent
Strong	Submissive

You could consider the needs of a sex or gender, but you should not overly focus on them.

FIGURE 3.2

It can be insulting and rude to use sex or assumed gender as a means of discussing ideas with your audience. For instance, I once attended a lecture in which a speaker used only masculine or commonly "male" associated examples because the audience was predominantly male. Football and baseball examples were constantly used. Several men in the audience were unable to understand many of the points the speaker was making because they simply didn't understand the analogies being made about certain sports the speaker assumed they understood based on their sex alone.

Some men were irritated with the speaker for assuming they would all "relate" to sports just because they were men. Other audience members clearly lost respect for the speaker. And still,

FIGURE
3.3 In some cultures piercings are decorative, protective, and ritual based whereas in other cultures it is considered defacing a sacred temple.

other men in the audience were confused because they didn't understand the complicated example. So, in sum, it is often not to a speakers advantage to make assumptions about their audience based on sex. There are cases in which it of course, makes sense to make assumptions, claims, or examples based on sex. For instance, if a speaker were giving a speech about the Nuva Ring (a form of female contraception) then the speaker could offer examples that only speak to women. Similarly, if you were giving a speech about the importance of prostate examinations, you could provide examples and instances that only refer to men.

ETHNICITY

Cultures of all types tend to have specific norms and ways of communicating. Ethnicity is an element of culture. Ethnic groups (often called **ethnicity**) can be understood as people who share language, nationality, or other cultural systems. The reason ethnicity can be an important consideration when constructing and delivering a speech is because different cultures have different expectations, rules, and systems of communicating.

Knowing these various norms can go a long way in helping you connect with your audience. Before constructing a speech you may want to consider the ethnic diversity of the audience. Appeal to as many cultures as possible and avoid potential misunderstandings or miscommunications.

Take for instance, when I was in college one of my good friends Shoko was reprimanded by a professor because she would not look at him in the eye when he asked her questions. She responded to him while looking down. The professor felt Shoko was rude and disrespectful. If the speaker had greater cultural awareness, he would have remembered that Shoko, being an exchange student from Japan, communicates differently with elders and people in positions of power. Avoiding eye contact in that particular situation was considered respectful in Shoko's culture. It is always the responsibility of the speaker to consider communication factors of culture and respect them.

Additionally, you will want to avoid using idioms. **Idioms** are distinct expressions used by a specific culture that other cultures might not understand because the denotative meaning of the words does not accurately describe the meaning. Avoid using idioms in your speech because others may be confused or even offended by them. If, however, you know that everyone in your audience is from a certain culture, using an idiom may be a nice way to bridge a connection with the audience. Common idioms are "get off my back," "you totally missed the bus," and "you look like you have the weight of the world on your shoulders."

Even those most well intentioned speakers will make mistakes and use examples, jokes, or analogies that are offensive to other cultures. It is essential that a speaker understand what is considered hurtful to certain cultures especially those that have been historically oppressed or subjugated. **Oppressive language** is any word or series of words that uses an identifier of a person or a certain group as a negative or undesirable characteristic. It is usually used to suppress and belittle, whether intentional or unintentional. It is considered a form of verbal violence. Keep in mind, the more you know about different cultures the better you can accommodate them. You should always examine your content for how it could be interpreted by different ethnicities. Please see the chapter in this book on language to get a deeper understanding and specific examples of oppressive language.

AGE

A great diversity of age in an audience should signal the speaker to use a diversity of examples and explanations. A good speaker will take note of the ages in their audience and adjust their examples accordingly. Using popular references to a younger crowd is a good bet. Using popular commercial slogans from the 1970's is not. Additionally, every generation has their commonly used slang terms, their quirks, and commonalities. A speaker will want to consider the age of their audience and adjust the terms they choose accordingly (see the chapter on language choices for more ideas).

Consider for example, a very polished presentation aimed at persuading the audience to not smoke marijuana. During the speech the speaker calls marijuana "a duby" and many members of the audience snicker and roll their eyes. Why do think this might happen? Perhaps it was because the term "duby" is used by older generations, and is no longer a popular way to refer to marijuana. Nowadays, the younger generations often refer to it as "pot" or a "joint." The speaker had been doing an excellent job of convincing the audience not to partake in a harmful illegal drug, but quickly lost momentum when a word choice that failed to consider the audience was used. It is important to create similarity with your audience and shared experience; using words that indicate you are different can have a detrimental effect as it creates distance rather than closeness.

Age may also be important to consider when you are deciding how much background information with which to provide your audience. Many speeches require some basic foundational knowledge and others must provide it. Consider the age of your audience and the likelihood they have learned, have experience, and or knowledge regarding your topic. For instance, if you have diverse age range and you are giving a speech on technology, do not assume that every member will know what Twitter or Skype are, or how to use them. You will need to provide some background before you can use examples or expand on these areas. Similarly, if you are giving a speech on an important historical event, you may have audience members who partook in it or lived through it, so you want to be sure you consider the effects of your words on those individuals.

OCCUPATION

You never want to use language with which the audience is unfamiliar. Doing so can pose a distraction, insult your audience, or even simply lose their interest. At the same time, you do not want to speak down to your audience either. If you knew the occupation of the audience before you gave a speech, you would be able to make language choices accordingly.

If you are giving a speech to an audience of two hundred medical doctors about

In this example, the speaker uses "diagnosis" because the audience is a group of medical personnel. Had it not been, he could have written "findings" or "what was found."

FIGURE 3.4

FIGURE
3.5

IF YOU (THE SPEAKER) HAVE A DISABILITY

Determine if your disability may affect how you deliver your speech and make accommodations as needed. If it will affect the way you deliver it, then you need to do one of two things or both:

Consider disclosing to the audience what your disability is. This will preserve your ethos in case that certain things arise. For instance, the author of this chapter is unable to sit or stand for long periods of time because of a spinal problem. When I give a speech, I let the audience know I may lean on the desk, sit on the desk, or walk throughout the presentation. This allows the audience to understand why I doing these otherwise inappropriate movements during my formal speech.

Make sure you have necessary accommodations present and ready well before the speech begins. You do not want to have to ask to be handed something latter on. Be prepared from the start.

a new machine that can be used in the case of heart attack, you should consider using the term "cardiac arrest" instead of "heart attack." When your audience clearly speaks the jargon specific to their occupation, you want to try to use language that is reflective of that occupation, but only if you can do so competently and accurately.

DISABILITY

A good public speaker will consider culture while constructing their speech and make adjustments during the speech as well. Able-bodied people often forget to make accommodations for the disabled community in general. During hurricane Katrina over seventy percent of those left behind were people with disabilities. Rescuers took able-bodied people first and frequently animals before the disabled. Was this a calculated effort? Were they told to take dogs and only people who could walk easily first? No. It happened because of the unconscious ways in which our able-bodied culture thinks about disability. As a speaker this mistake is one that cannot be made.

People with disabilities will likely be in your audience. Now, you might be thinking, "how on Earth am I supposed to know what disability someone might have and how to accommodate that disability during my speech?" The good news is I am not asking you to be able to see into the future or be a master planner. I am asking you to learn a few key things and use them consistently when you are the speaker. This list will help you be an inclusive, empathetic, professional speaker.

FIGURE
3.6

DISABILITIES ARE NOT RARE

8.1 million people have difficulty seeing.

7.6 million people have difficulty hearing.

30.6 million people have difficulty walking or climbing stairs.

According to the Disability Funders Organization, "people with disabilities constitute the nation's largest minority group, and the only group any of us can become a member of at any time."

According to the U.S Department of Education, workers with disabilities are rated consistently as average or above average in performance, quality and quantity of work, flexibility, and attendance.

Q13 answer

First, consider using off-colored paper for handouts instead of white paper. Many people have minor to severe conditions of the eye that make it very hard to see the words on a white background. Keep in mind a blue, green, purple, pink, or orange handout will be easier for these individuals to read. The color should not compete with your writing, so avoid the neon colors and anything that ruins the credibility of your handout by being distracting or unprofessional.

Second, consider placing a "reserved for a person with disability" sign on a couple chairs. Try to place at least one of these near the exits or on the outside of rows. When you walk with a cane, walker, or manufactured legs, it is exceptionally hard to get through tight spaces. Making sure these individuals have a seat that will make it more comfortable for them is important and professional. Note, however, that some people with a disability do not want to have a special seat and that is perfectly acceptable, they will simply not sit there. And, if by the time your speech starts, no one is sitting there, that is okay too.

Third, if you are using a presentation aid or a visual aid try to make the audience aware of this early on so that those with any sight impairments (near sighted or otherwise) and those who are hearing impaired may have the option to come forward before the speech actually begins. It is also important your videos be closed-captioned.

Fourth, if you have tables or chairs that are movable, be sure there is at least one row that is wide enough for a wheelchair to easily pass by without causing people to have to move and stand. People who use a wheelchair should not be put under stress because there is no safe and easily accessible place for them. Consider using a sign that indicates any row that is wheelchair accessible.

A good speaker will ensure their speech environment is as accommodating as possible.

FIGURE 3.7

Fifth, if there are no secure seats, which means the seats are not attached to the table or ground, you should remove one or two from the end of an aisle. This will ensure a wheelchair can easily slide in. Keep in mind, the bigger the audience, the more you will need to increase the number of wheelchair accessible seats.

Q13 answer Sixth, consider if you are using any sensory aids. Sensory aids are presentation aids that depend on the audience using one or more of their senses. For instance, in a speech on how to make carrot cake, you may be planning on asking the audience to smell the bit of spice you placed on their tables. To accommodate those who have a sensory disability, be sure to vividly describe the scent so that they can also enjoy and partake in the process. Take a look at the language chapter in this book for more pointers on incorporating vivid language.

Seventh, use meaningful gestures that enhance and correspond with what you are saying so that those with any form of hearing impairment may have a greater chance of understanding fully what you are saying. If possible, ask that someone who knows sign language be present for your speech.

Keep in mind that hearing aids do not fix hearing completely—they only enhance it—so you must still follow the accommodations.

FIGURE 3.8

Eighth, if you know someone has a sight or hearing impairment make sure you face them often, as they can understand much more by seeing your lips move. If you have to write on the board be sure to write on the board without talking. Hard of hearing people will not be able to hear you well when you are facing the board.

Ninth, make sure you use proper language regarding specific cultures of disability. Always use people-first language. People-first language places the person before the disability in a sentence and thereby communicates that the person is not defined by their disability but rather, one of many parts of their identity. For instance, you should say, "people with disabilities" or "a person with a disability" rather than "handicapped people" or "disabled people." If you need to let the audience know where restrooms are and they are located say, "accessible restrooms are just down the hall." Do not say, "Handicapped restrooms are down the hall." You would say, "Joey has Down syndrome," not "he is a Down syndrome baby." You would say, "Kim uses a wheelchair," not " Kim is confined to a wheelchair." Please see the language chapter in this book for a more in-depth discussion on language choices.

Tenth, don't try to over sympathize, become dramatic, or unnecessarily cater. Basic empathy is appreciated. You want to avoid making a person with a disability feel like they are being treated like a child. Avoid trying to over emphasize and applaud a basic accomplishment just because someone has a disability or impairment. We like to be treated like others as much as possible—remember that and respect us as people first.

Eleventh, be sure to ask before you help any person with a disability. Do not assume a person with a disability wants or needs your help even if they are clearly struggling with something. Always ask if the person needs assistance, once you have the "yes," then and only then proceed. Similarly do not touch people with a disability without asking permission. You would not appreciate strangers touching you without permission; show the same courtesy to the person with a disability.

Twelfth, keep in mind there are invisible disabilities. Invisible disabilities are disabilities that you cannot easily see, that the person would likely have to disclose in order for you to know. Invisible disabilities can also include people who simply choose not to disclose their disability. For instance, most people wouldn't know a person has dyslexia unless that individual disclosed it. If you use any handouts be sure to use simple and clear fonts like "Arial" because they are easier for people with dyslexia to see and comprehend. Generally, fonts with any fancy script writing, tags at the start or ends of letters, or even the common Times New Roman font poses a difficulty for some groups of people. Print materials and even presentational aids like PowerPoint® should be in simple clear fonts (sans-sharif fonts especially). Remember that even if no one has identified themselves as a person with a disability, it doesn't mean that a person with a disability is not in your audience. One in five people have some form of disability. Invisible disabilities can be emotional, physical, sensory or otherwise.

Thirteenth, evaluate your speech for its use of different types of learning strategies. People with learning disabilities often learn though different modes of learning. There are those who learn best with lecture, others with reading, and others with hands-on experience-based learning. Many people with learning disabilities learn best through the use of hands-on experiences. Try incorporating an activity, or several short hands-on moments during your speech—it will help not only those with learning disabilities but also others who just simply learn best and become more interested when speakers use multiple ways of engaging.

Generally, when approaching culture, be sensitive and considerate of needs. Remember, we are human, treat us as such. Recognize people with disabilities exist and treat us with respect as you would anyone. If you are ever in doubt about your accommodations, consider what that particular culture would feel like during your speech and adjust accordingly.

EDUCATION

The educational background of your audience may seem irrelevant but it can be very helpful. People who have an education tend to be more aware of current events, have a greater ability to consider multiple sides of an argument or issue, and more willing to tolerate and accommodate differences. If you know you have an educated audience, you can use more sophisticated language because research shows that educated people understand more sophisticated language choices. You run the risk of insulting or making an audience feel like you are talking down to them when you use language that is elementary to their abilities.

Educated audiences tend to be more open-minded but they also tend to have highly developed points of view.

FIGURE 3.9

Most important, you want to consider the basic knowledge level of your audience. What the audience knows about that certain topic is what is most important. You may be talking to a room of PhDs but it you are giving a lecture on coding for computers and their PhDs are in sociology you will still need to adjust jargon into simple language and explain the concepts as you would to anyone else. Consider the education, and then consider the degree to which it helps you determine an approach to your speech.

SOCIAL, POLITICAL, AND OTHER CULTURAL GROUPS

Belonging to certain groups outside ethnicity, age, sex, gender, disability, education, and occupation are also important to consider. Social groups refer to the various cultures people belong to based on interest, activities, political and religious affiliations, etc. This is an important construct to examine when constructing your speech because it will help you determine how to approach your topic. Religious affiliation can predispose an audience to hold attitudes and beliefs that may significantly impact the chances that the audience will accept a speaker's message, which means it is important for a speaker to keep in mind what values, beliefs and thus attitudes an audience may have as a result of their religion. Speakers must be careful to not make stereotypical comments or examples regarding religion in their speeches; assumptions and rumors are not valid, may perpetuate untrue notions, and be hurtful.

Considering the social and political cultures your audience identifies with is especially important in persuasive speaking. If you are trying to convince your audience to vote for greater gun control and you know the majority of your audience is Republican, you can alter your speech to accommodate appeals that will be better geared for that audience. If you know you are speaking to a group of Democrats, which is a political affiliation that is currently known to fight for increased gun control, then you don't have to work as hard on the basic foundationary levels of your argumentation. You are in essence "preaching to the choir" and can focus more on what the audience can do to accomplish this task as apposed to spending most of your time establishing why the task is important.

CONSIDER PSYCHOGRAPHICS

Psychological characteristics of your audience include an examination of attitudes, beliefs, and values. Although this can be a helpful process on any speech, it is especially helpful in persuasive speaking or other speeches where you plan to alter the ways your audience understands or acts. In order to change the ways in which people think of certain things or the ways they behave, you first need to have an understanding of what their attitudes and current behaviors are. Again, as was relevant in demographic analysis, we are not suggesting your rely blindly on stereotyping, we ask you avoid that. We are instead asking you consider where the audience may psychologically be and adjust your speech accordingly. This section discusses the ways in which audience attitudes, values, and beliefs can help you give a better speech.

ATTITUDES

An audience's attitude on a given issue refers to their tendency to think about that topic in a generally negative or positive way. For instance, if you felt Pop Tarts® were better than Toaster Strudel®, this would be an attitude you hold. Attitudes are psychological predispositions to feel a certain way about something. *answer*

© magdanphoto, 2013. Used under license from Shutterstock, Inc.

FIGURE
3.10

VALUES

The tendency to feel that something is right or wrong is a reflection of values. Values indicate an audience's perception of right and wrong. It does not reflect attitude or preference; it merely asserts a level of importance and desirability regarding a set of principles. For instance, you may value your personal rights, freedom, or independence.

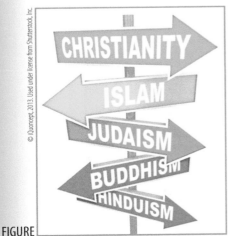

© iQoncept, 2013. Used under license from Shutterstock, Inc.

FIGURE
3.11 Religion is an example of belief-based perspective.

BELIEFS

Systems of beliefs are a set of accepted truths. A person comes to a belief based on interpretation and judgment. Beliefs are different than values because it is not concerned with right or wrong—beliefs are often "faith" based. An example of belief is a person's choice of religion or belief that humans have a responsibility to be forgiving and kind.

Knowing your audience's attitude, beliefs, and values about your topic beforehand is helpful because it can help you craft your overall message. If you can manage to have guessed the correct psychological and demographic characteristics, you can include appeals that appeal to your audience more directly. You can use valuative appeals that motivate different segments of your audience to agree, become interested, or merely openly listen to your message.

CONSIDER OCCASION

The occasion will tell you a number of key things that will allow you to adjust your speech to better suit your audience. The occasion will tell you what is appropriate in terms of dress, language, formality, time, and more. We have an entire chapter dedicated to discussing what is expected from a speaker at various occasions; visit that chapter to find your occasion and its expectations of you as a speaker. A special occasion speech is a presentation delivered for a celebratory, congratulatory, or ceremonial event. The general purpose of a special occasion speech is to entertain or inspire the audience.

FIGURE 3.12

A wedding speech that fails to accommodate the expectations and follow the rules of the occasion can end up devastating the couple and embarrassing the speaker.

Part of your responsibility as a speaker is to analyze and adjust to the customs, traditions, and general expectations of the given occasion. Each occasion has a different set of expectations, rules, roles, and judgments. In an effort to meet the needs and norms of any given occasion ask yourself a few questions:

1. **What is deemed appropriate for the specific time and place of this speech?** You will want to be sure you are dressed appropriately, use the expected style of speech and language choices, and that your speech is the "right" length for the given occasion. To assess these questions more fully, visit the chapter on language and special occasion speaking.

2. **What is considered appropriate for this specific type of speech purpose?** You may want to find out if it is customary for the audience to ask questions during the speech or after. You may discover the speaker can make these rules and therefore you should let the audience know early on when you would prefer questions to be asked. You also want to consider appropriate titles that you should use. Using improper titles can be offensive to your audience and embarrassing for you. Consider when it is appropriate to use titles like "doctor," "your honor," "the honorable _____," and other business position type titles like "CEO," or "executive assistant."

3. **Are there any special rituals or cultural processes I should facilitate?** Are you expected to speak to inform, persuade, entertain, or otherwise? If you are giving a speech at a church be sure to investigate the requirements and expectations of that speech. Not all religious ceremonies are the same.

FIGURE 3.13

A woman sets the flowers for a morning ritual.

4. *Is the audience voluntary or captive?* Whereas voluntary audiences attend because of interest. Captive audiences require more in terms of persuasion and entertainment. **Voluntary audiences** already come with some interest in the subject so you may not need to be more persuasive, but you should emphasize what they can do to create a change.

CONSIDER THE NEEDS OF THE AUDIENCE

FIGURE 3.14 Preserve the character of the person you are giving a speech about.

A speaker that constructs a speech purely based on their own needs will risk upsetting an audience, being judged as selfish, careless, rude, or inconsiderate. Taking into consideration what your audience needs is essential to the success of your speech. For instance, let's pretend you were asked to give a speech at a funeral (known as a eulogy) and you happen to know that the family was very close to the man who died, let's call him Frank. Frank was eighty-seven years old and was known as the funny man in the family. He was known for always telling jokes and chasing the grandkids with bugs, toads, and snakes. He was the man who always cracked a smile at the most reserved and sad of times. Knowing this information about Frank, you might consider that the audience would need his eulogy to honor that characteristic of Frank, by incorporating a little humor. You could remind the audience of Frank's funny ways and tell a joke or two.

You could also ask a few family members for their favorite memory of a time Frank made a sad day happy. The point is that, when you compose a speech, you must consider what the audience needs to hear not just for the occasion (that which is expected) but what will heal them, help them, and complete them.

Ask yourself these questions when considering the needs of the audience:

1. **Does my approach consider the unique person or situation in a way that will make others react positively?**
2. **Does my approach consider the unique needs of my particular audience?**
3. **Does my speech consider the audience's predisposition to the subject and adjust in a way that makes them feel comfortable and yet maintains my intentions?**

CONSIDER THE SPEECH SETTING

Knowing your **setting** for the day of the speech is just as important as constructing the speech itself. Failure to properly plan for your setting may result in a plethora of misunderstandings and problems. The speech setting includes several things, but the most important is the size of the space and the size of the audience.

You should first know the size of the room in which you will be speaking. The size of the room can determine many things. It may determine how you dress, affect your choice in audio enhancers, change the persuasive appeals (if you are persuading), it may alter how you move during your speech as well. Larger rooms will require a great attention to lighting details.

Next <u>you want to consider the expected size of the audience</u>. I say "expected" for a reason. You will rarely know exactly how many people will be in your audience, but you can usually have some idea. Just because your room is big doesn't mean your audience will be.

For example, once I was told I would be giving a thirty-minute speech in a large lecture hall that held about three hundred and twenty people. I prepared my speech in a grand style (which will be discussed in the language chapter); I practiced larger gestures, and general examples for my points. I failed, however, to ask the expected audience size. Instead I assumed the lecture hall would be generally full. You can imagine my surprise when I showed up to deliver my speech to an audience of about thirty people.

I had previously planned to use a standing microphone and audio equipment to ensure my voice was heard. But, if I used that method now, it would seem almost egotistical and certainly unnecessary. The choice in a big microphone would create a barrier between the audience and myself rather than make a greater connection. To a room so small I should rely on my own voice and ability to be heard.

My preplanned choices in grand gestures and vocals seemed forced and a little weird as I began. Being an inexperienced speaker at the time, I continued using my grand style of gesture and speaking, even though I knew it felt wrong. Continuing poor delivery choices for your specific audience must be avoided; when you recognize something isn't going well make a change. I could have at any moment walked away from the microphone and the big gestures and stately verbal language, and I should have.

Additionally, had I asked how many people were expected, I could have prepared more audience-centered examples in my speech. Instead of having broad examples, I could have prepared to ask questions of my audience. I would have planned on entering into audience discussion more frequently. Had I been more experienced, I could have done this on the spot as well. Remember, you can always drop your general planned examples and start interacting more with your audience when you feel you need to create a connection and add some participation. Audiences are more likely to be motivated or persuaded by a speaker who can actually keep their attention. One of the best ways to get audience attention is to include them through questions, stories they relate to, and discussions. It's important

FIGURE 3.15

Adjust delivery for smaller audiences.

FIGURE 3.16

Consider the size of your audience.

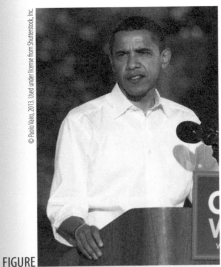

FIGURE
3.17 President Obama often gives speeches outdoors, but he always makes sure his audio equipment is ready to compensate for any weather disturbance.

to gather relevant setting information in advance and yet, regardless, be prepared to make adjustments.

Questions you should know the answers to:

1. **Will the speech be delivered outside or inside?** If it is outside, knowing the weather expectations is key to how you dress and even the visual aids you may use.

2. **What presentation aids are available and usable given the setting?** On a windy day using poster boards may be an issue. Using technology for your presentation aid is helpful but, if it is going to rain, you may want to double check that the technology will still be available and safe.

3. **What kinds of accommodations can I make for disabled members of my audience?** Ensuring persons with disabilities can easily access a seat at your speech is important.

4. **What size audience should I expect?** Knowing how many people are expected to attend will help you plan activities, discussions, types of microphones and technologies to use and give you a basis for the type of delivery style you should use in order to have the greatest impact.

5. **What size room will I be presenting in?** Knowing the size of the room in advance will help you plan how you will navigate the room, light the room and plan for various audience interactions and appropriate technologies that can aid in meeting your audience expectations.

CONSIDER THE:

Occasion	Demographics
Needs of the audience	Psychographics
Speech setting	Gender not sex
Means of delivery	

CONSIDER MEANS OF DELIVERY

You then want to consider delivery methods. You will want to consider all available technological options of delivery. You will want to determine which option is right for you given the occasion, audience needs, room size, and audience size. There are many delivery options you may have available to you. You may also want to ask if you can bring some delivery tools yourself. Various delivery methods you may want to consider include: standing microphone, hanging microphone, headpiece microphone, podium, lectern, media, stage, etc.

In the personal example, I had planned on using a large standing microphone for my speech to hundreds. When it ended up being just thirty people, and I stood there with my giant microphone, I looked a little silly and I certainly created distance between the audience and myself. In a room of only thirty people, you should rely on the three delivery tools you know best: your left lung, your right lung, and your diaphragm. In a small setting, ditch the microphones. Projection is your best friend in a small group of people. It sends a more personal feeling and lessens the formality and stiffness of the occasion. Projection refers to the quality of your voice as produced through volume and ability of your voice to be heard generally.

Ask yourself the following questions when analyzing your modes of delivery options:

1. **Is the type of delivery best for the setting?** Consider time of day, audience likelihood to be tired, light and darkness of the setting, etc.

2. **Is the type of delivery best for my audience? Does the delivery method present undue separation between the audience and the speaker?** Assess whether you need a volume-enhancing device and whether that device is appropriate for the occasions formal or informal expectations.

3. **Will you have advanced contact with the delivery method?** If you have never used a hanging microphone or a large podium, you may want to practice with it ahead of time.

SUMMARY

We addressed the various components of demographics as well as the dimensions of psychographics. We discussed how attitudes, values, and beliefs can influence how an audience perceives and reacts to your message and thus how you should approach your message. We learned how to be more accommodating of diverse audiences and a general understanding for how important analyzing your audience can be. This chapter also tackled the issues surrounding how to effectively analyze your audience without being stereotypical or insulting. The process is an interesting one to navigate, but if you keep with the main skills taught in this chapter, you should do well.

Review Questions

1 What are three demographics discussed in this chapter and their role in audience analysis?

2 What are the three psychographic areas this chapter discussed?

3 What are important things to know about the setting and occasion of your speech?

4 In what ways can a speaker accommodate a person with a physical disability?

5 In what ways can a speaker accommodate people with learning disabilities?

Glossary

Attitudes: Psychological predispositions to feel a certain way about something.

Audience adaptation: When the speaker adjusts their message for a specific audience based on demographic and psychographic information of their audience.

Beliefs: A set of accepted truths.

Demographics: are various sociological categories to which an audience may belong.

Ethnicity: Understood as people that share language, nationality, or other cultural systems.

Gender: The tendency for men or women to exhibit characteristics of masculinity or femininity and the degree to which they act in ways that are expected of their sexes.

Gender expression: for example, refers to the ways people tend to communicate their gender externally. This may come in the form of clothing, jewelry, tattoos, hairstyles and color, and even the sounds of their voice.

Gender identity: refers to how a person perceives themselves and how they prefer to refer to themselves.

Gender roles: refer to the various expectations, roles, and behaviors that have been assigned to men and women based on the idea that men should be masculine and women should be feminine.

Heterogeneous: refers to an audience that holds mostly dissimilar traits.

Homogeneous: means the audience shares several similar characteristics.

Oppressive language: Any word or series of words that uses an identifier of a person or a certain group as a negative or undesirable characteristic.

Projection: refers to the quality of your voice as produced through volume and ability of your voice to heard generally.

Sex: Whether a person is biologically male, female, or unisex.

Setting: The environment in which your speech will occur.

Values: An audience's perception of right and wrong.

CHOOSING A SPEECH TOPIC

Michael M. Korcok

Learning Objectives

❶ Move from the general purpose to a topic and specific purpose and to an effective thesis statement.

❷ Generate creative and challenging topic ideas from your experience, the media, and current events.

❸ Craft the right thesis statement for the speaking situation, your audience, and you

Julio Martinez is a veterinarian. He was recently invited to speak at a charity event for a local animal shelter. He believes his audience expects to hear a speech about animals but doesn't know how to focus his speech to encourage donations.

Joe Kelly's grandfather recently passed away and his grandmother has asked him to speak at the funeral. Joe has strong, positive memories of his grandfather but doesn't know how to express his feelings to an audience of family and friends. He's also worried about becoming emotional in front of so many people.

Kate Black is a sophomore enrolled in an introductory public speaking course. The first speech is an informative one and students are allowed to pick their topic. Kate feels lost. She doesn't feel like she knows enough about anything that would be interesting to the other students and she doesn't want to make a fool of herself.

In each of the introductory scenarios, the prospective public speaker must clarify a purpose, topic, and thesis in order to develop an effective speech. The process of speech preparation formally begins with topic development. For both novice and experienced speakers, the identification of an appropriate topic can appear daunting. The selection of an appropriate speech topic requires precision, organization, and planning.

Even when you are happy with your topic, you must refine and narrow it to fit the speech's purpose. Pick too broad a topic and you won't have time to address it well within your time

© ollyy, 2013. Used under license from Shutterstock, Inc.

FIGURE
4.1 Thinking of the right speech topic can be a challenge.

limit. On the other hand, too narrow a topic will likely fail to keep an audience's interest. You also may not be able to fill the time allotted if your subject area is too small.

CHAPTER OVERVIEW

This chapter presents strategies for the selection and refinement of a speech topic and purpose. The chapter begins with a discussion of the various factors likely to influence the development of the speech topic and purpose. These include the speaking event, the audience, and the characteristics of the speaker. These factors can place constraints and requirements upon the speech topic and purpose.

Much of this chapter focuses upon the process of developing a speech topic and purpose, which involves three steps: the general purpose, the specific purpose, and the thesis statement. The goal of topic selection is to move from broad considerations of the speech event, the knowledge and interests of the audience, and the speaker's own competence through a process of refinement that leads to the fashioning of a clear thesis that describes the central idea of the speech.

The general purpose describes the overarching goal of the speech. Three types of general purposes exist: to inform, to persuade, and to entertain. Selecting a general purpose provides the foundation for the development of the specific purpose and the thesis statement. The specific purpose is the combination of the general purpose and the speech topic. The topic is the general theme or subject of the speech. Many strategies for topic selection may be used, including brainstorming, personal interest lists, mind maps, and media prompts. The thesis statement is the key argument or idea of the speech.

The chapter concludes with a discussion of the most common mistakes made when choosing a topic and purpose. These mistakes include overgeneralization, the selection of a topic that doesn't interest the audience, the selection of a topic that doesn't interest the speaker, and the selection of an unfamiliar subject.

GETTING TO YOUR THESIS

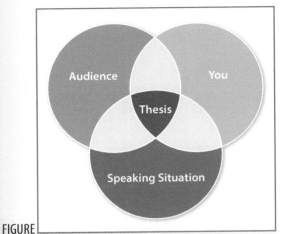

4.2 The right topic is constrained by the speaking situation, the audience, and you.

Speech topics do not occur in a vacuum. A **topic**, which is the general theme or subject of a speech, arises through the interaction of place, time, and person. Your topic must be appropriate for the context, or surrounding environment. The context is composed of three factors. They are the speaking situation, the audience, and you, the speaker.

Each of these factors may place constraints and requirements on the speech topic and purpose. A **constraint is a restriction or limitation**. Within some contexts, you are likely to find the range of topics limited to an acceptable list of topics. Within your public speaking class, for example, your instructor may place constraints on the topic of your speeches. He or she may specifically ask you to avoid particular topics that are overdone, too controversial, or too technical to treat adequately within the given speech assignment.

A **requirement is an obligation or expectation.** For example, you are likely to be given a time requirement for your speeches in class. Your instructor is likely to ask you to deliver an informative speech that is between five and seven minutes long, with penalties imposed for speeches that are too short or too long. This requirement will influence the selection of your speech topic and purpose because you must talk about something that can be sufficiently covered within the designated time.

THE SPEAKING SITUATION

The speaker's freedom to select topics is often limited by the event at which they will present. Outside of the classroom, the speaking event will likely help to dictate the general purpose. For example, if you are asked to speak at a wedding, you know that the content of your speech must involve congratulating the new couple. Similarly, the topic of a eulogy or a speech of presentation will often be readily apparent. The eulogy will involve speaking about the deceased being honored at the funeral, whereas the speech of presentation will discuss the award and the recipient.

The classroom also serves as a speaking event that will include particular constraints and requirements imposed by your instructor. For example, time requirements are a common restriction imposed by instructors. This requirement is instructive, requiring you to condense your topic into a manageable speech length. The requirement is also practical allowing several speeches to be delivered within a single class period.

Another common requirement is the use of references in class. For a speech assignment, your instructor is likely to require that you use a minimum number of references to support your main points. References increase the credibility of your speech and illustrate your effort as a researcher.

Often, instructors avoid placing many restrictions on the topic of a speech. Instead, they will give their students considerable latitude to select a topic of interest to them. Students should view this freedom as both an advantage and an encouragement to be creative. Experienced public speaking instructors hear hundreds of topics a semester. They want to hear topics that are interesting and challenging. However, students often fail to view topic selection as an opportunity to share their interests with others. Instead, they become paralyzed by the fear of coming up with a topic.

THE AUDIENCE

Audiences can impose particular constraints on the topic of a speech. As a speaker, part of your job is to consider how your audience will respond to potential speech topics. The first relevant consideration is the demographics of the audience. **Demographics** are the characteristics that describe the audience as a collective whole. Examples of demographic features include size, age range, level of educational attainment, and socioeconomic status. In addition, the heterogeneity of the audience, or the level of diversity among its individual members, will help to determine how much each individual demographic characteristic is likely to influence the audience's response to a given topic.

The response of the audience to your speech will also be influenced by the audience's psychology. The **psychology of the audience** reflects the prevailing moods, attitudes, and feelings of the individual audience members. Audience members have their own self-interests and needs that shape their interpretation of the speech.

Audiences also enter the event with their own collective expectations about the content of the speech. The expectations of the audience will reflect the prevailing culture. **Culture** is defined as the collective social development of values, meanings, knowledge, attitudes, beliefs, experiences, and institutions. Cultures shape communication norms, such as the rate of speech delivery, the expected degree of eye contact, and the type of language used. They also influence the appropriateness of potential topics. A diverse audience may contain individuals representing many different cultures, with each culture characterized by their own set of preexisting expectations.

The interaction between the speaking event and the audience can shape audience expectations and their ultimate response to a given speech. For example, the psychology of an audience at a wedding listening to a toast offered by the best man will be very different from the psychology of an audience attending a funeral. One audience is feeling happy and celebratory whereas the other is in mourning. Members of the audience within the wedding expect a toast that is positive and congratulatory. Members of the wake are dealing with their own feelings about the death of an individual. Both events may have religious significance for some members of the audience and members of the audience may attach particular cultural expectations to a speech delivered for each occasion. Both audiences reasonably expect that the content of any speeches offered at their events will appropriately reflect the overall mood.

The brief discussion of audience demographics, psychology, and culture serves to highlight some of the ways that audience characteristics can influence topic selection. Ideally, your job as a speaker is to understand your audience and select a topic appropriate for the audience. However, you must also be aware of the risk of stereotyping your audience. **Stereotyping** is an overgeneralization based on the assumption that all members of a group are the same.

Ultimately, successful topic selection begins with an audience analysis. The process of audience analysis was explored in Chapter 3 and prior to selecting a topic. You should review that chapter and conduct a formal audience analysis. The analysis of your audience will help you to identify any relevant topic constraints and requirements. It will also help you to select a topic that will suit your audience's characteristics. The failure to conduct an audience analysis can undermine your speech's purpose through the selection of an inappropriate topic. If your audience is apathetic or skeptical about the topic, their bias will make delivering your speech much more difficult.

THE SPEAKER

Finally, the topic selection process is influenced by the characteristics of the speaker. Like an audience, your characteristics as a speaker include your demographic background, your psychology, and your culture. The same speech can be delivered by three different speakers to the same audience and elicit three very different responses. That is because the speaker's characteristics, including appearance, dress, voice, and delivery technique, will influence the audience's reception.

For example, audiences tend to respond favorably to a speaker with strong topic knowledge. As a speaker, your personal interests, knowledge, and experience will also frame the selection of your speech topic.

If Michio Kaku is invited to speak at a college campus, he will speak about a topic related to science. If Toni Morrison is invited to speak, she is likely to discuss American literature and politics. When they speak, these and other famous persons share their personal experiences and convey their expert knowledge to the audience. Their specific knowledge is why they are invited to speak.

Similarly, you have your own personal areas of expertise and topics of interests. Few aspects of speech writing are less frustrating than topic development. Many students, when working on their first speech, fear that they lack the knowledge needed to talk about anything interesting. However, the truth is that everyone is different and that difference provides rich opportunities for interesting topic development. Some students discuss their health conditions, or the condition of a family member. Others speak about their favorite sport or team. Your past vacations, jobs, schools, hobbies, favorite television shows, books, and video games may all provide fertile ground for topics.

Remember to view a speech as an opportunity, rather than an obstacle. A speech provides you with the chance to advance your goals and to explore your interests. If you support a particular charity, policy agenda, political party, or social organization, the speech will give you the chance to share that interest with others.

For example, Jerod is a forty-five-year-old firefighter enrolled in a public speaking class. The class is required for his professional advancement. As a nontraditional student, he enters the classroom apprehensive about his ability to deliver a speech to the other students, who he views as young kids. When assigned an informative speech, he does not feel that he knows enough about a subject that will appeal to his younger classmates.

However, Jerod can draw readily upon his professional experience as a firefighter to craft an interesting speech. He can choose to discuss topics such as fire prevention and safety or the most

FIGURE 4.3 The best topics are ones that come from your own knowledge and experience.

common causes of house fires. Alternatively, he can write an informative speech about a particular firefighting event, such as when his unit was flown to New York to assist in the recovery effort following the terrorist attacks on September 11, 2001.

Furthermore, Jerod's topic choices are not limited to his work. He can also write a speech about what it is like to be a nontraditional student. As a working adult, he chose to return to the classroom. Although his schoolwork is important, he also has to juggle his responsibilities to his wife, children, boss, and coworkers. If Jerod is correct about the relative youth of the other students, they will not be familiar with the challenges associated with being nontraditional students.

Any of these topics fit Jerod's background. They all have the potential to interest his classmates. However, to identify these topics as appropriate for a speech, Jerod must go through the three step topic selection process. This process begins with the identification of the speech's general purpose, which is the subject of the next section.

GENERAL PURPOSE

The **general purpose** describes the overarching goal of the speech. Outside of class, the general purpose is likely to be indicated by the event or person asking you to speak. For example, an invitation to give a guest lecture may ask that you help educate the audience about a new policy or initiative. Within the classroom, the general purpose will typically be assigned to you by your instructor. Three types of general purposes exist: informing, persuading, and the special occasion speeches.

SPEECHES TO INFORM

Speeches to inform provide new information to the audience. The general purpose of the informative speech is to convey new knowledge to others. When you give a speech to inform, you assume the role of an instructor.

Informative speeches take many forms. The process-demonstration is a common type of informative speech. This informative speech shows the audience how to do something. The speaker is typically an expert with specialized knowledge relevant to the topic. For example, chefs on cooking shows engage in process demonstration when they show their viewers how to cook a particular recipe. Another type of informative speech is the biography. This speech describes the life, challenges, and accomplishments of an individual person. The general exposition is a third type of informative speech. The structure and preparation of speeches to inform are discussed in greater detail in Chapter 10.

SPEECHES TO PERSUADE

Speeches to persuade aim to motivate or convince the members of the audience to hold a particular viewpoint. A persuasive speech begins by outlining a specific argument or position the speaker supports. The body of the speech then offers arguments to support the speaker's perspective.

The goal of the persuasive speech may take one of three forms. First of all, persuasive speeches may reinforce an existing belief. If invited to speak at a convention of Young Republicans, you are more likely to write a speech praising that party rather than trying to convince the members of the party to join the Democratic party. Your speech will aim to increase the commitment of the audience to the organization and to create a strong, positive feeling about the political party to the audience.

Second, a persuasive speech can seek to change the audience's belief. For example, politicians in Congress will offer persuasive speeches to endorse or reject a policy goal, prospective law, or political appointment. In such cases, persuasion may take the form of creating a positive or negative feeling that will motivate the change in belief. In addition, the persuasive speech may try to weaken the existing viewpoint in order to make change easier.

Finally, a persuasive speech may motivate the audience to take a specific action. The goal of this type of persuasive speech is to convince listeners that they should do something, such as give to a particular charity or register to vote. These persuasive speeches are sometimes referred to as speeches to actuate. The structure and preparation of speeches to persuade are discussed in greater detail in Chapter 11.

SPECIAL OCCASION SPEECHES

Special occasion speeches describe a diverse range of speeches and events. A special occasion speech is a presentation delivered for a celebratory, congratulatory, or ceremonial event. The general purpose of the special occasion speech is to entertain or to inspire the members of the audience. However, the method of entertainment can vary considerably. For example, some special occasion speeches call for the use of humor whereas, for others, the use of humor may be regarded as inappropriate. The different types of special occasion speeches are detailed in Chapter 15.

SPECIFIC PURPOSE

FIGURE 4.4 Moving from the general purpose to the specific purpose requires choosing the right topic.

Your general purpose gives you a broad understanding of the direction of your speech. However, the general purpose doesn't tell you the actual subject of your speech. Instead, the general purpose should point you in the direction for narrowing your topic. For example, if you are assigned to offer an informative speech in your public speaking course, you need to decide what you will discuss. Your general purpose is to share information in an efficient, accurate, and clear manner. You want to bolster the audience's interest in your topic. What do you want your audience to learn from your speech? On the other hand, if you plan to give a persuasive speech, you need to determine what you want your audience to believe. What argument or position will your speech support?

For a special occasion speech, you should question the needs of the event and the desired purpose of your speech. What do you hope to accomplish when you get up to speak?

The answer to these questions is your specific purpose. The **specific purpose** is the general purpose plus the topic. The specific purpose narrows your topic to focus upon a goal consistent with your general purpose. By crafting your specific purpose, you will gain clarity on what exactly you want to aim to accomplish during your speech.

As you develop your specific purpose, you will see how the general purpose directly influences your topic to create your specific purpose. Two speeches may discuss the topic of 3D printers but their specific purpose will vary considerably based upon whether the general purpose is to inform or persuade.

GENERATING IDEAS FOR TOPICS

Many strategies can be used by you to develop your specific purpose. Brainstorming is one popular strategy for topic development. The process of **brainstorming** involves the creation of a list of potential topics in an uncritical manner. You should think about potential speech topics, asking yourself, "What can I talk about?" Write down your first answer immediately. Then, continue to write out ideas as they come to you. During this initial stage of free writing, don't worry about whether an idea is good and don't cross out ideas. The goal of brainstorming is to produce many different options within a relatively short period of time. Even if you write down something that doesn't seem like a good idea initially, that idea could lead you to the ideal topic later.

Example: Develop a Specific Purpose	
General purpose: To inform	Topic: Three-dimensional printers
Specific purpose: To explain how 3D printers work.	
General purpose: To persuade	Topic: Three-dimensional printers
Specific purpose: To convince the audience to buy a 3D printer.	

After the initial list is generated, the process of refinement can commence. Review the list and cross out items that you don't want to talk about, that you don't think will appeal to your audience, or that won't fit neatly within a speech's time limit. Don't force yourself to follow the original ideas perfectly. Use them to inspire additional subjects or ideas until you find a useful topic.

Personal interest lists provide another method of specific purpose development. Like brainstorming, your goal is to identify many different potential topic options. However, personal interest lists are more structured than brainstorming.

These lists touch on subjects like your educational background, your hobbies and interests, your employment experience, and key events in your life. They also include subjects that fascinate you that you would like to explore further.

The completion of these lists will reveal potential subjects to integrate into your specific purpose. For example, if you like to read, compiling the list of things you enjoy may remind you of specific books that you really enjoyed. A biography could provide the basis for an informative speech about a person. Alternatively, if you ever experienced an earthquake, tornado, or other weather event, the development of the list may remind you of the subject, leading to a speech about how to best survive a natural disaster.

Often, novice public speakers fear that they aren't familiar with subjects that an audience would find appealing. However, some of the best speeches touch on one of these personal experience topics, areas that the audience members don't know or haven't experienced firsthand. For example, one student worked in retail and developed an informative speech on how to deal with difficult customers. Her audience was composed of individuals who had never worked in retail. They enjoyed her anecdotes about crazy customers and returns. They also learned strategies that could be applied to many professional settings outside of retail.

Personal Interest Lists
Things you know.
Things you enjoy.
Things you do and have done.
Things you have experienced.
Things you would like to know more about.

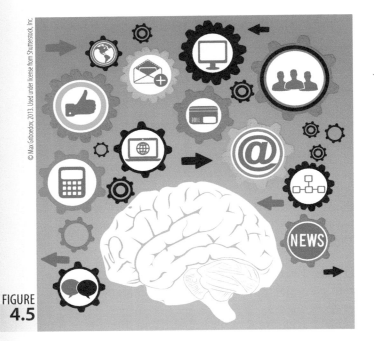

© Max Griboedov, 2013. Used under license from Shutterstock, Inc.

FIGURE 4.5

If you prefer a visual strategy for topic development, trying building a mind map. A **mind map** is a diagram illustrating connections between categories, words, concepts, and ideas. A mind map will typically begin when you write a word in the center of the page. Circle that word. Then, add subtopics that directly relate to your central idea. Draw lines to represent connections between the center word and the subtopics. Once you are satisfied with your list of subtopics, move to each subtopic, circle it, and surround it with lower level subtopics. Connect these ideas to each other in relationships that are meaningful to you.

The process of building a mind map is useful for several reasons. First, like brainstorming, the mind map encourages you to identify many different topics within a relatively quick period of time. In addition, the mind map offers more organization than the list generated by brainstorming. By requiring you to link subjects, you can begin to formulate ideas or consider potential main points to support your speech topic.

Media prompts provide another popular strategy for topic selection. Media prompts are references written by other authors. They include newspapers, magazines, websites, and other materials.

The review of media prompts can require a considerable time investment. Set aside some time to peruse some newspapers or magazines. Go online and surf the web. You can find topic inspiration through these references. As you read, make note of the stories and headlines you find most interesting. Explore those topics further to see if there is enough information to support a speech. Never limit yourself to just one type of media or one author. Other authors may be biased and referencing several different resources will help you to develop a balanced perspective. Media prompts can provide a very timely topic for a speech, such as a current campaign or political election, a policy being debated, or a recent crime.

> **EXAMPLE: BRAINSTORMING TOPICS**
>
> Books
> Television shows
> Local politics
> Campus activities
> Pet adoption
> Health issues
> Fashion trends

Media prompts can also be especially effective in helping you to narrow a topic. Let's say you are interested in talking about human health. However, health is a huge subject area. It includes topics related to biology, medicine, and psychology. It includes specific conditions, symptoms, and treatments. As you try to narrow your topic, you can visit the website of a major health organization, like the World Health Organization (WHO). WHO offers an alphabetical list of health subjects that may make excellent speech topics. Just perusing the list offered by WHO can inspire you to think of another topic not even listed on the website.

However, you need to be careful to not overuse media references during topic development. Your goal in selecting a topic is to provide your own point of view, not regurgitate the views of someone else. If you rely too heavily on the thoughts and arguments of someone else, your own interest and enthusiasm for the topic may be negatively affected. Furthermore, if you copy the words or ideas of media writers, you may quickly find yourself in trouble for plagiarism. Any references used should be noted in your speech's bibliography.

> **EXAMPLE: NARROWING TOPICS**
>
> 1. *The Turn of the Screw* by Henry James
> 2. *Mrs. Dalloway* by Virginia Woolf
> 3. *Game of Thrones* by George R.R. Martin
> 4. *Beowulf*
> 5. *Othello* by William Shakespeare
> 6. *The Age of Innocence* by Edith Wharton
> 7. *The Snow Queen* by Joan D. Vinge

When engaging in topic development, it is important to keep in mind that the different strategies for topic development and refinement are not mutually exclusive. Often, you will find that the best topics arise out of utilizing more than one strategy.

SPECIFIC PURPOSE WALKTHROUGH

Mia is an English major enrolled in a public speaking class. In order to develop an informative topic, Mia begins by brainstorming.

Mia's initial brainstorming attempt generates a diverse list of potential subjects that she may choose for her informative speech.

The list generated by brainstorming helps Mia to refine her general purpose into a specific purpose. Mia looks at her completed list and finds option #1 most appealing. For her informative, she decides that she wants to introduce the audience to a literary work. She feels comfortable talking about books and poetry because these are subjects she regularly covers within her major classes. She knows that she is enthusiastic about this subject and hopes that she can share her own enthusiasm with the audience.

However, Mia can't talk about all books or every piece of poetry. She needs to refine her topic further to something manageable within the allotted time. Mia continues to work on her topic by constructing a personal list. On her list of "Things You Know," Mia lists the books that she has read over the last year.

Mia feels reasonably confident that she could write an effective informative speech on any of these books. She has read them all recently and has discussed them with her peers. She knows that each of these books have published reviews that could help her to learn more about the book's themes, date of publication, and authors. However, none of these options really inspire Mia.

Therefore, Mia changes topic development strategies. She creates a mind map based on her personal list. On a blank sheet of paper, she draws several circles and places each of the seven books into a circle. Then, she takes the time to focus upon each book and draws lines to identify topics or points that each book inspires. For example, the *Game of Thrones* book leads Mia to reference the hit HBO television series, her favorite performers on the show, and her favorite characters. When she moves on to *Othello*, she draws lines connecting *Othello* to other works by Shakespeare, such as *Romeo & Juliet, Julius Caesar, King Lear,* and *Hamlet*. Persuasion similarly inspires notes about other Jane Austen classics, like *Pride & Prejudice* and *Emma*. The circle containing *Mrs. Dalloway* leads Mia to list other works by Woolf in addition to famous works by other significant early feminist authors, such as Mary Wollstonecraft's *A Vindication of the Rights of Woman*. The part of the mind map devoted to *The Snow Queen* leads Mia to consider other respected works of science fiction with themes similar to Vinge's novel, such as Frank Herbert's *Dune*.

As she works on her mind map, Mia also begins to note particular themes, such as marriage, female education, and social class. These themes begin to create links between works by different authors. For example, Mia connects the social class theme in *Persuasion* to *Othello* and *The Age of Innocence*. Mia also links themes about women's work and magic to several works. Mia's mind map gradually leads her to select a biography of Mary Wollstonecraft as the subject of her informative speech.

In Mia's case, her final specific purpose is not her original specific purpose. Mia expected to focus her speech on a book and instead changed the focus of her speech to a biography. There is nothing wrong with this and shifting topics is actually quite common. In fact, as you work on your speech topic, you may be surprised to find that your ultimate subject is very different from what you originally intended to discuss. Topic selection often requires considerable time and effort to select a specific purpose that is consistent with the general purpose, manageable within the time allotted, and capable of meeting all other speech requirements. Therefore, it is important for you to give yourself enough time to refine and revise your specific purpose until you settle upon a choice that you really like.

FIGURE
4.6 Topic selection is an opportunity for creative self-reflection.

© NLshop, 2013. Used under license from Shutterstock, Inc.

The attainment of a specific purpose is an important milestone within the topic development process. However, it is not the end of the process. Rather, once you have a workable specific purpose, you may engage in a further process of revision in order to craft your thesis statement.

THESIS STATEMENT

The process of topic selection is complete once the speaker crafts a thesis sentence. The **thesis statement** is a single-sentence statement of the one main idea developed by the speech. The thesis statement clearly and succinctly articulates the narrowed subject that will be discussed within your speech.

The thesis statement is said as part of the introduction in the speech. Often, it is the final line of the introduction. It should follow your catchy opening and come before the transitional shift into the body of the speech.

In addition, the thesis statement will reappear within the conclusion of your speech. You can choose to repeat it or you can rewrite it to change the language but keep the meaning of the thesis. When offered within the conclusion, the thesis statement will remind the audience of the content that they just heard within the speech's body.

Example of general purpose, specific purpose, and thesis statement:

General Purpose: To persuade
Specific Purpose: To persuade the audience to donate blood
Thesis Statement: Today, I am going to convince you to donate blood at next week's campus blood drive.

EXCEPTIONAL THESIS STATEMENTS

When crafting a thesis statement, remember to look for the hook. A speech is an opportunity to leave your personal imprint on your selected topic. You don't want to simply restate someone else's opinion or discovery. Instead, be creative. Take your topic, turn it and twist it to make it different from others, to grab the attention of your audience and to give your speech meaning.

For example, within your public speaking course, you will likely be asked to write and deliver a persuasive speech. Many students elect to write a persuasive speech to actuate—a speech that asks the audience to take a specific action. If your topic is automotive safety and your general purpose is to persuade, your specific purpose may be "to get more people to wear their seatbelts." With this specific purpose, you still have many options for your thesis statement. One option is "wear your seatbelt." Although simple and straightforward, this is a terrible thesis statement. It is too easy and obvious. It is also noncontroversial and will bore your audience.

Instead, you need to develop a thesis statement that makes seat belts interesting to your audience. For example, your thesis statement may become, "we should pass a law requiring automobile manufacturers to develop and install self-buckling seatbelts for new models." This is a much better thesis. It is a bit provocative due to its use of the law to enforce company behavior while still relying on your general purpose, specific purpose, and topic.

Cell phone technology would provide an alternative direction for a speech to persuade.

General Purpose:	To Persuade
Topic:	Automobile Safety
Specific Purpose:	To stop people from texting while driving.
Bad Thesis Statement:	You need to stop texting while driving.
Good Thesis Statement:	We should program cell phones to automatically disable when in a moving vehicle.

Sometimes, speakers will avoid stating their thesis directly during their introduction. This decision forces the audience to determine the speaker's thesis for themselves. This strategy is a mistake for several reasons. An unstated thesis invites room for misinterpretation and misunderstanding. One audience member may identify a thesis statement that is very different from the conclusion determined by another audience member. The difference in opinion may cause some in the audience to miss the speaker's intended point entirely. A clear stated thesis statement prevents such confusion.

Within your college level course, you should expect your instructor to require you to state your thesis statement. You should always take the time to carefully write a thesis statement during your topic development. A clear thesis statement will help you to keep your topic focused and avoid straying onto unnecessary tangents. As you continue to write your speech, always go back and reference your thesis statement. If you find yourself writing about issues that do not support your thesis statement, they likely do not belong within the speech.

COMMON MISTAKES

Both new and experienced speakers often make common makes during the process of topic selection. The first common error is overgeneralization. The purpose of your thesis statement is to offer a clear focus for the direction and content of your speech. Overgeneralization can also occur during the development of your specific purpose.

General Purpose:	To Persuade
Topic:	Feminist Movement
Specific Purpose:	To Show Support for the Feminist Movement
Overgeneralization:	All Men are Chauvinists

A second common mistake is the selection of a topic that won't interest others. In particular, you should be aware of the risk of apathetic or hostile audiences. An audience analysis will help you to avoid choosing a topic that will anger or bore your audience.

Topics that a speaker doesn't know much about often lead to poor speeches. Initially, you may find the prospect of researching a new topic appealing. However, if you aren't familiar with the topic, you'll quickly find that every part of the speech is more difficult and time consuming to write. Also, the lack of familiarity is likely to be evident to your audience. The translation of new information into a speech format is a difficult process and the risk of mistakes will be high.

Furthermore, the relationship between the speaker's psychology and topic selection is too important to be ignored. Early in this chapter, the significance of the speaker's psychology was discussed as a relevant consideration for the topic selection process. Speech delivery can be a very frustrating and frightening process.

Even experienced speakers often acknowledge struggling with anxiety or stage fright. However, the speaker's familiarity with the speech's topic can have a significant influence over the speaker's psychology. Knowledge and familiarity can bolster a speaker's confidence and decrease the associated anxiety. In contrast, if you are unfamiliar with your topic, you will be more likely to feel nervous about delivering the speech.

Your anxiety will be justified if members of the audience are likely to know more about your topic than you. You don't want to try to give a speech to an audience more knowledgeable than you. Embarrassment is likely if people in the audience know more about the topic than you do, particularly if they correct your errors. In general, sticking to what you know is the far safer topic selection strategy.

> **COMMON TOPIC CHOICE MISTAKES**
>
> Overgeneralization
> Choosing unfamiliar topics
> Lack of personal interest

The selection of a topic that doesn't interest you, the speaker, is another common mistake. You should strive to select a topic that you are passionate about, or at least one that you find interesting. With the near infinite number of potential speeches, you should be able to find something to excite you. Otherwise, you'll be unlikely to do the work to craft a quality speech. You may procrastinate and throw your speech together at the last minute. You'll be unlikely to creatively engage the topic. If you don't care about your topic, the audience will pick up on your attitude. If you don't care, why should they?

SUMMARY

For many, topic selection is one of the most challenging parts of speech-writing. However, the process of topic selection is relatively simple and structured. The development of your speech requires you to move from the general to the specific. The process of topic development involves three steps: the general purpose, the specific purpose, and the thesis statement. The general purpose identifies the overarching goal of the speech. The three general purposes are to inform (the speech to inform), to persuade (the speech to persuade), and to entertain or inspire (the special occasion speech). If you are writing a speech for a class, your instructor will often give you the general purpose.

Determining the general purpose allows the development of the specific purpose. The specific purpose is the combination of the general purpose and the topic. The best topics will promote enthusiasm and interest in both you and your audience. They reflect your personal knowledge and unique perspective.

Once you have your specific purpose, you must continue to refine your topic. The specific purpose should be narrowed in order to produce your thesis statement—the focused sentence that clearly identifies the key content of the speech. Good thesis statements will provoke audience interest and demonstrate your unique take on your topic. The topic selection process is complete once you have your thesis statement.

Topic selection can be enabled through the use of many different strategies, including brainstorming, mind mapping, personal interest lists, and media prompts. Brainstorming involves freely and uncritically developing a list of potential subjects. Mind mapping involves the creation of a diagram illustrating the connections between different topic options. Personal interest lists involve the structured identification of personal interests, knowledge, and experiences. The use of media prompts involves the search of different reference materials, such as newspapers, magazines, and Internet websites, for speech topic inspiration. These different topic selection strategies are not mutually exclusive. You may find one strategy works best for you or you may want to try a combination of strategies as you work toward the development of your thesis statement.

When developing your topic and thesis statement, you should be wary of common pitfalls. Common errors include overgeneralization, lack of familiarity with a topic, and a lack of interest. If working with media prompts, always be wary of the risk of plagiarism. Relying too heavily on someone else's words is a **serious mistake** that creates a host of ethical concerns. Your speech should be original. It should not regurgitate the views of someone else. Rather, recognize that the speech is your opportunity to convey your personal perspective on your selected topic.

Review
Questions

❶ Distinguish between a general purpose, a topic, a specific purpose, and a thesis.

❷ What are the three basic general purposes of a public speech?

❸ Describe brainstorming, personal lists, and mind maps.

❹ What media and social media do you participate in regularly?

❺ Why is audience analysis important for crafting a thesis statement?

Glossary

Brainstorming: A strategy used for topic identification that involves the process of quickly listing potential speech topics in an uncritical manner.

Constraint: A restriction or limitation.

Culture: The collective social development of values, meanings, knowledge, attitudes, beliefs, experiences, and institutions.

Demographics: The individual characteristics that help to describe the audience as a collective whole, such as size, age range, level of educational attainment, and socioeconomic status.

General purpose: The overarching goal of the speech. Three types of general purposes exist: to inform, to persuade, and to entertain.

Media prompts: Reference materials reviewed as inspiration for topic selection, such as newspapers, magazines, and Internet websites.

Mind map: A diagram illustrating connections between different categories, words, concepts, and ideas.

Personal interest lists: Structured identification of personal interests, knowledge, and experiences useful in the development of a specific purpose.

Psychology of the audience: The prevailing moods, attitudes, and feelings of the audience members.

Requirement: An obligation or expectation.

Specific purpose: The specific purpose is the combination of the general purpose and the speech topic.

Stereotyping: An overgeneralization based on the assumption that all members of a group are the same.

Thesis statement: The thesis statement describes the specific purpose of the speech by identifying the key content or argument.

Topic: The general theme or subject of the speech.

RESEARCHING FOR YOUR SPEECH

Andrea D. Thorson-Hevle

Learning Objectives

CHAPTER 5

1 Discuss the importance and role of research in public speaking.

2 Decide which sources are best for your specific speech.

3 Evaluate various research methods.

4 Effectively organize your research efforts.

5 Learn how to paraphrase, quote, and cite your research.

Research is a tool that benefits many different types of speeches. The goal of **research** is to aid you in forming a solid case so that you and your arguments are more likely to be accepted by the audience. If an audience is disappointed in your research efforts, it will significantly affect your ethos (credibility) for that speech. Research influences the effectiveness of the modes of persuasion that are critical to a speech. Failing to know the rules and expectations of research, can also affect your logos (logic). And, finally, even your pathos (appeal to emotions) can be affected by poor research.

In most cases, a formal speech, like an informative or a persuasive speech, requires research-based support. Researching for your speech entails finding evidence that supports your topic in the form of proof, clarification, and/or explanation. This chapter discusses the importance and role of research, discusses the types of research available, helps you decide which sources are best for your given speech, discusses research methods, teaches you how to effectively organize your research, and discusses issues of paraphrasing, quoting, and source citation.

EVIDENCE

Research materials can be divided into two categories: primary and secondary. <u>Primary research</u> *Q2* <u>refers to the collection of information that doesn't already exist.</u> An example of primary research is an interview. <u>Secondary research, on the other hand, is information that someone else has al-ready found, evaluated, presented, and/or concluded in some way.</u> *answer*

Because not all evidence is created equal, there is a general hierarchy of evidence. **A hierar-chy of evidence** refers to the idea that there are certain types of research and evidence that are deemed stronger than others. This is helpful to consider when choosing what types of evidence you will use for your speech and therefore what sources you will use in your research endeavors. Consider the diagram below.

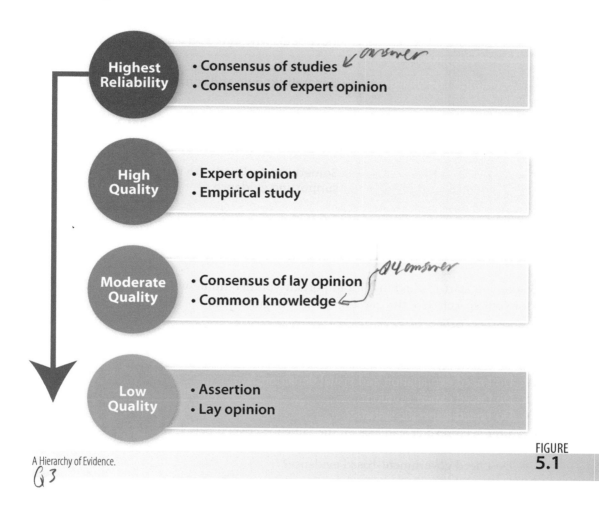

Highest Reliability
- Consensus of studies ← *answer*
- Consensus of expert opinion

High Quality
- Expert opinion
- Empirical study

Moderate Quality
- Consensus of lay opinion *Q4 answer*
- Common knowledge ←

Low Quality
- Assertion
- Lay opinion

A Hierarchy of Evidence. *Q3*

FIGURE 5.1

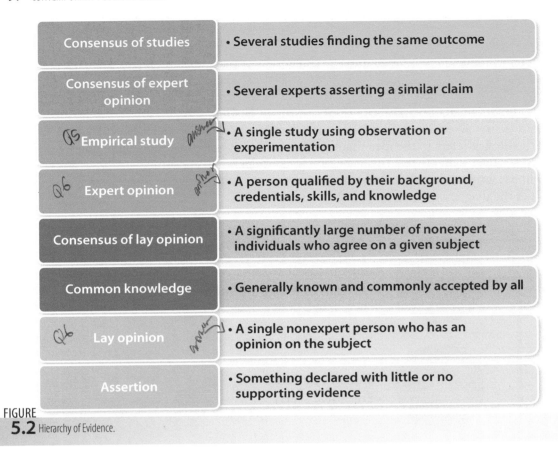

FIGURE
5.2 Hierarchy of Evidence.

Before you start researching, it's important you determine what type of evidence you will need for your speech. Use the questions below to guide you.

1. Do I need examples?
2. Do I need testimony?
3. Do I need reasoning and logic?
4. Do I need explanation and visual depictions?
5. Do I need expert opinion?
6. Do I need a specific statistic?
7. Do I need several statistics on the same idea over a period of time?
8. Do I need scholarly evidence?
9. Do I need government-based evidence?
10. Do I need to provide basic definitions for any concepts?
11. What evidence is essential to make my point?
12. What evidence can I use that will pack the biggest punch?
13. Do I need to know more generally?
14. Do I need to appeal to pathos through stories?

ORGANIZE YOUR RESEARCH

Once you have determined what type of evidence you need, you can start researching! But, before you get carried away and begin stacking up the books and scrolling through pages on the Internet, you need to have a way to organize your research efforts. This is a step many first time speakers and researchers skip. Often students tell themselves, "Oh, I'll remember where that quote was at" or "I'll figure out the citation information later." These procrastination moments can cost you several hours of time later on. It's best to start your research with a clear idea of what you are looking for, how you are going to use it, and how you are going to keep track of it. There are three principles to follow when organizing your information:

Organization is important. A well-organized research process will save you time and stress later on.

FIGURE **5.3**

1. Copy the important material; especially anything you might quote.
2. Create a working reference page.
3. Create a file to keep all of your materials.

COPY THE MATERIAL YOU WILL ACTUALLY BE USING

FIGURE **5.4**

This does not mean you have to copy all three hundred pages of a book, but it does mean you should copy the page in which your quote/statistic/information occurs. Once you have the copy made, you need to highlight and/or underline the piece of information you will use so that you can quickly and efficiently locate the information later. You also want to note on that copy exactly where in your speech this evidence will be used (introduction, conclusion, or one of the main points).

CREATE A WORKING REFERENCE PAGE

Most people wait until the last minute to start their reference page. This is a big mistake. You want to create a working reference page as you go, so that when you make your reference page, you are not struggling and stressed to find the source and locate all the pertinent information. I should note that not all instructors require a reference page. You should clarify your instructor's expectations. You should also clarify with your instructor as to which style of citing sources they would like

Collect for later reference use:

Author(s)

Title

Publication Date

Volume or Edition

Publisher

City & State of Publication

Page number

FIGURE **5.5**

Making note of these important areas will help you craft your reference page.

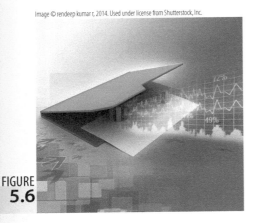

FIGURE 5.6

you to use. The American Psychological Association (APA) is the official form of citing for communication discipline, but again clarify the exact expectations of your instructor. Keep in mind that regardless of the official style of citing you use for your written work, your oral citations (which will be discussed later) always require the author's name and year at minimum.

PUT ALL OF THE ABOVE MATERIAL IN ONE FILE

Once you have collected all this information, the last thing you want to do is misplace a piece here and there. Have one dedicated file folder that you use only for the research on this particular topic and your days or weeks of researching and preparing will be worth it.

GENERAL PRINCIPLES FOR EVALUATING EVIDENCE

There are several key principles you should take into consideration when researching.

1. reliability
2. generalizability
3. currency
4. credibility
5. trustworthiness
6. competency
7. Ethical

FIGURE 5.7

Consider discussing various forms of evidence with others to be sure your choices are effective.

IT MUST BE RELEVANT

Using irrelevant information weakens your ethos as a speaker and your argument. Ensure the evidence is relevant and directly connected to your argument.

IT MUST BE GENERALIZABLE

The sample size must be representative of the population. For instance, let's say you find a study that found eight out of ten teenagers in America admit to smoking cigarettes before the legal age. You need to look at the sample size of that research to know it is generalizable. If the study was a sample of thirty teens from a Los Angeles City high school the findings are not generalizable because thirty teens from the city do not reflect the greater population of the United States, which has cities, farming areas, rural areas, and significantly more than thirty teens.

IT MUST BE CURRENT

Any information you gather from any kind of source should be no more than ten years old. The only exception to this rule is if you are using evidence or a source intended for an argument based in tradition. For example, you may want to quote a historical document, such as the Bill of Rights or the Declaration of Independence. Clearly, these sources are more than ten years old, but they are the exception to the rule. You also want to determine if there is more current information available. If so, you need to find out whether that information is similar or dissimilar to your less recent evidence.

THE EVIDENCE MUST BE CREDIBLE

Credibility concerns perceptions of competence, ethics, fairness, intelligence, reputation, and good will. There are two types of credibility: direct and secondary. Direct credibility is support you create yourself. An example of direct credibility is any time you mention your own personal experience or expertise. Secondary credibility is support you generate by using other people's credibility. For example, you may not be an expert in astrophysics, so you choose to cite an expert in the field instead. You are basically borrowing credibility.

Image © Feng Yu, 2014. Used under license from Shutterstock, Inc.

The reputation of your source can quickly heighten or ruin the validity of your argument.

FIGURE 5.8

THE EVIDENCE MUST BE TRUSTWORTHY

When considering whether or not a piece of evidence is trustworthy, consider the reputation of the source. Does the person or organization have a positive track record of being trustworthy, ethical, and unbiased? If it is a secondary source that you are considering using, ask yourself, "does it accurately and fully represent the original source's findings?" Determine whether the source is biased or not. One way to determine prejudice or bias is to consider who collected the data, and who paid for the research.

IT MUST DISPLAY COMPETENCE

Is the author or organization competent in that area? The author or organization must be an expert in the field, have substantial experience in that area, and/or have the necessary credentials. Competency is judged by the quality of someone's work as well as a clear and comprehensive understanding of the subject.

IT MUST BE ETHICAL

Use research ethically. When trying to maintain your ethics in research consider the following:

© marekuliasz, 2013. Used under license from Shutterstock, Inc.

1. Use unbiased sources
2. Be honest with counter examples

Good ethics are essential to making a strong speech.

FIGURE 5.9

3. Do not misconstrue information
4. Do not take a quote out of context
5. Be honest about "common knowledge"
6. Do not plagiarize
7. Do not copy any information from another source without giving the author credit in outline, reference page, and verbal citation.
8. Unintentional plagiarism is not an excuse and is punishable

| Relevant | Generalizable | Current | Credible | Trustworthy | Competent | Ethical |

FIGURE
5.10 Principles for evaluating good evidence.

POTENTIAL SOURCES FOR YOUR SPEECH

There are many different sources of research you can utilize for your speech. You should select the ones that best fit the needs of your specific speech (use the questions above to guide you). Keep in mind it is usually best to use different types of research support in your speech. The research sources are a list of commonly used and reliable forms of sources for your speech.

PRINT FORMS AND ONLINE FORMS

Print and online forms of research support wouldn't normally be lumped into the same category. With the changing times, our print world has quickly become an online world. To clarify, if something exists in print and also online they both count as print sources. Gone are the days that in order to read the *Bakersfield Californian* or *Los Angeles Times* you have to walk to your driveway and pick up a roll of gray papers. Nowadays, you can easily get your news online and often from the same sources as you would in print. As a general rule, if something is available in print and then subsequently online it is still considered a print source for this purpose of understanding research. Books and journal articles that were once only accessed by a trip to your local library or campus library are now available online.

Image © VectorZilla, 2014. Used under license from Shutterstock, Inc.

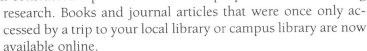

Given this constant blurring of available information in print and online, the two have been combined into one category for explanation purposes. There is an additional section herein that discusses how to evaluate sources online that are not scholarly in nature which needs to be considered whenever you are looking online for supporting evidence. Print forms that are commonly also available in print form include: scholarly journals, news, encyclopedias, dictionaries, almanacs, and documents and reports.

FIGURE
5.11

SCHOLARLY JOURNALS

FIGURE 5.12

Scholarly journals are collections of academic published articles, essays, and research authored by experts in their perspective fields and who are affiliated with a college or university. These are considered highly credible and reliable forms of research support. Academic journals are released monthly, bimonthly, quarterly, or yearly depending on the journal. The publisher does not pay authors for their work and other experts in the field put the article through an extensive peer review process. Scholarly journals should commonly be a top pick for supporting your ideas. Your college or university library will have an extensive selection for you to browse as well as expansive online databases of journals. EBSCO, Academic Elite, JSTOR, and Lexis Nexis are commonly used and highly reliable databases you may want to consider.

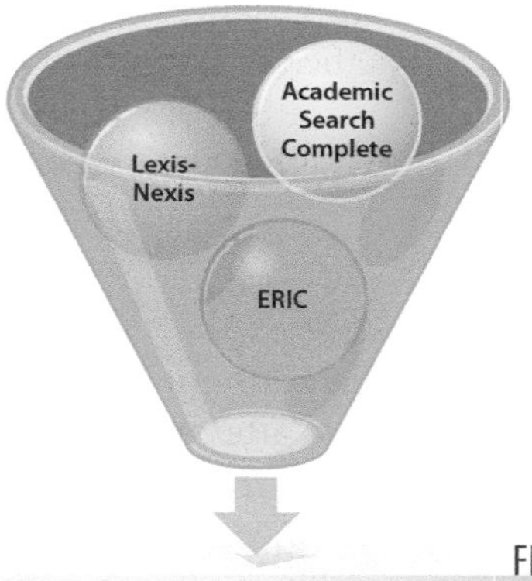

Scholarly indexes to consider.

FIGURE 5.13

NEWS SOURCES AND MAGAZINES

Various printed news sources and magazines can be credible sources. These are commonly authors who are paid by the publisher and intended for a general or mass audience. The writers are professional authors and/or journalists. These can be strong sources for credibility, but each news source and magazine varies significantly in its biases and fact-checking procedures.

FIGURE 5.14

DOCUMENTS AND REPORTS

State, national, and international government agencies as well as numerous independent organizations publish reports to the public on a wide variety of topics. Reports from the government can be on any topic ranging from health, business, agriculture, law, policy, engineering, and scientific experiments. These sources are generally considered acceptable sources of information. As with any source, however, you will need to specifically analyze its potential for biases against your specific topic. Common independent organizations that publish reports to the public include the League of Women Voters, various colleges and universities, Rockefeller and Ford Foundations, etc. As usual,

FIGURE 5.15

these sources should be examined on an individual basis for their potential biases on your specific topic. For instance, the National Rifle Association (NRA) publishes a great deal of reports; if we are looking at them as a potential source regarding gun violence, we should investigate whether their reports were based on findings from studies the NRA paid for.

ENCYCLOPEDIAS, DICTIONARIES, ALMANACS

Famous **encyclopedias** like the *Encyclopedia Britannica* and the *American Encyclopedia* are sources that attempt to cover every possible subject of interest. Encyclopedias are great references for background information and providing a foundation of knowledge. These are good to use when you need a historical fact or basic bibliographical information. However, many college professors will not accept encyclopedia-based information so it's important to consult your instructor if you are taking a college class. An additional important note is that *Wikipedia* is not considered a credible source for information because any layperson can add their opinion and therefore their credibility is highly questionable. However, Wiki pages often have links to credible sources that may work for your speech and can be evaluated on their own merit.

Dictionaries are sources that provide you definitions to terms. The most widely used *Merriam-Webster Dictionary* is available in print and online forms and is useful to provide a clear definition to any term that the audience may not know or may be unclear about. **Almanacs** like the *World Almanac* and the *Guinness Book of World Records* provide information on a range of subjects. These are not appropriate for most speeches but may come in handy for an attention-getter or as an audience engagement tool.

Newspapers are a great place to go if you need evidence regarding a current event. They can also provide expert opinions. Newspapers cover stories from personal to business to governmental. Use newspapers with caution. They tend to collect evidence very quickly and verifying their practices for collecting and verifying information can be difficult and can prove to be inaccurate to some degree as time passes. Be sure to recognize when a story is showing an opinion versus actual data or evidence. Be careful not to take an editorial as evidence. Editorials tend to be assertions and lay opinions, which hurts their ethos.

BOOKS

Books are excellent references when they are written by credible authors. There are books on every subject you can imagine. The key to using a book as a source is to check that it meets criteria for being credible, which will be discussed more later. The book needs to be authored and published by a credible and reputable source, be current, and unbiased to be used as a good source in your speech. Many books are now available in electronic form, also known as e-books.

EXPERIENCE-BASED RESEARCH
INTERVIEWS

Interviews are a great way to get specific information from experts. Interviewing can provide your speech with ethos because you are using credible experts and it can also help add pathos to your speech if you're interviewing someone regarding a potentially emotional issue. For example, if you were giving a speech on autism you could go to a local high school and interview their

Decide on a goal	What information do you need to obtain specifically?
Prepare questions in advance	Determine what questions you will pose and in what manner and order to best obtain your needed information. Be ready to ask follow-up questions. Open-ended questions are ideal as they allow the respondent to feel you would like more than a simple "yes" or "no"—you want an explanation as well.
Prepare to listen	Remind yourself that listening is not an innate ability, it is a skill that can be honed. It is important you decide to be a good listener during an interview. Good listeners get much more usable information from an interview.
Be open	Diminish the cynical side of yourself and biases you may have, be open to what they have to say.
Be honest	Be honest with your intentions and the time you expect the interview to take.
Build respect and trust	Building respect and trust is only possible if you are a sympathetic and engaged participant. Express emotions of goodwill and honest interest.
Decide how you will take notes	Before the interview, you need to determine if you will take notes, record, or both. If you are recording you need to ask permission when setting up the appointment.

special education specialist. This person is an expert in their field and could provide you great information and even potentially valuable quotes for your speech. If you ask the right questions, this person may also provide you with an emotional story you could retell in your speech.

PERSONAL EXPERIENCE *answer 6*

You may be thinking that your own personal experiences are valid representations of evidence. Why shouldn't you just use your own experiences? This is a good point—personal experiences are absolutely valid pieces of information. A person's experience is a truth, it is a form of evidence; however, it is weaker than many other forms of support. The second is our tendency to remember events that reinforce our beliefs and dismiss the experiences that prove our beliefs incorrect. In sum, yes, you can use personal experience as a form of example evidence but you must recognize that it is weaker than other forms and in order to have a successful speech you must employ other stronger support as well.

If you do choose to use your personal experience, be sure it meets certain criteria for being an acceptable use of personal experience. Ask yourself three questions before you use a personal experience in your speech.

Ask yourself three questions before you use a personal experience in your speech.

FIGURE 5.16

1. *Is it an appropriate self-disclosure?* You want to consider whether or not the audience may feel unsettled or uncomfortable with the level of disclosure. You do not want to disconnect with your audience through experience.

2. *Is your experience common and typical?* If your experience is the exception to the rule, then don't use it. You want to be ethical and you do not want to have your own personal experiences be the only evidence you have.

3. *Is it relevant and useful?* This means you want to consider the degree to which your example is actually dealing directly with your topic. You also want to make sure that even if your experience is relevant to the topic, that it also has a purpose and is useful to the audience. Don't tell a story, just to tell a story. It should have an intended effect.

NONPRINT MATERIALS

RADIO AND TELEVISION BROADCASTS

Image © RTimages, 2014. Used under license from Shutterstock, Inc.

FIGURE 5.17

Radio and television broadcasts include reporting, lectures, discussions, debates, meetings, investigations, and more. Television and radio often feature shows that attempt to be seen as legitimate news and expert opinion but are not—be sure to investigate. News programs in general are considered to be moderately to highly credible. Be careful, however, as not all news sources are created equal. Some news sources are funded by organizations with certain ideologies (ways of thinking) and they unconsciously and consciously promote those ideologies in their "news" reporting. MSNBC has been attacked for being liberal/left wing but it hasn't been officially found to be unethical or opinion based. A current example of this is *Fox News*, which has undergone attacks for its clear right-wing conservative viewpoints. Be sure to always check the newspapers for biases, reputation, and overall credibility.

ONLINE SOURCES

The Internet houses millions of opportunities to obtain information. Unfortunately, much of that information is weak in terms of its usability in a speech. There are some exceptions, however, and it is important you know how to identify trustworthy websites from the less credible and biased alternatives. Even seemingly credible websites still require your examination. A good rule is to find a piece of evidence from one source and then find two more pieces of evidence from two different sources that have similar findings. This increases your ethos as a speaker and it helps you feel assured you have collected credible evidence. When searching the Online there are basic searching tips and tricks you should be aware of. The term "boolean" for instance, is a word that you should be familiar with. Boolean searches permit you to use various combinations of words to

Image © alexmillos, 2014. Used under license from Shutterstock, Inc.

PREJUDICE

FIGURE 5.18 When researching we must be extra cautious of the sources we use online. Bias online sources are everywhere. You must make sure you use credible unbiased sources for your speeches.

broaden and limit your searches. The team Boolean derives from the 19th century Boolean Logic. Standard Boolean operations are (AND, OR, NOT, NEAR). You can also use the math form of these words in many search engines (+, −, =).

Now that we know what to look for in an online source, how exactly do we evaluate a potential online source? There are three steps you must take in evaluating the usability of an online source.

Address ending with...	What it means
.com	This is a commercial website that is likely to be biased but not necessarily wrong.
.edu	These are education websites. These sites are commonly held to higher standards than .coms, and if the source is directly from a specific department at a college or university the information can generally be considered credible. Exception: student blogs, websites, and pages are not credible unless used as an example of an experience not a generalization.
.org	These tend to be organizations that have a wide range of interests. These have low to high initial credibility; PBS, for example, is considered a highly credible source.
.gov	These are government-based websites that are held to high standards and come with automatically accepted credibility.
.net	These are networks. This ending indicates that this information was not published by an inherently credible organization. Anyone and any organization can obtain this. These are considered a high risk for credibility and bias.

Commercial Websites

- Are usually paid by advertisers and have their own interests at heart
- Use when you need to understand the way the company is marketing themselves, when their assertions are supported by other credible evidence, as potentially good places to obtain images and product basic information.

Organization Websites

- Have a preconceived agenda and purpose that may cloud or alter the way they present information or they may intentionally hide information from the public. Advertisers pay some organizations as well which lessens their credibility and increases their bias.
- Use when you need specific information about that particular organization, to obtain pathos evoking stories and perspectives, and as a starting point for research. These websites often share links to highly credible sources.

Personal Websites, Blogs, and Social Media Sites

- Are created by individuals who usually have no credentials or credibility in the subject. They are reflective of lay opinion, which is the lowest form of evidence and considered unreliable and ungeneralizable.
- Can be used when you need evidence that is based in personal experience. These areas can provide you with a story that can appeal to the emotions of your audience. These should be used in additon to more credible and generalizable data.

FIGURE 5.19

EVALUATING ONLINE SOURCES
DETERMINE IF THE SOURCE IS BIASED

You accomplish this by determining who is responsible for writing or publishing the information. Look at the site address (URL) as discussed above. The government and education extensions mean the item is more likely to be reliable. Take a look at the bubble diagram to get more insight into evaluating the other extensions. You also need to locate the copyright information, which is commonly at the bottom of the page in small type. Investigate the company and/or individual author to determine if they have any potential biases or credibility issues of concern. You can do this with a simple keyword search in a search engine. Sometimes you can locate a brief disclosure about the company by clicking on a link tabbed at the top of the page or posted near the bottom of the page. It may say "about us" or "our mission."

This is the information you found	Determine who is responsible and the level of potential bias	Determine if the information is current
According to Monsanto.com news (2013), genetically modified foods "delivers proven economic and environmental benefits" with a record of safety (para.1).	If you look at the bottom of the "news" page you can find the publisher is Monsanto. Do a quick *Bing* search and discover who Monsanto is.	If you look at the bottom of the "news" page you can find the publisher last updated the page in "2012–2013." No specific date is published with regard to the specific information offered. Because the information was updated within the last ten years it is considered current.
www.monsanto.com/ newsviews/pages/bioetech-saftey-gmo-advantages http://www.monsanto.com/ whoweare/Pages/default. aspx	Monsanto = the largest producer of genetically modified foods in America. They produce genetically altered seeds, agent orange, PCBs, DDT, and recombinant bovine growth hormone (all of which have had minor to severe effects on health and the environment).	You can infer that the information is within the acceptable time period of ten years because it was updated somewhere between 2012 and 2013.
	Based on this information you can quickly determine Monsanto is not a credible source to use. They clearly have vested interest in spreading the word that GMOs are safe and beneficial and therefore are considered a highly biased source you should not use in your speech.	Based on this information you can determine that this source meets the criteria for currency. However, because it did not meet the responsible and bias criteria, this is not a usable source for your speech.

DETERMINE IF THE INFORMATION PRESENTED IN THE WORK IS CURRENT

Outside of sources like the Constitution, policy, and historic events, sources used as evidence must be published within the last ten years. You want to make sure you have the most current information, because current information is relevant information, and can be generalized more easily. You also don't want to look foolish to your audience when they have knowledge that there are more recent findings. There should be a date somewhere near the heading or title of the work. If not, look near the copyright information at the bottom of the page. There is a difference between "date of publish" and "last updated." Date of publish refers to when the research was published or article written, etc. "Last updated" refers to the last time an administrator visited the website and updated any information on it. This doesn't necessarily mean they updated the information you are using. If there is not a publication date, or originally posting date, then using the "last update" is acceptable.

FIGURE 5.20

Ensure your information is current. Using old information harms your credibility, causes undue panic, and perpetuates fear, ignorance, and sometimes irreversible decisions.

DETERMINE THE DEGREE OF ACCURACY

Determining the degree of accuracy means checking for evidence that the information is correct and plausible. Online sources can be highly inaccurate. It is very important to be hypercritical of online information. You will want to check the citation information for any sources they cite as evidence for their own claims. Do a quick search to determine if those sources are credible and reliable and unbiased—the authors and the publisher as well. Consider issues of reputation, investigations, and unethical history. The biggest concern here is the existence of other information that replicated these findings. The degree of replication refers to the degree to which some finding has been found in other studies. In order to know if the information you have found has been replicated, you need to continue searching for information similar to it. If you find several credible sources that present the same findings, you can be better assured your findings are accurate.

FIGURE 5.21

Do not use inaccurate information. Your ethos depends on targeted precise information, as does the topic of your speech.

PARAPHRASING, QUOTING, AND CITING RESEARCH

How to successfully use quotes and paraphrasing in your speech is discussed in detail in the chapter on verbal support. It is also discussed in your workbook. Please refer to your workbook for exercises and tear out pages that will help you practice this skill. This section is meant to discuss paraphrasing, quoting, and citing from the researching perspective. It is first and foremost important to understand the difference between paraphrasing and quoting.

Q24 answer

Paraphrasing means rephrasing what someone else said or wrote in about the same amount of words. When citing your paraphrased material you need to have the author's last name and the year it was published. Quoting or using a direct quote means you are restating word-for-word exactly what was said or written. If you quote directly, you must place quotation marks at

Q24 answer

the start and end of the words being used. The period always comes after the quotation marks. You will always need the author's last name, year of publication, and page number to be presented somewhere in that sentence. It is usually best to have more information if possible. For instance, providing information about the authors' credentials or mentioning where the article was published, would be ideal and is often required. Consider the table here.

Paraphrasing in your outline in oral citation form	Quoting
Even expert Sarah Crachiolo admits in a 2014 lecture that half the battle of public speaking is making people believe you know what you are doing.	Professor of Communication Studies and Public Speaking Instructor at California State University, Long Beach Sarah Crachiolo candidly argued in a March 12, 2014 lecture that "Half the battle of public speaking is performing confidence and convincing the audience you know what you are doing."
Notice there is limited information provided about the author source of information.	Notice when directly quoting an expert the details are provided.

Weaving textual evidence into your speech is often essential, but it can be intimidating. Using quotes can substantially help your argument, but used in the wrong way, quotes can overwhelm a speech and the speaker. Paraphrasing is a nice option, but it too has its quirks to consider. When you are researching, keep in mind what would be best for your speech; a direct quote or paraphrasing and take notes for citations accordingly.

When to use paraphrasing	When to use direct quotes
To retell a story	If a person is famous for that exact quote
When an exact number or account is not necessary	If you are unable to capture the essence of the language in any other way
When you need to simplify the language used	If spoken another way, the words would lose their meaning
When you need to replace jargon with understood terms	If the specific word choice must be demonstrated
If you think your audience will understand it better if it was reworded or reorganized	If the way something is expressed matters
When you need to use information that is at two different parts in the source	If a formal element is needed

Regardless of whether or not you are citing a direct quote or paraphrasing you need to be sure to take note of the author's name, the year the work was published, and the page number where the information was found. Technically, if you are paraphrasing, you only need to orally cite the author's last name and the year of publication, but it is important to jot down the page number as well in case later you need to look back at your research to gather more evidence or get contextual information. You will need this information when you construct an outline, write your speech, and/or deliver your speech. If there is no author listed you need to record the name of the organization, text, journal, or website from which it came. Below are a few examples to give you an idea of what information you will need to make sure you collect while researching. For a more complete discussion on paraphrasing and quoting, please see the verbal support chapter.

	Example: How to write and orally cite
Direct Quote with an Author from a Journal, book, or other print source	In 2009, a study by Dr. Laura Khor found that "human rights violations are on the rise" (p. 132).
Direct Quote without an Author from a Journal	In 2009 a study released by the *Journal of Humanity* found "human rights violations are on the rise" (p. 132).
Direct Quote without an Author from a Website	According to a 2010 report from the surgeon general.gov, "there is no safe level of exposure to tobacco smoke" (para. 2).
Paraphrasing from a Website without an Author	The CDC's current website posted findings from a 2010 study that shows even the lowest level of tobacco smoke exposure is harmful.

SUMMARY

In order to construct a successful speech, a speaker must understand the tool of research. It is essential that we take a critical look at all potential sources and information we gather before we insert them into our speech. Unfounded, nongeneralizable, biased, or outdated sources can hurt our credibility, ethos, and, in the long run, have a detrimental effect on the success of the speech. It is important that researching be a planned process with a clear method of organizing, obtaining, and evaluating materials.

Review Questions

1. How can research support a speech?

2. What criteria must you use to evaluate online sources?

3. What is the difference between paraphrasing and quoting?

4. What are the three steps for organizing your research?

5. What are the four personal experience criteria?

Glossary

Almanacs: Provide information on a range of subjects such as the *World Almanac* and the *Guinness Book of World Records.*

Assertion: Something declared with little or no supporting evidence.

Consensus of expert opinion: Several experts asserting a similar claim.

Consensus of lay opinion: Significantly large number of nonexpert individuals who agree on a given subject.

Common knowledge: Generally known and commonly accepted by all.

Consensus of studies: Several studies finding the same outcome.

Dictionaries: Sources that provide you definitions to terms.

Empirical study: A single study using observation or experimentation.

Encyclopedias: References for background information and providing a foundation of knowledge.

Expert opinion: A person qualified by their background, credentials, skills, and knowledge.

Hierarchy of evidence: Refers to the idea that there are certain types of research and evidence that are deemed stronger than others.

Lay opinion: A single, nonexpert person who has an opinion on the subject.

Paraphrasing: Rephrasing what someone else said or wrote in about the same amount of words.

Primary research: Refers to the collection of information that doesn't already exist. An example of primary research is an interview.

Quoting or using a direct quote: Restating word-for-word exactly what was said or written.

Secondary research: Information that someone else has already found, evaluated, presented, and/or concluded in some way.

DEVELOPING VERBAL SUPPORT

Mark Staller, Andrea Thorson-Hevle, and Stef Donev

Learning Objectives

CHAPTER 6

① Define and describe ten common types of verbal support.

② Choose the right type of verbal support for your speech purpose and target audience.

③ Develop verbal support for the main ideas of your speech.

④ Evaluate the usefulness of paraphrasing versus quoting in a speech and how to cite verbal support during a speech.

A s Chapter 12 points out, there are three major areas that people often evaluate when they critique a public speech: content, structure, and delivery. Effective public speakers must have something to say (content), they must package their message in an easy-to-follow format (structure), and they must speak clearly and powerfully (delivery).

Think of these three major areas of public speaking as the legs on a three-legged stool: if public speakers are deficient in one of these major areas, then their speeches will collapse. Without effective delivery, their speeches are incomprehensible. Without clear structure, their speeches are confusing. Without well-developed content, their speeches are empty.

This chapter on developing verbal support will help you to develop solid content for your public speeches. Underdeveloped content in a speech usually indicates a lack of adequate verbal support. You may have a good idea for a speech, but this idea needs to be adequately expressed and developed in words that you can speak.

Verbal support is usually distinguished from visual support. Chapter 10 teaches you how to develop visual aids that reinforce your verbal and oral message. Although these visual aids may contain a few words, they also use other types of visual support such as pictures, drawings, charts, graphs, maps, and so on.

An effective speech has good content, structure, and delivery.

FIGURE 6.1

Types of verbal support are different ways to support an idea or assertion with words. Since this chapter focuses to some extent on how you use language, there is some overlap with two other textbook chapters. Chapter 14, on the one hand, teaches you that there are acceptable ways to support assertions (inductive and deductive reasoning) and there are unacceptable ways to support assertions (argumentative fallacies). However, Chapter 13 focuses on language at a very general level. Chapter 14, on the other hand, focuses on language at the very specific sentence level. Chapter 13 teaches you that you need to carefully consider your word choice at the sentence level in order to create vivid, simple, powerful language and in order to avoid oppressive language.

This chapter teaches you ten very specific, very common verbal vehicles that public speakers use to express and develop their main points and subpoints. A verbal "vehicle" is a rhetorical device or public speaking mechanism that is used to express or embody an idea. The ten types of verbal support that you will learn about in this chapter are 1) definitions, 2) facts, 3) surveys, 4) statistics, 5) comparisons, 6) testimonies, 7) proverbs and other pithy sayings, 8) examples, 9) stories, and 10) jokes.

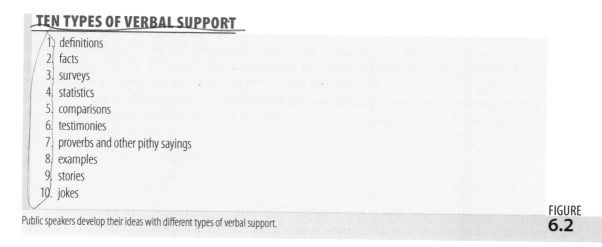

TEN TYPES OF VERBAL SUPPORT

1. definitions
2. facts
3. surveys
4. statistics
5. comparisons
6. testimonies
7. proverbs and other pithy sayings
8. examples
9. stories
10. jokes

Public speakers develop their ideas with different types of verbal support.

FIGURE 6.2

As a public speaker, you must speak, and speaking involves getting words to come out of your mouth. How do you get enough words to come out of your mouth? How can you adequately develop the content of your speech? Some speakers make the mistake of trying to cover too many ideas in one speech. They want to have enough to say, so they decide to speak about several different ideas or topics. This strategy often results in speeches that lack focus and that try to cover too much ground. Although speakers covering several topics may speak for a substantial amount of time, many of their ideas may also be underdeveloped and fairly shallow.

A much better approach to developing the content of a speech is to create a central thesis that gives your speech a clear focus and to then fully develop the supporting material you need to support or "prove" this thesis. Once you have learned how to use the ten types of verbal support described in this chapter, you will be able to present a well-developed speech even if you only have one main point to make. Instead of jumping from one underdeveloped idea to the next, you will be able to "go deep" and explain and develop an idea or assertion at least ten different ways.

FIGURE
6.3 Speakers must choose types of verbal support based on their target audiences and speech purposes.

However, you need to know about the different types of verbal support not just to ensure that you have well-developed content for a speech, but to ensure that you have the correct content (the right types of verbal support) for your particular audience and your particular speech purpose. A persuasive speech requires different types of verbal support than an informative speech or a speech to entertain, and a persuasive speech addressed to a skeptical audience requires different types of verbal support than a persuasive speech addressed to a friendly audience.

In addition to describing ten common types of verbal support used by public speakers, we will also give you some tips about when and how to use these verbal vehicles. At the end of this chapter, we also provide you with a chart that briefly describes all ten types of verbal support and then illustrates each type of verbal support using the common (and popular) topic of marijuana. After reading this chart, you will not only know a lot more about pot, but you will also be able to see the differences between the ten types of verbal support that we describe.

Now let us define and describe the ten types of verbal support that are often used by public speakers. The first six types of verbal support we describe are often used by speakers developing logos appeals (appeals to reason), whereas the last four types of verbal support we describe are often used by speakers developing pathos appeals (appeals to or through emotions). However, do not make too much of this organizing principle: you can find any of these types of verbal support in almost any type of speech.

1. DEFINITIONS

A basic type of verbal support that is quite useful is **definitions**: definitions are statements of the exact meanings of words. Before developing your ideas in detail in a speech, you need to clearly define the terms that you will use to express your ideas. Otherwise, your audience may not understand what you are talking about, or, even worse, you yourself may not think or communicate clearly about the ideas you are trying to develop.

Developing definitions for the terms that you are using in a speech involves more than referencing a dictionary: you must decide on the types of definitions that you need to provide to your audience. There are many types of definitions (some technical writing textbooks list 15 or more types of definitions), but we will list six different types of definitions that are especially useful for public speaking:

1.   **Dictionary definitions.** Dictionary definitions are compiled by dictionary writers and editors. If you look up a word in a dictionary, you will find a list of numbered definitions that give different explanations of the exact meaning of that word. If you decide to use a dictionary definition in a speech, do not give all the possible definitions of the word, and do not just pick one definition at random. Choose the dictionary definition that most accurately defines the word for the way you want to use it. Do not forget to orally credit the dictionary for this definition.

2. <u>Etymological definitions</u>. Etymological definitions are definitions that reveal the original meanings of words based on their root words. Usually most dictionaries provide brief etymological explanations of words before their lists of definitions are presented. If you want a full etymological definition of an English word, reference the *Oxford English Dictionary* or type in "etymological definition of (target word)" into your computer search engine.

Image © Dmitry Elagin, 2014. Used under license from Shutterstock, Inc.

A dictionary entry will often provide for a word an etymological explanation, various definitions, and synonyms.

FIGURE 6.4

Etymological definitions should be used when they shed significant light on the words you are trying to define. For example, the English word "companion" is formed from the root words "panis," meaning "bread" and "com," meaning "with," so the English word "companion" originally meant someone you were willing to break bread with—this etymological definition could be useful when trying to establish the intimate nature of companionship.

3. **Synonyms**. Synonyms are words or phrases having the same or nearly the same meaning as another word in the same language. In dictionaries, synonyms for a word are usually listed at the end of the list of definitions—the dictionary entry will end with the phrase "See also . . ." and then give the common synonyms for a word. You can also find many synonyms for a word by referencing a thesaurus.

Synonyms are useful in speeches because they give speakers a "shorthand" way of defining a term: speakers just need to replace the word to be defined with a more familiar or more understandable word. If you decide to clarify a term with a synonym, make sure your substitute word or phrase is actually clearer than the word to be defined.

4. **Negative definitions**. Negative definitions are definitions that specify what a speaker does *not* mean when using a word. For example, a negative definition for bread would be "When I speak of bread, I do not mean something to eat; I mean money." Negative definitions are especially useful when you think your audience might assign the wrong meaning to a term that you wish to use. You can clarify what you mean when using the term, and you can decrease the probability that your audience will misinterpret the word.

5. **Essential definitions**. Essential definitions are definitions that follow a particular logical form. You place the term to be defined in a category (the genus), and then you specify how the object or thing to be defined differs from everything else in this category (the differentiae): term + "to be" verb + category (genus) + distinguishing characteristics (differentiae). For example, an essential definition for the term dog is "A dog is a canine that has been domesticated." (Term "dog" + verb "is" + category "canine" + distinguishing characteristic "that has been domesticated.")

Essential definitions are particularly useful when speakers want to define a term with some precision, or when they want to appear to be thoughtful, intelligent people. However, essential definitions do not guarantee audience agreement: audience members can still argue about the category in which a term is placed or about the differentiae that supposedly distinguish an object or thing from everything else in a category. In other words, there are better and worse essential definitions.

6. Stipulative definitions. Stipulative definitions are definitions that give a specific meaning to a term for the purposes of argument or discussion in a given context. Speakers can stipulate what they mean when they use a particular term. For example, you might say "For the purposes of this speech, I define a person as . . . ," or "For the purposes of this speech, let us agree that the term 'person' means. . . ."

Stipulative definitions are very useful in a speech if you stipulate definitions to which your audience will agree. Stipulative definitions make sure that everyone is on the same page when a term is used, and they help to ensure that words are not misinterpreted or given different meanings during the course of a speech or conversation.

SIX TYPES OF DEFINITION

1. dictionary definitions	4. negative definitions
2. etymological definitions	5. essential definitions
3. synonyms	6. stipulative definitions

FIGURE 6.5 You must choose the right type of definition for your specific purpose.

WHEN AND HOW TO USE DEFINITIONS

Provide definitions whenever you think your audience may have difficulty understanding the meaning of a term or terms that you are using in a speech. Definitions often need to be provided towards the beginning of a speech. If you are using words with unambiguous meanings, then you do not necessarily need to provide definitions. However, sometimes seemingly simple words that appear to be unambiguous end up causing the most confusion or disagreement, so carefully consider whether definitions are necessary or dispensable in a speech.

Definitions can be used in any type of speech, even a speech to entertain. For example, here is a mock etymological definition that could enrich a humorous speech to entertain: "The English word 'politics' is derived from the Greek words 'poly,' meaning 'many,' and 'tics,' meaning 'blood-sucking insects,' so politics is an activity that involves many blood-sucking insects."

Definitions are especially necessary in informative and persuasive speeches. In informative speeches, definitions help to clarify meaning or aid in understanding: as you define your terms in an informative speech, you ensure that your audience has a clearer understanding of the concepts, principles, or objects that you are trying to explain or describe. In persuasive speeches, definitions provide common ground with your audience, and they decrease the probability of equivocation (the changing of the meaning of a word during the course of an argument).

2. FACTS

Very generally, facts are things known to exist or actions known to have happened. In the field of public speaking, statements of fact are distinguished from statements of definition, statements of value, and statements of policy. Argumentation theorists point out that the lowest, most fundamental level of argumentation is the definition level, the second level of argument is the fact level, the third level of argument is the value level, and the fourth and most complex level of argument is the policy level. In order to effectively argue a policy or to effectively argue a value statement, speakers must also pay attention to, and provide, fact-level statements.

THE FOUR LEVELS OF ARGUMENT

1. Definition level: Answers the question, "What is X?"   (X is a Y.)
2. Fact level: Answers questions like "Does X exist?" or "What does X cause?"   (X is.)   (X causes Y.)
3. Value level: Answers questions like "Is X good or bad?" or "Is X better or worse than Y?"   (X is bad.)   (X is better than Y.)
4. Policy level: Answers questions like "What should we do?"   (We should do X.)

Statements of fact are one of four types of statement recognized by argumentation theorists.

FIGURE 6.6

In a speech, after defining the things you are talking about, you will often need to provide factual statements related to these things. The next two subsections of this chapter (the subsection on surveys and the subsection on statistics) point out that statements of fact often involve numerical information, but facts do not necessarily involve numbers. For example, even though the statement "The Apollo moon landings actually occurred" does not contain numerical information, it is still classified as a statement of fact.

The example statement about the Apollo moon landings also illustrates that statements of fact are not necessarily "indisputable." Although it is commonly accepted that the Apollo moon landings actually occurred, you can find some human beings who will seriously dispute this claim. Since human beings have the ability to question and even disbelieve factual claims, it is best to classify and recognize statements as "statements of fact" if people would argue the factual status of these statements or claims. If people argue, "Is it a fact that . . .?", then they are arguing a fact-level statement, rather than a value-level or policy-level statement.

According to Aristotle's categories of being, in addition to providing a statement *that* something or someone exists (Mark Staller exists.), you can also provide factual statements about quality (Mark is white.), quantity (Mark is 5' 10".), relation (Mark is the son of Merlin Staller.), place (Mark is located on planet earth.), time (Mark wrote this paragraph at 7:00 a.m.), state (Mark is primarily a solid.), position (Mark is sitting.), active action (Mark is writing a textbook.), and passive action (Mark is getting a cold.)

WHEN AND HOW TO USE FACTS

Informative speakers are usually expected to provide several pieces of information or statements of fact as they develop the body of an informative speech. If you are presenting an expository speech, you will need to provide facts related to the basic questions asked and answered by news reporters: Who? What? When? Where? Why? If you are primarily describing an object or thing, you will need to focus on factual statements about quality, quantity, relation, place, state, and position. If you are attempting to give an informative speech but find yourself making a lot of value or policy claims (rather than fact-level assertions), then you need to re-evaluate the primary goal of your speech: perhaps your "informative" speech is really a persuasive speech.

Image © Oleksiy Mark, 2014. Used under license from Shutterstock, Inc.

An informative speech may need to answer the stock questions of news reporters.

FIGURE 6.7

Persuasive speakers need to provide factual statements that act as "evidence" or support for their larger or more complex persuasive claims. For example, if you want to convince apathetic audience members that they should wear their seatbelts, then you need to present factual evidence about the negative effects of not wearing seatbelts and/or the positive effects of wearing seatbelts. Or, if you want to convince a skeptical audience that gun control laws actually increase violent crime, then you need to provide factual evidence that establishes a causal connection between an increase in gun control laws and an increase in violent crime.

Be aware that asserting something as a "fact" does not adequately establish the factual nature of a statement: as a public speaker, you need to provide to your audience members verbal source citations that establish the credibility of your factual sources. Who asserts that something is a fact, or that something actually occurred? Why should your audience members consider this person or organization to be a credible and reliable source of factual information?

3. SURVEYS

Image © bloomua, 2014. Used under license from Shutterstock, Inc.

Surveys provide a means of collecting information from a group or community usually through written form. Surveys are typically distributed in mass contexts, such as through the mail, email or in mass phone calling initiatives. The same questions are asked each time to each person, consistency of questions is important. It is important that the interviewer, during verbal questioning, doesn't change the questions. There are three general types of surveys:

FIGURE 6.8

We can now conduct surveys on smart phones.

1. <u>Census Surveys</u>—are given to every member of the audience or population. This provides highly accurate information and is great to use in a classroom setting, but it's very difficult to mange for larger populations of groups.
2. <u>Case Study Surveys</u>—are given to a segment of a given population, but is not a representative sample. This means, the findings of the survey are not necessarily generalizable to an entire broader population.
3. <u>Sample Surveys</u>—are given to a carefully selected group of the population so that it can be generalized to a larger population.

Surveys do have some drawbacks however. Because of the nature of a written survey, there is a strong chance that you will have a low number of respondents unless you do a consensus survey. Two of the survey types are also limited in their generalizability and sometimes validity. Perhaps the most annoying drawback to the written survey is the likelihood that your respondent's will not answer some of your questions.

WHEN AND HOW TO USE SURVEYS

Surveys are ideal choices to obtain information when you need . . .

1. Information that isn't currently available
2. Information quickly
3. A written record of responses
4. Ability to decrease interviewer bias
5. Consistent information
6. A way to get data that doesn't require a trained expert in data analysis

7. Statistically valid information
8. Generalizable data

One of the most important things to remember is that your questions are the most important part of this process, so you need to put a lot of thought into them. Make sure your questions really ask what you want them to ask. Your questions should be specific, strategically planned, and organized in a planned and practical way. Nowadays, you also want to think about how you disseminate the surveys, mail is no longer as effective as it used to be, email is far more effective and efficient.

In order to create a survey, you should follow a few simple steps:

1. Know what you are looking for and generate questions that will get you that information.
2. Select the sample. Consider the types of surveys and thus the sample size that is appropriate. If you need this sample to be generalizable to a larger population, you need to be more sophisticated in the exact type of sampling you do. This isn't usually something you should be doing in a beginning level speech class.
3. Select the means of distributing the surveys.
4. Decide how you will analyze the answers.

4. STATISTICS

Statistics are one of the most impactful and compelling ways to reach your audience. They can also be boring and make your audience disconnect. These two ideas are so different, so how can they possibly be about the same thing? Well, because not all statistics are created equal. The trick about using statistics in public speaking, is that the speaker really needs to be critical in evaluating the quality, importance, impact, and need of that information. **Statistics** are a numerical representation of a given sample. Statistics make seemingly distant problems seem very close. Statistics can make topics that seem arbitrary become very real. And statistics can make an idea, concept, or problem seem more problematic than ever. Speakers use statistics in their speeches to:

1. Provide impact
2. Appeal to the emotions of the audience
3. Boost the speakers credibility
4. Enhance the reasoning established previously
5. Make concepts more understandable
6. Make things real
7. Help the audience understand how significant a situation/condition is
8. Make a concept memorable
9. Show a relationship
10. Demonstrate importance

WHEN AND HOW TO USE STATISTICS

Statistics should be used when you need your audience to believe you and you don't have a high amount of ethos or credibility yourself, because you are not an expert in the field. You might need statistics if you need the audience to understand a bigger picture or make an emotional impact with a surprising or startling piece of information. Whatever the case may be, there are a few things you should consider.

FIGURE 6.9

1. Make sure the source is credible. When using statistics it is important that you use credible sources. You should review Chapter 5 in this book again if you need to review what makes a reliable source. Sources that are reputable and unbiased will yield you powerful results. Be sure to verbally articulate the credibility of your sources, so that your audience can more easily accept your information.

Where you get your numbers matters. Are they from a government agency? A corporation? A university? A hospital? A blog? Something you kind'a sort'a more-or-less remember your Uncle Joe once mentioning? Or was it that crazy old man across the street? Getting an audience to remember numbers can be a hard sell. Convincing them the numbers are important because they come from an important and trustworthy source improves your odds.

2. You also want to be sure you don't use too many statistics. While one, two, or even three carefully placed and relevant statistics can be powerful and impactful in your speech, having too many can overwhelm your audience. Additionally, make sure your statistics make sense to your audience. Too many numbers that your audience can't make quick sense of will quickly turn them off to your cause.

The simple fact is that unless you are speaking to accountants, scientists, business people, or others who work with numbers on a daily basis, most people will not bother to—or cannot—remember very many numbers from a speech. Use too many numbers and you will confuse your audience; when people are confused, they resent the person who confused them.

3. Statistics are often best when followed up by a personal experience or story. Stories and personal experiences allow the audience to connect to the speaker and the ideas, when they follow statistics they are especially powerful.

4. Visual aids are also helpful reinforcement for statistics. Instead of just saying a statistic, show us the statistic. Represent your statistical information in a visually appealing way by using charts, graphs, or other visual representations.

How you present your numbers will have a major impact on whether your audience understands and remembers them. You need to give them a frame of reference and show how the numbers you do give them are related to one another as well as to the overall topic of your speech. You also need to repeat them several times in the speech if you want them to be remembered.

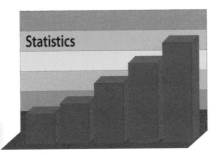

FIGURE 6.10

5. COMPARISONS

Comparisons are forms of verbal support that focus on two or more things in order to infer or point out that they are similar. Comparisons focus on similarities, whereas contrasts focus on differences. When a comparison is made between two things, it is assumed that they are alike or similar in one or more aspects.

Public speakers often use brief comparisons in the form of **similes** or **metaphors**. As you remember from those long-ago English classes, a simile says one thing (A) is *like* (is *similar to*) something else (B), whereas a metaphor says something (A) *is* something else (B).

Image © J. Helgason, 2014. Used under license from Shutterstock, Inc.

"Life is like a box of chocolates": metaphor or simile?   FIGURE **6.11**

"Life is Just a Bowl of Cherries" was a popular song in the 1930s. The title of the song is a metaphor. It claims that life REALLY IS just a bowl of cherries. If Buddy DeSylva and Lew Brown, who wrote the lyrics to a melody by Ray Henderson, had called the song "Life is Like a Bowl of Cherries," the title would be a simile, not a metaphor. What is the difference? Aside from the word "like," the big difference is that metaphors are usually stronger. Say your brief comparison out loud, first as a simile, and then as a metaphor. Which is the stronger and more interesting statement? In most cases it will be the metaphor: "Ralph is like an ox," (weaker simile) or "Ralph is an ox" (stronger metaphor).

EXTENDED ANALOGIES

Detailed comparisons are often called **extended analogies**. Whereas similes and metaphors are often very brief (only a sentence or phrase), extended analogies are developed at some length (often taking up several sentences or paragraphs). For example, Martin Luther King, Jr.'s *I Have a Dream* speech is filled with brief metaphors and similes, but in paragraphs three and four of this speech, King makes a detailed comparison of the Declaration of Independence to a check or promissory note—this detailed comparison is an extended analogy.

You can change a brief metaphor or simile into an extended analogy by making your comparison of two or more things explicit. If you say in a speech that "Smoking a cigarette is like sucking on the tailpipe of a car," you have presented a simile. However, if you go on to make this comparison explicit, you create an extended analogy: "No one in their right mind would suck on the tailpipe of a running car because, in addition to burning their lips, they would inhale into their lungs the harmful exhaust of an internal combustion engine; similarly, no one in their right mind should suck on a lighted cigarette because, in addition to messing up their lipstick, they would inhale into their lungs the many harmful chemicals that are created by the combustion of tobacco."

Analogies can be either literal or figurative. In a **literal analogy**, you compare two similar things, or two things that belong to the same category or class: a Ford pickup truck to a Chevy pickup truck, Red Delicious apples to Fuji apples, PC computers to Apple computers. In a **figurative analogy**, you compare dissimilar things, or two things that belong to different categories or classes: apples to linoleum, cars to coffee, planet Earth to a stage . . .as Shakespeare did in his play *As You Like It*: "All the world's a stage, And all the men and women merely players." Shakespeare puts these words into the mouth of his character Jaques, who goes on to present (in Act II, Scene VII) a wonderful extended analogy based on this figurative metaphor.

The extended analogy above that compares smoking a cigarette to sucking on the tailpipe of a car is classified as a literal analogy because it compares two fairly similar activities: both activities involve inhaling gases and chemicals into human lungs. Here is an example of a figurative analogy related to cigarette smoking: "Smoking cigarettes is like playing Russian roulette. The

FIGURE
6.12 Comparing smoking to playing Russian roulette can drive home the risk of cancer.

first time you pull the trigger when playing Russian roulette, you may not kill yourself. However, if you are stupid enough to pull the trigger again ("click") and again ("click"), the odds dramatically increase that you will blow your brains out. Similarly, the first time you smoke a cigarette, you may not contract cancer. However, the more you smoke and the longer you smoke, the odds dramatically increase that you will contract a fatal form of cancer."

WHEN AND HOW TO USE COMPARISONS

As Chapter 13 points out, you should use brief figurative metaphors and similes in a speech when you want to create vivid, powerful, passionate language. Figurative metaphors and similes are poetic devices that help to generate emotions in your listeners, so they are crucial when you are giving a persuasive speech primarily based on pathos appeals. When you are trying to motivate a neutral or apathetic audience, you can exploit the power of figurative metaphors and similes.

Extended analogies are also very effective rhetorical devices for persuasive speeches that are designed to motivate a friendly but apathetic audience to take action. For example, you can make apathetic audience members care about wearing their seatbelts by comparing people who do not wear seatbelts to people who do not pull down the safety bar on a rollercoaster ride (a literal analogy), or by comparing people without seatbelts to eggs without an egg carton (a figurative analogy). If you fully develop these analogies in detailed comparisons, you can drive home the importance of seatbelts in a powerful way.

Extended analogies are often employed in informative speeches. You can help your audience members understand an unfamiliar concept or principle by comparing this concept or principle to something with which they are more familiar. Teachers often use extended analogies. For example, to help people understand the hierarchical nature of the four levels of argument, you could compare these levels of argument to the levels of a parking garage: "The four levels of argument are like the levels of a parking garage. You cannot reach the fourth floor of a parking garage unless you drive through the first three floors. Similarly, you cannot effectively argue the most complex level of argument (policy) without also considering the three lower levels of argument (definition, fact, and value)."

When you use an extended analogy to clarify a concept or principle, make sure that you develop the description of the more familiar concept or principle first, and then end your extended analogy by focusing on the concept or principle that you want to clarify. Do not reverse the order: "The four levels of argument are like the levels of a parking garage. You cannot effectively argue the most complex level of argument (policy) without also considering the three lower levels of argument (definition, fact, and value). Similarly, you cannot reach the fourth floor of a parking garage unless you drive through the first three floors." Do you see how this reversed order is less effective, more confusing, and anticlimactic?

When you use an extended analogy to clarify a concept or principle, you also need to make sure that your comparison is based on the principle of "parallel structure": you need to compare a noun to a noun, or a verb to a verb, or an adjective to an adjective. Do not compare one part of speech to another part of speech. For example, do not compare a noun phrase to a participial phrase ("the levels of argument are like driving up the floors of a parking garage") or a participial phrase to an adjectival noun ("smoking cigarettes is like silliness"). Use parallel structure so that your comparison makes sense.

Literal analogies are often used in persuasive speeches that are designed to convince skeptical audience members to change their minds or to shift their position on a controversial point at issue. Since many skeptical audience members will be turned off by obvious pathos appeals, in a speech to convince, you need to rely primarily on logos appeals, and, as Chapter 11 points out, literal analogies are a well-recognized form of valid reasoning.

Literal analogies are considered to be a form of inductive reasoning. For example, in order to argue that criminalizing marijuana creates a "forbidden fruit" effect, you could compare the criminalization of marijuana in America in the 1950s and 1960s to Prohibition and the criminalization of alcohol in America in the 1920s and 1930s. Although this literal analogy is not guaranteed to convince a skeptical audience that criminalizing marijuana actually increases the demand for it, it is a logos appeal addressed to the audience members' reasoning capacity, rather than a pathos appeal designed to generate a particular emotion in the audience.

Literal analogies and other logos appeals are most appropriate for a skeptical audience.

FIGURE 6.13

6. TESTIMONIES

In public speaking, **testimonies** are statements given by individuals or organizations that a person presents in a speech as evidence or support for a point to be made. Testimonies as a form of verbal support used in public speaking need to be distinguished from legal testimonies or Christian testimonies. A legal testimony is a formal statement or declaration of a witness in a court of law while under oath or affirmation to tell the truth. A Christian testimony is usually a first-person account that explains why and how a particular person became a Christian.

In the field of public speaking, there are three main types of testimony. Peer testimony is the reported first-hand experience of a non-expert or layperson. Prestige testimony is the opinion of a recognized celebrity or famous person. Expert testimony is the opinion of a recognized expert. Let us take a closer look at these three different types of testimony:

Peer testimony: Since peer testimony is the reported first-hand experience of a non-expert, peer testimonies are usually presented as narratives or personal stories. Thus, most Christian testimonies qualify as peer testimonies. When Christians give their "testimonies," they often relate, in story form, the details of their particular religious conversions and/or experiences.

However, many peer testimonies are not specifically Christian. Anyone can give a "peer testimony" about anything they have personally experienced. Peer testimony is a great form of verbal support speakers can use to make a particular point hit home. For example, during congressional hearings, congresspersons will ask ordinary Americans to share their personal experiences in order to drive home how a particular situation or problem affects real human beings.

As a public speaker, you can incorporate peer testimony or personal stories into your speeches in order to add a more human element and to make an abstract point much more concrete and relevant. For example, if you are speaking to a group of college students in their late teens or early twenties, you can include a personal story from someone in their peer group so that they can identify with and relate to this person and the problem they faced or the issue they had to address.

Prestige testimony: You see a lot of prestige or celebrity testimony in advertising. Sports stars make hundreds of thousands, in some cases millions, of dollars endorsing shoes, golf clubs, skis, baseball bats and gloves, tennis rackets, skate boards, you name it. Movie stars endorse hair care products, clothing, cars, watches, beer, and such. Why? Companies know that people are impressed by star power. Deep down we all hope—as silly as it sounds when we say it out loud—that if we wear what stars wear, eat and drink what they eat and drink, support the causes they support, or use what they use, a bit of their talent, skill, fame, fortune, and glamour will rub off on us.

This is the same basic reason why charities and nonprofit organizations want stars and celebrities to represent their causes: people pay more attention when famous people talk than when you or I do. Actress Angelina Jolie has been a United Nations High Commissioner for Refugees Goodwill Ambassador since 2001. Bono, lead singer for U2, has supported, raised awareness of, and held charity concerts for groups such as Amnesty International, Band Aid, Live Aid, and the Global Fund to Fight AIDS, Tuberculosis, and Malaria. Tennis great Serena Williams created the Build African Schools foundation to build schools in Africa. These celebrities have leveraged their fame to influence the general public outside of the spheres of movies, music, and sports.

As a public speaker, you can also employ prestige testimony to leverage the fame of others for the purposes of your speech. Prestige testimony adds "star power" to a speech, and referring to and quoting celebrities that your audience members are familiar with lets them identify with the material better and makes the ideas in your speech more current and relevant.

Expert testimony: When you are in front of a room speaking, you are alone: just you, yourself, and your opinion. But if you can quote experts who share that opinion and who urge the same course of action that you are urging, then all of a sudden you are no longer alone. As they say in court cases, you have marshalled "expert testimony" to buttress your speech.

FIGURE **6.14**

Angelina Jolie is a UN Goodwill Ambassador.

Scientists, doctors, and other specialists are regularly called on by lawyers to add their expert opinions in court cases: people are asked to give their expert opinions in the fields of psychiatry, forensic pathology, chemistry, ballistics, accounting, computer security . . . the list goes on. Yes, it may be "only one person's opinion," but if that person's name is followed by a string of expert credentials, or if that person is considered a world-class expert on a particular topic, then that "one person" adds a lot of weight to an argument.

Expert testimony is one of the most effective forms of verbal support that you can use as a public speaker, especially when you are addressing a skeptical audience. Although your opinions may be reasonable and your arguments may be sound, when you reinforce them with expert testimony, you add authority to your opinions and arguments, authority that even skeptical audience members need to pay attention to and acknowledge.

WHEN AND HOW TO USE TESTIMONIES

Use peer testimonies and prestige testimonies primarily with friendly but apathetic audiences. Peer and prestige testimonies can get neutral or apathetic audiences to care about an issue or problem. However, if you are addressing a skeptical audience on a controversial topic, you need to exploit the power of expert testimonies.

Do not confuse peer or prestige testimonies with expert testimonies. Sometimes the dividing line is unclear. If experts are giving their opinion about a topic in which they have recognized expertise, then they are presenting expert testimony. If experts are sharing personal experience in narrative form, then they are presenting peer testimony.

Some experts are so well known that they have earned celebrity status. Albert Einstein, for example, was both an expert in the fields of mathematics and physics, and a celebrity—a person, some might say, who is famous for being famous. If you were to quote Einstein about the theory of relativity, you would be presenting expert testimony. If you were to quote Einstein about world peace, you would be presenting prestige testimony.

Some celebrities are recognized experts in their own field. If you were to quote Serena or Venus Williams giving tennis tips, you would be presenting expert testimony. If you were to quote Serena or Venus about buying a car or filling out a 1040 income tax form, you would be presenting prestige testimony.

Build up the credentials of your expert: When using expert testimony in a speech, you need to build up the credentials of your expert. Expert testimony, remember, is just the opinion of a person. The **credentials** of your experts are what make their opinions so authoritative and valuable, so you must convince your audience that the opinions they are offering are **expert** opinions. Why are they recognized as experts in their field? What special knowledge, skill, or experience do they possess that gives them expert status?

Let's see what happens when we do not identify the credentials of a quoted expert. Let's simply sat that "someone once said" or even that "Dale Carnegie once said": "**There are always three speeches, for every one you actually gave. The one you practiced, the one you gave, and the one you wish you gave.**"

This quotation is honest and funny. However, its impact is stronger when you first tell your audience that Dale Carnegie was one of the most famous speakers in US history. His best-selling book *How to Win Friends and Influence People* was published in 1936 and is still in print today.

And more than eight million people in eighty countries have graduated from Dale Carnegie training courses. When it came to public speaking, the man did know what he was talking about.

The same can be said for Peggy Noonan. She says that **"A speech is poetry: cadence, rhythm, imagery, sweep! A speech reminds us that words, like children, have the power to make dance the dullest beanbag of a heart."** Who is Peggy Noonan? What does she know about public speaking? Why should we listen to her? Aside from being a journalist and author, she was President Ronald Reagan's chief speechwriter, and she was also the chief speechwriter for President George H.W. Bush's presidential campaign. If you wanted to use her words in a speech, you would first let your audience know about the credentials that make her a recognized public speaking expert.

7. PROVERBS AND OTHER PITHY SAYINGS

Sometimes in a speech you will want to use a quotation that is not associated with a particular expert or celebrity. For example, you may access a book of quotations or search on a quotation website and find a pithy saying that has no clear source or that may even be listed as "anonymous." Although these pithy sayings do not qualify as prestige or expert testimonies, they still are a common form of verbal support that can enrich the ideas in a speech.

A "pithy" saying is a brief, meaningful, cleverly or clearly worded expression. Although we may not know the person who wrote or spoke these words, the words themselves are so well thought out that they carry obvious wisdom or persuasive force in themselves.

Proverbs are one well-recognized form of pithy saying. Every human culture amasses a storehouse of general cultural wisdom contained in proverbs. For example, different cultures have different proverbs related to speaking or talking. A Chinese proverb is "Talking doesn't get your rice cooked." An Italian proverb is "The cask can only yield the wine it contains." A Russian proverb is "The wise man has long ears, big eyes, and a short tongue." A Spanish proverb is "Talking about bulls is not the same as being in the bullring."

> ### Some Proverbs About Proverbs
>
> *Found on Bartleby.com and taken from the 1916 compilation by D.E. Marvin titled "Curiosities in Proverbs"*
>
> "A proverb is to speech what salt is to food." (Arabic)
> "Good sayings are like pearls strung together." (Chinese)
> "Proverbs are the daughters of daily experience." (Dutch)
> "A good maxim is never out of season." (English)
> "The maxims of men disclose their hearts." (French)
> "As the country, so the proverb." (German)
> "A man's life is often builded on a proverb." (Hebrew)
> "A proverb is an ornament to language." (Persian)
> "The common sayings of the multitude are too true to be laughed at." (Welsh)
> "A wise man who knows proverbs reconciles difficulties." (Yoruba—West African)

In addition to proverbs, there are many other types of pithy sayings. When trying to locate striking or memorable verbal expressions or statements for a speech, look for adages, analects, aphorisms, axioms, bon mots, bywords, catchwords, clichés, commonplaces, credos, dictums, epigrams, jests, maxims, memes, mottos, platitudes, puns, precepts, quips, saws, sententiae, slogans, sutras, truisms, and witticisms.

WHEN AND HOW TO USE PROVERBS AND OTHER PITHY SAYINGS

Use proverbs and other pithy sayings as attention getters, closers, general evidence, and transition devices in informative speeches, persuasive speeches, and speeches to entertain. Remember to credit your source when it is known, usually before you state the proverb or pithy saying. Although some memorable expressions speak for themselves, sometimes you will need to explain or restate the expression in your own words in order to clarify the point that you are trying to make.

8. EXAMPLES

In the field of public speaking, **examples** are forms of verbal support that help to explain what a speaker is saying or to show that a general statement is true. For example, if you were giving a speech on basic arithmetic and you wanted to explain that 2 + 2 = 4, you could present several specific examples to illustrate your point: two red apples combined with two green apples make four apples total, two trips to the bank and two trips to the store make a total of four trips taken, etc.

Specific examples can help to make general, abstract concepts or principles more concrete and understandable. For example, you could make the general principle "knowledge often decreases fear" more understandable by providing specific examples of situations where people could decrease their fear by increasing their knowledge: 1) people afraid of water could decrease their fear by learning how to swim, or 2) people afraid of public speaking could decrease their fear by learning the causes and symptoms of, and cures for, public speaking anxiety.

Examples can be hypothetical or real, fictional or factual. With a hypothetical or fictional example, you ask your audience to imagine specific examples that may not actually exist in the real world or have not actually occurred. (For example, the two examples in the previous paragraph are hypothetical examples—they do not refer to actual people who have reduced their fear of water or their fear of public speaking.) With a real or factual example, you present to your audience specific examples that actually exist or

FIGURE 6.15

A specific, concrete example can make an abstract truth about childhood illness hit home.

have occurred. You could give real, factual examples of particular people who have reduced their fear of water by learning to swim or of particular people who have reduced their fear of public speaking by learning the causes and symptoms of, and cures for, public speaking anxiety.

Some public speaking textbooks use the terms "example" and "story" interchangeably, but in this textbook we have listed examples and stories as separate forms of verbal support because the term "example" does not necessarily signify a story or narrative. The term "example" is a more general term than the term "story" because examples do not have to necessarily take the form of a story—they do not need to be arranged chronologically, as traditional stories are typically arranged.

For example, you could present a specific example about a particular person who decreased their fear of water by learning how to swim, and you could present this specific example as a story: you could begin the story by introducing the person and describing how they were afraid of water, you could relate how this person took swimming lessons at the local pool, and then you could end your narrative example with a some facts about how this person now plays and works around water without fear.

However, you could also present the same specific factual example without presenting it as a story. You could say in your speech, "For example, in 2005, my neighbor Laura Hemming decreased her fear of water by taking six months of swimming lessons." If true, this statement would be a factual example, but it would not be a true *story* because it is not presented as a narrative.

WHEN AND HOW TO USE EXAMPLES

Do not overuse or misuse the phrase "for example." If you begin a section of a speech with the phrase "for example," you should then present a specific, concrete example to back up or illustrate a more general, more abstract point. Specific examples are very effective forms of verbal support in informative speeches. When you want to explain or clarify a general, abstract point or principle, provide one or more specific, concrete examples.

On the one hand, provide enough details to make your specific examples specific: otherwise, your supposedly specific, concrete examples will be too vague to serve their purpose. On the other hand, do not get lost in minute details when providing specific examples. Specific examples, as forms of verbal support, are not ends in themselves, so only develop them as much as necessary to achieve your broader speech objectives.

Use examples wisely in persuasive speeches, especially persuasive speeches that address controversial issues. Make sure that you do not choose or construct examples that too easily prove your point. In persuasive speeches to convince, your examples need to be reasonable and representative. Otherwise, your skeptical audience can provide what they consider to be more reasonable counter-examples, or they can criticize your examples as unrepresentative.

9. STORIES

In his 1979 book *Mind and Nature*, anthropologist and cognitive theorist Gregory Bateson tells a story about a computer programmer who asked his computer if a machine could ever be built that would be able to think like a human being. Lights twinkled, circuits buzzed and hummed, and finally the printer spit out its answer: "That reminds me of a story. . . ."

As human beings, we are hardwired for stories. As kids, we asked our parents to tell us stories or to read and reread our favorite storybooks. Many of us had favorite TV shows that told the stories we loved to see and hear. Our lives are filled with the stories we grew up with, the stories we share with our friends and family, and the stories we tell about ourselves. When you get up to give a speech that contains a story, the better the story and the better you tell it, the better the speech will be.

As forms of verbal support, **stories** or **narratives** are verbal retellings of connected events that are usually arranged chronologically. The term "narrative" is the more technical term. The four text types commonly recognized by scholars are description, exposition, argumentation, and narration. Narration is primarily distinguished from description, exposition, and argumentation by its *form*. Narratives are stories, and traditional stories have a beginning, middle, and an end.

Stories and narratives have five traditional elements: Setting, Plot, Character(s), Conflict, and Theme. When you tell a story in a speech, you need to "set the stage" for the characters in your story by describing the setting. As your story unfolds, the characters must resolve some kind of conflict or solve some kind of problem—this is the "plot" of the story. The resolution of the conflict is usually the climax of the story. The story "theme" is the moral of the story or the point you want to make with the story.

Like examples, stories can either be factual or hypothetical. **Hypothetical stories** are fictional stories that have not happened in real life. One reason to present a hypothetical or fictional story in a speech is to get your audience to imagine what might happen in the future. Since the future has not happened yet, you can only tell hypothetical stories about the future. For example, you might get your audience to imagine what education might be like in the future: "Imagine that you wake up in the year 2020. After eating breakfast and brushing your teeth, you sit down at your computer to start your day of schooling. When you open your education program, up pops the face of your instructor and the faces of your fellow students on your computer screen. . . ."

Another reason to present a hypothetical or fictional story in a speech is help your audience relate to your speech topic. For example, you might tell the following story to get your audience to relate to victims of violent crime: "Imagine that you are in standing in line at the corner market with your bag of chips and soft drink when a voice behind your cries out, 'Everyone down on the floor—this is a stick-up!' Before you can turn around to see what is going on, you are shoved to the ground. You have just become the unwilling, unwitting victim of a violent crime."

A third reason to tell a hypothetical or fictional story is to teach a moral. Morality tales are stories that edify, inspire, illustrate, frighten, or caution. Many of the fictional stories that we grew up with are morality tales with lessons about the dangers of trusting strangers, of being lazy, of going into the woods alone—especially if you are a red-hooded female.

Let's take a look at some of the classic children's books that contain moral messages. Waty Piper's 1930 classic *The Little Engine That Could* is still being read today. It tells kids to have faith and keep on trying despite discouragement. Its mantra-like phrase "I think I can, I think I can, I think I can" reinforces the need for self-confidence. Judith Viorst's *Alexander and the Terrible, Horrible, Very Bad Day* stresses perseverance and points out that everyone has bad days . . . and survives them. Dr. Seuss' *Green Eggs and Ham* illustrates how hard it is to get some people to try something new. These fictional stories teach important moral lessons.

However, as a public speaker, a poor reason to tell a hypothetical or fictional story is that you do not want to do the research or put in the work necessary to tell a factual story. Why tell a hypothetical story about a person who contracts cancer when there are thousands of powerful, heart-wrenching, factual stories about real people who have contracted cancer? A common mistake of inexperienced public speakers is telling a hypothetical or fictional story when a factual story would be more appropriate and effective.

Factual stories are true stories that have actually occurred. They are usually the most effective stories because they report real events happening to real people, with actual consequences.

Image © Andy Dean Photography, 2014. Used under license from Shutterstock, Inc.

FIGURE 6.16 Factual stories report real events happening to real people, with actual consequences.

You make a factual story *seem* real by including specific names, dates, and locations. These specific details make your factual stories believable.

There is a temptation at times to "tweak" a factual story, to add—or delete—a few facts to make the story more effective or to "clarify" the moral of the story. Or maybe you think you can distort a factual story because your cause is so just and righteous that the ends justify the means. Don't! First, if anyone in the audience catches you, you lose your credibility as a speaker. Second . . . it is a lie.

Passing a hypothetical or fictional story off as a factual story is also, plain and simple, lying. If your audience discovers that you have lied to them and presented a fictional story as if it were really true, you have lost them and any chance you might have had to get their support. If they catch you in one lie, they will assume that most, if not all, of what you have said is also a lie. We all resent being lied to.

WHEN AND HOW TO TELL STORIES

As with ice cream, apple pie, and pizza, too many stories can leave your audience sleepy . . . and bloated. Unless you are giving a speech primarily to entertain your audience by telling amusing stories, you need to use stories judiciously. Too many stories, or stories that wander off the topic, detract from the purpose of your speech. In effect, they become a time suck.

How much time should a story in a speech take? Many politicians, salespersons, trainers, and others who speak regularly about the same topics usually have different versions of the same story. Let's take the topic of installing solar panels. A speaker might have a one- to two-sentence story about installing solar panels as part of an overview of various options. There might also be a one-minute extended illustration, a ten-minute very extended illustration, and a very lengthy, fully developed twenty-minute story. The time a speaker spends on a story—in this case the story of becoming energy efficient, helping the planet, and saving money—depends on how much time the speaker has to talk and on what else needs to be said. It is the same with any story that you might need to tell in a speech.

In a five- to ten-minute speech, an **extended illustration** or "long" story would last about a minute to a minute and a half. It might be 8–12 sentences long, and it might be comprised of about 150–200 words. A **brief specific instance** or "short" story would last about 20–30 seconds. It might be 2–4 sentences long, and it might be comprised of 30–60 words.

You could use an extended illustration (or a long story) in an informative or persuasive speech to make a point hit home. For example, after asserting that playing professional football can cause knee injuries, you could develop an extended illustration about fullback "Ickey" Woods who played for the Cincinnati Bengals, blew out both knees, and ended up selling food off of the back of a refrigerator truck.

You can string several brief specific instances (or short stories) together to show how prevalent an occurrence or a problem is. Using the same example of football causing knee injuries, you could follow an extended illustration about "Ickey" Woods with several brief specific instances about different professional football players playing other positions who also seriously injured their knees.

Whether you tell a long story or a short story, you need to add specific details. Have you ever watched television with a poor screen that was blurry and grainy? Telling a story without specific details is like making people watch television with poor reception. In order to have a high-definition story, you need lots of details and descriptive words to form precise, powerful images in the minds of your audience members.

When you use a story in a speech, you need to make the point or purpose of the story clear. Often, the "moral" or point of a story is presented *after* a story is told. Sometimes, however, you can present the point or purpose of a story *before* you tell the story: "Let me tell you a true story to illustrate the dangers of mixing prescription drugs together. . . ." If you want to make sure your audience gets the point of a story, you can make this point both *before* and *after* the story. Some speakers want to be subtle or sophisticated, so they do not want to make the point of a story obvious. However, do not be too subtle, or you audience may totally miss the point you are trying to make, and your story can become a distraction.

Image © blackboard1965, 2014. Used under license from Shutterstock, Inc.

A story lacking specific, clear details is like a television screen with poor reception.

FIGURE 6.17

10. JOKES

A joke is a statement that takes an unexpected turn. Here are two very old jokes that the late, great Henny Youngman used to tell that date back to the days of vaudeville, possibly earlier:

> "Take my wife . . . Please!" and, "A panhandler walked up to me on the street and said he hadn't had a bite in three days. So I bit him."

According to cognitive scientists, jokes create inconsistencies. They simply do not make sense. We try to make them make sense by solving the "cognitive riddle" to find out what is hidden within the sentence. When we do figure it out, we laugh with relief. This is the basis of the old joke: **He who laughs last . . . thinks slowest.**

The thing to remember, however, is that the audience has to understand the joke: they have to "see" the inconsistency and recognize that it is inconsistent—slightly out of whack—before they figure it out. Remember, if they don't get the joke, you don't get the laugh. So you have to make sure that your audience knows what it needs to know in order to get the joke—and give you the laugh.

TYPE OF JOKES

Portable jokes are jokes that speakers can tell anywhere by inserting the name of the city that they are in, or a city that the city they are in likes to make jokes about. Comedians and public speakers are always on the lookout for good lines that they can adapt to whatever they are talking about or to the place they will be talking in, like the fictional town of Gulp, a place so small that the town square has only three sides:

FIGURE 6.18 Jokes are cognitive riddles.

—You can tell that the toothbrush was invented in Gulp (OR NAME ANOTHER CITY). Had it been invented anywhere else they would have called it a teethbrush.

—You know the difference between Gulp and yogurt? Yogurt has live culture.

—The main difference between the Boy Scouts and the Gulp City Council is that the Boy Scouts have adult supervision.

Exaggeration jokes are jokes that take something that everyone is familiar with, and then take one aspect of it and exaggerate it past the point of all common sense. To tell an exaggeration joke, take a person, place, or object, and then think of the most ridiculous attribute or quality you can give to it. Once you have your "topic" make your "where to begin" list. The sample below is: "My car is so expensive that . . ." The "where to begin" list could include things like: cost, size, color, mileage, add-ons, special features, wheels, tires, trunk, engine, etc.

My car is so expensive that . . .

1. It doesn't have a stereo system because there wasn't room for that and an orchestra.
2. The hood and the trunk are in different zip codes.
3. The radiator is filled with *Perrier*.
4. The glove box seats six.
5. I let Bill Gates borrow it when he's trying to impress people.
6. Cops pull me over just so they can touch it.
7. It runs on gas from its own oil wells.
8. I keep a Lamborghini in the trunk in case of a breakdown.
9. Instead of a GPS I have my own Google Earth satellite.
10. My license plate has an unlisted number.

Story jokes or "narrative jokes" are jokes that tell a story with a punchline. Most standard "story" jokes involve three people or three occurrences (Three drunks walk into a bar, or three people jump out of an airplane, etc.). The first two narrated occurrences establish a pattern, and then the third and final occurrence breaks this pattern—this is the story joke's "punchline."

Not all funny stories are story jokes. Some of the best-known comedians in the world are known more for being storytellers than joke tellers. For example, Bill Cosby has won five Grammy Awards for his comedy albums and three Emmy Awards for his TV shows. While he does tell jokes, he is better known for his stories. (You can find and listen to many of them on YouTube.) The stories he does tell often have a moral as well as a punchline, and for the sort of motivational and inspirational speaking he often does, the message is as important as the laugh, in some cases, even more so. When you want to entertain an audience in a speech, you can tell funny stories, or you can tell jokes, or you can tell story jokes.

According to tallrite.com, the University of Hertfordshire undertook a research project to find the best jokes in the world. Since their best joke in the world has a somewhat violent punchline, we will paraphrase for you their second place winner, which happens to be a story joke:

"Sherlock Homes and Dr. Watson go on a camping trip. After a good meal, they retire for the night. After several hours, Holmes wakes up his faithful sidekick and says, 'Watson, look up and tell me what you see.' Watson replies, 'Thousands and thousands of stars.' Holmes asks, 'And what do you deduce from that?' Watson thinks deeply, and then declares, 'Astronomically, there are millions of galaxies and potentially billions of planets; astrologically, I see that Venus is in Scorpio; horologically, I infer that it is approximately four in the morning; meteorlogically, I deduce that we will have excellent weather tomorrow; and theologically, I comprehend that our Creator is omnipotent and that we are small and insignificant creatures.' Watson then asks, 'What do you deduce, Sherlock?' Holmes exclaims, 'Someone has stolen our tent!'"

WHEN AND HOW TO TELL JOKES

Most people would rather hear a joke or a funny story and have a good laugh than listen to a collection of dry and boring statistics, names, dates, and facts, even about a topic as phantasmagorically scintillating as public speaking. (Honest!) Successful informative speakers dealing with statistics, names, dates, and dry facts are often successful because they manage to weave interesting tidbits, trivia, and jokes into their presentations.

However, there is a difference between telling jokes and giving a humorous speech or a speech with humor. Some speakers open up a presentation with several minutes of jokes, jokes that they tell well and that get a lot of laughs, but then it seems almost as if they flip a switch, and that funny monologue turns into a dull, dry, and boring speech. The key is to find the humor in the material itself. So, if you are going to talk about microwave ovens and you want to make your speech interesting or humorous, tell microwave oven stories and jokes—funny ones.

The main problem with just telling jokes in a speech that do not tie into what you are talking about is that they do not tie into what you are talking about. Comedians will sometimes refer to such jokes as **joke-jokes**. Yes, they can be funny. They can be very, very funny. But if these joke-jokes do not fit with the rest of their act, if it interferes with the flow of their jokes, they drop them.

As a public speaker, you have a message, and everything you say has to fit into that message and help make it convincing and memorable. Throwing a joke-joke into the middle of a speech can interfere with the message you are trying to deliver. It can distract the audience. The goal is not just to make the audience laugh, but to make them laugh while keeping them focused on your topic and the points you are trying to make.

When you do tell a joke in a speech, watch your timing. Do not rush either the set-up or the punchline of a joke. The set-up is essential information your audience needs to "get" the punchline, and the punchline is the climax of the joke, so your audience needs to clearly comprehend both of these parts of the joke.

Raised eyebrows and palms facing up indicate to an audience that it is time to laugh.

FIGURE 6.19

Image © Accord, 2014. Used under license from Shutterstock, Inc.

After you give the punchline of a joke, nonverbally indicate to your audience that it is time for them to laugh by turning one or both palms upward and by raising your eyebrows. It is amazing how these simple nonverbal cues can call forth laughter from your audience. No one wants to look foolish because they are the only one in a crowd that is laughing. When you nonverbally signal that it is time to laugh, you make it "safe" for your audience members to respond to your joke with laughter or appreciative applause.

When your audience does laugh because you have told a funny joke, let them. Stop what you are doing, smile and nod, and wait for the laughter to finish before you continue. An audience enjoys laughing almost as much as you will enjoy creating that laughter. We must warn you, however, that creating laughter and hearing an audience laugh can be addictive.

Be very careful about using humor and jokes in persuasive speeches, especially persuasive speeches on controversial topics or issues. Humor is risky—what you find funny your audience may find trivial or offensive. When trying to win over a skeptical audience, the last thing you want to do is to offend and alienate them by telling them a joke that they do not appreciate. Even in persuasive speeches to motivate an apathetic audience, jokes are risky because they can create the wrong tone for your speech. If your speech to motivate is on a serious topic or has a serious tone, humorous jokes might not fit.

PARAPHRASING AND QUOTING

Once you have gathered verbal support, the next question is: Do you use actual **quotations** or do you **paraphrase**? As with everything else in public speaking and communication in general . . . it depends.

Do you have too many quotes? Your job is to deliver a speech that you yourself wrote. It is not to read a series of related quotations from others. So, how many quotations are too many? It depends on the subject, the length of the speech, and the length of the quotations. Limiting yourself to one or two a page is pretty safe, especially if you are dealing with short quotations.

Do not "steal" a quotation. Do not claim someone else's work as your own. Using the words or ideas of others without giving them credit is called **plagiarism**. If you use someone's words, you must place these words in quotation marks. If you paraphrase someone's work, you must rewrite it so that although the ideas may be the same, the words and structure are new and different. Be aware that paraphrasing does not relieve you of the burden of citing your sources: you still need to give credit to the people who originated these ideas.

Remember that the fact that you are using someone else's ideas that agree with your own adds weight to your own speech.

Students flunk courses for plagiarizing. Some get kicked out of school. Having plagiarism on your academic record could keep you out of graduate school, law school, medical school, or other professional disciplines. People have lost jobs, had their reputations and careers ruined, and been stripped of their degrees—even PhDs—when it was proved that part of their so-called "original work" was stolen—plagiarized. Think of plagiarism the way writers, speakers, and teachers do: *grand theft of intellectual property.*

Paraphrasing means rephrasing what someone else said or wrote in about the same amount of words. At minimum, when citing your paraphrased material you need to have the author's last name and the year

FIGURE 6.20 Plagiarism is grand theft of intellectual property.

it was published. It is again, recommended to have the works name and some additional credibility information.

Using a direct quote means you are restating word-for-word exactly what was said or written. If you quote directly, you must place quotation marks at the start and end of the words being used. The period always comes after the quotation marks in APA. You will always need the author's last name, year of publication, and page number to be presented somewhere in that sentence (if this is being used in a formal in-text citation).

Some instructors have you cite in your outline the same way you will verbally cite. This is a great method because it reinforces the specific language you will be using in your speech. Ask your instructors if they require the page number in their verbal citations. To be clear, it is a standard that in print forms of outlines (unless your instructors says otherwise) a page number where the quote is located must be present.

QUOTING

Be selective of what you choose to quote. In speechmaking it can become easy to over quote experts. Audiences don't like to be bombarded with long boring quotes. Consider how long the quote is. Long quotes can be dull, lose audience interest, and get confusing. Long quotes are only made worse when speakers put them on PowerPoint slides. Make sure your quote is necessary, impactful, purposeful and to the point. If you choose to use a long quote make sure it is adding to your pathos and you are delivering it in a way that adds to quality of your speech, not harming the quality of your speech. Novice speakers often have a hard time knowing when to directly quote a source and when to paraphrase. Here are some reasons it may be appropriate to use a direct quote:

1. If a person is famous for that exact quote
2. If you are unable to capture the essence of the language in any other way
3. If spoken another way, the words would lose their meaning
4. If the specific word choice must be demonstrated
5. If the way something is expressed matters

Note: Citation rules can change. Always check your most current APA manual before completing your reference page and formal in-text citations.

Some students think there is something wrong with using quotations in a speech; they believe that they should be able to say it all in their own words. They probably can, but can they say it as well? Can they say it with authority?

You know what you personally bring to the speech. So, ask yourself what you still need, and where—and from whom—to get it. Luckily, you do not have to go very far: the Internet, your favorite books, or lines from movies, TV shows, or songs that you can expect your audience to be familiar with. There are more "good quotes" available than any one speaker will ever be able to use in a lifetime of speaking. The job is to find the ones that work best for your speech.

PARAPHRASING

Paraphrasing allows the speaker to summarize information. Sometimes speakers are short on time, which makes paraphrasing a great choice. Paraphrasing allows a long explanation or story to be shortened, it allows a speaker to remove problematic word choice, improper grammar, leave out steps that are irrelevant to a given audience, and more. Paraphrasing can be very helpful to a speaker who needs to be able to lump several independent yet related research sources together. This process can help a speaker build credibility quickly by providing generalized findings. For instance, a speaker could waste several minutes quoting independent researchers from six studies that found the same basic outcome, or a speaker can paraphrase by saying that "Researchers have found 'insert finding here'" (insert names and years of publication dates for all research that supports that finding). Times when it is usually best to paraphrase include:

TO RETELL A STORY

1. When an exact number or account is not necessary.
2. When you need to simplify the language used.
3. When you need to replace jargon with understood terms.
4. If you think your audience will understand it better if it was reworded or reorganized.
5. When you need to use information that is at two different parts in the source.

When to paraphrase	When to quote
To retell a story	If a person is famous for that exact quote
When an exact number or account is not necessary	If you are unable to capture the essence of the language in any other way
When you need to simplify the language used	If spoken another way, the words would lose their meaning
When you need to replace jargon with understood terms	If the specific word choice must be demonstrated
If you think your audience will understand it better if it was reworded or reorganized	If the way something is expressed matters
When you need to use information that is at two different parts in the source	If a formal element is needed

VERBALLY CITING YOUR SOURCES

During your speech you need to verbally cite your sources. For example, you might say "According to communication experts Thorson, Staller, & Korcok, 2013, page 132, "insert quote here," or give your statement and in the end give the author, year, and optional page number where the quote is found. The idea with citing your source is that you are proving that your evidence is credible, that you are not plagiarizing, that the source is current, and that others could easily find this information themselves. If you are taking a college class ask your professor which formatting style they prefer. The American Psychological Association (APA) style is commonly used in the communication discipline and as such is what will be displayed in the examples below.

EXAMPLE OF HOW YOU WOULD VERBALLY CITE YOUR SOURCE

According to the book *Contemporary Public Speaking* by communication scholars, Thorson, Staller, & Korcok, 2013, p. 213, "research can be divided into two categories; primary and secondary."

EXAMPLE OF HOW YOU WILL USE IN-TEXT CITATIONS IN OUTLINES

Note: Some instructors will have their students write their citations in verbal format in their outlines, while others will have their students use the formal in-text citation format depicted in this section. Be sure to check with your instructor for their requirements and/or recommendations. Revisit this chapter in your workbook for more citation discussion.

"Research is a tool that benefits many different types of speeches. The goal of research is to aid you in forming a solid case so that you and your arguments are more likely to be accepted by the audience. If an audience is disappointed in your research efforts, it will significantly affect your ethos (credibility) for that speech. Research influences the effectiveness of the modes of persuasion that are critical to a speech. Failing to know the rules and expectations of research can also affect your logos (logic). And, finally, even your pathos (appeal to emotions) can be affected by poor research" (Thorson, Staller, & Korcok, 2013, p. 92).

If you were instead paraphrasing (not using word-for-word what the author said) then you could leave off the page number.

Basic public speaking standards insist a speaker cite the author(s) and the year of publication at minimum. However, given that ethos is always important, more information is usually beneficial, which is why most public speaking instructors will require their students provide the title of the work (book title, article title, lecture title, etc.) and the credentials of the source. How you manage to fit all that information in is up to the speaker, but it best to vary the way you cite information. For instance, don't say "according to" every single time you quote or paraphrase a source.

EXAMPLES OF PARAPHRASED RESEARCH IN ORAL CITATION FORMAT

True Story:

In their May 17, 2004 *US News and World Report* article titled "The Secrets of Sleep", Nell Boyce and Susan Brink tell the story of Pacy Erck, a Health Education teacher at Edina High School in Minnesota. Ms. Erck struggled for years to keep her morning students awake. She says they were "always nodding off". That is, until school officials made a change that helped all of the students at Edina High School get 5 more hours a week of sleep. The change was surprisingly simple: They moved the start of classes from 7:30 to 8:30 in the morning. Erck has seen a dramatic change. She says her students are no longer dropping their heads constantly and classes are "livelier".

Surprising Fact:

Elizabeth Ward reports some startling discoveries in her September, 2004 article for *Environmental Nutrition*, "Good night, sleep tight. Weight, immunity and memory will benefit". Ward writes that sleep researchers at the University of Chicago found that missing just 3–4 hours of sleep nightly over less than a week sends people into a metabolic tailspin so severe that they begin to exhibit early signs of diabetes.

Expert Opinion:

In "The Family Sleep Cure," published in the January 2009 edition of *Prevention* magazine writer Camille Noe Pagán reveals one cure she learned from Susan Zafarlotfi, PhD, director of the Institute for Sleep-Wake Disorders at Hackensack University Medical Center, that will help the whole family sleep. Zafarlotfi cautions that artificial lighting from TV and computer screens confuses our brains, making us think it is still daylight. This prevents the release of a chemical that helps us sleep, melatonin. As a result, we are wakeful, tossing and turning instead of getting the sleep we need.

OR

Dr. Douglas A. Gentile found a startling risk factor connected with video gaming and children's health when he published his research that resulted in his article "Pathological video game use among youths: A two-year longitudinal study," which was published in *Pediatrics*, 2011. Gentile says, his research shows that the more time kids spend playing video games and the lower their social competence levels are, the more at risk they are for becoming addicted to playing video games.

Statistic:

In 2011, media expert and award-winning research scientist Douglas A. Gentile, Ph.D. published an article "Pathological video game use among youths: a two-year longitudinal study" found that kids addicted to video games were more than twice as likely to be diagnosed with ADD or ADHD."

ORAL CITATIONS WITH DIFFERENT TYPES OF VERBAL SUPPORT

In order to increase your understanding of the ten types of verbal support that we have presented and described in this chapter, we now present to you a chart which briefly describes each type of verbal support and gives you a specific example of this type of verbal support related to the topic of marijuana. If you read through the specific examples contained in this chart, you should have a clearer understanding of the similarities and differences between these common types of verbal support, and you should have a better idea of how to orally cite these sources.

Type of Verbal Support	Example
1. Definitions: Statements of the exact meanings of terms.	
A. Dictionary definition	According to the online dictionary *dictionary.com*, marijuana is the dried leaves and female flowers of the hemp plant used in cigarette form as a narcotic or hallucinogen.
B. Etymological definition	The etymology of the term "marijuana" is unclear. Some think that it derives from the American Spanish word "marihuana" or "mariguana," and these words may be a composite of a personal name, "Maria Juana," or "Mary Jane." According to the *Oxford English Dictionary*, the term "marijuana" became a preferred word for cannabis in American in the 1930s.
C. Synonyms	When I use the term marijuana, I am referring to what many people call "pot" or "weed" or "cannabis."
D. Negative definition	When I mention "weed" in this speech, I am not talking about weeds that need to be pulled out of your flowerbed: I am referring to cannabis or the dried leaves of the hemp plant.
E. Essential definition	Marijuana is an hallucinatory drug made from the leaves and flowers of the hemp plant.
F. Stipulative definition	When I use the term "marijuana" in this speech, I mean to signify the recreational drug that can be eaten or smoked.
2. Facts: Things known to exist or actions known to have happened.	
A. Factual statement of quality	The cannabis sativa plant, it is commonly known, has a green color.
B. Factual statement of quantity	According to the US Drug Enforcement Administration Museum and Visitors Center, found online at *deamuseum.org* and which I accessed on June 14, 2014, more than 3 million marijuana plants have been found and destroyed in US National Forests since 1997.
3. Surveys: Studies that gather information through questionnaires.	
	According to an October 22, 2013 online article I accessed last Tuesday written by Art Swift and appearing on the official Gallup website at *gallup.com*, the year 2013 was the first time ever a majority of Americans, 58%, favored legalizing marijuana. Results of this Gallup survey were based on 1,028 telephone interviews with a random sampling of adults living in all 50 states.
4. Statistics: Facts or information represented numerically, or by numbers.	
	The National Institute on Drug Abuse, an official US Government agency, publishes statistics about marijuana and other abused drugs. On the NIDA DrugFacts page, found at *drugabuse.gov* revised in January 2014 and accessed in June 2014, it is stated that the amount of THC in marijuana samples confiscated by police has been steadily increasing over the last few decades. In the 1980s, THC levels were around 4%, but in 2012, THC concentrations averaged around 15%.
5. Comparisons: Types of verbal support that focus on similarities.	
A. Metaphor	Marijuana is a magical potion.
B. Simile	Pot plants are like the deadly poppies in the Land of Oz.

(continued)

Type of Verbal Support	Example
C. Literal analogy	Smoking pot is like inhaling a medical vapor. Some anesthesia is administered in vapor form, and when you inhale the anesthetic, you lose consciousness. Similarly, when you inhale marijuana smoke, your lungs fill with cannabis chemicals, and you lose touch with the mundane.
D. Figurative analogy	Smoking weed is like falling in love. When you fall in love, time seems to stand still, you feel fully alive, and you only care about your beloved. Similarly, when you smoke weed, time slows down, your senses are heightened, and you care only about the high you are on.

6. **Testimonies: Statements made by persons or organizations and used as support in a speech.**

A. Peer testimony	On November 16, 2011, Max Schwartzberg testified before the New York City Council at hearings about the use of medical marijuana. His detailed testimony relating his personal use of marijuana starting at age 12 can be found at *preventteendruguse.org*. I accessed his testimony on June 14, 2014 under the title "A Teen's Story." Max testifies that marijuana turned him from a bright, caring, sensitive child into a paranoid, emaciated, psychotic teen.
B. Prestige testimony	The website *healthadvocate.net* lists 42 celebrities that are in favor of the legalization of cannabis, including Bill Maher, Danny Devito, Jesse Ventura, Johnny Depp, Oliver Stone, Stephen King, and Zach Galifianakis. Oliver Stone, the HealthAdovcate website reports, stated: "I went to Vietnam, and I was there for a long time. [Using marijuana] made the difference between staying human or, as Michael Douglas said, becoming a beast."
C. Expert testimony	Nora D. Volkow, M.D., is Director of the National Institute on Drug Abuse. On April 1, 2004, she testified before the House Committee on Government Reform concerning the effects of marijuana. Her expert testimony can be found on the US Department of Health and Human Services official website at *hhs.gov*. In the conclusion of her testimony, she states, "Marijuana is not a benign drug. It has . . . significant adverse health and social consequences associated with its use."

7. **Proverbs or Other Pithy Sayings: Brief, meaningful, cleverly or clearly worded expressions.**
An anonymous quotation found on *searchquotes.com* says, "I don't need pot to be hungry, lazy, and paranoid."

8. **Examples: Types of verbal support that show that a general statement is true.**
Canada is a great specific example of how the use of medical marijuana will likely play out in the US. Marijuana is legal in Canada nationwide, and licensed operators can mass-produce marijuana for medical use. According to the June 13, 2014 article "Canada is Primed to Be a Global Example for Medical Marijuana" written by John Tilak for *Reuters* news agency, the medical marijuana sector will grow tenfold in its first 10 years.

Type of Verbal Support	Example
9. Stories: Verbal retellings of connected events usually presented chronologically.	
A. Extended, factual illustration	When I attended Medford Senior High School in the late 1970s, I had a classmate named Brian Smith. We all thought Bryan would get a music scholarship because he was a brilliant clarinet player. However, in his sophomore year, Brian began to smoke weed heavily. He dropped out of both concert band and jazz band in his Junior year, and he barely graduated from high school. Several years after leaving my hometown of Medford, Oregon, I learned that Brian was still smoking large amounts of weed, jobless, and living in his parent's garage.
B. Brief, specific instance	Brian is not the only person who found his drive and motivation decreased by smoking pot. My brother-in-law, whom I will call "Bob" for privacy purposes, began smoking pot while in Vietnam in the late 1960s. He has smoked pot regularly for the past four decades, and he is content to live in a trailer with his wife who has raised his children and has been the primary bread-winner in the family.
10. Jokes: Statements that take an unexpected turn.	
A. Portable joke	You know that folks in Gump are true stoners because their bongs get washed more than their dishes.
B. Exaggeration joke	Smoking pot made me so high I got altitude sickness.
C. Story joke	Three sinners end up in hell, an alcoholic, a sex addict, and a stoner. The devil tells them he will give them a thousand years to get over their addictions; if they can, they will get to go back to live on the earth. The alcoholic is locked in a room full of beer, the sex addict is locked in a room full of virgins, and the stoner is locked in a room full of weed. After a thousand years, the devil checks in with each addict. The alcoholic says, "I am so hung over, I will never have another beer" and, poof, he is back on the earth. The sex addict says, I am so tired of meaningless sex, I want to become celibate" and, poof, she is transported to the land of the living. When the devil opens the door of the stoner's room, the stoner punches the devil in the face and angrily exclaims, "You forgot my lighter!"

SUMMARY

In this chapter we looked at ten types of verbal support that you can develop to make yourself a more effective and dynamic speaker, and to ensure that you have fully supported the main ideas and assertions of a speech. In addition, you learned when and how to use these different types of verbal support, depending on your target audience and your speech type and purpose. We also discussed the difference between paraphrasing and quoting and how you might go about citing your sources in your outlines and verbally during your speeches.

FINDING FUN FACTS

How do you discover interesting or just plain odd facts about things?

Research. There is a tendency to Google something and then just grab the first "facts" that show up. The fact that they are the first ones that show up indicate that they are the ones most people look at. They are the facts that everyone already knows . . . including the people in your audience. Because you are not telling your audience anything new, they tune you out. They do not pay attention. You are wasting their time.

So, how do you give them something new? Do more research. Think of better ways to phrase the questions you ask Google or whatever search engine you are using. Dig a little deeper. Look for something that you yourself did not know, and then ask your friends if they knew it.

Here, for example, are three facts that most people are probably not aware of, but that can be found by doing a little bit of digging on the Internet:

1. Donating blood is an easy way to lose a pound since that's about what a pint of blood weighs.[1]
2. The first artificial Christmas trees were made in Germany in the 1800s by painting goose feathers green and sticking them on wire "branches" wrapped around a wooden dowel, the tree's "trunk." Then, in 1930, the U.S.-based Addis Brush Company made them from wires and brush bristles painted green, using the same machines and materials it used to make the brushes it was best known for the rest of the year—toilet brushes.[2]
3. Serving Diet Cokes drives flight attendants crazy, according to an article in Mental Floss magazine by author and flight attendant Heather Poole: "Diet Coke takes the most time to pour—the fizz takes forever to settle at 35,000 feet." A flight attendant can serve three passengers different drinks in the time it takes one cup of Diet Coke to be ready to serve.[3]

When you do find a "fascinating fact" or "startling statistic," ask yourself it the source of the information is credible. Just because it is on the Internet does not make it true. And also remember that Wikipedia and all the other "Wikis" are not acceptable in academic papers because anyone can post anything they want to there. Your best bet for "true facts" are educational and government sites, and the established news media. Again, it's not what you are talking about, but the stories you tell and the way you tell them that make a speech interesting and memorable.

---

[1] http://www.cicbc.org/BloodFacts.asp
[2] http://urbanext.illinois.edu/trees/facts.cfm
[3] http://mentalfloss.com/article/31044/10-shocking-secrets-flight-attendants#ixzz2PEw1I1N8

Review Questions

❶ What are ten different types of verbal support that you can use to develop an idea?

❷ What types of verbal support work well for an informative speech?

❸ What types of verbal support work well for a speech to entertain?

❹ What types of verbal support work well for a speech to motivate an apathetic audience?

❺ When is it appropriate to paraphrase versus quote during a speech?

Glossary

Brief, specific instances: Short stories or verbal illustrations.

Comparisons: Forms of verbal support that focus on two or more things in order to infer or point out that they are similar.

Definitions: Explicit statements of the meaning of a word or term.

Essential definitions: Definitions that follow a particular logical form: you place the term to be defined in a category (the genus), and then you specify how the object or thing to be defined differs from everything else in this category (the differentiae).

Etymological definitions: Definitions that reveal the original meanings of words based on their root words.

Expert testimonies: One of three primary forms of testimony. Expert testimonies are statements of people who are recognized as experts in their particular field of knowledge.

Extended analogies: Fully developed, detailed comparisons.

Extended, factual illustrations: Long, true stories.

Factual stories: Narratives relating actual events.

Facts: Forms of verbal support based on things that actually or have actually existed or on actions that have actually occurred.

Figurative analogies: Comparisons in which you compare dissimilar things, or things that belong to different categories or classes.

Hypothetical stories: Make-believe or fictional narratives.

Jokes: Short stories or statements with unexpected twists or surprise endings.

Literal analogies: Comparisons in which you compare similar things, or things that belong to the same categories or classes.

Negative definitions: Definitions that specify what a speaker does *not* mean when using a word.

Peer testimonies: One of three primary types of testimony. Peer testimonies are statements or personal accounts of individuals who have experienced a particular life event.

Plagiarism: Taking credit for someone else's words or ideas without giving them the credit they deserve.

Prestige testimonies: One of three primary forms of testimony. Statements of famous people or celebrities.

Proverbs and Other Pithy Sayings: Brief, meaningful, clearly or cleverly worded expressions.

Statements of fact: Statements made on one particular level of argument. Whereas statements of definition proclaim what a thing is, statements of value proclaim that a thing is good/bad, better/worse, right/wrong, and statements of policy proclaim what should or should not be done, statements of fact proclaim that something or some state exists, or give information about how this thing or state exists.

Statistics: Numerical data. Facts or information presented in numbers.

Stipulative definitions: Definitions that give a specific meaning to a term for the purposes of argument or discussion in a given context.

Stories: Verbal retellings of connected events that are usually arranged chronologically.

Surveys: Studies that gather information through questionnaires.

Synonyms: Words or phrases having the same or nearly the same meaning as another word in the same language.

ORGANIZING YOUR SPEECH

Michael M. Korcok

Learning Objectives

CHAPTER 7

❶ Structure your thoughts to communicate logically and powerfully.

❷ Design effective speeches to introduce, develop, and conclude your ideas.

❸ Choose and create the right opening and closing for your speech.

❹ Design your speech with a great choice for ordering your main points.

Sera just received her first speech assignment for her public speaking class: an informative presentation. She wants to talk about the history of volleyball, a subject she feels qualified to discuss due to her status as the college's junior varsity team captain. She's narrowed her topic and has even written a preliminary thesis statement that she likes. Now what? She stares at the blank page, wondering what to do next.

Marcus is very excited to have been invited to speak at his city's annual Chamber of Commerce convention. He wants to use the opportunity to persuade the members of the audience to support a newly proposed city ordinance that will encourage entrepreneurialism through tax incentives. Marcus has collected several books and economic articles containing evidence that support his position. However, as he looks at all the material, he wonders how he will possibly fit everything he needs to discuss within his twenty minute time allotment.

The dilemmas faced by Sera and Marcus are faced by everyone charged with writing a speech, from the most experienced professional speechwriter and to the novice public speaking student. Once a topic is selected and refined into a clear thesis statement, you must actually write your new speech. The key to success is speech organization, the focus of this chapter.

By reading this chapter, you will achieve three objectives. First of all, you will develop an appreciation for the value of speech organization. Speech organization provides important benefits to both the speaker and the audience. Organized speeches are clear, enjoyable, and effective.

They can hold the attention of the audience and reduce the anxiety felt by the speaker. In contrast, disorganized speeches create confusion, undermine the rapport between the audience and speaker, and typically fail to achieve their purposes.

Second, you will study the function and structure of the three components of every speech: the introduction, the body, and the conclusion.

The introduction is the beginning of the speech. It is composed of three parts: the opening, the thesis statement, and the preview. The introduction should account for between ten and fifteen percent of the total speech.

The body is the middle part of the speech, falling between the introduction and the conclusion. The body is the bulk of the speech, accounting for approximately eighty percent of total speech length. The development of the presentation's main ideas occurs in the body.

The body contains between two and five main points. A main point is a block of time used to develop the thesis statement. The organization of the body includes the selection of an order for the presentation of the main points. Common options for main point ordering include time order, topic order, cause-effect, problem-solution, comparative advantage, and Monroe's motivated sequence.

The Three Parts of a Speech in Proportion	
I. Introduction	10–15%
II. Body	75–80% Q9
III. Conclusion	5–10%

The conclusion is the end of the speech. It is the last opportunity for the speaker to leave a lasting impression upon the audience. Like the introduction, the conclusion also contains three parts: the restatement of the thesis statement, the review of the preview, and the closing. The conclusion is the shortest part of the speech and should only account for between five and ten percent of the total speech time.

Finally, through this chapter, you will learn how to effectively use transitions and signposts. A transition is a single sentence bridge that connects one main point in the body to the next. A signpost is a short, often numerical, cue used within a speech to explain the structure of a complex main point. By the end of this chapter, you will understand how to organize the parts of your speech through effective design in order to produce and deliver an effective, efficient speech.

Organizing your thoughts on a subject is a prerequisite to communicating them.

FIGURE 7.1

© olbyy, 2013. Used under license from Shutterstock, Inc.

BENEFITS OF SPEECH ORGANIZATION

Speech organization is very important. The successful organization of a speech provides benefits to both the speaker and the audience. As the speaker, you will immediately enjoy the psychological benefits of knowing that you've adequately prepared and organized your speech. If your speech is organized, you will look and feel more confident during your delivery. You'll also be less likely to make an error. Ultimately, successful organization will decrease the stress associated with speech presentation. The level of anxiety you experience will be reduced because organization will improve your knowledge of the material.

In addition, speech organization can improve the delivery of the speech. Through the process of organization, you will gain a greater sense of familiarity with the material. This familiarity will increase the ease of delivery. You won't have to constantly worry about checking your note cards because you'll remember much of the material.

Your audience will also enjoy important benefits associated with your speech organization. Imagine you are sitting in a physics class listening to your professor discuss the Higgs boson. You are very interested in the topic and are trying to take notes. However, your notes are confusing because the speech does not have a clear structure. Instead, the speaker bounces randomly from the work of Peter Higgs, to the current related experiments, to the media's use of the term "God particle," and then back to the technical aspects of particle physics. While your professor appears knowledgeable, you and most of the audience are lost by the disorganization of the speech. As a result, your mind wanders and you leave the lecture hall frustrated with the class.

In contrast, a well-organized speech about the Higgs boson could have bolstered your enthusiasm and interest in the subject. You would have been able to follow the professor's lecture, leaving the lecture hall with a better understanding of particle physics.

This example illustrates some of the benefits of speech organization enjoyed by the audience listening to the speech. In general, the audience enjoys comprehension benefits when a speech is structured and organized. The audience's ability to understand the thesis and content of the speech is bolstered by a clear organizational format that leads the audience through the speaker's train of thought. A speaker who takes the time to preview and review important points increases the likelihood that the audience will remember the speech's most important points.

Organization also helps to establish a rapport between the speaker and the audience. In a previous chapter, you learned the difference between ethos, pathos, and logos. Ethos describes the perception of competence or incompetence of the speaker. Speech organization helps the speaker to establish ethos by illustrating the credibility of the speaker. In addition, a speaker who is confident and organized will project an interest in the speech's subject, encouraging the audience to be interested as well.

Benefits of Speech Organization
1. Speaker ethos and confidence improve.
2. Speech apprehension drops.
3. Organized content improves delivery.
4. Audience interest and comprehension improve.
5. Fewer speaker errors occur.

In contrast, a lack of organization will undermine the speaker's ethos. If a speaker is disorganized, it creates the perception that the speaker didn't take the time to prepare and doesn't value the speech. Members of the audience may start to question the speaker's credibility. Why should they care about the speech if the speaker does not? The audience members may also begin to feel unappreciated by the speaker, determining that the speaker didn't value the speech enough to engage in sufficient preparation. These negative feelings will influence the audience's response to the speech. Members of the audience will be more likely to view the speaker with hostility or ignore the content of the speech.

When considering the benefits of speech organization, consider your own educational experience. Chances are your favorite professors were organized. They took the time to explain important topics and check your comprehension before moving on. Their lectures were structured, creative, and focused. You could pay attention and learn something because the information was clearly presented to you.

In contrast, your least favorite professors were probably like the professor in the physics lecture example given above. When a speaker doesn't bother to organize or structure a speech, it is easy for the audience to feel unappreciated and frustrated. Although the speech may contain important information, that information is unlikely to be conveyed to the audience.

SPEECH ORGANIZATION OVERVIEW

From an academic perspective, a speech is divided into three sections. They are the introduction, the body, and the conclusion. Each part of the speech does different work in a presentation, and those jobs dictate how we organize each part.

The Parts of Every Speech Another Way	
Introduction	Tell 'em what you're gonna tell 'em
Body	Tell 'em
Conclusion	Tell 'em what you told 'em

A layperson's understanding of a speech also recognizes three parts: tell 'em what you're gonna tell them, tell 'em, and tell 'em what you told them. In the introduction, you tell 'em what you're gonna tell them. In the body, you tell 'em. In the conclusion, you tell 'em what you told 'em.

And you don't really need the next explanation, but just in case this isn't very clear . . .

Every speech is like a hamburger. A hamburger has three parts: the top bun; the juicy middle with all those ground beef patties, ketchup, mustard, tomatoes, lettuce, and pickles; and the lower bun. In the speech, the introduction is the top of the bun that hints at what is inside. When you look at a warm hamburger bun, you know that the hamburger is inside. The body is the meaty, juicy hamburger and fixings. The conclusion is the bottom bun, which holds it all together.

Ultimately, the development and organization of a speech requires you to divide your speaking time between the introduction, the body, and the conclusion. These three parts should not be equal in time, however, and part of the process of organizing a speech involves budgeting your allotted speech time. Roughly, the speech should give between ten and fifteen percent of the total time to the introduction, while the conclusion should get between five and ten percent of the total time. The body, the largest part of the speech, should command roughly eighty percent of the speech time. So, for a seven-minute speech, the introduction should be about forty-five seconds, the body should be about five minutes, thirty seconds long and the conclusion would receive the remaining thirty seconds or so.

Often, instructors will ask students to create an outline when preparing a speech. An outline summarizes the major points within a speech. The outline will identify the introduction, body, and conclusion. It will also identify the thesis statement, main points of the body, and closing statement. Although not all speech writers use an outline, the creation of an outline can be a powerful tool for organization because it forces you to clearly identify and organize your speech's content.

THE INTRODUCTION

The **introduction** is the start of the speech. Your audience is forming their first, most important, and longest-lasting impression of you during the introduction and this part of the speech is your only chance to make a great first impression.

Despite their importance, introductions make up a relatively short portion of the total speech. When you work on writing a speech, keep in mind that your introduction should only fill between ten and fifteen percent of your total speaking time. That means, for a speech intended to last around seven minutes, for example, the introduction should only be between forty-five seconds and one minute long.

The preparation and organization of the introduction is very important. The introduction of a speech should be written-out, word-for-word. Once the introduction is written, you should take the time to memorize it completely. Although this may initially appear to be a difficult task, it is important to keep in mind that the introduction is really only a small portion of the overall speech.

Memorization of the introduction is important. Looking at the audience will establish your credibility and confidence. By memorizing your introduction, you can deliver the beginning of your speech while scanning the audience instead of grasping for words or fidgeting with your notes.

FUNCTIONS OF THE INTRODUCTION

The Functions of the Introduction
1   Tell 'em what you're gonna tell 'em.
2   Begin the speech.
3   Get the audience's attention.
4   Establish speaker credibility.
5   Generate audience goodwill.
6   Communicate speech relevance.

The introduction of your speech has many different jobs, or functions, to do. What is the most important job? Tell 'em what you're gonna tell 'em. In other words, the first job of the introduction is to let your audience know what they are about to hear. This prepares the audience to organize and understand the content to come. Two of the three parts of the introduction perform just that function: the thesis and preview both "tell 'em what you're gonna tell 'em." That means all the other jobs we will discuss need to be accomplished by the opening.

In addition, the introduction is the formal beginning of the speech. Although this function may appear self-evident, it is a good reminder of the nature of a speech. Any public speech presentation is always an event, a block of time with a defined beginning, middle, and end. The introduction always begins the event that is your speech. How you begin the speech is, unavoidably, your introduction.

A key function of the introduction is to get the audience's attention. Many believe that getting the audience's attention is so important that every introduction needs to do it. Attention-getting is important because members of the audience have their own interests, concerns, and problems. For those audience members, the introduction needs them to set aside their other thoughts for the duration of the speech and pay attention to you and your ideas.

Many speakers spend a lot of time crafting the perfect opening, one that will quickly grab the audience's attention. However, attention-getting is not always the most important function of the introduction. Although you should never assume that you have the audience's attention simply by virtue of giving a speech, some audiences in some situations will give you their attention without doing anything special. For example, if you are a famous or distinguished person, a friendly audience is likely to give you their attention even if you do not open your speech with an attention-getter.

Alternatively, some audiences are captive audiences. A **captive audience** is composed of individuals required to attend the speech and pay attention. For example, in your public speaking class, you will likely be required to give one or more speeches in front of your classmates. The attendance of your classmates will be required and they will have to pay attention to your speech. They may even be required by your professor to offer a verbal or written critique after you complete your speech. In this example, your introduction does not really need to have an attention-getter. However, an attention-getter is still likely to garner appreciation from the members of your audience due to its entertainment value.

The fourth function of the introduction is establishing the speaker's credibility, or ethos. The introduction provides you with an opportunity to explain why they should listen to you. Credibility is important for all speeches because audiences need to take a speaker seriously. However, it is particularly important for persuasive speeches and for speeches about complex, technical, and controversial topics. If the audience members think you are an expert, they are more likely to listen to your reasons, arguments, and analysis. In contrast, if they don't think you're an expert or have no real experience with your topic, the members of the audience will be less likely to consider your judgment.

Being a recognized authority on the subject you are addressing is helpful. Fortunately, you can establish your credibility in other ways as well. For example, you may also establish credibility by referencing the expertise of others, such as academic researchers or successful professionals. Referencing other experts shows that you have taken the time to review the related literature and have a working familiarity with the topic that the members of your audience likely lack.

In some cases, the credibility of the speaker may be established prior to the speech. For example, event flyers or other advertisements may be circulated to promote the identity of the speaker as an expert on the speech's subject. However, such external actions need not replace the introduction's role in illustrating the speaker's credibility. Even if your credibility has been established prior to the speech, it's not a bad idea to build credibility-enhancing strategies into the introduction. After all, the speaker cannot assume that everyone in the audience is cognizant of the speaker's relevant credentials.

The fifth function of the introduction is to create goodwill. Goodwill encompasses factors such as likeability and trust. Goodwill is important for all speeches but particularly significant for the success of persuasive speeches. An audience that likes and trusts a speaker is more likely to be swayed by that speaker to support a particular argument. Goodwill shouldn't be taken for granted, but speakers sometimes convince themselves that an audience is hostile because their communication apprehension has gotten the best of them. While that might rarely occur, audiences typically begin with a neutral or somewhat positive attitude toward speakers. Nonetheless, if creating goodwill is deemed important for a speech, the opening is the time to do it.

The sixth and final function of the introduction is establishing the relevance of the speech in the minds of the audience members. Speakers often take for granted that if they have the audience's attention that their listeners will understand why the speech matters to them. An explicit statement drawing the connection between the content to come and the lives of audience members can go a long way to establish interest in the speech to come.

As previously noted, the introduction should involve only about ten percent of your total speech. That is not very much time to try to achieve all five of these functions. Therefore, an important part of crafting your introduction involves prioritization. When writing your introduction, you should think through which of the above jobs are most important for your speech topic, the speaking event, and your audience. The introduction should be crafted with those jobs in mind.

STRUCTURE OF THE INTRODUCTION

The basic structure of the introduction should always include three sections: the opening, the thesis statement, and the preview. The opening is the first section of the introduction, which also makes it the first part of the speech. Openings have to do all the jobs of an introduction except telling them what you will say. As a result, openings should take most of the time in the introduction; the other parts are short.

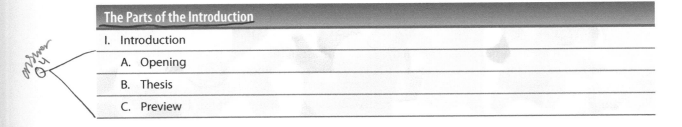

The Parts of the Introduction
I. Introduction
A. Opening
B. Thesis
C. Preview

Openings should take the biggest share of time available to the introduction. The other two parts of the introduction, the thesis and preview, are single sentences and quick. Openings are also your chance to be creative in the introduction. In contrast, the other parts of the introduction are pretty formulaic. Openings have to achieve all of the important functions of the introduction except the first one. The only job the opening doesn't do is to tell 'em what you're gonna tell 'em.

Since the opening does so many jobs in the introduction, the speaker needs to make some hard choices here. Begin by assessing what really needs to be accomplished in the introduction. Is getting their attention the most important function, while generating goodwill, establishing credibility, and drawing relevance are lower priorities? Perhaps establishing oneself as an authority on the subject while pointing out topic relevance are the most important tasks to accomplish in the introduction. Each speaking situation, with its own topic, speaker, audience, and occasion will have its own priorities to achieve in the introduction.

Once the speaker has decided which functions should take precedence, they should choose how to accomplish those tasks. One way to proceed is to treat the opening as an undivided whole: a single opening type will need to accomplish all the important jobs. For single functions, a specialist opening type may be a good choice. If the most important task is to create goodwill, for example, a joke to begin the speech is a great choice. To accomplish multiple functions with a single undivided opening, a generalist opening type such as a story might be the way to go: good stories can be effective attention-getters, can generate goodwill, and can draw topic relevance for the audience. The advantage of a single, undivided opening is the elegance and flow of an introduction: this choice allows the words of an introduction to move simply and seamlessly from opening to thesis and preview.

Sometimes, rather than a single, undivided opening to do the jobs the speaker concludes need to be done, an opening with several parts is called for. In this approach, the opening might begin with an attention-getter, move to building speaker credibility, and finish by drawing a connection between the topic and the members of the audience. Each of the functions of the introduction gets its own part of the opening. The primary advantage of this way of constructing an opening is that a speaker can focus on how best to achieve each of the priorities they have identified without trying to force them into a single, undivided opening. If performed artfully, these subdivided openings can work as smoothly and effectively as undivided openings.

The second part of the introduction is the thesis statement. In Chapter 4, we defined the thesis statement as a single sentence statement of the one main idea that the speech will develop. The thesis statement gives the big picture to the audience: it tells 'em what you're gonna tell 'em as a whole. Often, you will begin the formal organization of your speech with the thesis statement, building the other parts of the speech around that central idea.

When writing your introduction, it is important to frame your thesis. You want to ensure that your thesis statement clearly stands out from the rest of the introduction. One way to do that is to pause for a second or two before and after stating your thesis. By emphasizing your thesis, you ensure that your audience knows what to expect from your message, which will bolster their ability to comprehend the rest of the speech.

The final part of the introduction is the preview. The preview is a single-sentence, ordered list of the main points in the body of the speech to come. Like the preview of a movie, the preview within the introduction gives your audience a sneak peek into the structure and direction of your speech. The preview tells 'em what you're gonna tell 'em in more detail than your thesis statement alone. In fact, the preview works with the thesis statement to mentally prepare your audience for the speech's message.

TYPES OF OPENINGS

Crafting a great opening begins by deciding which of the functions of the introduction are most important for the speech being presented. The thesis and preview take care of telling the audience what the speech will be about. That leaves five functions for the opening to take care of: begin the speech, get the audience's attention, build credibility, generate goodwill, and draw relevance. How you prioritize those jobs for your speech for a given audience is the most important consideration in choosing which type of opening to present.

Every opening begins the speech, and how you begin the speech is your opening, whether you want it to be or not. Speakers often make the mistake of introducing themselves at the very beginning of a speech or of asking if everyone is ready or of muttering under their breath about how they are really nervous or even that they hate speaking in public. Speakers don't typically consider these as openings in a speech, but that's exactly what they are. Effective public speakers will let silence settle a bit and then begin with their opening.

Question openings aren't usually a good opening choice, but they do begin a speech. Every opening choice does that, though, even inadvertent ones. Question openings are rarely effective at any of the tasks openings can accomplish, but you might think they are a good choice since they are so often used.

Question openings are so common not because they are effective, however, but because they are easy to construct. Once a speaker has a thesis statement worked out, a question opening requires almost no effort to write. Just turn the topic into a question to ask the audience. And that's why so many speeches begin with a question: the speaker didn't have to do any work to come up with one. Using a question opening is a surefire way to communicate to your instructor and your audience that you didn't want to go to the effort of constructing a good opening. Question openings do begin a speech, however.

When the most important job for the opening is getting the audience's attention, you should consider a **startling statement opening**. Startling statements present a surprising fact or unique perspective or make a stunning claim which compels listeners to focus on the speaker. Startling statements as openings are a "specialist" opening in that they typically don't do any of the other jobs of an opening especially well: they are the attention-getter openings.

FIGURE 7.2 Startling statement openings are attention-getting specialists.

Startling statements need care. It is easy to go wrong with a poorly chosen startling statement: a startling statement that isn't that startling is a wasted opportunity to do a useful opening while a too startling statement runs the risk of annoying the audience, creating bad will. A startling statement that is too startling might also leave audience members "stuck at the beginning," ignoring the rest of the introduction as they work through the opening itself.

Don't yell "YAAARRRGH!" at the beginning of a speech, for example. You will surely startle your audience into paying attention to you, but it won't be in a good way. Similarly, beginning a speech with "government programs to help the poor cost taxpayers MILLIONS of dollars every year!" is unlikely to startle anyone.

Beginning a speech with an attention-getting claim like "the terrible air quality in our area will lower the lifespan of each of us in this room, on average, by about six years." will likely get most or all of your audience to listen.

When the most important job for the opening is building your credibility, you should consider an **opening quotation**. Quotations work to establish credibility by letting the audience know that you are well-read on the subject you are about to discuss. Quotations identify the person who made a statement followed by quoting their statement. Quotations can, if well-chosen, also get the audience's attention or create goodwill, but they are a specialist opening for building credibility.

Quotations by well-known authorities or well-liked celebrities are often safe openings that can build your credibility. Quoting an authority that the audience is likely unfamiliar with requires that you qualify them after stating their name: the more detailed the qualification, the more you demonstrate your familiarity with the content. Quotations are rarely a risky opening, but their safety often comes at the cost of not being especially snazzy. Quotations are also fairly easy to research: there are numerous collections of quotations online.

When the most important job for the opening is creating audience goodwill, you should consider **opening with a joke**. A good joke gets the audience laughing with the speaker, and once someone laughs with you, they are much more likely to think you're okay. Those successful in sales learn quickly that goodwill with a customer or client goes a long way to closing the deal: that's why so many salespersons will look to tell a joke early in a conversation. A well-chosen and told joke can get the audience's attention, but jokes are a specialist opening to generate goodwill.

Jokes are risky openings. A joke that falls flat wastes the opportunity of a good opening, but a bad choice of joke can do real damage to a speech. Some of the most effective humor is risk-taking: famous comedians often make their living by telling cutting jokes that tweak controversial issues. Jokes about sex or race or ethnicity or religion that go after stereotypes, contradictions, and social absurdities are the bread and butter of cutting-edge comedy. Unfortunately, these are also the jokes that risk alienating or even angering audience members. A speech is not the time to tell that hilarious joke you first heard at the bar a few days ago.

Story openings aren't specialist openings like startling statements, quotations, or jokes. Story openings are generalists: they can accomplish any of those jobs and even more than one. A well-chosen story can get the audience's attention, build the speaker's credibility, and create goodwill. A good speaker will develop their ability to craft and tell stories well, since stories are a skilled speaker's opening of choice.

The problem with stories as openings is that you have no time to tell them well. A seven-minute speech, for example, should have an opening that is about one minute long. Sixty seconds isn't much time to tell a tale. A minute is enough time for about one-hundred-eighty to two hundred words and that's not many words at all. Polished public speakers learn to tell stories efficiently.

Types of Opening	What It Does Best
Questions	Bad but begin a speech
Startling Statements	Attention getters
Quotations	Build credibility
Jokes	Generate goodwill
Stories	Generalist openings

A good story needs details and a tale without the details isn't worth telling. Stories with important elements missing are a mistake: the time would be better used with one of the other opening types. Except questions, because questions aren't good openings. The following is a story: "Yesterday I woke up, I did things, and then I went to sleep." It's a terrible story precisely because it lacks key details that could make it worth the telling.

Good stories have all of the **basic narrative elements**: a protagonist, an antagonist, a setting, a plot, a theme, and a narrative structure. A protagonist is the central figure of your story, the heroine or hero who acts. An antagonist is the main villain of the tale, the bad guy or the terrible fix our heroine is in. The setting is the time and place that the action occurs. The theme is the lesson to be learned, the reason the tale is worth telling, or the worthwhile point the story makes. Finally, the narrative structure is the dramatic flow of the tale: tension or mystery or complexity building until a resolution, the climax, occurs. That's a lot to pack into just a few words.

There are many other types of openings, nearly as many types as there are openings themselves. But these few, the question, the startling statement, the quotation, the joke, and the story are the basic openings every speaker should master. Knowing what functions they perform and when to choose which type of opening will serve you well.

THE CONCLUSION

The **conclusion** is the end of the speech. It offers the speaker one last chance to be memorable. During the conclusion, your audience is forming their final impressions of you. Although last impressions are not as important as first impressions, they are still significant and likely to be remembered. In addition, the conclusion is the final opportunity to ensure that the audience understands your thesis statement.

Conclusions are important but also relatively brief when compared to the other parts of a speech. Conclusions should make up between five and ten percent of your total speaking time. So, for a speech planned to last about seven minutes, with an introduction written to require between forty-five seconds and one minute for delivery, the conclusion should only be about thirty seconds long.

The preparation of the conclusion is just as important as the preparation of the introduction. Conclusions should always be prewritten, word-for-word, and memorized. This preparation will allow you to look at your audience while ending your speech, which can leave a powerful impression upon your audience. If you used notes or an outline while delivering your speech, you don't want to spoil your final words and undermine your ethos by struggling to find your place on the page.

FUNCTIONS OF THE CONCLUSION

The conclusion of a speech fulfills three basic functions. The first is to tell 'em what you told 'em. In other words, remind your audience of what they just heard. This is the most important job of the conclusion because it reinforces the significance of your points and conveys a lasting message to the audience. If the audience didn't recognize a main point as important, you will have this last chance to remind them.

The second function of the conclusion is inevitable. The conclusion is the end of the speech. The conclusion always ends the communicative event that is your speech. Once your conclusion is over, your speech is over. How you end the speech is, unavoidably, your conclusion.

The final function is to give the audience a reason to remember your speech. You should always aim to finish the speech memorably. A speech comes to not much, no matter how good the content and passionate the speaker, if most of the audience soon forgets what they heard, or even that they listened to a speech.

The Functions of the Conclusion Q6 ←
Tell 'em what you told 'em.
End the speech.
Get them to remember the speech.

answer

STRUCTURE OF THE CONCLUSION

The structure of the conclusion should be divided into three parts: the restatement of the thesis statement, the review of the preview, and the closing. The parts of the conclusion are designed to accomplish the functions outlined in the previous section. The first part of the conclusion is a restatement of the thesis statement. Restating the thesis reminds the audience what the speech was about: it tells 'em what you told 'em as a whole. You can choose to reword your thesis statement for the conclusion or you can repeat your original statement from the introduction verbatim.

The second part of the conclusion's structure is the review of the preview. Reviewing the preview reminds the audience what the main points in the body were. It tells 'em what you told 'em in more detail than the restatement of the thesis.

The final component of the conclusion is the closing. Closings don't remind the audience of the content of the speech, but they do end the speech and have to do so memorably. The closing is the last chance you have to get the audience to remember you. For example, you may want to refer back to the beginning of your speech. Alternatively, you may want to finish with a relevant quotation. If you started a story in the introduction, the conclusion is your opportunity to finish it. Ultimately, you want to be careful and creative when you craft your conclusion. Make it memorable and end on a high note.

The Parts of the Conclusion
III. Conclusion
A. Restatement of the thesis
B. Review of the preview
C. Closing

answer
Q7

The function and development of the closing is equivalent to the opening within the introduction. Closings should demand most of the speaking time allotted to the conclusion. The other two parts are short. In addition, whereas the other parts of the conclusion are pretty formulaic, the closing provides you with another option to be creative.

The types of closing are similar to the types of openings. Startling statements make little sense at the end of a speech, of course: it is too late to get the audience's attention. Questions are even worse as a closing than as an opening. That leaves jokes, quotations, and stories as sensible basic closing types.

Bookending the opening and closing is often an effective choice. To bookend an opening and closing, one would pair these parts of a speech with matching or complementary texts. If the opening is a quotation, then a closing quotation with a different take on the same topic or a different quote from the same author might work well. Similarly, beginning with a joke and delivering a second punch-line or a matching joke as a closing can be effective. Bookending with a story can be as simple as reserving the story's ending for the closing or telling a continuation of the tale at the end of a speech.

THE BODY

The **body** of the speech is found in the middle, between the introduction and the conclusion. The body of the speech takes the majority of the speaking time in the presentation. Approximately eighty percent of the total allotted time for the speech should be devoted to the body. This means that the previous two sections, the introduction and conclusion, only account for about one fifth of the total speech. For example, in a seven-minute presentation, the body should account for about five and one half minutes.

The preparation of the body differs somewhat from the preparation of the introduction and conclusion. The short lengths of the introduction and conclusion help you to memorize them before your presentation. In contrast, unless the speech event calls for a memorized or manuscript presentation, the body should not be memorized and, unlike the introduction and conclusion, it shouldn't be written out. Outline, organize, and structure the body. Then, practice delivering the body without worrying about trying to get the exact wording of the body to be the same every time.

MAIN POINTS

Main points are blocks of time in the body used to develop one main idea each. A speech should contain between two and five main points. The main points should demand roughly equal lengths of time and importance. In general, a thesis statement can be well-supported with two or three main points.

The Structure of the Body
II. Body
A.   Main point 1
Transition from mp 1 to mp 2
B.   Main point 2
Transition from mp 2 to mp 3
C.   Main point 3

A few decades back, three main points was considered the standard for a well-made speech. Quite a few stock main point orders were designed with three main points in the body of the speech in mind. In recent years, however, bodies with two main points have become popular, especially for shorter speeches.

The reason two main points have become more popular is that fewer main points allows more time in each main point to develop ideas with examples, stories, statistics, and visual aids. In a five-minute speech, for example, with the body getting about four minutes of the total time, a speech with three main points allows about eighty seconds per main point whereas a speech with two main points allows about two minutes per main point. And for a speech that short, an extra forty seconds per main point to develop key ideas can make all the difference.

The main points of a speech should all support the thesis statement. When considered together, they provide sufficient support to render the thesis accurate. Only ideas that directly develop and support the thesis should be included as main points. When planning your body, remove from the main points any ideas that do not develop the thesis statement.

TRANSITIONS

The body should always contain transitions. A transition signals to the audience the speech's movement from one point to another, or one part of the body to another. You should expect to include a transition between each main point within the body. If you wish to add transitions from the introduction to the body and from the body to the conclusion, you may, but many speakers don't feel these are needed.

A transition is a bridge that connects two main points and so reminds the audience of two things. The transition reminds the audience of the previous point and it introduces the new point.

The successful development and use of transitions requires full transitions, rather than half transitions. A full transition will signal both the point previously discussed and the point about to be discussed. In contrast, the half transition will fail to include both points. It may repeat the previous point or identify the new point but it will fail to mention or connect the two.

The main points in the body may also contain signposts. Signposts are short, often numerical, cues used by the speaker to highlight a transition to a new sub point within a complex main point. Examples of signposts are "first," "second," or "finally." For example, you may choose to give a process demonstration style of informative speech within your public speaking class. Although transitions are required, signposts are optional.

ORDERING MAIN POINTS

Once you have selected the main points to support your thesis statement, you must determine their order within the body. Order is an important part of organization. The choice of ordering should be made deliberately in order to facilitate comprehension by making your main points appear logical and easy to understand. Six main point orders commonly used to develop a speech are time order, topic order, cause-effect, problem-solution, comparative advantage, and Monroe's motivated sequence.

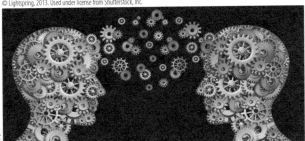

FIGURE 7.3 Ordering your main points well helps convey the structure of the speech's thesis.

Time order moves the speech in a sequence based on the chronological occurrence of events. The speech begins with the earliest event and moves forward in time to conclude with the events occurring last. For example, you may use time order to arrange an informative bibliography about Abraham Lincoln. With your body, you would begin with Lincoln's birth, continue to discuss his education and his political career, before ending your main points with his assassination. The time order signals to the audience that the chronology of Lincoln's life is important. In addition to biographies, time order is particularly useful for process demonstration speeches and other historical speeches.

The second design option is **topic order**. Topic order divides the subject of the speech into its component parts. The order will make intuitive sense to the speaker and the audience. Topic order is ideal for expository presentations.

Topic order is a very common method of arranging main points within a speech because it gives the speechwriter a greater deal of control over the order of the main points. Almost any speech subject can be subdivided into subpoints or categories. Then, the order of the main points can be organized in a way that makes logical sense to the speaker. The topic order can move from the general to the more specific, or from the least significant to the most important, depending on what makes sense to the speaker.

EXAMPLE OF THE USE OF TOPIC ORDER

Topic: Holidays Celebrated by Catholics
Thesis: In order to promote interreligious dialogue, I'm going to talk about three holidays celebrated by members of the Roman Catholic Church.
Main Point 1: First of all, Catholics remember those designated as saints on November 1, All Saints' Day.
Main Point 2: In addition, Catholics celebrate the birth of Jesus Christ on December 25, Christmas.
Main Point 3: For Catholics, the most important holiday is Easter, the day that celebrates the resurrection of Jesus Christ.

For example, John decides that he wants to deliver an informative speech on holidays celebrated by Catholics to his public speaking class. After researching the different holidays, he identifies three as the most important for explaining the beliefs of the religion. He then uses topic order to structure his speech.

In this example, the main points are organized according to the three holidays John wants to discuss.

The third type of design, the **cause-effect order of main points**, is useful primarily for persuasive speeches and noncontroversial informative speeches. This order aims to establish and explain a relationship between two subjects or events. It shows that one subject or event caused the other.

For example, you may want to use a cause-effect order of main points for a speech explaining the causes of lung cancer.

EXAMPLE OF THE USE OF CAUSE-EFFECT ORDER

Topic: Lung Cancer

Thesis: In order to promote health, I'm going to discuss three behaviors proven to cause lung cancer.

Point 1: Lung cancer is linked to the inhalation of asbestos.

Point 2: Exposure to second-hand smoke, or passive smoking, can also contribute to an increased risk of lung cancer.

Point 3: The most common cause of lung cancer is smoking tobacco products, which include cigarettes.

The speech's identification of the causes of lung cancer is noncontroversial. The points of the speech are backed by substantial scientific evidence. No one seriously argues that cigarette smoking is not linked to lung cancer. Therefore, you can fulfill your general purpose of informing the audience using this structure.

However, the cause-effect order of main points will not work as well for an informative that explores a controversial topic. In fact, the use of the cause-effect order of main points can cause an intended speech to inform to become a speech to persuade. For example, the human causes of global warming are a generally settled speech subject that continues to be somewhat controversial. The cause-effect design is less appropriate for this speech topic because members of the audience are likely to question your selected structure and your conclusion. Although you may intend for the speech to be informative, the use of the cause-effect order will likely skew it to become more persuasive in nature.

The cause-effect structure is clearly not appropriate for informative speeches that aim to discuss only one cause among many. For example, you may select as your informative topic the cause of crime. You then craft a thesis statement that states that crime results from insufficient government spending on antipoverty programs. This design is no longer an informative speech. It has become a speech to persuade.

The **problem-solution order** divides the body of the speech into three basic sections. The first section outlines the problem. The second section discusses the solution to the problem. The third section then argues that the solution proposed in the second point will solve the problem outlined in the first point. The problem-solution order is well-suited for persuasive speeches to actuate.

If you watch television commercials, you are likely already very familiar with the problem-solution order. Many commercials start with a problem, such as bad breath, as their first point. They then present a branded product, like mouthwash, as the solution for bad breath. Their commercial argues that all your bad breath problems will be solved if you purchase and use the recommended mouthwash.

The **comparative advantage order** also divides the body into three sections. The first part is the plan or course of action that you want to propose to your audience. The second main point explains the advantages caused by the use of the plan outlined in the first point. The third main point then answers potential objections to your plan. This order is effective for persuasive speeches to actuate.

For example, Sheila's persuasive speech urged the audience members to volunteer their time to a local animal shelter. In the final section of her speech, she addressed objections related to time, stating:

"Now, you may agree that volunteering at the animal shelter is a good idea but you may worry that you just don't have the time. This is a valid concern but I am one of the most busy people in this room. I have three children, a full-time job, I go to school here, and I still find time to volunteer at the local animal shelter. If I can find two hours a week to support this worthwhile cause, so can you."

Within this third point, Sheila identified a likely objection and then argued against it. By the end of her third point, she had successfully given reasons why the potential objection was not a reason to support her plan.

The sixth potential order is **Monroe's motivated sequence**. This order was developed for persuasive speeches by Alan Monroe, a Purdue University Professor. This ordered sequence is composed of five parts: attention, need, satisfaction, visualization, and action. The attention step grabs the audience attention with a powerful opening. The need then shows how the subject of the speech meets a particular need. This step may be supported by evidence, such as statistics or personal example. The third step, satisfaction, details how to solve the need. The fourth step, visualization, explains to the audience the outcome of the proposed solution. Visualization relies heavily upon sensory details to show why the solution must be accepted, either for the good it will produce or the bad that will result in its absence. The final step, action, then directs the audience to act in a particular way that will help to solve the problem.

SUMMARY

This chapter began with an overview of the importance of speech organization. Speech organization provides important benefits to both the speaker and the audience. The speaker will enjoy greater familiarity with the speech content, increased confidence, and decreased anxiety. Speech

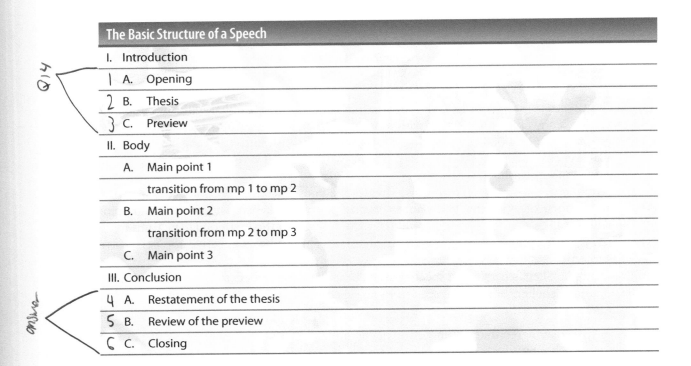

The Basic Structure of a Speech

I. Introduction
   A.   Opening
   B.   Thesis
   C.   Preview

II. Body
   A.   Main point 1
       transition from mp 1 to mp 2
   B.   Main point 2
       transition from mp 2 to mp 3
   C.   Main point 3

III. Conclusion
   A.   Restatement of the thesis
   B.   Review of the preview
   C.   Closing

organization also helps the speaker to establish ethos with the audience. The audience will enjoy benefits associated with speech organization, including increased comprehension and interest.

The organization of a speech recognizes three components: the introduction, the body, and the conclusion. Each part of the speech has specific functions and style options. The introduction is the beginning of the speech. The introduction can fulfill five distinct functions. The most important function is to begin the speech and to explain to your audience what they are about to hear. In addition, the introduction can get the audience's attention, establish your credibility as the speaker, and establish goodwill between you and the audience. The introduction is divided into the opening, the thesis statement, and the preview.

The conclusion ends the speech. The conclusion has three functions: end the speech, remind your audience what they just heard, and finish memorably. The conclusion also contains three parts: the restatement of the thesis statement, the review of the preview, and the closing. Many different types of closings are available for your consideration, including the joke, the story, and the quotation.

The body is the middle of the speech, found after the introduction and before the conclusion. The body contains the main points that support the thesis statement. Once the main points are developed, the speaker must order them within the body. Effective order designs include the time order, topic order, cause-effect, problem-solution, comparative advantage, and Monroe's motivated sequence.

Speakers should signal movement from one main point to another through the effective use of transitions, and from one subpoint to another using signposts. Transitions let the audience know that you are moving on to a new main point within the body of the speech. Signposts may be used as additional cues, such as between subpoints of a main point.

Review
Questions

1. Give three reasons why it's important to structure a speech.

2. Describe the three parts of every speech in three different ways.

3. List and briefly explain five different types of speech opening.

4. List and briefly explain six different ways to order the main points of a body.

5. Give three different functions of a speech conclusion.

Glossary

Attention getter: An action used to draw the attention of the audience and convince them to set aside their personal concerns in order to listen to the speech.

Body: The body is the middle part of the speech, accounting for eighty percent of total speech time. The body contains main points that support the thesis and transitions that let the audience know when you are moving from main point to main point.

Cause-effect order of main points: The arrangement of main points to illustrate that one event or thing caused another.

Captive audience: An audience composed of individuals whose attendance was required and who must pay attention to the speaker.

Closing: The final part of the conclusion, which closes the speech in a memorable manner.

Comparative advantage order of main points: Method of main point ordering that divides the body into three sections: the proposed plan, the advantages generated by the plan, and the answering of any potential objections to the recommendation.

Conclusion: The end of the speech, accounting for between five and ten percent of the total speech time, containing three parts: restatement of the thesis statement, review of the preview, and closing.

Introduction: The beginning of the speech, composed of three parts: the opening, the thesis statement, and the preview. The introduction should account for between ten and fifteen percent of the total speech.

Main point: A block of time in the body used to develop one main idea that develops the thesis.

Monroe's motivated sequence: A five-step main point order developed for persuasive speeches by Alan Monroe.

Opening: The first and largest section of the introduction, which does all of the introduction's jobs except for explaining what your speech will say.

Opening quotation: A specialist opening type for building the speaker's credibility on a topic.

Opening with a joke: A specialist opening type for generating goodwill with an audience.

Outline: A rough draft of the speech that illustrates hierarchal relationships of the speech components through numeric organization.

Problem-solution order of main points: Method of ordering main points by dividing the body of the speech into three parts: the problem, the solution, and the explanation of how the solution solves the problem. Most commonly used for persuasive speeches.

Preview: The final part of the introduction is an ordered list of the main points in the body of the speech to come.

Question openings: Easiest type of opening to write, so one of the most common openings, but also rarely effective.

Restatement of the thesis statement: The first part of the conclusion. It restates the thesis statement offered in the introduction, reminding the audience of the central theme or argument of the speech.

Review of the preview: The second part of the conclusion. It serves to remind the audience of the main points of the speech.

Signpost: A short, often numerical, cue used by the speaker to explain the subpoint structure of a complex main point.

Startling statement opening: A specialist opening type to get the audience's attention.

Story openings: A generalist opening type, a well-told story can do any of the jobs openings can do, or even several at the same time.

Thesis statement: A single-sentence statement of the one main idea developed by the speech.

Time order of main points: The arrangement of the main points by chronological order within the body. Sometimes called sequential order.

Topic order of main points: The arrangement of main points into subdivisions or categories of the speech's subject. One of the most common methods of arranging main points.

Transition: A single sentence bridge that connects one main point in the body to the next.

OUTLINING YOUR SPEECH

Mark L. Staller

Learning Objectives

① Understand basic outlining rules and procedures.

② Make brief scratch outlines.

③ Develop detailed preparation outlines.

④ Develop abbreviated delivery outlines.

⑤ Recognize similarities and differences between preparation outlines and delivery outlines.

Whereas Chapter 7 taught you how to organize a speech, this chapter teaches you how to make the organization of your speech obvious to both yourself and others by constructing a speech outline. A written outline is a logically structured document having its sections and sub-sections labeled with numbers and letters. The obvious structure of an outline makes it a good tool for quickly revealing the content and organization of a longer work. For example, you could take a half hour or so to read this entire textbook chapter in order to understand what it covers and where it covers it, or you could take a minute or so to scan the following brief outline of this chapter:

CHAPTER 8 OUTLINE

I. The general purposes of outlining
    A. To develop and organize ideas
    B. To receive feedback from others

II. The general guidelines for outlining
    A. How to label an outline
    B. How to format an outline
    C. How to subdivide an outline

III. The specifics of a detailed preparation outline
  A. Why to use a preparation outline
  B. How to make a preparation outline
  C. A sample preparation outline

IV. The specifics of an abbreviated delivery outline
  A. Why to use a delivery outline
  B. How to make a delivery outline
  C. A sample delivery outline

V. The specifics of an impromptu scratch outline
  A. Why to use a scratch outline
  B. How to make a scratch outline
  C. How to use a scratch outline

VI. The less conventional ways to prepare and present a speech
  A. Storyboards
  B. Mindmaps

This brief outline makes your job as a reader much easier, don't you agree? You now know that if you read this chapter, you will first get an understanding of the general purposes of outlining and the general guidelines for outlining. Next, you will learn about three specific kinds of outlines related to public speaking: 1) detailed preparation outlines used for preparing extemporaneous speeches, 2) abbreviated delivery outlines used for presenting extemporaneous speeches, and 3) scratch outlines used for preparing and presenting impromptu speeches. Finally, you will learn about some less conventional ways to prepare and present a speech. This brief Chapter 8 outline demonstrates the usefulness of an outline for you, the reader. Read on to further understand the usefulness of an outline for you, the public speaker.

PART 1: THE GENERAL PURPOSES OF OUTLINING

One important purpose of outlining is to help writers and speakers organize and develop their ideas. An outline can be compared to the framework of a skyscraper. Once a well-engineered, solid framework is constructed, a towering skyscraper can be erected. Similarly, once some well-thought-out ideas are put together in a solid outline, a much longer, much more detailed essay or speech can be developed.

A two- to three-hundred-page novel, for example, may begin as a five-to-ten-page outline. Many novelists first create brief story outlines that contain all of the important plot twists to be developed in

© Pavel Ganchev - Paf, 2013. Used under license from Shutterstock, Inc.

A massive skyscraper is built upon a solid framework.

FIGURE 8.1

their novels, and then they write out all of the description and dialogue that "fleshes out" their stories. In his article "The Architecture of a Thriller" (published in the June 15, 2012, Word Craft section of *The Wall Street Journal*), suspense writer Jeffery Deaver shares how outlines are the blueprints for his novels:

FIGURE
8.2 Long books often begin with short outlines.

"By the end of the outlining process, I know exactly what happens in every chapter . . . Outlining is the most efficient way to structure a novel to achieve the greatest emotional impact. The most breathtaking prose and most brilliantly drawn characters are wasted if the plot meanders and digresses. Outlining lets you create a framework that compels your audience to keep reading from the first page to the last."

Outlining helps Jeffery Deaver write blockbuster novels, and outlining can help you prepare a knock-out speech. You do not want to give a speech where you meander and digress. You want well-developed, well-organized ideas that will compel your audience to keep listening from the first word out of your mouth to your last. An outline can provide your speech with a clear framework for all of your ideas. Once you have outlined the major ideas you want to cover in your speech, you will be able to "flesh out" these ideas with researched evidence and verbal support.

A second important purpose of outlining is to help writers and speakers make the content and structure of their texts obvious so they can receive feedback from others. An outline can be compared to a full-body x-ray machine. To verify the basic soundness of a person, physicians need to perform a thorough physical examination. A full-body x-ray machine makes their job much easier because it allows them to see all the major organs, all the bones, and all the connective tissues in a body at once.

Similarly, to examine the basic soundness of any communicative text, we need to be aware of the ideas in that text, and we need to be aware of the relationships among these ideas. An outline can quickly reveal the basic content and structure of any essay or speech.

This textbook, for example, was written with the aid of chapter outlines. Because there were multiple writers and editors working on this project, the writers were asked to prepare preliminary chapter outlines that could be examined by everyone involved in the textbook production. Before the writers wrote their chapters, the preliminary outlines were checked for balance and development of ideas. Editors looked for underdeveloped or overdeveloped ideas. They also looked for missing or out-of-place ideas. With helpful editorial feedback, the writers were then able to correct problems and improve their chapters *before* their chapters were actually written.

Outlining helped the writers of this textbook improve their textbook chapters, and outlining can help you improve any speech you have to deliver. If you prepare an outline that clearly re-

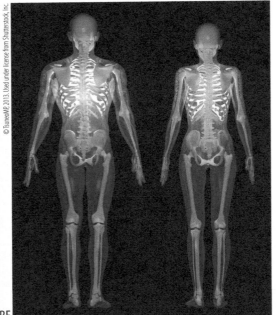

FIGURE
8.3 Like an x-ray machine, an outline reveals the basic content and structure of a speech.

veals the content and structure of your speech and you share this outline with others, they can give you helpful feedback. They can point out any underdeveloped or overdeveloped sections of your speech. They can point out missing or out-of-place ideas. With helpful feedback from others, you can improve your speech *before* you deliver it.

An outline helps you to share your ideas with others.

FIGURE 8.4

PART 2: GENERAL GUIDELINES FOR OUTLINING

Before you learn about the specific types of outlines you can use to improve your speeches, this section will help you learn (or review) some very general outlining guidelines. These general guidelines apply to the standard outline format widely taught in American colleges and universities. If you know these general guidelines, you can outline your speeches using an outline format that many people are already familiar with. The abstract outline that follows will help you to visually grasp these general outlining guidelines.

I. First main point
   A. First first-level subpoint
   B. Second first-level subpoint
   C. Third first-level subpoint

II. Second main point
   A. First first-level sub point
      1. First second-level subpoint
         a. First third-level subpoint
         b. Second third-level subpoint
            (1). First fourth-level subpoint
            (2). Second fourth-level subpoint
      2. Second second-level subpoint
         a. First third-level subpoint
         b. Second third-level subpoint
         c. Third third-level subpoint
   B. Second first-level subpoint
      1. First second-level subpoint
      2. Second second-level subpoint
      3. Third second-level subpoint

III. Third main point

An abstract outline.

FIGURE 8.5

GENERAL GUIDELINE #1: USE NUMBERS AND LETTERS TO LABEL YOUR MAIN POINTS AND SUBPOINTS

Q3 answer

Numbers and letters are used to clearly mark the sections and subsections of your outline. The standard outlining format uses Roman numerals (I, II, III,) for main points, capital letters (A, B, C) for first-level subpoints, Arabic numerals (1, 2, 3) for second-level subpoints, and lowercase letters (a, b, c) for third-level subpoints. Fourth-level subpoints, rarely used, are marked off by Arabic numerals in parentheses—(1), (2), (3).

If you were the only person using your outline, you could deviate from this standard labeling system, but if other people are going to be looking at and referring to your outline, you can save time and avoid confusion by sticking to these standard numbers and letters. Roman numerals are created on a keyboard with the capital i, v, x, and l keys (I, V, X, and L).

Roman numeral one is represented with a capital i (I); Roman numeral two is represented with two i capitals (II); Roman numeral three is represented with three i capitals (III); Roman numeral four is represented with a capital i and a capital v (IV); Roman numeral five is represented with a capital v (V); Roman numeral six is represented with a capital v and a capital i (VI); Roman numeral seven is represented by a capital v and two ii capitals (VII); Roman numeral eight is represented by a capital v and three i capitals (VIII); Roman numeral nine is represented by a capital i and a capital x (IX); and Roman numeral ten is represented by a capital x (X). In a speech outline, you should rarely have to go higher than a Roman numeral ten.

Arabic Number	Roman Numeral	Arabic Number	Roman Numeral
1	I	6	VI
2	II	7	VII
3	III	8	VIII
4	IV	9	IX
5	V	10	X

FIGURE 8.6 Converting Arabic numbers to Roman numerals.

© K. Oksana, 2013. Used under license from Shutterstock, Inc

FIGURE 8.7 Too many numbers and letters decrease the effectiveness of an outline.

Do not use too many numbers and letters in your outline. You do not necessarily need a number or a letter for every single phrase or sentence in your outline. Numbers and letters are used to label and clearly mark your *ideas*, and sometimes a single idea may be developed in two or three sentences. If you have gone through half the alphabet in order to label a subsection of an outline, you are probably adding too many label markers. It is unusual to go beyond half a dozen numbers or letters in any section of an outline, and it is quite common to top out at around three numbers or letters per section.

Do not use too few numbers and letters in your outline. If you visually scan an outline and see a "paragraphy" section, this section probably needs to be further subdivided. General guideline #3 will give you more explanation of when and how to subdivide in an outline.

Do not use "bullet points" in an outline, especially a formal outline. Bullet points tell the reader that some information or ideas have been marked off in the outline, but they do not reveal how many ideas have been marked off. A major purpose of the number and letter markers used in an outline is to help people keep track of how many ideas are present in an outline section.

If you have three Roman numerals in your outline, you know that you have three main ideas you need to track; and when you see Roman numeral three (III), you know you are reading the third and final point. If you have four capital letters in a subsection, you know that you have four supporting points to develop, and each letter—A, B, C, D—provides a visual cue for each separate supporting point.

GENERAL GUIDELINE #2: INDENT TO MAKE YOUR MAIN POINTS AND SUBPOINTS STAND OUT

Q3 answer

Notice that in the example abstract outline, the Roman numerals are located at the far left margin of the paper, then the capital letters are indented about five spaces or so to the right, then the Arabic numerals are indented another five spaces or so, and then the lowercase letters are indented another five spaces, etc. This indentation makes your main points and subpoints stand out from one another. In addition to the number and letter markers, the white spaces created by the outline indentations provide further visual cues to distinguish main points and subpoints.

If you were to turn a standard outline ninety degrees to the right, you would see that the main points stand out like the high points of a line graph or EKG reading. The subpoints, which have been indented to the right, would be lower on the line graph, and the least important points of the outline correspond to the lowest points on a line graph. Thus, the standard indentations used in an outline create a secondary visual representation of the most important and least important ideas contained in the outline. Used in conjunction with number and letter markers, indentations make it very easy to visually scan and recognize the main points and supporting points of a speech or essay.

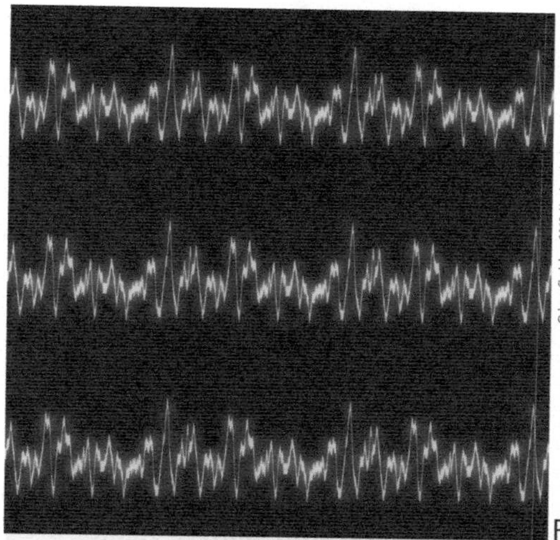

If you are using a computer or word processor, the word processing program you use may have a default setting for outline indentations. Once you start inserting Roman numerals and capital letters, the word processing program may automatically format your outline. If you want help with your outlining, make sure the outlining function is activated on your computer. If you want to format your own outline, you need to turn off the automatic outlining function. In order to create a standard outline, you also have to make sure your computer is not set to "center align." You do not want the lines of your outline centered on the paper. You want each Roman numeral in your outline to be located at the far lefthand margin of the paper, and you want all of your subpoint lines to be uniformly indented and aligned.

© Ivan Cholakov, 2013. Used under license from Shutterstock, Inc.

Like an EKG reading, an outline distinguishes main points from subpoints.

FIGURE 8.8

GENERAL GUIDELINE #3: SUBDIVIDE WHEN YOU HAVE TWO OR MORE POINTS TO MAKE

Q3 answer

When you have two or more points that you want to make in a section of an outline, then you need to subdivide that section. For example, if your first main point (I) has two supporting points, these two supporting points would be indented and marked with the capital letters A and B. If your first main point (I) has three supporting points, these three supporting points would be indented and marked with the capital letters A, B, and C.

FIGURE 8.9 Subdivide in an outline when you have two or more things to say.

However, you do not subdivide in an outline if you only have one thing to say in a section. In other words, you should not have a subpoint A if you do not also have at least a subpoint B, and you should not have a subpoint 1 if you do not also have at least a subpoint 2. Look at the example abstract outline, and you can see this principle being consistently followed. There is a Roman numeral I, but there is also a Roman numeral II and Roman numeral III because there are three main ideas to be developed. Under Roman numeral I, there is a capital letter A, but there is also a capital letter B and C, because there are three supporting points to be made in this section. Wherever there is a subdivision in the abstract outline, there is at least two points to be made, and sometimes there are three.

When you violate this subdivision guideline in an outline, you are making the outline more complicated than it has to be. If you only have one point to make in a section, then you can make this one point after the number or letter marker for this section, and you do not need to add any subpoint markers. For example, in the example abstract outline, the third main point is represented only by the Roman numeral III because evidently there is only one point to be made in this section. No subpoint A is necessary. No subpoint 1 is necessary. No subpoints are necessary.

There are several other principles of subdivision which can help you create a well-structured outline; these are the principles of coordination, subordination, and balance.

Coordination: The principle of coordination is that equal ideas should be expressed on the same level of an outline. For example, if you have three main points to make in a speech, you need to make sure these three main points receive equal treatment by assigning each of them a Roman numeral. You want to make sure one of these ideas doesn't get lost by being placed on a lower level of the outline.

Subordination: The principle of subordination is that secondary or lower-order ideas are placed beneath, or subordinated to, higher-order ideas. For example, if you have three pieces of supporting evidence for a main point assertion, you need to make sure that these three pieces of evidence are placed beneath this main assertion, and that they are marked off with the appropriate subdivision markers. You want to make clear that the three pieces of evidence are support for, and not equal to, the main assertion.

When you analyze and evaluate outlines, you sometimes discover that ideas are located in the wrong place, usually because they violate either the principle of coordination or the principle of subordination. You can improve an outline (and a speech based upon an outline) by ensuring that equal ideas are on the same outline level (coordination) and that lower-order ideas are placed beneath higher-order ideas (subordination).

Q4 answer

Balance: Q4 answer The principle of balance ensures that ideas are not underdeveloped or overdeveloped. The different sections of an outline do not have to be perfectly balanced, but some attention needs to be paid to the balance between ideas and their supporting points. Notice, for example, that the sample abstract outline has more subpoint levels in the second main point than in the first or third main points—this is not necessarily wrong or inappropriate. The second main point may need to be more fully developed than the other two points. Note also that the first main point has three supporting points, whereas the second main point has only two supporting points. Again, the difference in number of subpoints is not necessarily wrong or inappropriate.

The ideas in your speech outline should be properly balanced.

© Syda Productions, 2013. Used under license from Shutterstock, Inc.

FIGURE
8.10

However, when you scan the sample abstract outline, the third main point does seem to be underdeveloped compared to the first two main points. The third main point does not need to have the exact same number of subpoints as either main point one or main point two, but the fact that the third main point has *no* subpoints indicates that there is a lack of development and verbal support for this point. The supporting evidence for the main ideas in this outline seems unbalanced.

Now that we have reviewed these very general principles of outlining, you should be able to construct and critique outlines that follow the standard format. Now let us consider how to adapt and use a standard outline for specific public speaking purposes.

PART 3: EXTEMPORANEOUS PREPARATION OUTLINES

The detailed **preparation outline** (and its corresponding abbreviated **delivery outline**) is what distinguishes extemporaneous speaking from the other types of delivery used for public speaking. Impromptu speakers use a scratch outline at the most to prepare and deliver their impromptu speeches. Manuscript speakers may or may not use an outline when preparing their speech—they often just write their speeches out in manuscript or "essay" form.

Extemporaneous speakers, however, move way beyond scratch outlines when they prepare their speeches. They usually construct detailed, logically structured preparation outlines that help them work out all the ideas in their speeches and that make the relationships between these ideas obvious. Once they are satisfied with the content and structure of their speeches, extemporaneous speakers then shrink their detailed preparation outlines down into abbreviated delivery outlines. While preserving the structure of the detailed preparation outlines, extemporaneous delivery outlines use only key words and phrases to remind the speakers of the ideas that were more fully developed earlier in the preparation outlines.

It is important not to confuse transcripts of extemporaneous speeches with the outlines actually used to prepare and deliver these speeches. People may listen to and transcribe extemporaneous speeches into "essay" format and then publish these speeches in manuscript form for others to read. However, extemporaneous speeches do not begin as manuscripts. The two outlines described above—a detailed preparation outline and an abbreviated delivery outline—are the hallmark of the extemporaneous speaking method taught in the majority of public speaking classes in America.

Although I try to expose my public speaking students to different types of delivery, I focus, like most instructors, on extemporaneous delivery. Since outlining is such an important part of extemporaneous speaking, I deliver a model speech at the beginning of the semester on the importance of preparation outlines. I prefer a complete-sentence preparation outline, so that is what I model for my students. I will now share this speech with you, in preparation outline form:

INTRODUCTION

I. In the past, I have had students in my public speaking classes approach me with an honest, sincere question: "Mr. Staller, can I skip the speech preparation outline and jump right to my key-word delivery outline? I can save a lot of time and effort by skipping the detailed, complete-sentence outline."

II. I told these students, and I would like to tell you, that preparing a fully developed speech preparation outline is a crucial step in the extemporaneous speech-making process. I want to assure you that the preparation outline is a very valuable, useful tool. It is not a waste of time. It is not a waste of effort.

III. Let me give you six reasons why a preparation outline is important for extemporaneous speaking:
   A. It helps you develop specific, concrete content for your speech.
   B. It helps you manage your speech time effectively.
   C. It helps you avoid "dead air" when you are speaking.
   D. It helps you work on your speech on the "style" level.
   E. It helps you organize and internalize the ideas in your speech.
   F. Most importantly, it helps you improve your speech <u>before</u> your deliver it.

Let me explain each of these reasons in greater depth.

BODY

I. Why does a dog whine when it sees an empty food bowl? The bowl is empty! It doesn't have any content. That is what is wrong with some speeches—they are empty of specific content. You don't want your audience to whine that you don't really have anything to say.
   A. A preparation outline helps you develop specific, concrete ideas for your speech.
   B. Content is a foundational element of a speech. The three main elements of a speech are content, structure, and delivery. Without content, you are not even to first base—your speech can't really get off the ground.
   C. Impromptu speakers have to think up much of their content on the spot, but extemporaneous speakers can develop their speech content in their preparation outlines.

II. The second reason preparation outlines are important is that they can help you to manage your speech time effectively.
   A. Most of your speeches in this class will be timed, and you have a fairly narrow time window to aim for.
      1. A preparation outline gives you an idea how long your speech is—about one and a half minutes per page of a typed, double-spaced outline. A typed, three-page preparation outline translates into about a four to five minute speech.

      2.   You won't be saying the exact words in your preparation outline, but you will get close to these words, so your outline gives you a general idea of the length of your speech.

  B. You want your speech introduction, speech body, and speech conclusion to be balanced and in the right proportion. You don't want your introduction and conclusion to be too long, and you don't want your speech body to be too short.

      1.   If you want a one-minute introduction, you need about a half-page introduction.

      2.   If you want a four-minute speech body, you need about two pages of your outline devoted to your speech body.

      3.   When you have a fully developed preparation outline to look at, you can visually see the time length of your speech on paper.

  C. I once had a speech student skip her preparation outline for a cooking demonstration speech. All she did was jump to her note cards and write at the beginning of her speech, "Tell story about Aunt Maggie" for her attention-getter.

      1.   Unfortunately, her "Aunt Maggie" story took five minutes! She did not have enough time to give her cooking demonstration and had to stop about half-way through the recipe.

      2.   If I could have looked at her "Aunt Maggie" story on paper in a preparation outline, I would have been able to tell her that her attention-getter was way too long.

III.   The third reason a preparation outline is important is that it helps you to avoid "dead air."

  A. Have you ever been listening to the radio or watching television and had the sound stop or the screen go blank? When this happens, I say, "Oops! Someone just lost their job at the radio station!" or, "Oops! Somebody just lost their job at the television station." "Dead air" is a big "no-no" in broadcasting.

  B. "Dead air" is also a big "no-no" in public speaking. Public speakers are supposed to speak to their audiences, not stand there silently. A well-developed preparation outline guarantees that you will have plenty to say to your audience and can avoid "dead air."

  C. Another one of my public speaking students skipped her detailed preparation outline and only wrote for Step Two of a cooking speech, "Mix ingredients together." She never wrote out in sentences what she wanted to say about all of these ingredients.

      1.   When she got to this part of her speech, she said, "Now mix your ingredients together," and then mixed her ingredients in total silence for the next three minutes. It was very uncomfortable for both her and her audience.

      2.   A complete-sentence preparation outline would have given her plenty to say as she mixed her ingredients together.

IV.   The fourth reason a preparation outline is so important is that it gets you all the way to the "style" level when working on a speech.

  A. The five processes of classical rhetoric are invention (developing your ideas), arrangement (putting those ideas in some order), style (choosing words to express your ideas), memory (committing these ideas and words to memory), and delivery (speaking these words to your audience)

  B. If you skip the preparation outline and jump right to a key-word delivery outline, you have some idea of your content and speech structure, but you never actually get to work on the precise words you will use to express your ideas. You don't get to work on the "style" level.

  C. A complete-sentence preparation outline lets you think about the exact words you would like to use in your speech. Even though these may not be the words you use in your speech when you deliver it from keyword note cards, the fact that you thought out your words ahead of time on paper will help you say something similar when you are speaking to your audience.

(continued)

V. The fifth reason a preparation outline is important for extemporaneous speaking is that it helps you to organize and internalize your thoughts.

    A. A preparation outline differs from a manuscript (written in paragraphs) because it has a logical structure indicated by numbers and letters. These numbers and letters act as memory markers to help you remember how many things you need to talk about.

        1. You can count off the tasks of your speech introduction.

        2. You can count off the main ideas in your speech body.

        3. You can count off the tasks of your speech conclusion.

    B. Since you transfer the logical structure in your preparation outline over to your keyword note cards, the numbers and letters help you remember all the little "chunks" of your speech.

    C. As you practice delivering your speech from your brief keyword note cards, you can always go back and re-read your detailed preparation outline until the ideas are internalized. Then your note cards will be enough to remind you of the ideas that are in your mind.

VI. The sixth and most important reason to prepare a preparation outline is that it lets you improve your speech *before* you deliver it in front of an audience.

    A. If I listen to you deliver a speech in class and hand you back an evaluation sheet with a grade on it, is there anything you can do to improve your speech or speech grade at that point? No. It is too late to make improvements—the speech is now over.

    B. However, if you write out your speech on paper and share it with me and other people ahead of time, we can help you improve your speech before you have to deliver it in front of an audience. Preparation outlines should be shared ahead of time so revisions and improvements can be made.

CONCLUSION

I. Now that I have explained why preparation outlines are important, I should not have any of you coming to me and saying, "Can I skip the preparation outline?" You now understand why preparation outlines are so valuable.

II. A preparation outline helps you to develop specific content, manage your time, avoid dead air, work on the style level, organize and internalize your thoughts, and improve your speech before you deliver it.

III. Let me conclude by emphasizing that both the preparation outline and delivery outlines are important for extemporaneous speaking. Don't get these outlines confused, and don't try to skip either one or the other.

© Monkey Business Images, 2013. Used under license from Shutterstock, Inc.

FIGURE 8.11 Your instructor may want to give you feedback on your speech preparation outline.

As you can see, I expect my students to construct detailed, complete-sentence preparation outlines for their extemporaneous speeches. Some public speaking instructors may not require such a detailed outline. Some public speaking instructors may require an even more formal outline than the one I have modeled. Your instructor may ask you to bring your preparation outline to class or to his or her office so you can receive feedback. You may also be required to turn in the final draft of your preparation outline right before you deliver your extemporaneous speech as evidence for the time and effort that you put into the preparation process.

We have already gone over some very general guidelines for outlining. These general guidelines should be followed while constructing a detailed preparation outline for extemporaneous speaking. However, there are specific elements of speech preparation outlines that we have not yet considered. In the next section, you will learn about some of the particulars of speech preparation outlines, and you will consider your outlining options.

HOW TO MAKE A PREPARATION OUTLINE

Here are six specific suggestions for speech preparation outlines. These six suggestions are sometimes followed by alternate suggestions, so make sure you read each section all the way through to have a full understanding of your outlining options.

1. **Label the three main parts of your speech preparation outline.** Most instructors want you to separate and clearly label your speech introduction, your speech body, and your speech conclusion. You usually do not need to label these sections with a number or letter. Just use the words, "Introduction," "Body," and "Conclusion."

2. **Use Roman numerals for the main ideas in your speech body.** If there are five main sections in your speech body, these sections should be labeled with the Roman numerals I, II, III, IV, and V. All the supporting evidence and arguments for each section will be placed beneath and subordinated to these main ideas.

   Some speech instructors also want you to use Roman numerals for the main tasks of your speech introduction and conclusion. If there are four tasks in your speech introduction, you will label these tasks with the Roman numerals I, II, III, and IV. If there are three tasks in your speech conclusion, you will label these tasks I, II, and III. You will then subdivide in your introduction and conclusion as needed.

   Since the numbers and letters used in outlining are supposed to help you keep track of the ideas in your speech, make sure you begin renumbering in your speech body and conclusion. If you do not begin renumbering in each major section of your speech, the Roman numerals will be more confusing than they are helpful. For example, if you continue numbering your speech body after numbering four tasks in your introduction, the first main idea in your speech body will be labeled "V." In order to have your first main idea labeled number one, after you have numbered the tasks of your introduction, begin at Roman numeral I again for the first idea of your speech body. After you have numbered the main ideas in your speech body, begin at Roman numeral I again for the first task of your speech conclusion.

   Some instructors do not want you to use Roman numerals in your speech introduction and conclusion. Instead, for your introduction, they may want you to use task labels such as "attention-getter," "thesis," "audience relevance," "speaker credibility," and "preview." For your conclusion, they may want you to use task labels such as "restated thesis," "review," "call to action," and "closer." If this is the case, use the Roman numerals for the main ideas in your speech body.

3. **Use either complete sentences or incomplete phrases in your preparation outline.** Some public speaking instructors have a strong preference for complete sentences. Some public speaking instructors have a strong preference for incomplete phrases. For your speech class, follow the lead of your instructor.

Outside of speech class, the principle of parallelism requires you to choose between complete sentences or incomplete phrases—it is confusing and awkward to go back and forth between the two options. If your speech instructor doesn't have a strong preference, here are some advantages and disadvantages of both incomplete-phrase outlines and complete-sentence outlines:

Advantages of incomplete-phrase outlines:
1.   You can generate an incomplete-phrase outline fairly quickly.
2.   You do not get hung up on grammar, punctuation, and fine details.
3.   You never create even the possibility of reading your speech word-for-word.

Disadvantages of incomplete-phrase outlines:
1.   You never fully develop your ideas.
2.   You do not actually choose precise words for your ideas.
3.   You cannot get very detailed feedback from others.

Advantages of complete-sentence outlines:
1.   You fully develop your ideas, even down to the "style" level.
2.   You can see the entire speech on paper and estimate speech length accurately.
3.   You can get detailed feedback on your speech content, structure, and language.

Disadvantages of complete-sentence outlines:
1.   You need time to fully develop your speech in this format.
2.   You can neglect your abbreviated delivery outline.
3.   You may be tempted to read this complete-sentence outline like a manuscript.

© Monkey Business Images, 2013. Used under license from Shutterstock, Inc.

FIGURE
8.12 An incomplete-phrase outline may work best for informal meetings.

Outside of your public speaking class, for real-world speech situations, I think there is a time and a place for both the complete-sentence and the incomplete-phrase preparation outline. For speeches with very short deadlines, or for speeches that you have to present fairly regularly (like a weekly report at work), an incomplete-phrase outline will probably be your best choice. For important extemporaneous speeches that are given on rare occasions (like a one-time shot at landing a multimillion-dollar contract for your business), take the time to prepare and get feedback on a complete-sentence preparation outline.

49.   <u>Make sure to include "connectives" and transition sentences in your preparation outline.</u> In a complete-sentence preparation outline, transition sentences can usually be placed right after the Roman numerals in the outline: you can introduce a main idea, and then you can subdivide and present supporting evidence and verbal support. In an incomplete-phrase preparation outline, transition sentences are often labeled "transition sentence" and set apart from the Roman numerals. Again, follow the lead of your public speaking instructor for transition sentences in your classroom-speech outlines.

5. **Include oral source citations in your outline.** Make sure you understand the difference between written source citations and oral source citations. If your instructor requires a complete-sentence preparation outline, make sure your outline includes oral source citations written out in sentences.

Written source citations are used in written essays. They are usually placed in parentheses at the end of a quotation or paraphrase. Written source citations follow formatting rules: MLA formatting is used by the Modern Language Association, whereas APA formatting is used by the American Psychological Association. Written source citations are not usually vocalized. A person reading an essay usually sees a written source citation, and then turns to a Bibliography or Works Cited page to learn more about the source cited.

Oral source citations, on the other hand, are spoken out loud by speakers. Oral source citations are presented in complete sentences because people usually speak in complete sentences. Oral source citations have no set format. The speaker must give enough information about the source so the audience can find and check the source if they so desire. In addition to *who* said something, oral source citations usually also reveal *where* and *when* they said it.

Unlike written source citations, oral source citations are usually shared *before* the related evidence or verbal support is presented to the audience. For example, if you were using a statistic in a speech, you would not give the statistic first and then say, "This statistic came from such and such a source." Instead, you would first establish the credibility of your source and prepare your audience to hear the statistic. You might say, "I have a startling statistic to share with you. Although this statistic is hard to believe, the source of this statistic is solid. According to . . ."

Thus, oral source citations differ from written source citations in two important ways: oral source citations usually come *before* the evidence they support, and oral source citations are written out (and spoken) in complete sentences.

A complete-sentence preparation outline lets you prepare and practice your oral source citations before you deliver your speech. An incomplete-phrase preparation outline often just contains written source citations, so there is still a lot of work for a speaker to do before he or she can share this source information effectively with a live audience. Work with your instructor so you know the kind of source citations you are expected to have in your outline and to give during the delivery of your speech.

6. **Clarify if your instructor expects a basic preparation outline or a more formal "classroom" preparation outline.** A basic preparation outline is something that a speaker can use to prepare and improve a speech whether giving a speech in a public speaking classroom or out in the world at large. A formal classroom preparation outline is designed to help not only the student speaker, but also the instructor.

In addition to the speech itself, a formal classroom preparation outline may include a speech title, a general purpose statement, a specific purpose statement, a thesis statement, and a complete bibliography. This formal classroom outline quickly reveals to the instructor what the stu-

FIGURE **8.13**

Oral source citations allow you to credit your sources during the course of your speech.

dent speaker was trying to accomplish as well as all the research sources that were used in the speech.

Some instructors only require a basic preparation outline. Some instructors require a formal classroom outline with the preliminary speech information added before the speech introduction and the formal bibliography added after the speech conclusion. Make sure you know what type of preparation outline your public speaking instructor requires and expects.

If you do turn in a formal classroom outline with preliminary speech information and a complete bibliography, remember that these sections of your speech preparation outline are never seen by or heard by your live audience. Your audience does not see your speech title or specific purpose statement. The first thing they should usually hear and see is your "attention-getter."

Similarly, your live audience never sees your bibliography attached to the end of your formal preparation outline. It is important to realize that the only information your audience receives about your research sources is the verbal information you provide them during the course of your speech. A bibliography does not eliminate the need for oral source citations.

A sample student preparation outline has been provided for you to analyze and evaluate. For the sake of thoroughness, we have decided to provide as a model a formal classroom preparation outline that includes both preliminary speech information and a formal bibliography. Your public speaking instructor may or may not require such a detailed outline. Good public speakers construct their speeches with their audience in mind. Similarly, good public speaking students need to construct their speech outlines with their particular speech instructor in mind!

A SAMPLE PREPARATION OUTLINE

SPEECH TITLE:	"Exercise for Every Body"
GENERAL PURPOSE:	To inform
SPECIFIC PURPOSE:	To inform people about the types of exercise appropriate for different body types
THESIS:	Everybody, and every body type, can benefit from exercise

INTRODUCTION

I. Can everyone please stand up? Now I want each of you to reach up high and then reach down to your toes. Okay, thank you. Please have a seat. Can you tell me when was the last time you have done that?

II. How many of you exercise regularly? How many of you do not exercise? Okay now, how many of you do not exercise because you simply have the excuse, "I'm too busy," or "I don't have time to exercise"?
    A.   If you think you do not need exercise because you aren't "fat" or you just think, "Whatever, I'm fine," think again.
    B.   Keep in mind what you think about yourself and your health as I inform you about what exercise can do to your body.

III. In my speech today, you will learn that everybody, and every body type, can benefit from the right kind of exercise.

IV   Let me preview the main points I will make in my speech today.
    A.   First, I will briefly define exercise and describe its benefits.
    B.   Second, I will inform you about the risks associated with the lack of exercise.
    C.   Third, I will share the types of exercises you can do for your specific body type.

BODY

I. Now that I have given you a preview of what I will inform you about, I would like to tell you exactly what exercise is and what benefits comes from it.

    A. What is exercise?

        1. In their 2011 article in volume 46 of the *Nursing Journal*, Ceria-Ulep, Serafica, and Tsa identified exercise as the use of skeletal muscles in the body for any movement, resulting in an expenditure of energy.

        2. They state, "Exercise is planned, structured, and repetitive body movements performed to improve or maintain one or more components of fitness."

    B. What are the benefits of exercising?

        1. The 2012 article "Exercise and Longevity" found in *Maturitis* and written by Gremeaux, Gayda, Lepers, Sosner, Juneau, and Nigam, discovered that there is improved health functioning due to exercise.

            a. Exercise can reverse the effects of the aging process on psychological functions.

            b. Exercise decreases the risk of death.

            c. Daily exercise can decrease certain cancers.

            d. Exercise can lower the risk of osteoporosis.

            e. Exercise can improve muscle function.

            f. Exercise can improve respiratory functions.

        2. Exercise also improves both cognitive functioning and psychological well-being.

            a. Exercise elevates mood.

            b. Exercise increases alertness.

        3. Now that you understand what exercise is and the benefits of exercise, I will move on to the risks associated with the lack of exercise.

II. Without exercise, you put yourself at risk for chronic diseases, obesity, and depression.

    A. Several chronic diseases are associated with the lack of exercise.

        1. The 2012 article I mentioned previously reports that there are two types of cardiovascular disease that may occur when someone does not exercise.

            a. Ischemic heart disease is a problem with the circulation of blood to the heart.

            b. Cerebrovascular disease blocks the circulation of blood in the blood vessels of the brain.

        2. Without exercise, high blood pressure can also increase.

            a. The article "Exercise and Longevity" points out that high blood pressure puts people at risk of heart failure.

            b. Hypertension also puts people at risk for obesity.

    B. Obesity is on the rise in America due to the lack of exercise.

        1. According to a 2009 article in volume 72 of the *Journal of Environmental Health*, statistics show that obesity has "doubled since the 1980s from 15% to 30%."

        2. In a 2010 article of volume 100 of American *Journal Of Public Health*, it is reported that in the past thirty years obesity in fourteen to nineteen year olds is up seventeen percent.

        3. M.A. Fitzpatrick's September 2002 article in *Nursing Management* reports that "18% of American adults are obese and about 300,000 obesity-related deaths occur annually in the United States."

    C. Symptoms of depression can come from the lack of exercise.

        1. Eriksson and Gard's 2011 article "Physical Exercise and Nutrition," found in volume 16 of *Physical Therapy Review*, states that the lack of exercise causes depression in which the person has "no focus or concentration" leading to feelings of worthlessness or thoughts of suicide.

            a. The lack of exercise also causes the loss of enthusiasm for the activities of daily life.

            b. The sedentary person may feel isolated most of the time.

(continued)

    2.   Difficulty of sustaining weight is a problem when depression comes along.

        a.   On the one hand, an individual can gain excess weight.

        b.   On the other hand, an individual can lose necessary weight.

   D.   I have told you what exercise is and its benefits; I have told you what can happen with the lack of exercise; and now, I want to tell you the types of exercises that you can do for your body type.

III.   According to a 1992 article in volume 162 of the *Journal of Social Psychology*, there are different kinds of exercise for three different body types: ectomorph, mesomorph, and endomorph.

   A.   One body type is called "ectomorph."

      1.   Ectomorphs are thin and skinny.

      2.   Ectomorphs don't gain weight easy, have a flat chest, and a fast metabolism.

      3.   American society encourages all ages to become this way or remain this way to prevent sickness and promote longevity.

      4.   The workout types for ectomorphs are usually short and intense, and they focus on one specific muscle group at a time.

   B.   Another body type is called "mesomorph."

      1.   Mesomorphs are athletic and rectangular shaped.

        a.   Mesomorphic males have broad shoulders, and their waists cave in, forming a V-shape.

        b.   Women now tend to want this body type because there have been an increasing number of women entering competitive sports such as cross-fit training and bodybuilding.

      2.   Mesomorphs are naturally strong and gain muscle very easily.

      3.   A mesomorph's workout type would be cardio and weight training, but their bodies respond to weight training better.

   C.   A third body type is called "endomorph."

      1.   Endomorphs tend to have more fat underneath their skin than ectomorphs and mesomorphs.

      2.   This body type usually gains fat very easily and finds it hard to lose fat—just the opposite of ectomorphs.

      3.   They have a slower metabolism.

      4.   People that are endomorphs need cardio exercise and weight training.

CONCLUSION

I.   Hopefully, you can now clearly see that everybody, and every body type, can benefit from the right kind of exercise.

II.   I have shared with you the benefits of exercise, the risks of not exercising, and the different kinds of exercises appropriate for different body types.

III.   Technology has advanced in the twenty-first century, so there are many ways for society to take part in multiple exercise routines.

   A.   There are many gyms that are available to those who want to exercise such as the Student Recreation Center at CSUB, In Shape, Body Exchange, and 24-hour Fitness.

   B.   Exercising in your own home can also be done by using treadmills, elliptical trainers, and dumbbells.

   C.   Many people also use guided video exercises like p90x, Wii Fit, and Insanity.

IV.   So, now what do you think about yourself and your health? You are now more informed about the importance of exercise to be able to make good choices for yourself and your future.

Bibliography

Babey, S. H., Hastert, T. A., Wolstein, J., & Diamant, A. L. (2010). Income disparities in obesity trends among California adolescents. *American Journal of Public Health, 100*(11), 2149–2155. doi:10.2105/AJPH.2010.192641

Ceria-Ulep, C. D., Serafica, R. C., & Tse, A. (2011). Filipino older adults' beliefs about exercise activity. *Nursing Forum, 46*(4), 240–250. doi:10.1111/j.17446198.2011.00238.x

Eriksson, S., & Gard, G. (2011). Physical exercise and depression. *Physical Therapy Reviews, 16*(4), 261–268. doi:10.1179/1743288 X11Y.0000000026

Fitzpatrick, M. A. (2002, September). A healthy nation starts with you!. *Nursing Management.* p. 6.

Gremeaux, V., Gayda, M., Lepers, R., Sosner, P., Juneau, M., & Nigam, A. (2012). Exercise and longevity. *Maturitas, 73*(4), 312–317. doi:10.1016/j.maturitas.2012.09.012

Ryckman, R. M., Dill, D. A., Dyer, N. L., Sanborn, J. W., & Gold, J. A. (1992). Social perceptions of male and female extreme mesomorphs. *Journal of Social Psychology, 132*(5), 615–627.

Statistics from the U.S. obesity epidemic. (2009). *Journal of Environmental Health, 72*(2), 29.

PART 4: EXTEMPORANEOUS DELIVERY OUTLINES

A detailed preparation outline for an extemporaneous speech, especially a complete-sentence preparation outline, contains the content of a speech almost word-for-word; however, unlike a manuscript, a preparation outline has a logical outline structure. This logical outline structure lets the speaker and others quickly evaluate the speech. This logical outline structure also allows the speaker to quickly develop an abbreviated delivery outline.

Why are *two* outlines necessary for extemporaneous speaking? It might seem that making two outlines for a speech is extra work, but creating two outlines—the detailed preparation outline and the abbreviated delivery outline—actually makes your speaking job easier in the long run. The preparation outline and the delivery outline serve different functions, as their names imply: the *preparation* outline helps you prepare and improve your speech, whereas the *delivery* outline helps you deliver your speech to a live audience.

The most important difference between a preparation outline and a delivery outline is length. A delivery outline is much shorter than a preparation outline. Although a delivery outline has the exact same logical structure as its corresponding preparation outline, it is abbreviated. Like an impromptu scratch outline, a delivery outline for an extemporaneous speech only contains key words or phrases. The complete sentences or longer phrases of a detailed preparation outline are shrunk down to just a few key words on a delivery outline.

Why should you expand your thoughts in a detailed preparation outline and then condense these same thoughts in a delivery outline? There are at least four benefits of creating and using an abbreviated, "key word" delivery outline. *answer*

Q6 First, a key word delivery outline helps you recall your speech. The logical outline structure that is transferred from your preparation outline to your delivery outline acts as a memory recall device. Since both outlines have the exact same logical structure, the numbers and letters in your

© Neil Overy, 2013. Used under license from Shutterstock, Inc.

In the long run, the two outlines used for extemporaneous speaking makes your job easier.

FIGURE 8.14

delivery outline help to trigger your memory. For example, when you scan your delivery outline and see the letters A, B, and C under Roman numeral I, you remember that you have three supporting points for your first main idea, and the key words after these letters help you to recall and recover these three points.

Second, a key word delivery outline can greatly reduce your public speaking anxiety. If you have created a detailed preparation outline for your speech, you gain confidence because you know that you have worked through the invention, arrangement, and style stages of the speechmaking process. If you have created a clear delivery outline, you gain confidence because you know that you have a "safety net" in case you blank out. Your delivery outline is your fall-back mechanism if you have a memory lapse or lose your place. Although you may not need to look at your delivery outline very much, it is there for you if you need it. An abbreviated delivery outline helps you stay on track.

Third, a key word outline forces you to speak to your audience. Because there are no complete sentences in your abbreviated delivery outline, you cannot read your speech to your audience as if it were a manuscript. The key words in your delivery outline only remind you of the *ideas* you want to share, so you must choose the words to express these ideas "extemporaneously." Even though you may have spent much time and effort preparing and practicing your speech ahead of time, delivering your speech from a key word delivery outline will give it a feeling of freshness and spontaneity.

Fourth, a key word delivery outline allows you to easily interact with and engage your audience. Since you do not have to scan complete sentences, you can scan your live audience and establish good eye contact with your audience members. Since you are not reciting your speech word-for-word, you can also more easily develop a give-and-take rapport with your audience. You can interject comments referring to the unfolding speech situation, and you have the freedom to field audience questions and adjust to audience feedback. An abbreviated delivery outline gives you a lot of flexibility as a speaker.

FIGURE 8.15 A brief delivery outline gives a public speaker a lot of flexibility.

© Rihardzz, 2013. Used under license from Shutterstock, Inc.

HOW TO MAKE A DELIVERY OUTLINE

Your delivery outline is an abbreviated version of your detailed preparation outline. To aid in memory recall, it should have the exact same logical structure as your preparation outline. If you label the three main parts of your speech (Introduction, Body, and Conclusion) in your preparation outline, use these exact same labels in your delivery outline. Do not use "bullet points" in your delivery outline. Every Roman numeral, capital letter, Arabic number, and lowercase letter that appears in your preparation outline should appear in your delivery outline. Each letter and number in your delivery outline should trigger your memory and help you recall the detailed information in the corresponding section of your preparation outline.

You also want to use indentations for the main points and subpoints in your delivery outline. Just like your preparation outline, your delivery outline should place Roman numerals at the far-left margin for the main ideas in your speech, and indent uniformly for subpoints. This indentation is even more crucial for your delivery outline. When delivering your speech, you only have a few seconds to scan your delivery outline, so you want helpful visual cues and markers to help you locate your ideas and supporting points quickly.

The major difference between your detailed preparation outline and your abbreviated delivery outline is what follows the numbers and letters in the outline: whereas the detailed preparation outline may have complete sentences following the numbers and letters in the outline, the abbreviated delivery outline should only have key words or short phrases after each number and letter. This difference is crucial. DO NOT WRITE OUT COMPLETE SENTENCES IN YOUR ABBREVIATED DELIVERY OUTLINE. You only want to trigger your memory with a key word or phrase so you can speak extemporaneously about the idea being addressed.

There is one exception to this general rule regarding key words and phrases in a delivery outline: if you are directly quoting someone else's words in your speech, then you may include a quotation in complete sentences. Make sure you place quotation marks around this quotation written out in complete sentences, and make sure you give a full oral source citation so your audience knows that you are reading someone else's words at this point in your speech.

Because your delivery outline is used to help you deliver your speech in front of a live audience, you may also want to incorporate delivery prompts and visual aid cues into this outline. For example, if you think you might be tempted to rush through your speech, you could place at the top of your delivery outline the reminder, "Speak slowly! Do not rush." If you have several visual aids to display, you can insert visual aid cues in parentheses throughout your delivery outline: (Show Visual Aid #1 here.) (Remove Visual Aid #3 now.)

Your delivery outline can be typed out on one piece of paper, or it can be written out on one or more note cards. If you decide to place your delivery outline on a piece of paper, use a standard eight-and-a-half-inch by eleven-inch piece of paper. Type your outline using an easy-to-read font. Use only one side of the paper. If you write out your delivery outline on note cards, write legibly on three- by five-inch or four- by six-inch cards. Use only one side of each note card. You should only need a few note cards for a short speech. A good method is to place each major section of your speech on a different note card—you can then "feel" the different parts of your speech in your hand as you deliver it. If you are speaking in a class, your instructor may limit the number of note cards you may use.

There are advantages and disadvantages of placing your delivery outline on paper. One advantage of typing your delivery outline on a piece of paper is that the outline is easy to see and read. There is also only one piece of paper to keep track of on the podium. The disadvantage of a paper delivery outline is that a podium may not be available. It can be fairly awkward to hold a large piece of paper in your hand, especially if your hands are shaking.

There are also advantages and disadvantages of placing your delivery outline on note cards. An advantage of note cards is that they can be held in one hand. Their size and stiffness makes them easy to manipulate and move around as needed. The disadvantage of note cards is that they can be hard to read if you do not write them out clearly. They can also be distracting if you use too many of them.

The following sample delivery outline is presented as a typed paper outline, not handwritten note cards. Ask your public speaking instructor what type of delivery outline—paper or note cards—he or she prefers. If your instructor does not have a preference, consider the advantages and disadvantages mentioned above, and construct the type of delivery outline that will work best for your public speaking situation.

A SAMPLE DELIVERY OUTLINE

INTRODUCTION

I.   Stand up, reach up, touch toes, sit down—when was last time?

II.   Exercise regularly? Do not exercise? "Too busy," or "Don't have time?"
      A.   Fine or not fat? Think again.
      B.   Will inform you about exercise.

III. Everybody, every body type, can benefit

IV.   Main points:
      A.   Definition and benefits
      B.   Risks from lack
      C.   Exercise/body types

BODY

I.   What it is/what it does
      A.   What is exercise?
           1.   (2011 article, volume 46, *Nursing Journal*) Use of skeletal muscles/expenditure of energy
           2.   Planned, structured, and repetitive body movements
      B.   What are benefits?
           1.   (2012 article in *Maturitis*) Improved health functions
                a.   Reverse aging effects
                b.   Decrease death risk
                c.   Decrease certain cancers
                d.   Lower osteoporosis risk
                e.   Improve muscle function
                f.   Improve respiratory functions
           2.   Improves cognitive functioning/psychological well-being
                a.   Elevates mood
                b.   Increases alertness
           3.   Will move on to risks from lack

II.   At risk for chronic diseases, obesity, and depression
      A.   Several diseases
           1.   Two types of cardiovascular disease
                a.   Ischemic heart disease
                b.   Cerebrovascular disease
           2.   Increased high blood pressure
                a.   At risk of heart failure
                b.   At risk for obesity
      B.   Obesity on the rise
           1.   (2009 article, volume 72 of the *Journal of Environmental Health*) Has doubled
           2.   (2010 article, volume 100 of *American Journal Of Public Health*) fourteen to nineteen years over thirty years up seventeen percent
           3.   (September 2002 article. *Nursing Management*) 18% obese/300,000 obesity-related deaths annually

    C.   Symptoms of depression
        1.   (2011 article, volume 16 of *Physical Therapy Review)* Lack can cause depression, feelings of worthlessness, suicidal thoughts
            a.   Also lack of enthusiasm
            b.   Feelings of isolation
        2.   Weight problems
            a.   Excess weight
            b.   Loss of weight
    D.   Now types of exercise for body types

III.   (1992 article, volume 162, *Journal of Social Psychology*) Ectomorph, Mesomorph, and Endomorph.
    A.   Ectomorph
        1.   Thin and skinny
        2.   Don't gain weight, flat chest, fast metabolism
        3.   Body type encouraged
        4.   Short and intense workouts, specific muscle groups
    B.   Mesomorph
        1.   Athletic, rectangular shaped
            a.   Males—broad shoulders, V-shape
            b.   Women now want
        2.   Naturally strong
        3.   Cardio and weight training
    C.   Endomorph
        1.   More fat underneath skin
        2.   Gains fat easily, finds hard to lose
        3.   Slow metabolism
        4.   Cardio exercise and weight training

CONCLUSION

I.   Everybody, and every body type, can benefit

II.   Shared benefits, risks, and the different types

III.   Many ways to exercise
    A.   Many gyms
    B.   Treadmills, elliptical trainers, and dumbbells
    C.   Guided video exercises

IV.   Now what do you think? Now more informed. Can make good choices

PART 5: IMPROMPTU SCRATCH OUTLINES

Very few public speaking textbooks provide instruction on how to outline an impromptu speech. (The dozen contemporary public speaking textbooks I consulted before writing this outlining chapter were zero for twelve.) This lack of instruction on how to outline an impromptu speech is unfortunate, because many public speaking instructors have their students do some kind of impromptu speaking activity or exercise during the course of a public speaking class. If you ever

FIGURE
8.16 Impromptu speakers often have little or no time to outline a speech.

have to speak in public with very little preparation time, you will appreciate learning about a **scratch outline** that you can put together quickly for an impromptu speech. all answer

In an impromptu speaking situation, you have very little time to work through the "invention" and "arrangement" stages of the speech-making process. You have to come up with some ideas quickly, and you have to arrange them in some order quickly. You may have a few minutes, or you may have only a few seconds, to prepare your impromptu speech. There is no time to write out your impromptu speech in sentences. There is no time to even outline the introduction, body, and conclusion of your impromptu speech separately.

I will teach you how to literally "scratch out" and label a few thoughts on a piece of paper in order to survive and even thrive as an impromptu speaker. The following figure presents a simple abstract impromptu scratch outline.

A.G.—	(Attention getter)
Th.—	(Thesis)
I.	(First main point)
II.	(Second main point)
III.	(Third main point)

FIGURE
8.17 An abstract scratch outline for an impromptu speech.

The "A.G." in the scratch outline reminds you that your impromptu speech needs to begin with an attention getter or attention grabber. The "Th." reminds you that you need a clear thesis for your impromptu speech. The Roman numerals I, II, and III remind you that you need to come up with about three main points for your speech. If you can write out five key words or phrases in these five sections of a scratch outline, you should be able to deliver a five-minute impromptu speech.

HOW TO MAKE AN IMPROMPTU SCRATCH OUTLINE

It is important to note that an impromptu scratch outline is not necessarily filled out from top to bottom—you do not need to come up with your attention-getter first. The first section of a scratch outline that needs to be filled out is the "thesis" section. For example, if you are given three abstract topics in an impromptu speech competition or exercise, you would need to take one of those topics and turn it into a thesis, an assertion you want to make about your topic. (The letters on the scratch outline are "Th," and not just "T," because you do not want to confuse your general speech topic with your specific speech thesis.)

Once you have scratched out a thesis on your impromptu outline, you need to quickly decide on a speech structure. (Impromptu speakers often use "topical" structure because they just need to come up with three independent points supporting their thesis. Impromptu speakers also like to use "inductive" or "argument by example" structure because they just need to come up with three stories or examples that illustrate their thesis.) Once you <u>decide</u> on a speech structure, you quickly develop your main ideas. Each <u>main idea</u> is represented on the scratch outline with just a key word or phrase.

An impromptu speaker does not have to make three points, but if you decide to make only two points, you will have to fully develop these points and have lots of supporting ideas and evidence. You can make more than three points, but then you have to manage your time very wisely. If you are trying to give a five-minute impromptu speech, make about three points. Jot down three key words or phrases to the right of the three Roman numerals.

Make about three points in a short impromptu speech.

FIGURE 8.18

Once your main ideas are jotted down, tack on an <u>attention-getter</u> that can help you introduce your topic and that will lead into your thesis. If you have any preparation time remaining, go back to the body of the scratch outline and add any subpoints you can think of that will help you more fully develop your main ideas. If you are only writing key words or phrases, you should be able to fill out a scratch outline in about a minute. If you have more time to prepare, definitely add subpoints to your scratch outline.

HOW TO USE AN IMPROMPTU SCRATCH OUTLINE

Once you have filled out a very brief impromptu scratch outline, you have everything you need on paper to deliver a well-structured, well-developed impromptu speech. Reading the scratch outline from top to bottom reminds you to accomplish three very basic introductory tasks. The "A.G." reminds you to gain attention, the "Th" reminds you to state your thesis, and the Roman numerals I, II, and III remind you to preview your main ideas.

The three Roman numerals (and any subpoints you have added) remind you to present and develop the main ideas of your speech body, and they remind you to present these ideas in the correct order. After developing your first main point as much as you can, the second Roman numeral reminds you to transition into your second main point. After developing your second main point as much as you can, the third Roman numeral reminds you to transition into your third and final main point.

Reading the scratch outline from bottom to top reminds you to accomplish three very basic conclusion tasks. The Roman numerals remind you to review the main ideas you have covered, the "Th" reminds you to restate your thesis in a memorable way, and the "A.G." reminds you to close your speech with a "wrap-around" closer that refers back to your attention getter.

If you would like to get further instruction on delivering an impromptu speech using a scratch outline, turn to Chapter 9. Chapter 9 describes the four primary methods of delivery in detail, including impromptu delivery. There you will find a "Quick Guide to Impromptu Speaking" and more tips on delivering an impromptu speech effectively. Your public speaking instructor may also have additional impromptu outline formats for you.

Impromptu scratch outlines can also be used to "rough out" ideas for any type of speech. Since scratch outlines can be constructed so quickly, they can be used to quickly generate ideas for a possible speech, and they let you experiment with different possible speech structures. For example, if you wanted to prepare a speech to entertain on the topic of "dating," you could experiment with several possible structures by first making some scratch outlines on this topic.

(Since these are very rough scratch outlines for a possible speech, we will not worry about attention getters.)

"Ideal vs. Real" Contrast Structure

Thesis: My prom date was not what I thought it would be

I. What I thought my prom date would be like
    A. Limousine
    B. Dancing and dining
    C. Sweet memories
II. What it was actually like
    A. Borrowed car
    B. Moping and groping
    C. Embarrassing moments

Contrast Structure

Thesis: A date can be worse than a car wreck

I. Level of risk
    A. You only crash car once
    B. Multiple chances to crash and burn on a date
II. Level of suffering
    A. Car wreck injures your body
    B. Bad date injures your ego
III. Level of responsibility
    A. You don't choose to get in a wreck
    B. You chose to go on the date

Inductive Structure

Thesis: My blind dates are almost always disasters.

I. My date with the personal ad woman
II. My date with John's cousin
III. My date with my ex-friend Carla

Chronological Structure

Thesis: Dating practices have changed dramatically.

I. Traditional dating in the 1940s and 1950s
II. New rules in the 1960s and 1970s
III. Confusion in the 1980s and 1990s
IV. Dating in the new millennium

Classification Structure

Thesis: Be aware (and beware) of different dating types

I. The "serious" dater
II. The player
III. The "rebound" dater
IV. The stalker
V. The self-discloser

Hopefully you now see how useful scratch outlines can be both for impromptu speaking and for developing ideas and experimenting with speech structures for any type of speech. Since it only took a few minutes to throw together these scratch outlines, a very small time commitment has resulted in a variety of approaches to take for a speech to entertain. Once an approach has been decided on, the scratch outline with the most potential can be fully developed and transformed into a manuscript (for manuscript delivery) or a detailed preparation outline (for extemporaneous delivery).

PART 6: LESS CONVENTIONAL WAYS TO PREPARE AND PRESENT A SPEECH

In the preceding sections of this chapter, I have tried to give fairly general guidelines for outlining a speech without being overly prescriptive. While presenting a "standard" outlining method that is used by many speech instructors and their public speaking students, I have tried to acknowledge that other speech instructors have different preferences. You need to work with your public speaking instructor to find out what kind of outline (if any) he or she expects. Your instructor may ask you to master a particular outlining method, or your instructor may give you the freedom to experiment with different methods.

There are other, less traditional ways, of preparing and presenting public speeches. Some people like to develop their ideas in a less-structured format called a **storyboard**. A storyboard has columns for both words and images. People who are visual thinkers may prefer to use storyboards to develop their ideas. A less traditional way for delivering a speech is to use a **mind map**. A mind map relates ideas together visually. Instead of using numbers and letters in a linear fashion to signal main ideas and subpoints, a mind map places a main idea in the center of a piece of paper, and then has "spokes" radiating out from this main idea to several subpoints.

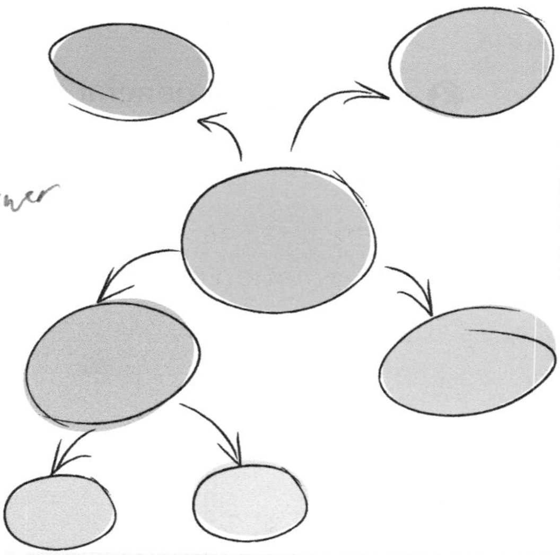

To become an effective public speaker, you will need to discover which methods of preparing and delivering a speech work best for you. For your in-class speeches, try to master the methods that your public speaking instructor recommends or requires. With solid instruction and practice, these methods will probably yield excellent results. After you have completed your public speaking course, you can continue to use these methods, or you can develop your own methods for preparing and delivering your speeches.

Mind maps present information more visually.

FIGURE 8.19

© phigabig, 2013. Used under license from Shutterstock, Inc.

SUMMARY

After reading this chapter, you should now have a grasp on the general purposes and principles of outlining. Outlines are used to develop ideas and to make the relationships among ideas obvious. You now know about three specific kinds of outlines used by public speakers: 1) detailed preparation outline used to prepare an extemporaneous speech, 2) an abbreviated delivery outline used to present an extemporaneous speech, and 3) a scratch outline used to prepare and present an impromptu speech. You also now know that there are other, less traditional methods for preparing and presenting speeches.

Review Questions

1. Why do speakers and writers use outlines?

2. What essential information needs to be included on a scratch outline for an impromptu speech?

3. What are the general guidelines for outlining?

4. Why does extemporaneous speaking require two outlines?

5. What are the important similarities and differences of a speech preparation outline and a speech delivery outline?

Glossary

Coordination: An outlining principle that places equal ideas on the same outline level.

Delivery outline: An abbreviated, key word outline used to present an extemporaneous speech.

Extemporaneous speech: A speech that is prepared ahead of time but not delivered from a manuscript. A detailed preparation outline is used to prepare an extemporaneous speech, but the speech is then delivered with the aid of a brief, key word delivery outline.

Impromptu speech: A speech delivered with little or no preparation. An impromptu scratch outline, developed in a few minutes or seconds, may be used to prepare and present an impromptu speech.

Manuscript speech: A speech written out word-for-word in essay form. Short manuscript speeches are often constructed without the aid of a speech outline.

Mind map: A less traditional, more visual way of capturing the ideas to be presented in a speech.

Oral source citation: A complete sentence inserted into a speech outline or manuscript that allows the speaker to orally credit the source being referenced.

Outline: A logically structured document that reveals the content and structure of a speech or essay.

Preparation outline: A detailed, logically structured outline that helps a speaker develop the ideas and words to be used in an extemporaneous speech.

Scratch outline: A very abbreviated key word outline used to prepare and present an impromptu speech. Scratch outlines may also be used to develop and explore possible ideas and speech structures for an extemporaneous speech.

Storyboard: A less traditional, more visual method for developing the ideas of a speech.

Subordination: An outlining principle that places subordinate, lower-order ideas on a lower outline level than higher-order ideas.

Transition sentence: A sentence placed in a speech outline that helps the speaker move from one speech idea to the next. Transition sentences are sometimes set apart from the other sections of a speech outline.

Written source citation: An abbreviated reference to a source placed in parentheses. Written source citations are usually combined with a works cited page or bibliography to reveal to a reader the sources used in a speech or essay.

DELIVERING YOUR SPEECH

Mark L. Staller

Learning Objectives

© Vitaly Korovin, 2013. Used under license from Shutterstock, Inc.

CHAPTER 9

① Describe and effectively use the visual elements of delivery.

② Describe and effectively use the aural elements of delivery.

③ Understand the four major types of delivery for public speaking.

④ Decide which method of delivery to use for any specific speaking situation.

On the one hand, effective **delivery** cannot make up for a lack of thought and organization. You cannot neglect or ignore the first three canons of Rhetoric—invention, arrangement, and style—and then rely on effective delivery alone to make your speech a success. Speaking clearly and enthusiastically, gazing boldly into the eyes of your audience members, and waving your hands around dramatically will not make up for the fact that you have nothing substantial to say. You can speak with sound and fury, but you may signify next to nothing.

On the other hand, ineffective delivery can absolutely ruin a speech. No matter how much time you have put into developing and organizing the ideas in your speech, without effective delivery, all your preparation effort is wasted. Delivery is more than just "icing on the cake." Delivery is an essential element of an effective public speech. The invention, arrangement, and style stages of the speech-making process are complemented and completed by good delivery. When a speaker develops good ideas, arranges these ideas clearly, expresses these ideas in appropriate words, and then *delivers* these words effectively, speaking excellence can be achieved.

In the first half of this chapter, you will learn about two primary aspects of delivery: 1) the visual elements of delivery, and 2) the aural elements of delivery. Knowledge of the visual and aural elements of delivery will help you use both your body and your voice more effectively when you deliver your speeches. After reading this chapter, you will also have a fuller, more precise vocabulary to analyze and describe what you see and hear when you observe a speech.

In the second half of this chapter, you will learn about the four primary methods used in the modern world: impromptu delivery, manuscript delivery, memorized delivery, and extemporaneous delivery. You will learn: 1) what each type of delivery method entails, 2) when each type of delivery method is appropriate, 3) some specific situations when each type of delivery method is used, 4) the drawbacks of each method, and 5) tips for using each method effectively.

THE VISUAL AND AURAL ELEMENTS OF DELIVERY

Preparing your speech is very much a matter of the mind: you must use your intellect to discover and create your ideas, to organize and expand your ideas, and to express your ideas in words. *Delivering* your speech, however, is very much a matter of the body: you must encode your verbal message in visual and aural symbols, and you must use your body to transmit these symbols to your audience through the visual and auditory channels. Therefore, the two main aspects of delivery that you must be aware of are: 1) the visual elements of delivery (what your audience sees), and 2) the aural elements of delivery (what your audience hears).

When you become consciously aware of the visual and aural elements of delivery, you can use your voice and body more effectively when you communicate your oral message. In addition, learning the specific vocabulary for the visual and aural elements of delivery gives you the language you need in order to give useful feedback to other speakers. If you know the specific terminology for the many different visual and aural elements of delivery, you will be able to go way beyond vague, unhelpful comments like, "Work on your verbal delivery," or, "You look good." Instead, you will be able to give very specific feedback, like, "Vary your voice inflection and eliminate your vocal clutter," or, "Your effective use of hand gestures and facial expressions enhanced and reinforced your verbal message." (Chapter 12 gives you more advice about how to give effective feedback to other public speakers.)

As you learn the specific visual and aural elements of delivery, you will also more fully appreciate the complexity of the delivery task: when a speaker stands in front of an audience to deliver a speech, there are a host of visual and aural elements to consider and control. We will now consider eight visual elements of delivery and eight aural elements of delivery.

THE VISUAL ELEMENTS OF DELIVERY

In addition to any visual aids and visual aid presentation technology they may use, public speakers must also consider the visual presentation of their own bodies. There are at least eight visual elements to be aware of when standing before a public speaking audience.

Use of space: Where you position your body in relation to the audience

Posture: How you hold your body when you are sitting or standing

Lower body movement: The movement of your hips, legs, and feet

Upper body movement: The movement of your head, shoulders, and torso

Hand gestures: Hand movements used to reinforce your verbal messages

Facial expressions: Combinations of facial features used to convey emotions

Eye contact: Direct gaze between the speaker and audience members

Personal appearance: Appearance of the speaker created by grooming and clothing

Eight visual elements of delivery.

FIGURE 9.1

Use of Space. Speakers must decide how they will position themselves in relation to their audience. Typically, speakers are expected to position themselves at the front of their audience, toward the center. If the room is very shallow, you need to avoid invading the "personal space" of audience members in the front row. In America, the "personal space bubble" for individuals extends approximately three feet around a person, so avoid standing closer than this to anyone during your speech.

"Public distance" is considered to be four to twelve feet from a person, so you should try to position yourself in this space parameter. If you stand closer than four feet, your audience may think you are being too intimate. If you purposely stand farther than twelve feet away, your audience may think that you are trying to distance yourself from them. If the room is very deep and the audience extends back quite a distance, you need to elevate yourself to help those in the back get a good view. (That is why a raised dais is often provided for speakers. If you are speaking in a large room with a big crowd, use the raised dais provided for the occasion.)

You need to decide whether you are going to remain in one area during your presentation or whether you are going to roam around as you speak. Sometimes the presentation technology or sound system may influence where you position yourself. Make good decisions about how to use this technology so you can still use your speaking space effectively.

FIGURE
9.2 Public speakers must avoid popping the personal space bubbles of their audience members.

Posture. In addition to *where* you stand, you need to think about *how* you are standing. Your posture is the way you hold your body while you are sitting or standing. Usually, you will not sit down when delivering a speech in public. For many speech occasions, sitting is too informal, and sitting down while speaking often makes it difficult for all of your audience members to see you. (Sitting is appropriate and necessary when you are not able to stand due to a disability or injury.)

Be aware that your posture sends messages about your emotional state to your audience. For example, if you stand slumped over with your head down, your spine curving forward, and your arms hanging at your sides, your audience may think that you are very tired or that you are feeling defeated, or that you have very low self-esteem. On the other hand, if you stand with your chest thrust out, your spine curving back a bit, and your arms stiff at your sides, your audience may think that you are assertive or aggressive, or even that you are belligerent and ready to fight.

The standard public speaking posture is to stand straight with your feet slightly apart and your weight evenly distributed on both feet. Your head should be up, and your arms should be hanging loosely at your sides. This position indicates that you are alert and that you are ready to engage the audience. Evenly distributing your weight on both feet allows you to move freely around the room. Holding your head up allows you to observe and

FIGURE
9.3 Poor posture can send a negative message to your audience.

make eye contact with your audience. Allowing your arms to hang down at your sides allows you to use hand gestures if you so desire.

Practice standing in this standard public speaking position. Some public speaking students tell me, when they first stand this way, "I feel like an ape!" Get comfortable with your own body. Your arms are designed to hang down at your sides. You do not look odd if you stand this way—you look fine. (There may be other reasons you look odd, but you do not look odd because you have arms.)

Lower body movement: Lower body movement occurs primarily in your legs and feet. (Hip thrusting and shaking is appropriate for some dance forms, but is usually inappropriate for public speaking.) A lack of lower body movement can distract from your speech message: what is very natural for a tree (standing in one place rooted to the ground) seems very unnatural for a human being. Your audience may think that you are very "stiff" and uncomfortable.

Good posture allows you to use your body effectively for your speech delivery.

FIGURE 9.4

On the other hand, too much lower body movement can also distract from your speech message. You should not pace around the room like a caged tiger, nor should you tap your toe constantly like a blues guitar player. Do not cross and uncross your legs repeatedly like a country line dancer. Instead, use purposeful lower body movement to enhance your message. Moving laterally from side to side can signal that you are changing your speech topic, whereas moving toward your audience can signal that you have something important to say.

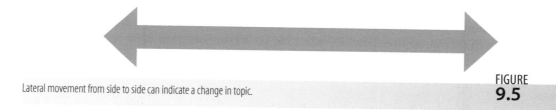

Lateral movement from side to side can indicate a change in topic.

FIGURE 9.5

Upper body movement: Upper body movement occurs primarily in your head, shoulders, and upper torso. In America, you can nod your head up and down (to signal affirmation), or you can wag your head from side to side (to signal negation). You can also throw your head back as you raise your eyebrows to indicate surprise. You can shrug your shoulders to indicate either resignation or uncertainty.

As you are speaking, watch out for unconscious head bobbing or body swaying. Some speakers create a distracting "Mr. Bobble Head" effect by unconsciously bobbing their head up and down as they speak. Other speakers seem to be "rocking out" at their favorite concert when they unconsciously sway their upper torsos. As with lower body movement, your upper body movement should be conscious and intentional, and it should reinforce your verbal speech message.

Hand gestures: Technically, hand gestures belong in the category of "upper body movement," but hand gestures are so important we will place them in their own category. There are four main types of hand gestures. First, some hand gestures are used to reinforce verbal messages. For ex-

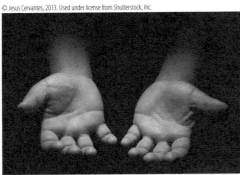

FIGURE 9.6 Think of your hands as inexpensive, low-tech visual aids.

ample, you can point at the audience when you say, "You can make a difference," or, you can spread your hands wide when you say, "This is huge!"

Second, some hand gestures are used to substitute for verbal messages. For example, you can form a circle with your index finger and thumb as you hold your other three fingers up in the air to indicate that everything is "okay," or you can hold one hand up in the air and wave at your audience at the end of your speech to acknowledge their applause.

Third, some hand gestures are used to direct the flow of communication. For example, you can cup your ears with your palms facing your audience to indicate that you want a verbal or vocal response from them, or you can turn your palms up in the air after delivering the punch line of a joke to indicate that it is now time for the audience to laugh.

Sometimes hand gestures are not used to communicate a message: the fourth type of hand gesture is used to regulate the external or internal environment of the speaker. For example, you can fan your face with your hands when you are hot, or you can twirl your hair with your fingers when you are nervous. Public speakers must be careful when they use these "environmental regulators" because these hand gestures can distract or confuse an audience. The audience may have difficulty determining whether a speaker is scratching his or her nose because it itches, or whether a speaker is scratching his or her nose to convey a message. As a public speaker, you want to fully exploit the first three types of hand gestures, and you want to limit the number of hand gestures that are used to regulate your environment.

Think of your hand gestures as inexpensive, low-tech visual aids. Your hands can visually express and reinforce many of your verbal signifiers. Your hands are almost always available when you speak in public, so use them. Do not hide your hands behind your back, and do not "lock up" your hands by getting a death grip on the podium. Think carefully about how you will hold your delivery aids and visual aids—you want to keep your hands free for effective hand gestures.

Be aware that the use of hand gestures is influenced by culture. Some ethnic groups and nationalities (Germans, for example) are less comfortable with flamboyant, very expressive hand gestures. Other ethnic groups and nationalities (Greeks and Italians, for example) often use and expect very expressive hand gestures. The dominant American culture is fairly comfortable with the use of hand gestures. You may need to exaggerate your hand gestures slightly when you are speaking to a very large crowd in order to get the visual impact you desire.

Facial expressions. Facial expressions are primarily used to indicate the emotional state of the speaker. The human mind is programmed to "read out" the emotional state of anything that looks like a human face. Look at the following figures. What is the emotional state indicated by face number one? What is the emotional state indicated by face number two? What is the emotional state indicated by face number three?

You were quickly able to read out the emotional states indicated by these simple "faces," but these "faces" do not belong to real human beings—they are just a few circles, dots, and lines contained in two-dimensional illustrations. Cartoonists can

FIGURE 9.7 Face number one.

portray a wide range of "human" emotions with just a few lines, dots, and circles. Similarly, computer "emoticons" are now inserted in emails and text messages to indicate the emotional states of people who are using computer-mediated communication. These examples and diagrams show how powerful and important facial expressions are when it comes to communicating emotions.

Face number two.

FIGURE 9.8

As a public speaker, the main thing you need to remember about your facial expressions is that they should match the content and tone of your speech. If you are delivering a serious message with a somber tone of voice, you need to make sure you have a serious, somber facial expression. If you are delivering a light-hearted, humorous message with an animated tone of voice, you need to make sure you have an appropriate facial expression to match.

Face number three.

FIGURE 9.9

An obvious contradiction between your speech content and your facial expression can confuse your audience. For example, one of my public speaking students had the habit of smiling and laughing when she became nervous. Unfortunately, when she got nervous while delivering a seatbelt safety speech, she began to laugh and smile broadly as she related a gruesome, true story. The story involved a traffic fatality and a decapitated head, so laughter and broad smiles were definitely not appropriate when telling this factual illustration! Make sure your facial expressions match the content and tone of your speech.

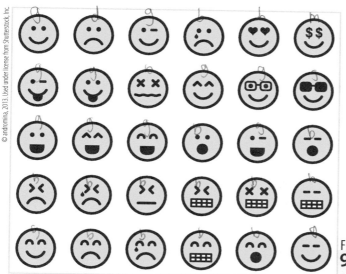

FIGURE 9.10 Emoticons are used to express emotion online.

Eye contact: Many communication experts consider eye contact to be the most important visual element of public speaking. Direct eye contact commands the attention of an audience. Direct eye contact can connect human beings together even without the use of words. Romantic partners sometimes trace the beginning of their relationship back to the moment in time when they looked across a crowded room and "their eyes met."

Like hand gestures and facial expressions, eye contact is also culturally influenced. In the Western world, eye contact is expected of a speaker. If a public speaker avoids eye contact in America, the audience may assume that the speaker is dishonest, shy, unconfident, unsure, or

FIGURE
9.11 Direct eye contact is crucial for public speakers in the Western world.

bored. You do not want your audience to make any of these negative assumptions about you, so you need to look them in the eye.

Here are some tips for using eye contact. "Scan" your entire audience by moving your head from side to side. Do not stare at just one person or one part of the audience. If you get distracted when you look people directly in the eyes, you can scan foreheads instead of eyeballs. Some speakers like to establish two focal points on the back wall, and then they direct their gaze back and forth from one focal point to the other. Another "focal point" variation is to find two supportive audience members on both sides of your audience, and then direct your gaze back and forth from one supportive audience member to the other. You *appear* to be scanning the entire audience while only focusing on two very supportive faces. As you get more comfortable, you can then look at other audience members.

Scanning your entire audience and looking every audience member in the eye can have a very positive effect on both you and your audience. On the one hand, your audience members will feel like they are being personally "drawn in" to your speech message, and they will think that you are speaking directly to them as individuals. On the other hand, if you establish direct eye contact with many audience members, you can more effectively monitor audience feedback, and you can draw psychic energy from your audience members.

Personal appearance: Your personal appearance is determined by two primary components: your clothing (or attire) and your grooming (or hygiene). How you dress and how you groom yourself make a big impression on your audience. Your personal appearance sends important nonverbal messages to your audience about what you value, about how you think and feel about yourself, and about the kind of relationship you want to establish with them.

Here are some general clothing guidelines for public speaking. First, dress appropriately for your audience. You want to avoid dressing in a way that will offend your audience even before

FIGURE
9.12 Professional look for a man.

you open your mouth to speak. Since you often will not know the personal clothing preferences of a large, diverse audience, play it safe—avoid extremes in clothing and fashion. When you speak in public, if you are wearing a hat or cap, it is usually best to remove it. (Some people think that it is disrespectful to wear a hat while speaking.) You may not personally have a problem with speakers who wear hats, but you cannot assume that all your audience members think and feel the way you do.

Second, dress appropriately for the speaking occasion. Determine how informal or formal the occasion is going to be, and dress accordingly. Since you are going to be "on stage" as a public speaker, it is best to err on the side of formality: dressing up indicates your respect for the audience and your respect for the speech situation. For a formal classroom speech, you may want to dress "professionally," as if you were going to an important white-collar job interview.

If you are male, your "professional" ensemble should include dress shoes and socks, slacks, a dress shirt and tie, and a sport coat or jacket. If you are female, your "professional" ensemble contains a few more options: you can wear dress shoes and slacks, and a dress shirt; or, you can wear a pantsuit; or, you can wear a dress skirt and a blouse with a jacket; or, you can wear a business-style dress.

Third, dress appropriately for your speech topic. Would it ever be appropriate to wear a baseball cap for a speech? How about if you were giving a speech on how to pitch a fastball? Would it ever be appropriate to wear a tuxedo for a classroom speech? How about if you were demonstrating how to wear a tuxedo, or you were talking about your experience as the best man at a recent wedding? Sometimes the general guideline "dress appropriately for your speech topic" will trump the first two guidelines mentioned above.

The final general clothing guideline I will mention is worded in the negative: do not dress in a way that will distract from your speech message. For example, avoid wearing t-shirts and jackets with symbols, logos, or messages on them. You may think that something as innocuous as a basketball jersey with your favorite team logo on it would be fine to wear, but what if that basketball team is the team that some of your audience members love to hate? When they notice your jersey, they are certainly not going to focus their minds on your speech message.

Here are a few grooming tips for public speaking situations. If you are having a "bad hair" day, go to a barber or hairstylist: do not stick a hat or cap on your head. If you have long hair, you may want to wear it up or pin it back so your hair does not fall in your face while you are speaking. Wearing your hair back will also decrease the odds that you will twirl your hair with your fingers or "whip it back" with a distracting head roll. If you are speaking after a meal, make sure you brush your teeth: you do not want to sit down after a speech and find out that you had a piece of lettuce stuck between your two front teeth. Finally, applying a good deodorant can help decrease the amount of anxiety sweat you may experience.

If you have made good decisions about your clothing and grooming, you should be able to speak in public with confidence. The attention you have paid to your appearance will create positive internal feelings for yourself, and it should set the stage for a positive interaction with your audience.

Professional look for a woman.

FIGURE 9.13

THE AURAL ELEMENTS OF PUBLIC SPEAKING

The aural elements of public speaking include paralanguage, the nonverbal but vocal elements of your communication. To clearly understand what paralanguage is, let us distinguish verbal communication from nonverbal communication, and let us also distinguish vocal communication from nonvocal communication.

Verbal/Vocal (speaking)	**Verbal/Nonvocal** (writing, texting, etc.)
Nonverbal/Vocal (sighing, grunting, groaning, paralanguage)	**Nonverbal/Nonvocal** (posture, facial expressions, body movement, eye contact)

Verbal and nonverbal communication can be distinguished from vocal and nonvocal communication.

FIGURE 9.14

Verbal communication is human communication that is expressed with words. Verbal communication can be nonvocal (e.g., communicating through writing or texting), or verbal communication can be vocal (e.g., communicating through the spoken word). Nonverbal communication can be nonvocal (e.g., many of the visual elements of delivery that we discussed above, such as facial expressions, eye contact, and posture) or nonverbal communication can be vocal (e.g., grunts, sighs, shouts, laughter, and paralanguage).

Paralanguage is not the words you say, it is *how* you say these words. Some vocalized sounds (such as grunts and sighs) are not words, but most vocalized sounds humans make are words. The loudness or softness of your spoken words, the rate at which you speak these words, the tone of voice you use when saying your words—these are all elements of "paralanguage," which encompasses most of the aural elements of delivery. There are at least eight aural elements of delivery to be aware of when speaking to an audience.

Pitch: When you change your voice pitch, you change how "high" or "low" your voice is. Every human being is born with a natural pitch range. A woman who sings comfortably in the high pitch range is called a "soprano," whereas a woman who sings comfortably in the low pitch range is called an "alto." A man who sings in the high pitch range is called a "tenor," whereas a man who sings in the low pitch range is called a "bass."

For effective public speaking, you need to use your entire natural pitch range. You want to avoid a **monotone** delivery. Someone using a "monotone" voice never changes his or her pitch. Sometimes a monotone voice is described as "flat" because there are no high or low pitches included—almost the same exact pitch is used for every single word spoken. It is very difficult to listen to a monotone voice for any length of time.

Sometimes people with little public speaking experience use a pitch pattern that is almost as excruciating as the monotone voice—they lower the pitch of their voice at the end of almost every sentence. This pitch pattern may be used as an unconscious defense mechanism: in order to give the impression that giving a speech is "no big deal," inexperienced speakers will lower their pitch at the end of each sentence. Unfortunately, this pitch pattern produces a "bored" tone of voice: the speakers sound like they are bored by their own speech.

Experienced speakers realize that they must motivate their audience to pay attention, so they strive to convey through their paralanguage that the speech they are giving is a "big deal." These speakers convey enthusiasm for their speech topics simply by raising the pitch of their voice right before the ends of their sentences. Just a simple change in pitch pattern can help to change a "boring" speech into an "interesting" speech.

1. **Pitch:** How high or low your voice is
2. **Rate:** How fast or slow you speak
3. **Volume:** How loudly or softly you speak
4. **Enunciation:** How clearly you say your words
5. **Pronunciation:** How correctly you say your words
6. **Accent or dialect:** Regional variations in how words are pronounced
7. **Voice quality:** The particular quality of your voice, such as "raspy" or "nasal"
8. **Verbal clutter:** Filler words that clutter your verbal communication

FIGURE 9.15 Eight aural elements of public speaking.

Rate: Your speaking rate is how fast or slow you are speaking, and it can be quantified by counting the number of words you speak per minute. The average extemporaneous speaking rate is about one-hundred-twenty-five to one-hundred-fifty words per minute, but debaters who practice "speed" drills can reach speaking rates around three hundred to three-hundred-fifty words per minute. Speaking rate can be further subdivided into two components: 1) the duration of sound, and 2) the use of pauses. One person may speak in quick, staccato sentences but use long pauses. Another person may sustain word sounds but have very few pauses. Both could be speaking at the exact same speaking rate.

Be aware that the adrenaline rush that often accompanies public speaking can cause your speech rate to increase dramatically: a speech that you practiced and timed at home at eight minutes may turn out to be only six minutes long when you deliver it in front of a live audience. The only substantial difference between your practiced speech and your "live" speech may be your speaking rate—the adrenaline boost which kicks in with the "fight or flight" response can easily cause your speaking rate to increase.

An increased speaking rate will not necessarily "ruin" your speech. A quick pace and a fast speaking rate often make a speaker come across as "energetic" and "enthusiastic." Instead of thinking that you are nervous, your audience might think that you are excited about your speech topic. However, if you are obviously speaking very quickly, you will give your audience the impression that you are rushing through your speech in order to "get it over with."

Speaking too slowly can make it difficult for your audience to follow you. Since your audience can think at about eight hundred words per minute, too slow a speaking rate will create a lot of "internal" noise in your audience—they will have too much time to think their own thoughts, and they will find it difficult to keep paying attention to your words. Practice your speech until you can deliver it at a decent rate and with very few unnecessary pauses.

Volume: Your voice volume is how "loud" or "soft" your voice is. Some people get very quiet when they speak in public and their voice can hardly be heard. A good rule of thumb is to project your voice loudly enough so that the people in the back of the room can easily hear what you have to say.

Some speakers think that they will maintain the attention of their audience members if they continually shout at them. However, if you present a continuous barrage of loud words, your audience will eventually tune you out. The key to maintaining the attention of your audience is to *vary* your voice pitch, rate, and volume. Sometimes a whisper can be more effective than a shout. Sometimes your words will have more force if you take a step toward your audience and *decrease* your voice volume.

Shouting continually at your audience will not necessarily maintain their attention.

© oilyy, 2013. Used under license from Shutterstock, Inc.

FIGURE
9.16

Enunciation: Enunciation is an issue on the "phonetic level" of language: it is how *clearly* you say the sounds of your words. Some synonyms for "enunciation" are "clearness," "clarity," and "articulation." Public speakers need to enunciate their words clearly so their audiences can easily receive their vocalized verbal messages.

Compared to English speakers in other countries, Americans are somewhat "lazy" with their enunciation; it is not uncommon for Americans to clip off the ends of their words, or to run their words together. When you are using informal American English, you can get away with a lot of enunciation errors, but even an American audience demands some minimal level of articulation. For example, on several American television reality shows, some people have such poor enunciation, the television producers have added subtitles to help people understand what they are saying. If your audience wishes that they could read some subtitles when you are speaking, then you have an enunciation problem!

You can improve your enunciation by reading out loud and clearly articulating the sounds of your words. Do not read out loud by yourself, or you may just reinforce bad enunciation habits: you need to have feedback so you can become aware of when you are mumbling or running your words together. To develop the ability to distinguish and vocally represent fine distinctions in letter sounds, you can practice enunciation drills and "tongue twisters."

Pronunciation: Do not confuse the term "pronunciation" with the term "enunciation": these terms sound similar, but they refer to two different aspects of spoken language. "Enunciation" refers to how *clearly* you are saying your words, whereas "pronunciation" refers to how *correctly* you are saying them.

Pronunciation is a phenomenon of human culture. Human beings do not know how a word is "supposed" to be said until they are taught by their culture group. You become part of the "in" group when you pronounce your words the same way that others in your culture group pronounce them. Since pronunciation is primarily a matter of enculturation, what may be the "correct" pronunciation of a word for one culture group may be incorrect for another culture group.

Audiences are typically less forgiving of pronunciation errors than they are of enunciation flaws. If (American) English is your native language, then your American audience will expect you to pronounce your words correctly when you give a speech. If you mispronounce words, they may consider you to be "ignorant" or "uneducated." If English is a second language for you, relax and focus on your overall message: your audience does not necessarily expect you to pronounce every word correctly. Usually audience members are much more forgiving of pronunciation errors when they realize that someone is not speaking his or her native language.

To avoid pronunciation errors, use words with which you are familiar. Check the pronunciation of unfamiliar words before using them in a speech. Be especially careful when you are quoting the words of others or reciting from other sources. Practice delivering your speech out loud in front of other people so you can get feedback on your pronunciation.

Accent or dialect: Accent and dialect are closely related to pronunciation. Accents or dialects arise when people using the same language pronounce their words differently in different geographic regions. (Technically, "dialectic" is a broader term that can also include variations in grammar and punctuation, but "dialectic" is commonly used as a synonym for "accent," which refers specifically to regional variations in oral pronunciation.) Some linguists can identify a person's geographic place of origin by noticing subtle variations in his or her word pronunciation.

With the advent of a national television news media that promotes a "standard" American pronunciation, very heavy regional accents have diminished in America. However, there are still distinct regional differences in pronunciation. When discussing American accents with my college students in California, they often mention friends or family members who have "New York" accents or "Minnesota" accents or "Arkansas" accents. Some of these students are surprised to learn that Americans on the East coast or in the Midwest would say that they have a "California" accent.

As a public speaker, should you cultivate or eliminate your regional accent? That depends on the effect you want to have on your audience. If you want to stand out, then you might need to emphasize your accent; if you want to fit in, then you might need to decrease or eliminate your accent. My friend Pierre is originally from Newfoundland but now lives in Los Angeles. He married an American woman and became an American citizen. You could not guess from his West coast American accent that he ever set foot in Canada. He has worked very hard to eliminate his Canadian accent. On the other hand, several years ago I had an international student from Canada in my public speaking class. She was very proud of her Canadian citizenship, and she spoke confidently and effectively using a thick Canadian accent.

Voice quality: Voice quality refers to the particular quality of your voice. Some voices have a natural "nasal" quality—it sounds like people are speaking through their noses when they talk. Other voices have a natural "raspy" quality—it sounds like people are hoarse or have a sore throat when they speak. A person with a "sonorous" voice produces full, deep vocal sounds.

You are a unique human being, so you have your own unique natural voice quality. However, you can change or modify the quality of your voice. For example, you probably have already developed a "spooky" voice for telling a scary story: "It was a dark and stormy night, and all the campers were gathered around the campfire . . ." You can also cultivate a more effective "public speaking" voice if your natural voice quality seems inappropriate. For example, if you have a natural "breathy" voice quality, you may need to speak from your diaphragm and project your voice more forcefully.

Verbal clutter: Clutter is annoying and distracting. Public speakers are annoying and distracting when they clutter their speeches with unnecessary "uhs," "ums," and "ya knows." This distracting speaking habit is often caused by a speaker's unconscious desire to avoid even a split second of silence in between words, so "vocalized pauses" is also a helpful phrase to describe this phenomenon. In order to avoid even a brief moment of silence, speakers replace every silent pause with a vocalized pause— "uh. . .," "um. . ."

Like a cluttered room, verbal clutter is annoying and distracting.

FIGURE 9.17

Unfortunately, if you are guilty of using a lot of verbal clutter, some audience members will start to count how many times you use a certain "filler" word. Once audience members start counting your filler words, you have lost them. Although the human mind has the ability to multitask, it is almost impossible for human beings to count and process verbal messages simultaneously. If an audience member approaches you after a speech and asks, "Did you know you said 'um' thirty-two times during your speech?" you can be sure your speech message was not received.

Here are some suggestions for eliminating verbal clutter. First, give yourself permission to pause now and then. You do not have to fill every second of your speech with sound. Second, since verbal clutter is usually an unconscious habit, you need to become aware of your own verbal clutter. One way to do this is to overemphasize your vocalized pauses to make them obvious to yourself: practice your speech, but force yourself to say "um" or "uh" (or whatever filler word you use) after each word of your speech. For example, you might practice the beginning of your speech and say, "Today, um, I, um, will, um, be, um, talking, um, about, um, a, um, very, um, important, um, issue, um." If you annoy *yourself* with your favorite filler word, you have a better chance of keeping it in your conscious awareness.

If you are not easily provoked and want to have some fun, you can become aware of your verbal clutter by practicing your speech in front of a live audience. However, before you begin practicing your speech out loud, give a squirt bottle to one or more audience members and instruct them to squirt you in the face each time you use a filler word. Employing this "squirt bottle" method, you will quickly become highly aware of any unconscious filler words you have been using!

THE FOUR MAJOR TYPES OF DELIVERY

© ioloto, 2013. Used under license from Shutterstock, Inc.

FIGURE 9.18 Effective speakers choose the delivery method that is appropriate for their audience and speaking situation.

For your public speaking class, you will most likely be asked to focus on and master extemporaneous delivery—the most commonly used method of delivery in America. However, you need to know about the other methods of delivery because these other methods may be more appropriate for some speaking situations. Sometimes you may need to speak with very little preparation, and sometimes you may need to carefully craft and deliver every word of your speech. Thus, before learning about extemporaneous delivery in this chapter, you will first learn about the other three methods of delivery: impromptu, manuscript, and memorized delivery.

Each method of delivery has its place. The best method of delivery will be determined by your speaking situation and the expectations of your audience. The most effective speakers focus on the needs of their audience. If you want to be an effective speaker, you will not just use the delivery method you prefer; you will use the delivery method that the speaking situation demands and that your audience expects.

IMPROMPTU DELIVERY

Explanation and description of impromptu delivery: The adjective *impromptu* means that something is prompted by a present occasion, rather than being planned in advance. A synonym for the adjective *impromptu* is "improvised." An impromptu speech is one that is improvised or thrown together quickly, with little or no preparation. When speakers give authentic impromptu speeches, at most they only have time to prepare a scratch outline to speak from, but they may not even have time for that. They suddenly find themselves in a situation that requires them to speak, so they must speak "off the cuff" or on the spur of the moment.

When impromptu delivery is appropriate: Impromptu delivery is the appropriate delivery method to use when you truly were not given the time to prepare a speech. Do not believe everyone who claims to be speaking "impromptu": *claiming* to be speaking spontaneously is a strategy that some speakers use to generate admiration in, or to lower the expectations of, their audience. If you know that you are going to be asked to say a few words at some event or special occasion, you should prepare your comments ahead of time.

You may have to use impromptu delivery for a wedding toast.

FIGURE 9.19

Specific impromptu speaking situations: 1) answering an unexpected question during a job interview; 2) demonstrating how to use a machine at work to some visitors; 3) accepting an unexpected award; 4) participating in an impromptu speaking contest; 5) giving a last-minute wedding toast; 6) saying a few words at a funeral when asked to honor the memory of the departed one.

Drawbacks of impromptu delivery: Impromptu delivery is a very stressful, high-stakes approach to public speaking—you may shine, or you may barely survive, or you may crash and burn. Compressing the invention, arrangement, style, and delivery stages into just a few minutes or seconds demands quick thinking and split-second decision making. If you try to improvise a speech, you may find yourself having difficulties generating and organizing ideas. You may also have difficulty finding the right words to say, or saying any words at all. You may also experience a high level of public speaking anxiety.

Tips for effective impromptu delivery: First, in your public speaking class, if your instructor has asked you to prepare and practice your speech ahead of time, do *not* use impromptu delivery. You may be an adrenaline junky who likes living on the edge, or you may be a slacker who enjoys the challenge of "bluffing" your way through an assigned speech, but your instructor and classmates will most likely not be impressed with your improvisation.

If other student speakers have spent hours researching, organizing, outlining, and practicing the delivery of their speeches, they will probably consider your "thrown-together" speech a waste of their time. An unprepared speaker who tries to "wing it" on an assigned speech shows a lack of respect for the audience and a lack of understanding of what is expected from a public speaker. A public speaker that has time to prepare should have a focused, well-organized message that has been developed with care.

You will have other, more appropriate opportunities to try out impromptu speaking. For example, in an impromptu speaking contest, each competitor is usually handed three different general topics or three specific quotations right before they are expected to speak. They are given about two minutes to prepare a five-minute speech that they then must deliver to the judge and the other competitors. Your speech instructor may ask you to try

Your audience will not be impressed with impromptu delivery when you are expected to prepare and practice your speech ahead of time.

FIGURE 9.20

out impromptu speaking in a formal impromptu speech contest, a formal class assignment, or an informal class exercise. The next few paragraphs give you tips for preparing and presenting an impromptu speech in these types of situations.

To prepare an impromptu speech, quickly choose a topic. Do not agonize over your choice. Either pick a topic that you have lots to say about, or pick a topic to which your audience can relate. Once you have picked your topic, form a thesis about this topic. Decide on a primary, specific assertion you want to make about your topic—this is your thesis. Once you have formed your thesis, decide on a speech structure or organizational pattern for your main ideas.

Chapter 7 (Organizing Your Speech) describes various organizational patterns you can use for a speech body. Chapter 15 (Speaking to Inform) and Chapter 16 (Speaking to Persuade) give examples of organizational patterns for informative and persuasive speeches, respectively. Use one of these organizational patterns to develop the main ideas of your impromptu speech. Don't forget to also create an attention-getter to introduce your topic and lead into your thesis.

You can keep track of the ideas you want to present in your impromptu speech by quickly making a scratch outline. Impromptu speech scratch outlines are described in detail in Chapter 8 (Outlining Your Speech). (In this same chapter, you will also find several sample scratch outlines.) You only have time to write a few key words on your scratch outline to remind you of your attention-getter, your thesis, and the main ideas of your speech. If time allows, you can also add subpoints to your scratch outline to flesh out your main ideas. The entire process of preparing your scratch outline should only take one or two minutes.

To deliver an impromptu speech, you just need to remember to count to three. In your speech introduction, 1) gain attention, 2) state your thesis, and 3) preview your main ideas. In your speech body, develop about three main points with specific, concrete details. Make the transitions between these points obvious with verbal "signposts" or "signal words." (Words like "first," "second," "third," "next," and "finally" can be used to signal where you are at in your speech body.) In your speech conclusion, 1) review your main ideas, 2) restate your thesis, and 3) provide closure. (Most impromptu speakers use a "wrap-around" closer that refers back to their attention-getter.) If you have a speech with three main points and you accomplish the tasks described in this paragraph, you should be able to deliver a five-minute impromptu speech.

When you deliver an impromptu speech, remember the importance of acting competent and confident. (Speaker poise is often an important judging criteria in an impromptu speech contest.) Stand straight, establish eye contact with your audience, and speak with authority and enthusiasm. Do not panic if you blank out. Do not draw attention to any mental lapse. Pause, breathe, and smoothly continue when you get your train of thought back.

If you develop your skills as an impromptu speaker, you will not only *act* confident, you will actually become a more confident person. Take advantage of any opportunity you are given to hone your impromptu speaking skills. If you master impromptu speaking and impromptu delivery, you will have confidence and poise that you can apply to many other life situations.

In addition, impromptu speaking assignments and exercises can drill into you the minimum standards for any public speech. If you can accomplish the basic preparation and delivery tasks listed below

FIGURE 9.21 Developing impromptu speaking skills can give you confidence for many different life situations.

in the "Quick Guide to Impromptu Speaking" in one or two minutes, then you can easily accomplish these same tasks when you have much more time to prepare your speeches.

QUICK GUIDE TO IMPROMPTU SPEAKING

To prepare an impromptu speech:
1. Choose a topic ✓
2. Form a thesis ✓
3. Decide on a speech structure ✓
4. Make a scratch outline ✓
5. Develop your main ideas ✓
6. Create an attention-getter ✓
7. If time allows, add subpoints ✓

To deliver an impromptu speech:
In your introduction,
1. Gain attention
2. State your thesis
3. Preview your main ideas

In your speech body,
1. Make about three points
2. Fully develop your ideas
3. Provide clear transitions

In your conclusion,
1. Restate your thesis
2. Review your main ideas
3. Provide closure

A QUICK GUIDE

MANUSCRIPT DELIVERY

Explanation and description of manuscript delivery: A manuscript speech is written out word-for-word in essay format (usually with paragraph breaks) and then read directly from a typed manuscript or teleprompter or other device. Be aware that not every speech you see in manuscript form was actually delivered from a manuscript. Any speech—manuscript, memorized, impromptu, or extemporaneous—may be recorded and then transcribed into manuscript form. The speaker may have been improvising, or using key word note cards, or speaking from memory, but all the reader sees is the transcribed script of the speech. With manuscript delivery, the speech begins in manuscript form and is actually delivered by reading the speech text.

Teleprompters are used to deliver manuscript speeches.

© Kjpargeter, 2013. Used under license from Shutterstock, Inc.

FIGURE 9.22

FIGURE
9.23 Most modern political speeches are scripted and delivered from a manuscript.

When manuscript delivery is appropriate: Manuscript delivery is the appropriate method of delivery when every word of a speech needs to be controlled and accounted for. If you are addressing very sensitive matters or need to be very accurate or careful with you words, you may want to speak from a manuscript. For very formal occasions, where every word of a speech is expected to be well-crafted and weighty, manuscript delivery is appropriate. It is necessary and appropriate to use manuscript delivery when giving an eloquent speech using "high" style.

Specific manuscript speaking situations: 1) a radio or television newscast; 2) an official proclamation; 3) a formal graduation speech; 4) an eloquent "inspirational" speech; 5) an official statement on a legal matter; 6) almost any political speech in the modern media age. (Television news "sound bites" often highlight the verbal mistakes and speaking "faux pas" of politicians, so most political discourse is now—wisely—scripted.)

Drawbacks of manuscript delivery: Preparing a speech manuscript is a time-consuming process that takes specialized writing skills. That is why politicians have full-time speech writers on their paid staff. In addition to a good speech writer, manuscript delivery requires a good speech reader. The major drawback of manuscript speaking is delivery problems. A poor reader can butcher a well-written manuscript speech. If you are not properly trained in manuscript delivery, you may bury your head in your manuscript and have little or no eye contact with your audience. And if you are reading a manuscript speech written by someone else, you may mispronounce their words, or you may come across as insincere or inauthentic.

Manuscript delivery is too formal a delivery method for many public speaking situations. Audiences—especially American audiences accustomed to informal, direct discourse—expect speakers to *speak* to them, not read. You may be tempted to deliver a class speech by reading a manuscript, but if this is not the assigned delivery method, you should avoid this temptation.

Tips for effective manuscript delivery: Only use manuscript delivery when it is called for—for very formal occasions, or for public speeches that require very eloquent, very accurate, or very careful language. To guarantee you have an authentic voice, write your own manuscript speech.

Once you have written and fine-tuned your manuscript, you need to read it over and over until your speech has been internalized. Practice reading your manuscript out loud, with appropriate facial expressions and hand gestures.

For a typed manuscript, use an easy-to-read font. Experiment with different font sizes—the standard eleven- or twelve-point font may not be as easy to read as a fourteen- or sixteen-point font. To avoid re-reading a line of text, double space your manuscript. Use only the top two thirds of the paper so your eyes do not have to scan all the way to the bottom of the page. If your manuscript is several pages long, do not staple these pages together. Leave the pages separated so you can avoid "flipping" pages over. If you are speaking outdoors, place the manuscript pages in heavy, low-gloss, see-through plastic covers so they will not be blown away by any gusts of wind.

Before delivering your manuscript, check out the equipment you will be using. Make sure a podium is available. If there is a microphone attached to the podium, make sure it will not obscure your manuscript. If the podium is not adjustable, make sure it is not too tall or too short for your height. (A music stand functions well as a makeshift or substitute podium, and it can easily be adjusted up and down.)

When you deliver your manuscript speech, you can track each line of the manuscript with the index finger of one hand to help you keep your place. Remember to make eye contact with your audience. Do not rush. The formal occasion that calls for a manuscript speech also calls for a more stately speaking rate. You should have chosen the words for your manuscript speech with great care, so give just as much care to how you deliver these words. Speak them clearly and forcefully. When you have finished your manuscript speech and received your applause, exit the stage with the same gracefulness you used to the deliver your speech.

MEMORIZED DELIVERY

Explanation and description of memorized delivery: Memorized delivery is a step beyond manuscript delivery: a speech is written out word-for-word, and then it is committed to memory and delivered from memory word-for-word. The manuscript is set aside and the speaker relies solely on his or her power of memory to recall the speech.

When memorized delivery is appropriate: In ancient Greece and Rome, when the art of public speaking was first developed in the Western world, memorized delivery was recognized as the only appropriate method for delivering a speech. Greek and Roman societies were primarily "oral" cultures that were transitioning into literacy, so these societies had a basic distrust or suspicion of written language. If a person had something important to say, then they were expected to say it without the aid of the written word.

Actors and actresses are expected to deliver their lines from memory.

FIGURE
9.24

Ancient Greek and Roman public speaking instructors and students had ingenious methods for memorizing and recalling speeches. For example, one standard method for recalling a lengthy speech was to associate different parts of a speech with different rooms of your house: during your speech introduction, you might imagine that you were standing on your front porch; when you were ready to move on to your speech body, you would mentally "walk" from room to room to recall the main points you wanted to remember.

In modern "literate" cultures, there is no automatic stigma involved in using or consulting a written text. In fact, as the specific manuscript speaking situations presented in the previous section indicate, when people now have something important to say, they are often *expected* to read it from a manuscript. However, there are still certain public speaking situations where memorized delivery is the most appropriate method for presenting a speech.

Speeches are often memorized when they are given repeatedly. If you have to deliver the same speech dozens or hundreds of times—maybe even daily or hourly—it is appropriate and

FIGURE
9.25 Formal religious services may include oral prayers recited from memory.

even necessary to memorize it. You may also memorize a speech to impress your audience. In our modern literate world, where the power of memory is not often exercised or used, presenting a speech from memory is considered to be quite an accomplishment. Memorized delivery is also appropriate when you want to make your speech a true "performance" without a script or delivery aid of any kind getting in your way.

Specific memorized speech situations: 1) a standard sales pitch delivered repeatedly to customers, 2) a political "stump" speech delivered out on the campaign trail, 3) a live narration delivered on an amusement park ride, 4) a recitation at a formal religious service, 5) a monologue in a theatrical play, 6) a contest speech delivered at a speech tournament.

Drawbacks of memorized delivery: Memorized delivery is very time-consuming. It can take days or weeks to commit a speech to memory, so memorized delivery is not practical for many short-term speaking situations.

Like manuscript speaking, the primary drawback of speaking from memory is delivery problems. Delivering a speech from memory is a specialized skill. Actors and actresses can deliver their lines from memory and make it seem natural because they have studied and practiced their craft. Without special training and practice, you probably will not be able deliver a memorized speech effectively. Without this special training and practice, people who attempt to deliver a speech from memory often "tune out" the audience as they focus on recalling their words. They may speak in a "robotic," detached voice, their body may be frozen in one position, and they may look up and to the right, as if receiving a message from above.

Like impromptu speaking, delivering a speech from memory is also a high-stakes proposition—either you will recall your speech, or you will not. When you attempt to deliver a speech from memory, you are adding to the pressure of public speaking the additional pressure of recalling every word of your speech. Because there is no delivery aid to consult or fall back on, if you forget your speech, you are sunk.

Tips for effective memorized delivery: Begin the process of memorizing your speech by reading your entire manuscript repeatedly until the general flow of the speech is internalized. Break the manuscript into sections, and then memorize these sections in order: memorize and recite the first section, then memorize and recite the first and second sections, then memorize and recite the first, second, and third sections, etc.

As you memorize the words of your speech, develop and memorize the visual and aural elements of delivery that will enhance these words. One primary purpose of memorized delivery is to pro-

FIGURE
9.26 Ilf you forget your memorized speech, you are in trouble.

mote and highlight the effective use of your body and voice, so these visual and aural elements need to be well thought out. How will you stand? What tone of voice will you use? What facial expressions are appropriate? What hand gestures need to be added to reinforce your words?

Practicing and memorizing your speech as a holistic performance that involves your words, your voice, and your body will actually make it easier to remember your speech. Your verbal memory will be reinforced by your visual memory and your kinesthetic or "muscle" memory. Standing in a certain position, looking in a certain direction, or making a particular hand gesture will help to trigger the words associated with these actions.

When you are delivering your memorized speech in front of a live audience, take full advantage of the absence of delivery aids. There is nothing to get in the way of you and your audience. Engage your audience with appropriate eye contact. Use your voice and body to reinforce the words you have taken such effort to memorize.

If you have put in the necessary preparation and practice to memorize and deliver your speech effectively, then have confidence in yourself and your abilities. Do not undermine yourself by placing a "backup" manuscript nearby that you can consult "just in case." If you think you need a manuscript, then you should speak from a manuscript. If you think that memorized delivery is appropriate, then deliver your speech from memory.

An effective memorized speech can entertain and impress an audience.

FIGURE 9.27

Sometimes a "prompter" is allowed to give a verbal prompt to performers who are having difficulty recalling their words. If you are speaking in such a situation, decide ahead of time on the nonverbal signal you will give to the prompter if you need a verbal prompt. However, do not over-rely on verbal prompts. Have a strategy for handling memory lapses yourself. If you blank out, pause. Give yourself a few seconds to remember the next words. If necessary, repeat the last line you just said. Often, repeating this previous line will jar your memory and allow you to recover the next line.

Remember, your audience doesn't necessarily know what you are supposed to say next. Do not draw attention to or apologize for any memory lapses. Get back on track as quickly as possible, and calmly continue on with your speech. A brief memory lapse in a well-delivered memorized speech is not that big a deal, unless you the speaker make it a big deal.

EXTEMPORANEOUS DELIVERY

Explanation and description of extemporaneous delivery: In the discipline of public speaking, the extemporaneous speaking method can be thought of as a cross between manuscript speaking and impromptu speaking. Extemporaneous speakers develop detailed preparation outlines that may be written out even down to the sentence level (like manuscript speeches). However, to deliver their speeches, extemporaneous speakers shrink these detailed preparation outlines down into abbreviated delivery outlines that contain only key words or phrases (like impromptu speech scratch outlines).

Working with *two* outlines—the detailed preparation outline and the abbreviated delivery outline—allows the extemporaneous speaker to fully develop the ideas of the speech without

FIGURE
9.28 An extemporaneous speech is often delivered from note cards.

worrying about word-for-word delivery. The ideas of the speech are fully developed in the detailed preparation outline, but since the speech is delivered from the key word delivery outline, these ideas may be expressed a little bit differently each time the speech is practiced or delivered.

Outside the discipline of public speaking, the adjective "extemporaneous" is generally used as a synonym for the adjective "impromptu," so many people have difficulty clearly understanding or explaining the difference between an impromptu speech and an extemporaneous speech. An extemporaneous speech is sometimes defined as a speech that is unplanned and improvised—this definition equates extemporaneous speaking with impromptu speaking. An extemporaneous speech can also be defined as a speech that is planned and prepared ahead of time, but delivered without the aid of a manuscript—this second definition is the definition primarily used within the discipline of public speaking.

When delivered effectively, a good extemporaneous speech can easily be confused with a good impromptu speech because an effective extemporaneous speaker talks freely without too much concern for the precise words used to express the ideas of the speech. Audience members unfamiliar with the extemporaneous speech-making process may mistakenly think that the speaker just threw these thoughts together quickly, whereas the speaker may have spent hours researching, organizing, outlining, and practicing the delivery of the speech.

When extemporaneous delivery is appropriate: Extemporaneous delivery should not be used when the formality of a speaking occasion requires either manuscript or memorized delivery; otherwise, extemporaneous delivery is appropriate for almost every other public speaking situation. Extemporaneous delivery lends itself well to informal public address which is the dominant, most prevalent speaking style in America.

In the majority of day-to-day public speaking situations, American audiences want speakers who will speak to them as if they were having a conversation with them. Extemporaneous delivery promotes this conversational, engaging speaking style—that is why the majority of public speaking textbooks and the majority of public speaking instructors focus primarily on this method of delivery.

Specific extemporaneous speaking situations: 1) a classroom lecture; 2) a student presentation; 3) a speech at a conference or symposium; 4) a courtroom speech; 5) a business presentation; 6) an informal sermon or homily.

Drawbacks of extemporaneous delivery: Extemporaneous delivery may be considered too informal for some very formal occasions. Because every word is not necessarily thought out ahead of time, extemporaneous delivery also has drawbacks when you need to choose your words carefully. Extemporaneous delivery does not promote the use of eloquent language and "high" style. In order to speak poetically and to incorporate many figures of speech into your discourse, you will need to write out your words and deliver them from a manuscript or from memory.

Tips for effective extemporaneous delivery: Chapter 8 (Outlining Your Speech) gives you specific instructions on how to develop both a detailed preparation outline and an abbreviated delivery outline for an extemporaneous speech. Read the appropriate parts of Chapter 8 for more advice on developing and using these outlines.

Although Chapter 8 gives you specific, detailed advice on preparing outlines for an extemporaneous speech, here are some tips and reminders related to outlining that directly impact the delivery of your speech.

First, make sure you subdivide and "chunk down" all the major ideas and supporting ideas of your speech in both your preparation outline and your delivery outline, and preserve the exact same logical structure in both of these outlines. The numbers and letters in your outlines act as memory recall devices: these numbers and letters help you remember how many points you have to make in each section of your speech.

FIGURE **9.29**

Lawyers often speak extemporaneously in the courtroom.

Second, do not fixate on your detailed preparation outline. This outline is primarily used to help you prepare your speech, but you will not have this outline in front of you when you deliver your speech. You also need to put time and effort into your "key word" delivery outline. You have not adequately prepared to deliver an extemporaneous speech if you are scribbling out delivery note cards right before your speech.

Third, if given a choice, use index cards for your delivery note cards, rather than a piece of paper. If a podium is not available, you will have to hold this paper, and a thin piece of paper can shake if you are nervous. Note cards can be easily held in your hands if there is no podium. If you write out your note cards, make sure you write legibly. Write on only one side of your note cards so you do not have to flip them over. Number your note cards so you can easily rearrange them in case you drop them. Only place key words and phrases on every other line of your note cards—the white space around the words will help these words stand out.

In addition to "key word" reminders about the main ideas and supporting ideas to be covered in your speech, you can also place visual aid cues and delivery reminders on your notes cards: "Show Visual Aid #2 Now," "Don't rush! Speak slowly," etc. You will need to experiment with delivery outlines and note cards to determine which type of delivery aid works best for you.

Fourth, DO NOT WRITE OUT COMPLETE SENTENCES ON YOUR DELIVERY OUTLINE OR NOTE CARDS! Do not give yourself the opportunity to "read" your speech to your audience. You may be tempted to include complete sentences in your delivery outline because you are afraid you might forget something. Resist this temptation. Once complete sentences are placed in your delivery outline or on your delivery note cards, you will likely resort to "reading" these sentences to your audience if you get nervous. The only words on your delivery outline should be key words and phrases to help you remember the ideas of your speech.

STAY RELAXED AND CHILL OUT

FIGURE **9.30**

Delivery outlines can contain delivery reminders.

Now that we have reviewed how to prepare your delivery note cards, here are some tips about using them during the delivery of your speech. Practice delivering your speech using your note cards and presentation aids. You need to practice manipulating these items during your speech. Hold your note cards in one hand, not both. (You want to be able to make hand gestures.) You can place your note cards on a table or podium in front of you, but pick them up and look at them if you need to. (It is more distracting to the audience if you are trying to peer down at the note cards from several feet away.) Your main focus should be on your audience—keep your eyes on them. Do not look at your note cards if you do not need to. If you have internalized your speech properly, you should only need to glance at your note cards a few times throughout your entire speech.

During your extemporaneous speech, the audience will be aware that you are sometimes referring to your delivery note cards. They will also focus their attention on your presentations aids when you ask them to do so. However, the focus of your speech is not your delivery outline or note cards. The focus of your speech is not your presentation aids. The focus of your speech is you and the message you have to share with your audience.

SUMMARY

In the first part of this chapter, you learned about eight visual elements and eight aural elements of delivery. You now know that your audience *sees* your: 1) use of space, 2) posture, 3) lower body movement, 4) upper body movement, 5) hand gestures, 6) facial expressions, 7) eye contact, and 8) personal appearance. When you speak, your audience *hears* your 1) pitch, 2) rate, 3) volume, 4) enunciation, 5) pronunciation, 6) accent, 7) voice quality, and 8) verbal clutter.

In the second part of this chapter, you learned the strengths and weaknesses of the four primary delivery methods (impromptu, manuscript, memorized, and extemporaneous delivery), and you learned when it was appropriate and inappropriate to use each method.

If you have assimilated the information in this chapter, you now have the knowledge you need to become a complete, well-rounded public speaker. You have the potential to both prepare and *deliver* an excellent speech. However, this potential can only be realized if: 1) you have the motivation to develop your delivery skills and 2) you have an effective method for developing these skills.

It can be overwhelming to consciously think about all of the elements of delivery when you are in the middle of a speech. If you find yourself "freezing up" or struggling with delivery because you are trying to keep track of all the different delivery elements, focus your mind back on your speech message. You do not want to forget *what* you have to say because you are so worried about *how* you are saying it.

To quickly improve your delivery skills, you should record and observe your speech performances so you can analyze how you are using your body and voice and then make necessary adjustments in your future speeches. You should also observe and listen to good public speakers. Use these public speakers as learning models. As you observe and listen to excellent public speakers, you will find yourself unconsciously incorporating many of their effective delivery techniques. However, seek to develop your own delivery style—what works for another speaker may not work for you.

Your public speaking instructor, with the aid of this textbook, can help you develop the knowledge and skills you need to deliver a speech effectively. You need to provide the motivation and desire. Can you deliver?

Review Questions

❶ What are the four major types of delivery you can use for a public speech?

❷ What are the drawbacks of each major type of delivery?

❸ When should you use the different delivery methods?

❹ What are eight visual elements of delivery?

❺ What are eight aural elements of delivery?

Glossary

Accent or dialect: Regional variations in oral pronunciation.

Aural elements of delivery: What you hear when a speaker speaks.

Delivery: The fifth canon of Rhetoric. Presenting your speech to your audience.

Enunciation: How clearly you say the sounds of your words.

Extemporaneous delivery: One of the four major methods of delivering a speech. Extemporaneous speakers plan and prepare their speeches ahead of time, but they do not speak from a manuscript.

Impromptu delivery: One of the four major methods of delivering a speech. Impromptu speakers deliver their speeches with little or no preparation.

Inflection: Another name for pitch. When you raise or lower the pitch of your voice, you change your voice inflection.

Manuscript delivery: One of the four major methods of delivering a speech. Manuscript speakers read their speeches word-for-word from a manuscript.

Memorized delivery: One of the four major methods of delivering a speech. Speakers commit a speech to memory, and then they recite the speech from memory word-for-word.

Monotone voice: A voice that has no pitch variation.

Paralanguage: The nonverbal but vocal elements of oral delivery, such as sighs, grunts, groans, and tone of voice.

Pitch: How high or low a voice sounds.

Posture: The way a person holds their body when sitting or standing.

Pronunciation: How correctly you say your words.

Rate: How fast or slow you say your words. Speaking rate is usually determined by the number of words you speak per minute.

Verbal clutter: Another name for vocalized pauses. Filler words that clutter your verbal messages.

Visual elements of delivery: What you see when a speaker speaks.

Vocalized pauses: Filler words that are vocalized to avoid silence or pauses.

Volume: How loudly or softly you speak.

MAKING AND USING PRESENTATION AIDS

Andrea D. Thorson-Hevle

Learning Objectives

CHAPTER 10

❶ Usefulness and roles of presentation aids.

❷ Deciding which types of presentation aids to use.

❸ Knowing when to use presentation aids.

❹ Effectively using and managing presentation aids

Presentation aids are devices that serve to clarify, exemplify, explain, and support a given speech. Presentation aids can be visual, audio, audio/visual, and even sensory. Although the speech should always remain the star, presentation aids are essential and can provide some of the most memorable moments of a speech. This chapter provides information on the different types of presentation aids, when to use them, and how to use them effectively. However, if you are thinking about using presentation aids during a speech in class, you should always consult your instructor regarding their specific requirements and suggestions for presentation aids for your in-class speeches.

The presentation aid should be thought of as a supporting performer. It has its role, at times that role is significant, but that actor/actress (presentation aid) should never steal the spotlight from the main actor/actress (the speaker). This means they need to fulfill a function within your speech, but they should not become more important than the speech. You may be wondering why presentation aids are important. What could a little board with some picture on it, or a graph in a PowerPoint presentation really offer? The answer is, if the presentation aid is done poorly, nothing. However, if the presentation aid is used properly and with purpose, everything! Visual aids can be the final element needed to ensure your audience is swayed in the "right" direction.

There are many reasons presentation aids are important. Fundamentally, they are important because they provide further explanation, illustration, and clarification. They also increase audience interest and they are an alternative way of understanding and emphasizing a point. Presen-

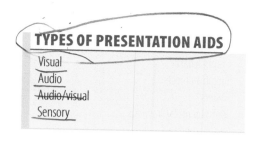

TYPES OF PRESENTATION AIDS

Visual
Audio
Audio/visual
Sensory

tation aids appeal to a different part of your audience. As we know, different people learn differently and as such different people are persuaded by different approaches. Listening to an eight-minute or hour-long speech can be tedious, and they may tune out the moment they get a little confused with the language the speaker uses. In this situation, having a presentation aid can be the apparatus that brings those audience members back to life. There are different types of presentation aids: visual, sensory, audio/visual, and technological/software-based.

Visual aids (VAs) are a type of presentation tool used to provide support to a speech. Examples of visual aids include graphs, charts, posters, models, drawings, photos, images, and tangible objects you show the audience. Visual aids make a topic or concept that seemed theoretical, rare, or otherwise seem real. Words can convey a great amount of emotion and generate empathy, but a visual aid can provide that last bit of information needed to make the point and bring an audience to full emotional investment.

Now, what can visual aids offer that actual words cannot? I once had a student give a persuasive speech urging the audience to quit drinking energy drinks. One of her points was that energy drinks actually have an excessive amount of unhealthy sugar in them. She compared and found energy drinks have substantially more sugar than soda (pop for those of us from the North) and even Kool-Aid! This was clearly interesting to the audience, but it hadn't really deterred anyone yet. She then brought out a poster board, on which she had glued various types of drinks from tea, soda, coffee, and energy drinks. Underneath each type of drink she had a plastic bag with sugar in it. Each bag was full of the amount of sugar that is typically found in each drink.

When the students were able to see the disgustingly large amount of sugar they were consuming they were stopped in their tracks. To add further precautionary power, she tossed one of the bags to an audience member whom had previously admitted to consuming several energy drinks a day and who argued he thought they were actually healthy. The young man held the heavy bag of sugar in his hand with shock, embarrassment, and disgust. "I guess I won't be drinking these anymore," the student replied. Now that was a great use of a visual aid! The speaker was able to actually convince an avid energy drink consumer to change his behaviors through the visual appeal. Her words alone had not convinced him, but a sack full of sugar went a long way.

FIGURE 10.1

Visual aids are a public speaker's good friend; they are supportive, illustrative, and back you up.

There are several different types of VAs and we discuss each one in depth. Some types of VAs are simple, easy to create, clear, and straightforward. Others are more complex, requiring technological understanding and equipment. Each type has its rewards and risks. The right visual aid will have a tremendous effect on your speech.

GRAPHS AND CHARTS

Graphs and charts are unique visual aids because they are able to communicate information in a way that other visual aids cannot. **Graphs and charts** can show trends, demonstrate complex numerical data, display information over a long period of time, and demonstrate relationships. There are several types: bar graph, line graph, pie chart, doughnut chart, pictogram, table, flow chart, and picture chart are the most common. This is by no means a comprehensive list of all charts and graphs out there, but it is the commonly used and most likely to be useful for your presentations in a public speaking course.

BAR CHART :

A bar chart should be used when you want to compare two or more individual things in a simple and direct way. A bar chart will show two or more different categories next to each other, which makes for a fast comparison and understanding. Consider the bar chart depicted in Figure 10.2. You can see how the bar chart is helpful in determining which groups are doing what and how much of it.

© Fisheess, 2013. Used under license from Shutterstock, Inc.

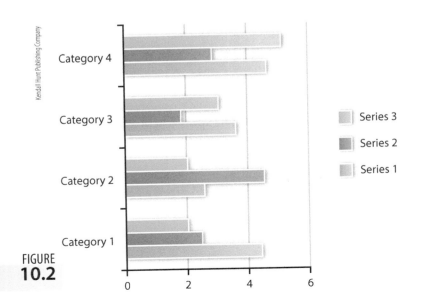

Kendall Hunt Publishing Company

FIGURE 10.2

Legend: Series 3, Series 2, Series 1

LINE CHART

A line chart is best to use when you want to illustrate that a trend exists. Line charts show data at equal intervals. A simple line chart will have two variables, one is shown on the *x* axis, and the other variable is depicted on *y* axis. If you want to display multiple trends, you can use a line chart to show the correlation of trends for different groups. If you do this, please be sure to use different colors for each line. Using different colors ensures the audience will not get confused. I used the same data that was used in the bar graph example to construct the line graph depicted in Figure 10.3. You can see how for this information the line graph provides a different way of displaying the same data. The information is distributed in a similar, yet different way. You can often use any number of graphs or charts for your information. I recommend making a couple and seeing which one shows your findings in the best way.

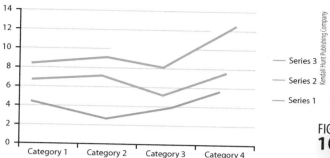

FIGURE 10.3

PIE CHART:

A pie chart is best to use when proportion is a point you are trying to demonstrate. It only contains one data series and as such, it is highly useful if you are trying to explain one major concept. A pie chart shows the parts of a greater whole out of one-hundred percent.

DOUGHNUT CHART:

A doughnut chart is very similar to a pie chart, except as you might guess at the center, which means it can illustrate several different data series at a time unlike the pie chart. At the center of the round chart is another ring; each ring represents another data series. In the doughnut chart below each color represents a quarter of the year. There are three rings so we are showing the results over three years. You can see what quarter did the best which year and compare.

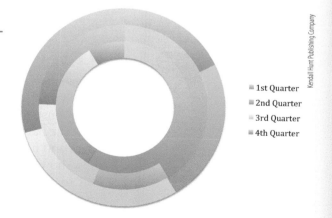

■ 1st Quarter
■ 2nd Quarter
■ 3rd Quarter
■ 4th Quarter

PICTOGRAPH

A pictograph uses a series of photos as symbols for ideas. Because of our society's recent affinity toward pictures and icons, this type of graphical representation has become popular. The benefits of using A pictogram for a VA, is that it appeals to audiences that like pictures and those who learn best through pictures. Pictograms are also nice because they can really jazz up a normally boring chart. Pictograms can even add a bit of humor. You have likely seen many pictographs in your life especially during your elementary school years.

TABLE

A table uses columns and rows to provide information. Usually tables contain words or numbers. Tables are intended to make summarizing, comparing, or contrasting information simple. Consider for example the table below where the costs of two cell phone plans are compared.

Provider	Carrier A	Carrier B
Cost	$69.99 + $10 for each additional line	$49.99 + $19.99 for each additional line
Speed/feature	3G	4G
Extras	Free navigation and hot spot	Free hot spot and access to more applications

FLOW CHART

A flow chart is an excellent choice for a visual aid when you need to demonstrate a step-by-step process. They are great for illustrating stages and a nice organized way to show how one thing can or will lead to another. Hierarchal structures are common with flow charts. There are many ways to create a flow chart. Be creative.

GUIDELINES FOR CHARTS AND GRAPHS

Use color! The first tip in making charts and graphs is to use color and use color effectively. Charts and graphs in black and white are boring and confusing. Color can make a statement and clearly define the areas of interest. Use the more captivating or bold color on the concept you most want you audience to pay attention to.

Use lighter, less bright or bold colors on the areas that are not the center of attention but still need to be displayed. Use colors in high contrast. For instance, if you choose light pink, medium pink and dark pink it would be more difficult to see what you want the audience to pay attention to and what is important.

You also want to consider the words that you choose. If you can shorten the description of an item and not lose its identification by doing so, then do it! For instance, on the above graph, notice how clear it is. The audience knows exactly where they should be looking in the first option. In the other option there is far too much information being communicated at once. The audience won't know what to look at and will likely give up trying to figure it out. Remember the simpler the better; graphs can be confusing so keep it simple and clear.

ALWAYS . . .

Use color
Keep it short
Make it big!

The third tip for making a great chart or graph is to make it big enough! This is very important. You may have created the most visually appealing, accurate, amazing graph, but if your audience can't see it then it has no value. The bigger your audience, the bigger your graph must be. If you are going to be delivering a speech in an auditorium or a lecture hall then a simple poster board graph is not sufficient. In that case, you should consider using handouts. If you had planned on showing graphs to the audience you should consider putting the graphs on the actual handouts and simply referring to them during your speech. Alternatively, you may want to use an overhead or PowerPoint projection to help with the size difficulty.

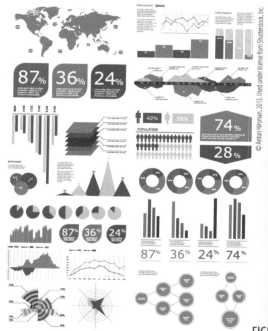

If your audience has to strain for even a few seconds to see what you are trying to show them, they will stop trying, become irritated, or even disconnect from your presentation entirely.

Avoid using too much information on one aid.

FIGURE 10.4

Always remember the more complicated your chart or graph, the bigger it must be as well. You should make all important graph lines thick enough to be seen from all the way in the back of the room. You should always inquire about the size of the room before making your graph,

TANGIBLE OBJECTS

Be safe
Pick the right moment
Have a plan
Make sure it's worth it!

chart, or any visual aid for that matter. An important tip: If your audience has to strain for even a few seconds to see what you are trying to show them, they will stop trying, become irritated, or even disconnect from your presentation entirely.

TANGIBLE OBJECTS/PROPS

Tangible objects or props are just a fancy way of referring to any object or item you bring to show the audience. Do you remember the days of show and tell? Wasn't it so much better to bring in your pet spider than to just tell the class about it? Tangible objects are great for letting the audience see what you are talking about and bring your speech to life.

For instance, when I was in college, I gave a demonstration speech on oral health. One of my points was how to tell a good toothbrush from a harmful toothbrush. I explained to the class how to identify the good from the bad toothbrushes. When I actually passed out the good toothbrush to everyone, I also had a picture of the bad type on the screen for the audience to compare. My point was made much more quickly. I also let students take a toothbrush home with them. If you can provide something for your audience to take home with them, they are more likely to remember your speech.

One minor caution for these types of visual aids is potential risks to safety. Take the spider example, if you plan to bring an actual deadly spider to class in an attempt to reinforce how we can identify this dangerous spider, it would be important to ensure that the deadly spider was in a safe and secure cage.

There are some general rules you will want to keep in mind when using a tangible object.

THREE GUIDELINES FOR USING TANGIBLE OBJECTS AS VISUAL AIDS

1. **Reveal your object at the right time**. You need to pick the best moment to show us your object. Make sure that the unveiling of your item at that particular time is ideal for your speech. You may want to use it as an attention-getter, a closing device, or to exemplify a point that you feel your words inadequately describe.

   You also want to consider how the object will impact pathos and adjust to make that object have as big of impact as possible. If you are using the object purely for explanation purposes, make sure you use it during the point in the speech that you are explaining the concept.

2. **Make sure you have a plan.** Prior to your speech, consider how you will introduce your item. Where will you put it? How will you put it away? The use of the object should be fluid and seamless. An object is a great visual aid, but if the speaker keeps the object visible the entire speech, or worse, holds the item for the entire speech, it becomes a distraction. Holding visual aids can also significantly hinder a speaker's ability to gesture.

For example, Joe delivered a polished, researched, organized, and perfectly constructed speech about eating organic foods. But, Joe made one mistake, which made it impossible for his audience to take him seriously, damaged his pathos, and ruined his delivery grade. As his attention-getting device in the introduction of his speech, Joe held up two apples for the class to consider. He asked them which apple was organic and which was genetically modified with a virus and reptile DNA. This was a great attention gaining moment.

The students examined the apples. One was clearly three times the size of the other, it was glossy, and was a solid red compared to the inconsistent coloring and dull nature of the other. Many of the students guessed correct. The larger, brighter, glossy apple was the genetically modified one. This was brilliant! It got everyone interested and engaged. Students were whispering with intrigue. The student continued onto his first point, and then his second, and then his third. During all this time he still had the apples in hands! He delivered an eight-minute speech carrying one giant apple and one mini apple in each of his hands! At one point he even switched them from one hand to another, rubbed them, and tried to stick one in his pocket (without luck).

The class giggled at his inability to gesture when he tried. They laughed when he realized what he had done but had nowhere to put the apples. At the point he realized the apples were an issue, he was at the far end of the room, away from the desk he had originally kept the apples. In order to place the apples back on the desk, he would have to walk in front of the class about forty feet and turn his back to the audience (a big no-no in public speaking). It was easy to see that he was in a state of anxiety over holding the apples, and wondered if the walk was worth the embarrassment and distraction. Meanwhile, he was quickly forgetting his speech due to all the stress, sweating from his brow, and had begun a nervous sway.

What this student needed to do to avoid all of this was have a plan. Before the speech ever began Joe should have decided where and when he was going to use the apples and when he would need to put them down. He would need to plan how he was going to get rid of the apples in a confident, nondistracting way, at the right time. You see, even the cleverest visual aids can ruin your speech if you don't think them through.

3. <u>Make sure it's worth it</u>! I can't tell you how many times I have had a student give a speech with a single photo as their visual aid. Photos are great. They are wonderful visual aids, but only if they are used in the proper way. If you give a speech and have a single photo as your visual aid, do not pass it around the class for all to see. One, it takes too much time. Second, a photo isn't all that interesting when you are waiting three minutes to finally see it. And, third, it would be better placed in a presentation slide or under an overhead projector so that all could see the photo at the exact same moment and it could also be magnified to more greatly validate your point.

If it appears you have used a tangible object just for the sake of having one, you also lose points with your audience. You don't want to hurt your credibility (ethos) over a visual aid choice. The audience will appreciate a speaker who takes the time to determine which type of visual aid is best for that given speech, at that given venue, on that given subject. Be sure to consider all the factors and be sure it's worth it. Can you imagine passing about a photo or two to an audience of three hundred? How on Earth would anyone stay interested? Well, they wouldn't.

POSTER BOARD/LARGE IMAGE BOARD

When you hear "poster board" you may be thinking about your seventh grade science project in which you had this giant board that folded at each end so that at just the right moment you could reveal the earth shattering results of your brilliant experiment. The poster boards referred to in speech-making are not like that. **Poster boards** in speech-making are large poster boards that are two-sided. One side is left blank and the other side has an image or stimulating visual that enhances, explains, exemplifies, or illustrates a point in a speaker's speech. Often speakers have several boards. They may use a board at each point in their speech or several boards at one point or scattered throughout.

There is no rule about when and how many you can or cannot have. Rather, it is important to follow the rules that you should only use the aid when you need it in order to make your point or enhance your persuasive power. Too many boards can become distracting, but the right amount can have a great impact on your speech. While there is no magic number of boards to use in a given speech, there are many rules and guidelines for this type of visual aid and for good reason. A poorly constructed, unpolished, messy, overwhelming poster can ruin a brilliant speech in seconds.

Let me first start by reminding you that you should always consult with your professor for their expectations. Some professors do not even allow poster boards to be used as a visual aid while others require it. A poster board does have some great advantages. A poster board can be taken with you and does not require electricity or some technology to make it work. You never have to worry about the Internet being down, a "clicker" not working, a slide formatting issue, or a picture all of a sudden disappearing from your PowerPoint presentation.

FIGURE 10.5 Poster boards.

The disadvantages to a poster board are ironically similar to the advantages. Using a poster board doesn't involve technology, which seems to be the visual aids that audiences today are looking for. Poster boards can run the risk of looking "homemade," in a bad way, whereas a technology aid looks sleek and professional. The key to using poster board visual aids is to follow the rules.

POSTER BOARDS

Big is best
Use simple words
Limit images
Professional quality
Clear images

GUIDELINES FOR POSTER BOARD VISUAL AIDS

BIG IS BEST

Consider the size of the audience, the size of the room, and the height at which you will display it. The person at the very back of the room should be able to easily see your poster and understand exactly what the point of it is.

If for even a moment the person in the back has to strain to see, read, or decipher your poster, you have lost them. An example of a good visual aid would be when a student painted a big strawberry on her poster board. It was beautiful and looked quite yummy. It took up about ninety percent of the poster board space. She soon removed a section of the middle part of the strawberry to reveal a fish and bacteria underneath. The fish and bacteria were large and looked quite unsavory. This visual aid was great! It was a simple image easily seen and clearly made her point about genetically modified foods containing things that do not naturally occur in our foods. In this case a fish and bacteria in a strawberry.

USE SIMPLE WORDS ONLY

You should never, ever, ever, ever use full sentences or long fragments on a poster board. Too many words are overwhelming and even annoying to an audience. If you must use words, then keep it simple; single terms are best. Do not use your poster as an alternative note card. Overloading your poster board only hurts your credibility and underutilizes a great opportunity to appeal to your audience with emotion.

DO NOT USE MULTIPLE IMAGES ON ONE BOARD

One picture per board is ideal. If you are giving a speech persuading the audience to adopt dogs you shouldn't show us twenty-five pictures of different dogs all over the board. A good board will have one nice solid big picture of a dog that looks lovable and hungry for love. You may even want to have a couple boards, but never more than one image.

When a poster has too many images on it, the audience doesn't know which one to look at. From far away, a poster board with multiple images can blur together, look messy, unplanned, and even harm your ethos and pathos. Pick your best images and place them on separate boards.

The exception to this rule is if you are showing a before and after set of images. Even then, you should evaluate the cost of placing two images on one aid for the audience to process and be sure the advantage is worth the risk. The advantage is ease of comparison. The disadvantage is the images must be sized down in order to fit both images on a single board. This means it may be more difficult for certain people to see your board. Generally, if you have a small enough room you can put two images on a single board, but you need to ensure that they are clear and visible from the farthest corner of the room.

I once had a student give a speech on drinking and driving. His visual aid was a poster board with about twenty images of cars and human bodies after car crashes involving intoxicated drivers. Up close these images were startling, disgusting, terrifying, but from where the audience was sitting, the poster board might as well have been a finger-painting by a two year old. From far away, all you could see was a blur of colors. Not only did the pictures not make an impact because there was too many of them, but it also hurt the success of the speech overall. If the student had selected just one single image and placed it on the board in full-board size, the speech would have been much more impactful and persuasive.

Make it look professional. If you are going to hand draw a graph, chart, word or otherwise, you need to make sure they look nice. Use a ruler to draw lines and mark where items should go. Draw everything out in light pencil first so you can see any mistakes. Be sure everything is centered and evenly placed. Make sure you buy an extra board in case you make a mistake. Bottom line, you are giving a speech in college not in a fourth grade class, so make it look college level. You do not want your board to hurt your appeals to logos, ethos, and pathos.

Only use quality images. Sometimes you will find a perfect picture for your speech. But when you print it off in a size big enough for the occasion, it gets fuzzy or pixilated. Many speakers will use it anyway, and to their detriment. Do not ever use a photo or image that became disproportional or fuzzy from maximizing its size. Be sure to double check that your image is clear and easily seen from the farthest spot in the room in advance of your speech.

TRANSPARENCIES

© chungking, 2013. Used under license from Shutterstock, Inc.

Transparencies are see-through thin plastic sheets that you can write on with removable or permanent pen. They are used under a magnifying apparatus and a bright light, which together transfers a magnified version of whatever is on the sheet to a wall or screen. To be quite honest, transparencies are seen as a bit "old school." They are what we used before we had PowerPoint, or Internet and computers in general. So, why am I teaching you about this dinosaur? Well, because sometimes old things are still great things and because sometimes technology will not be available or will fail you and you need to have a backup plan—transparencies are brilliant little backup plans. Transparencies also have a unique advantage in that you can write on them while you are presenting your speech. For certain speeches, this is a great advantage.

There are some avoidable disadvantages you should be aware of that come along with using transparencies. The nonpermanent markers can smudge. Be sure to hold your hand in a way to avoid this. If you print the transparencies from a copier, be sure to buy the transparency sheets that are safe for copies. Some copiers/printers can heat the sheets to a point that they actually melt. To adjust the focus you have to turn knobs that tend to be either hard to turn or really loose. You may also have to adjust the focus for each sheet. If there are no focus knobs, you have to actually move the projector forward and back to achieve a clear image, which you will need to practice before your speech. Visit the Online portion of this chapter to learn about ARMs and other projection-based aids you may like.

HANDOUTS

Handouts are basically any paper, pamphlet, or paper based information item you provide your audience and that they are encouraged to keep you audience's attention. Handouts are a nice option and also a great "in addition to" type of visual aids, which means they are nice in addition to some other form of presentation aid. Handouts are intended to provide additional information to your audience that they can consider during your presentation or when they go home.

For instance, a student gave a persuasive speech on the effects of alcoholism and had a great handout. One of her main points was the effect on relationships. Her handout had a simple quote on the top that demonstrated how greatly alcoholism affects children and other loved ones. She also had a mini "are you, or is your friend an alcoholic?" questionnaire. She followed the questionnaire with two support groups in town intended for anyone needing help for their addictions and two places in town that people could go to for anyone who has been harmed by an alcoholic. She also provided national help lines at the very bottom of the handout.

4X9 RACK CARD BROCHURE TEMPLATE

FRONT

BACK

FIGURE
10.6 Handouts.

4x9 RACK CARD TEMPLATE

FRONT

BACK

FIGURE
10.7 Handouts allow the audience to continue learning even after the speech is over.

The student's handout was intended to help the audience long after the speech was over and it was very effective. Her handout considered the various possible audiences, those with alcoholism those who know someone with a problem, and those who want to know the signs so they can access themselves or others in the future. She also managed to use pathos, logos, and ethos appeals in one simple handout.

FIVE GUIDELINES FOR USING HANDOUTS

Cite any sources. Any information taken from other sources needs to be given credit on the document. This includes statistics, images, quotes, etc.

Plan when you will pass them out. Be sure the time you choose to hand them out is appropriate. It is advised to pass out handouts before the speech begins if you will refer to them in your speech. Just politely ask they remain face down until you ask they be turned over. This ensures less distraction and more focus on you.

Consider when it will be read. If your handout's purpose is for the audience to have something to refer to later on, then you need to provide it once the speech has ended. You also want to be sure the information on the handout is clear and easy to understand since they will be reading it once you are no longer available for clarification.

Make it inviting. Your handout needs to be visually appealing and conform to the general principle for any visual aids: be clear, be simple, be interesting, use color (if you can—we know color copies are expensive so don't feel tremendous pressure to do this in college unless your instructor requires it, but just know that in the real world color is essential).

Have a clear purpose and stick to it. Is the purpose to give them startling statistics and information to further inform the audience? Is the purpose to provide more persuasion? Is the purpose to provide them with contact information or options of where they can go?

WHITEBOARDS/CHALKBOARDS

© CLS Design, 2013. Used under license from Shutterstock, Inc.

FIGURE 10.8 Chalkboards have their disadvantages, but they can be useful.

Whiteboards and chalkboards are very similar. They are large boards found commonly in classrooms and business meeting rooms on which a speaker can write. **Chalkboards** are the old messy version of whiteboards that use chalk to write on a black surface and can be wiped clean but leave behind a dusty residue that transfers onto clothing easily. **Whiteboards** permit users to use multiple colored markers, which lessen transfer to clothes and wipe off nicely to give the audience a truly clean background, whereas the blackboards, once wiped, remain in a used state, with smudges and white debris everywhere.

These aids are really nice to use when you need to spontaneously respond to an audience member's questions that requires demonstration. It is also great to use when technology is not available or has been historically unreliable. If any of your other aids fail you at the last moment, the board will be an excellent stand in. When you know the room has a whiteboard or chalkboard come prepared just in case you may need to use them by bringing a whiteboard marker or chalk with you. The other reason this is a great aid is that it can allow you to work with the audience. For instance, if you want to get the audience involved and ask them to brainstorm and toss out a bunch of terms, you can write these terms on the board and interact with the audience.

White boards are great because you can use color, wipe it clean quickly, and there is no dust.

FIGURE **10.9**

Although they do have their advantages, whiteboards and chalkboards are not the ideal presentation aids because they require you to break a very important rule of public speaking: do not turn your back to your audience. In order to write (in a way that doesn't look like a child wrote it) you must turn your back to the audience. If this happens throughout your speech your audience may disconnect. Once you lose the power of eye contact, you open yourself up for the audience to disengage. Another drawback to these aids is that they require you to spell perfectly. If you spell a word wrong in front of your audience, it can be devastating!

AUDIO/VISUAL

Audio and visual aids are those aids that have one or both audio capability (hearing) and/or a visual capability (seeing). Audio clips are recordings of sound whether it be a person's voice, music, or otherwise. An example of an audio aid would be a recording of two birds singing (you can't see them, you can only hear). Video clips are parts of a recorded movie, television program, or home video, which can greatly impact your audience's attention. An example would be a video of two birds singing. They are actually used often as an attention-getter in speeches. They are also great to enhance the audience's understanding of an idea. These can also be used in conjunction with SMART boards and software-based aids like PowerPoint, which can make a presentation look very polished and professional.

Bring backup cables when you are using audio/visual aids.

FIGURE **10.10**

The drawback to this aid is that it can require a lot of preparation and time. It can be a long process finding a specific clip and recording it onto another device. It can also end up having poor recording quality, which can result in the speaker looking unprofessional or underprepared. They can also quickly become too much for the audience. A clip that is too long can make an audience tune out and lose interest. If possible, keep clips to no more than one minute, fifteen seconds. Research suggests that after that point audiences tend to lose focus and become disinterested.

SENSORY AIDS

Sensory aids are aids that appeal to the senses of the audience. These aids focus the audience in a different way. For instance, a sensory aid could be allowing your audience to smell certain items in order to enhance your point. Going back to our previous discussion of GMO, if you are giving us a speech and one of the main points is on the benefits of growing your own food at home, you could place several home grown strawberries in a container and several genetically modified or nonorganic strawberries in another. Having students close their eyes and simply smell the two bowls is a sensory experience and thus a sensory aid. They will quickly find the homegrown strawberries have a stronger, sweeter smell to them. You can see how these aids are wonderful in certain situations.

You will want to consider how and when to use this aid. You want a plan that includes knowing whether or not there may be a mess and if you need to bring cleaning materials in case there is an accident. You will want to practice ahead of time and see how long the activity will take. You want to consider how many items you will need given the size of the audience and the time you have to give the speech. You also want to consider any potential risks to allergies if you bring foods in. Additionally, allow people to opt out of the activity if they are allergic or simply do not want to participate. For instance, my mother is highly allergic to lilies. If she was a member of an audience where a speaker was giving a speech about how to make beautiful flower arrangements and one of the many flowers present in the room was a lily, my mother would immediately have a reaction regardless of whether it was in front of her or not. In many sensory aids cases it is wise to address the audience and ask if anyone may have an allergy to the items you have brought and, if so, be prepared to accommodate.

FIGURE
10.11 Sensory aids add impact and reinforce your ideas in a unique way.

TECHNOLOGICAL/SOFTWARE-BASED PRESENTATION AIDS

SMART BOARDS

If you have a SMART board in your classroom or the place you will deliver your speech, the possibilities are endless. SMART boards are amazing visual aids that are fundamentally interactive whiteboards. A SMART board has the capabilities of the everyday whiteboard and also the video, audio, interactive abilities of a touch screen computer. The integrated system allows an entire audience to see and interact or specifically allow several students to use the board at a time. The SMART board permits the teacher to control the projector from their computer or anywhere in the room for many technologies. SMART boards are one of the newest innovations used for business, education, and even government agencies.

FIGURE 10.12

Smart Boards let an audience become involved in your speech and ideas.

The reason technology is a wonderful visual aid choice is it allows you to explain, exemplify, and then interact with the concepts you are teaching! You can use the SMART board as a standard computer, you can show a video from YouTube or a PowerPoint slide, you can even show a movie and at the same time be writing on it all! These boards are considered great for audience participation, engagement, and to increase the appeals to different learning styles. The presentation quality is high and the attractiveness of the product has been known to keep audiences participating and listening faster and longer than the more traditional options.

GUIDELINES FOR USING A SMART BOARD

Don't make it too complicated for your specific audience and determine what will be overwhelming for some audiences and underwhelming for others.

FIGURE 10.13

Software-based aids can simplify complex ideas and illustrate your points.

Make it an inviting process not an intimidating one. Because the audience can come up to the board and answer questions or participate in an interactive activity, you want to be sure to provide an environment of empathy, compassion, and humor. This makes the audience feel like a wrong answer is not a big deal and mistakes can be fun instead of demeaning or embarrassing.

Conform to the general rules of the other devices that you are co-using. For instance, if you are using a PowerPoint along with the SMART board, be sure to follow the general rules for PowerPoint as well as the rules for a SMART board.

GENERAL TIPS FOR SOFTWARE PRESENTATIONS

Make sure your presentation works on the computer you will be using the day of your speech.

Double check that all images are visible. Sometimes images will translate as question marks or not show up at all.

Practice your speech with the technology. This means using a clicker or clicking manually. If this is not seamless it hurts your credibility.

SOFTWARE-BASED TECHNOLOGIES

PowerPoint refers to a software program created by Microsoft that allows a user to create multiple slides that are projected onto a screen. The slides can have images, text, embedded links to the Internet, video, audio, and more. PowerPoint and other presentation software (Prezi, Keynote) can be an amazing tool in keeping your audience on track and interested. However, as wonderful as it can be, it is still the most frequently misused and poorly utilized presentation aids.

DESIGN PRINCIPLES

Repetition
Alignment
Proximity
Edit nonessentials
Creativity
The rule of five to eight

You will want to use this type of presentation aid when you feel it will more effectively explain your idea, is necessary for understanding, equipment is present, and when you feel comfortable with the technology. I have listed some major things to consider when making a PowerPoint presentation.

When creating a presentation using PowerPoint, Prezi, or otherwise, you should approach it will it with visual style in mind. The first design principle is repetition. Speakers need to consistently remind their audience of key ideas. Previously in this book we discussed the importance of previewing the main points of your speech, transitioning into each main point, and reviewing all the main points again at the end. In short, we have already discussed the importance of repetition in public speaking.

Repetition is also important in technology presentations like PowerPoint and Prezi. Repetition refers to the restatement of a concept multiple times at different points in time. You should have a preview slide and a review slide in most informative and persuasive speeches. If you are taking a class, clarify the requirements with your professor, but the general rule is to have a preview and review slide at minimum. These slides give the audience a map of where you are going and what they have covered and results in a clearer understanding. The other slides should be impactful and consider the purpose of your speech, the specific audience, and the given occasion.

© jljbjbdesigns, 2013. Used under license from Shutterstock, Inc.

FIGURE 10.14 Using variations of the same image or idea can keep your presentation coordinated and consistent, but interesting instead of expected and boring.

REPETITION

You should strive for consistency in your slide themes, background, and overall look. This does not mean that every slide must be exactly the same color and have the exact same types of images. Creativity is good too and will be discussed later. You also don't want to have every single slide with the exact same image background or color background because it can cause the audience to lose focus and miss information because it becomes too expected. What I mean when I say "keep it consistent" is that your presentation should seem cohesive and you should have at least one common element present in the majority of the slides. For instance, if I was delivering a persuasive speech on volunteering at local elementary school, I might have a little crayon icon on the majority of the slides. Instead of having that icon in the exact same place and the exact same size, I would vary its presence. For example, on a slide where I have a list of five things, I could use the crayon as the bullet icon. In one slide I could set the crayon as a large background and fade it so it isn't distracting. In another slide I could have the crayon at the top header where it looks like the crayon actually wrote the heading.

PROXIMITY AND ALIGNMENT

This is just a fancy way of saying you need to make sure your items are centered on your page or placed in alignment with other items on your slide so that your slide looks planned and professional. Slides that are misaligned look sloppy and thrown together last minute. A well-aligned slide will look crisp and reflect well on the speaker. You can indicate what is most important and what is a subpoint, for instance, simply by placing things in a different way.

Proximity refers to how close items on the slide are to one another and what that communicates. Things that are close together tell the audience they are related in some way. When we put things farther apart, we are generating an idea of dissimilarity. Take for instance a title slide. On a title slide you will have the tile of your presentation, who authored it, and perhaps an image that represents the idea. If you put all this information together without a space it becomes hard to discern what is the title, who is the author, and what is important. The title of the presentation should be the largest and if there is a semicolon used and the title continues, simply make that part smaller and put in underneath the title. Your name as the author should be significantly smaller, you are not the important concept the audience needs to remember, your speech is.

© DT10, 2013. Used under license from Shutterstock, Inc.

Try to use space to your advantage. Notice in this slide there is a significant amount of white space in the lower third. This is an excellent trick. If your slide seems boring or lacks impact, use white space like this, it draws your attention to the term.

FIGURE
10.15

So your name should not only be smaller but also much farther away from the title. The spacing indicates to the audience what is most important; the title of the presentation and thus the topic. The image should be rather small on a title slide and should not steal the show but still be present and visible.

Alignment is the proper adjustment of various components that creates harmony and desirable coordination; this often refers to things in a straight line. Alignment will help your audience easily process the important information. A slide that is poorly aligned will look unprofessional and have less impact. Take the time to be sure your photos and text are aligned properly. Your software will come with various tools to help you accomplish this task. Do not rely on "eye-balling it." Your presentation software will allow you to view "grids, guides, and rulers." These tools will help you ensure your items are perfectly straight and/or properly placed. Good alignment will create a nice flow to your presentation. Experienced presenters know that images or text boxes that float without purpose on a page are one of the easiest ways to lose credibility.

HIGH QUALITY IMAGES

Images must be relevant to your subject and have a clear purpose in adding something to the presentation. The images should be easily seen and understood. This means the audience member in the back should easily see the image and understand its importance or function. If your audience has to strain to see or take time to think about what a given image means to the speech, then you have failed to use your aid well and hindered your speech in the process.

EDIT NONESSENTIALS

This means you need to examine your presentation and access what elements are not essential and do not have a clear purpose that helps your intent. Any visual clutter needs to go. Visual clutter is any information in the form of words or images that overwhelm a slide or have little purpose. The slides should be clean and easy to understand, not messy and full. Animation effects are usually ineffective and tend to be more distracting than helpful. If you animate a slide show with a noise or an image that moves, be certain it is necessary and helps your explain your point or increase your appeal to the emotions. Otherwise, transitions on slides with loud noises that occur over and over get annoying and seem juvenile.

PowerPoint slides should not have full sentences. Full sentences are reserved for the speaker. There is one small exception and this and exceptions should rarely be used. A direct quote can be a full sentence. However, if you use a quote, if must be more powerfully captured on a PowerPoint slide than if it were verbally spoken—it must be more impactful, meaningful, and effective delivered in that way. If the quote is only present to act as a fancy note card for the speaker it is not acceptable. Statistics as quotes are ineffective and useless. A great speaker can deliver a powerful quote far better than the symbols on a slide.

© ifong, 2013. Used under license from Shutterstock, Inc.

Using high quality vivid images captures your audience's attention.

FIGURE 10.16

© DT10, 2013. Used under license from Shutterstock, Inc.

PROCESS

Simple and few make a bigger statement that complicated and many. Editing your slides is a process and very important.

FIGURE 10.17

© beerlogoff, 2013. Used under license from Shutterstock, Inc.

FIGURE 10.18 Unique and creative images will pique the audience's interest.

CREATIVITY

Your presentation needs to have cohesiveness but that doesn't mean you can't put a little pizazz in there. A speaker is an artist and words and images are your tools with which you create a captivating work of art. That art can be informative, persuasive, or any number of other intents, but in its sum any speech is a form of art. It's up to the speaker to paint the canvas the way they want the audience to see it. So, amidst all these rules I just gave you, remember to also consider the artistic and creative approach to making a presentation. Creativity and imagination are incredibly powerful tools. Try to think outside the box and discover alternative ways to explain, examine, or persuade while using your presentation aid.

Again, I remind you of the most famous speeches in our history, what did they have in common? They all had passion; they all meant what they said to the core of who they were. Their words had power because it came from deep within. Allow your passion and creativity to shine through during your oral presentation and the images and technologies you use.

THE FIVE TO EIGHT RULE

There should only be about five to eight words per slide. The rule in the past was called "the rule of six" which argued there should never be more than six line lines on a given slide. There should never be more than six words on a given line. There should never be more than six words in the header. We have found that when presenters are given the option to use more words they will and often to the detriment of the audience and themselves. Please note your citation does not count in the five to eight word count.

Don't be afraid of colorful ideas.

© art4all, 2013. Used under license from Shutterstock, Inc.

FIGURE 10.19

Keeping your slide to five to eight words makes the slide impactful and also forces you to pick only the best and most relevant ideas. The five to eight rule also keeps the speaker from continually glancing or reading from the slides and using the slides as a fancy note card, which I like to call a baby blanket. You are fundamentally Linus from *Charlie Brown* when you read word-for-word from your PowerPoint slides. As Lucy might say, "Grow up, put down the baby blanket, and start presenting like a big kid."

A PRESENTATION AID CHECKLIST—ARE MY AIDS . . . ?

Big enough to see at the farthest seat in the room

Aiding my explanation or furthering my point

Used at an appropriate time

Helping my speech and not distracting from it

Professional quality

Being used effectively and competently

Appropriate for my audience

Appealing to my specific audience

Clear and consistent with other aids I use

Planned—where it will be in the room, how I will use it, and how I will manage it

POWERPOINT DESIGN

Don't Split Audience Attention	Focus Audience Attention Instead
1 Don't use the presentation as a note card	• You should know your information so well that you wouldn't need a slide to help you along the way. • The audience will be irritated with your lack of preparation and lose interest in the speech. If all of the important information is in the slides, why are you there? • Practice and know your speech instead of relying on your aids.
2 Don't use full sentences	• There is only one exception to the rule of "never use full sentences in a PowerPoint;" you may use a full sentence when that sentence is a direct quote. • If you use a direct quote, the quote needs to be relevant, memorable, and incredibly necessary.
3 Don't use bullet points	• Most of the time bullets are not necessary. • If you are demonstrating a list of things then it is okay, otherwise avoid placing bullets on everything. And remember if you don't have a #2 you can't provide a bullet for #1. Ask yourself if there is a more visually stimulating way to get points across without typing them in bullets. • Consider one word for each idea and a picture for an example.
4 Don't allow clutter	• Noise can come from unnecessary graphics or images that compete with what you are really trying to communicate.
5 Don't use multiple images per slide	• You should generally have one image on a slide. • More than this and your audience will be overstimulated and your point becomes blurred. • One image per slide is best.
6 Don't use backgrounds, themes, or templates that don't consider your needs and the needs of the audience	• Your background should not compete with your information. • Your general scheme should be clear and consistent and provide something that enhances the presentation, not takes away from it.
7 Don't use distracting fonts	• Use fonts that can be easily read from far away. • Resist the temptation to have the beautiful script and calligraphy, they just can't be seen from far away.
8 Don't use hard to see text	• Always shoot for high contrast between the color of your font and the background color.
9 Don't use fuzzy, small, odd, or watermarked images	• You may need to stretch an image to make it big enough on the slide; doing so can make the image odd and unclear. • Make sure you double check all images and be sure they can be easily seen from far away. • Never use small, disproportional, or fuzzy images. • Never use watermarked images. They scream to the audience: "Thief!"
10 Don't use multiple ideas per slide	• Each slide should have one clear idea being presented. • More than one and the audience can become overwhelmed and lost and your slide will appear messy.
11 Don't rely on text	• Limit words to five to eight per slide beyond source citations. • Ask yourself if all those words and lines are really helping your audience understand. If not, delete and reshape the slide so that it has as few words as possible but gets the point across.

The slides on the right side of the page have violated the rules. The slides on the left are constructed according to the rules. Can you locate the problems with the slides on the right?

Just say No to GMO's

© Reinhold Leitner, 2014. Used under license from Shutterstock, Inc.

Today I will demonstrate the harms associated with Genetically Modified Organisms and convince you to stop buying GMO products

© Reinhold Leitner, 2014. Used under license from Shutterstock, Inc.

The Monarch Butterfly

© , 2013. Used under license from Shutterstock, Inc.

Claimed Benefits of GMO's

- Increased Yield and Hardiness
- Conserve natural resources
- Ability to stop world hunger
- People will die without it

© Camilo Torres, 2013. Used under license from Shutterstock, Inc.

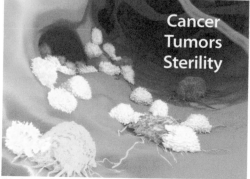

Cancer Tumors Sterility

© Juan Gaertner, 2013. Used under license from Shutterstock, Inc.

Animal studies show

GM foods cause:
Breast cancer
Liver damage
Immune disorders
Female sterility
Rapid cell growth – cancer
Death
Kidney Damage

SUMMARY

This chapter focused on teaching you the various tools available to make your speech come to life. We discussed the choices you have in presentation aids and the advantages and drawbacks to each. We addressed the standards for each type of presentation aids that must be taken into consideration and how your ethos will be adversely affected if you don't. This chapter provided information on the different types of presentation aids, when to use them, and how to use them effectively. Rules and guidelines are there for a reason, they help us create successful effective speeches. Remember, each speech purpose, topic, and occasion will determine what types of aids are appropriate, useful, and effective. Please visit the Online website and the technology guide in this book for more information.

Review
Questions

❶ How can a presentation aid enhance your speech?

❷ What are the benefits to using tangible objects? What are the drawbacks or risks?

❸ How do you know when you should use a presentation aid?

❹ What are the basic design principles you should follow for a PowerPoint presentation?

❺ What are the basic guidelines for crafting a poster board?

❻ When presentation aids are used, is the rule of simple and few best or more and complex preferred?

Glossary

Alignment: The proper adjustment of various components that creates harmony and desirable coordination; this often refers to things in a straight line.

Audio and visual aids: Have either or both an audio capability (hearing) or a visual capability (seeing).

Blackboards: Boards with a black background that are written on with chalk.

Graphs and charts: Show trends, demonstrate complex numerical data, display information over a long period of time, and demonstrate relationships.

Handouts: Any paper, pamphlet, or paper-based information item you provide your audience.

PowerPoint: A software program created by Microsoft that allows a user to create multiple slides that are projected onto a screen.

Proximity: How close items on a slide are to one another and what that communicates.

SMART board: The capabilities of the everyday white board and also the video, audio, interactive abilities of a touch screen computer.

Sensory aids: Aids that appeal to the senses of the audience.

Tangible objects: Any object or prop you bring to the speech that can be passed around the audience or given to the audience to take home with them.

Transparencies: See-through thin plastic sheets that you can write on with removable or permanent pen.

Whiteboard: Board with a white background that allows users to write on it in multiple colored dry-erase markers.

USING TECHNOLOGY: A QUICK REFERENCE GUIDE

Helen Acosta

Learning Objectives

CHAPTER 11

1. Learn what presentation technology to look for in a speaking space.

2. Reach to the cloud when presenting your speech.

3. Create technological presentation aids using the principles of good design.

4. Purge your slides of poor design choices.

5. Use mediated technology presentation aids effectively.

I was the keynote speaker at the Association for Retired Teachers Convention in San Jose. I had been booked several months in advance. When I called to confirm the week before I was told that there would be a break before my presentation, I was assured that the break would give me time to work with the tech guys to connect my laptop to their projection system. I arrived forty-five minutes before my scheduled appearance and the organizer let out an exasperated sigh, "You're late! Well, c'mon! Let's get you started." I was flustered but I smiled and went over to talk to the tech guy for my setup. The tech guy explained that one of the morning speakers had cancelled at the last minute so, instead of speaking right after lunch as planned I would speak during lunch. In other words, there was no time to set up my technology. I had to speak immediately. The situation wasn't ideal but I was hired to deliver and my reputation was on the line. It's a good thing I had a backup plan. While the organizer introduced me, I pulled just one page from the handouts I had forwarded to the organizers for the convention packets.

FIGURE 11.1

The vital page that would keep me on track was a single sheet with pictures and reminders of my presentation for my audience to take home with them. I stepped onto the stage, knowing that everything would be okay.

I got three more convention bookings from that appearance. Apparently, my presentation was more than okay.

Presentation technologies, in their current incarnation, _are a mix of multimedia hardware and_, now, most often, _cloud-based software used for audio visual enhancement of presentations._ We've recently entered an age in which much of the cloud-based software is now provided via a freemium sales model. "Freemium" means that the basic software packages that most of us need to deliver presentations tend to be provided without charge. Premium users who need loads of storage and bandwidth pay a fee but the rest of us get to use the technology for free.

In this chapter we consider:

FIGURE
11.2

- The presentation space
- The preparation process
- Presentation design
- Mediated presentation strategies
- Backup planning
- Delivery tips for presenters using technology

CONSIDER THE SPACE

While presentation technologies are really cool tools, there is some hardware that must be present in order to use these technologies. Unless you own the hardware and plan to bring it with you, you'll need to depend on your speaking venue to provide the hardware.

CONSIDER THE PREPARATION PROCESS

Cloud-based presentation technologies are exciting to use because they are more fully integrated with the Internet than the more traditional desktop presentation technologies. Best of all: Most cloud-based presentation technologies are free. However, once we get beyond the novelty, most of us will experience a typical learning curve.

QUESTIONS TO ANSWER BEFORE YOU CHOOSE A PRESENTATION TECHNOLOGY

1. What technologies will be available in the presentation space?

Computer	Large Screen TV or Projector Q3	Internet Connection/ Wi-Fi Q4	Presentation Remote Control
If not, load your presentation on your laptop, tablet, or smartphone. If there is a TV or projector in the room ask: • What types of inputs are on the device? • What types of connector cables are provided in the room? • What adapter should I bring? (Do a web search for adapters from your device to the device in the room.)	If neither is available in the room and the audience small, view the presentation slides on your laptop (no more than five to seven audience members for this option). • Images should be simple and large • Fewer, if any, words	If you won't have access to the Internet, plan to use a simplified desktop-based presentation technology like Adobe Acrobat Presentation.	High-tech solutions: • Bring your own remote • Load a free remote app onto your smartphone • Use a wireless mouse as a presentation remote
When you must provide your own device you are only limited by its power. • Presenting from an iPad or iPhone? Use Haiku or Google Presentation. • Presenting from an Android tablet or phone? Use Deck Slideshow or Google Presentation. • If your device is slower/older, use Adobe Acrobat Presentation.	If you know your entire audience will have smart devices and access to Wi-Fi, send them a link to the online meeting ahead of time so they can view your graphics while you talk with them. Most online presentation tools include an "online meeting" mode. This will allow you to advance the slides for the audience so you can hold their attention.	If you have an existing presentation save it as a PDF. Load the PDF on your device and present from the PDF.	Low-tech solution: Deputize a member of the audience to press the forward arrow each time you nod at them.

2. If any of the above are not provided will I have the time/resources to set up my own technologies?
   • If not, use a low-tech solution like a flip chart or presentation boards.

3. Will I have time to test the technology in the room where I'll present?
   • If not, use a low-tech solution like a flip chart or presentation boards.

FIGURE 11.3

LEARNING TO LOVE THE CLOUD

In a typical learning curve our reactions move from:

"This is so cool . . . oooh . . . what does this thing do?"

to

"Hmmmm . . . How did that work?"

to

"Wait, last time all I had to do was . . . DAMN . . . it didn't work! Let's try this . . . Noooooooooooooo! Why aren't you working!!! NO! NO! NO! NO!"

When we start yelling at and pleading with the computer we go into a spiral of hate. If you can replace that momentary hate with the curiosity you began with you'll be able to learn any new cloud-based technology quickly. If, however, you just reject the technology and build a fortress of anger then you'll retreat to your mental cabin in the woods and start mouthing hermit-like curses at every new technology. In other words: You will become a cantankerous curmudgeon well before you reach old age.

Before you begin using any cloud-based technology there are some issues you should be prepared for:

FIGURE 11.4

1. There is no standardized structure between cloud-based presentation technologies. Be prepared to spend an hour or two exploring and playing around with the technology before you start to prepare your presentation.
2. The technology is cloud-based. As a result, all of your work will be done on the Internet. If your Internet access is spotty, you will have problems working in the program and saving your work.
3. Each technology works well on at least one of the big four Internet browsers: Internet Explorer, Safari, Mozilla Firefox, and Google Chrome. If you are having trouble using a highly rated technology on one Internet browser, close that browser and try another. All four Internet browsers are easy to install on any computer. Just do a web search for the browser and follow the instructions on the "install now" page.
4. Every browser will encounter virtual memory issues if you work for more than an hour without saving and closing the browser. You'll know when you're encountering virtual memory issues because the program will stop working properly and you'll experience lag times between operations.
5. Cloud-based presentation technologies are all hosted and have a large but not limitless bandwidth. If you are trying to work at the same time that millions of people are working you will experience performance issues. For instance: Students often report that Prezi.com experiences issues between ten and noon on weekday mornings. So, plan to work on your presentation during less traditional hours in order to avoid workday rush hours.

FIGURE 11.5

CONSIDER DESIGN

GOOD DESIGN VS. BAD DESIGN

Good design, regardless of technology choice, follows some basic principles that have been used in Eastern art for millennia and Western art since the renaissance. Design principles in the United States came into their own from the 1950s to 1980s. Unfortunately, in the 1990s, good design in presentations was lost with the advent of PowerPoint. Everything we once knew was forgotten until we began sharing our presentations online and found our way back to the design principles that have always drawn and focused audience attention:

- Vision trumps all other senses
- Present one idea at a time
- Simple is better
- Stimulate multiple senses
- Use evocative, emotion-provoking images (featuring people)

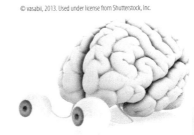

© vasabii, 2013. Used under license from Shutterstock, Inc.

VISION TRUMPS ALL OTHER SENSES

"Hear a piece of information, and three days later you'll remember 10 percent of what was said," explains developmental molecular biologist, Dr. John Medina. "But add a picture to it and you'll remember 65 percent." (Medina, 2008)

FIGURE 11.6

SHARE ONE IDEA AT A TIME

When multiple ideas are presented on a single slide we feel obliged to read the whole slide while trying to pay attention to the speaker's words as well. However, since our minds can't actually multitask but, instead turn off from one task and turn on to another, when our attention is split we don't effectively process any of the information presented, orally or visually. According to Dr.

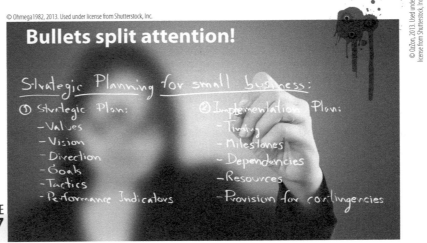

© Ohmega1982, 2013. Used under license from Shutterstock, Inc.

© OzZon, 2013. Used under license from Shutterstock, Inc.

FIGURE 11.7

Medina multitasking actually slows us down by over fifty percent and increases error rates by over fifty percent. Want your audience to process the information you share? Present one idea at a time (Medina, 2008).

SIMPLE IS BETTER

"We are biologically incapable of processing attention-rich inputs simultaneously."
—Medina, 2008

FIGURE 11.8

FIGURE 11.9

It is harder for audiences to process information presented simultaneously in oral form and written text. Your audience will get lost in the text and miss much of your message (Pass, 2003).

"Pictures beat text . . . because reading is so inefficient for us. Our brain sees words as lots of tiny pictures, and we have to identify certain features in the letters to be able to read them. That takes more time than a single image." (Medina, 2008) . . . or an image the mind interprets as a single image as in figures 11.12 and 11.13.

FIGURE 11.10

FIGURE 11.11

FIGURE 11.12

FIGURE 11.13

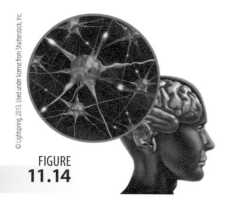

FIGURE
11.14

STIMULATE MULTIPLE SENSES

Every sensory experience we have is saved in a different place in our brains. When we connect sensory experiences together with factual and emotional support, we build a web of meaning that is easier for an audience to remember.

USE EVOCATIVE IMAGES

(rather than generalized images)

Evocative images are images that tend to cause an emotional response. People don't pay attention to boring things. If the image is generalized, doesn't evoke emotions, or connect to previous experiences, people will daydream rather than pay attention.

FIGURE
11.15

FIGURE
11.16

FIGURE
11.17

Use emotion-provoking pictures of people whenever possible. As humans, we have a natural curiosity about all other humans.

The and symbols are © Bodrillius Amadeus, 2013. Used under license from Shutterstock, Inc.

FIGURE
11.18

POWERPOINT DESIGN REMINDERS FROM CHAPTER 10

Don't Split Audience Attention	Focus Audience Attention Instead
Don't use the presentation as a note card	• You should know your information so well that you wouldn't need a slide to help you along the way. • The audience will be irritated with your lack of preparation and lose interest in the speech. If all of the important information is in the slides, why are you there? • Practice and know your speech instead of relying on your aids.
Don't use full sentences	• There is only one exception to the rule of "never use full sentences in a PowerPoint"; you may use a full sentence when that sentence is a direct quote. • If you use a direct quote the quote needs to be relevant, memorable and incredibly necessary.
Don't use bullet points	• Most of the time bullets are not necessary. • If you are demonstrating a list of things then it is okay, otherwise avoid placing bullets on everything. And remember if you don't have a 2) you can't provide a bullet for 1). Ask yourself if there is a more visually stimulating way to get points across without typing them in bullets. • Consider one word for each idea and a picture for example.
Don't allow clutter	• Noise can come from unnecessary graphics or images that compete with what you are really trying to communicate.

Don't Split Audience Attention	Focus Audience Attention Instead (continued)
Don't use multiple images per slide	• You should generally have one image on a slide. • More than this and your audience will be overstimulated and your point becomes blurred. • One image per slide is best.
Don't use backgrounds, themes, or templates that don't consider your needs and the needs of the audience	• Your background should not compete with your information. • Your general scheme should be clear and consistent and provide something that enhances the presentation, not takes away from it.
Don't use distracting fonts	• Use fonts that can be easily read from far away. • Resist the temptation to have the beautiful script and calligraphy, they just can't be seen from far away.
Don't use hard to see text	• Always shoot for high contrast between the color of your font and the background color.
Don't use fuzzy, small, odd, or watermarked images	• You may need to stretch an image to make it big enough on the slide; doing so can make the image odd and unclear. • Make sure you double check all images and be sure they can be easily seen from far away. • Never use small, disproportional, or fuzzy images. • Never use watermarked images. They scream to the audience: "Thief!"
Don't use multiple ideas per slide	• Each slide should have one clear idea being presented. • More than one and the audience can become overwhelmed and lost and your slide will appear messy.
Don't rely on text	• Limit words to five to eight per slide beyond source citations. • Ask yourself if all those words and lines are really helping your audience understand. If not, delete and reshape the slide so that it has as few words as possible but gets the point across.

FIGURE **11.19**

DESIGN CHECKLIST

- Limit words to labels and headings.
- Cite each source (small) on the slide where you'll present the information from the source.
- Use one or two evocative images per slide.
- Create enough slides so you don't have to hold notes.
- Insert blank slides when you want your audience to focus only on what you are saying.
- Avoid distractions such as unnecessary animations and/or sound effects.
- Embedded video clips should not exceed thirty seconds.

FIGURE **11.20**

For most of us, when we think of presentation technologies, the traditional PowerPoint-type slide presentation comes to mind. However, over the last decade, we've been introduced to a much wider variety of presentation technologies that have allowed us to share ideas more widely than any other time in human history. We've entered the age of the mediated presentation.

FIGURE
11.21

MEDIATED PRESENTATIONS

Computer mediated communication occurs when two or more technological devices are used. Mediated presentations are simply presentations that use computer based technologies in order to present to an audience. Mediated presentations can be found all over the Internet. Whether it's a ranting vlog on Youtube, a slidecast on slideshare, an open courseware lecture by a superstar professor, or a TED talk by a futurist with big ideas, we've all seen mediated presentations. Think back to the model of communication. The CHANNEL is the method through which the speaker and audience communicate with one another. In mediated presentations the CHANNEL is a form of electronic media (video, audio, online conference, chat, etc.).

Mediated presentations range from simple YouTube videos with a single person talking to interactive, multimedia, multimodal presentations (translation: presenter talks, audience talks, everyone can interact with and manipulate a shared desktop that includes video, graphics, and sound). There are two types of mediated communication: synchronous and asynchronous. Synchronous communication is immediate; all participants are online and communicating at the same time. Asynchronous communication has lag time between communication and participants are not online and communicating at the same time.

IMPORTANT TERMS to Understand Regarding Mediated Presentations

	Same Place	Different Place
Same time (synchronous)	**Face-to-face, simultaneous interaction** *unmediated* traditional meetings traditional classroom	**Simultaneous interaction across distances** *mediated* Chat rooms, phone/video conferencing, team editing on cloud-based technologies
Different time (asynchronous)	**Same place, different time** *mediated* Hallway bulletin boards, self-guided tours, historical markers	**Interaction across time and distance** *mediated* Online learning classrooms, discussion threads on social networks, email, texting, vlogs, blogs, online videos (and comments)

FIGURE
11.22

PREPARING FOR MEDIATED PRESENTATIONS

Your preparation process for a mediated presentation will depend on how deeply mediated the presentation is. The more distant your audience feels to you, the harder you will have to work to create a human connection with them.

When you prepare for a mediated presentation you need to use a few tricks in order to capture and keep your audience's attention:

1. Assume that your audience will be participating in a room that is full of distractions. Use emotion-provoking graphics and short, action and image-packed sentences to keep their attention.

2. Simplify your background to avoid distracting your audience. Ideally, use a single-color backdrop to help your audience focus only on you and your slides.

3. Use a side-by-side presentation tool such as Present.me, Vcasmo, or Zentation (Figure 11.23), so the audience can clearly see your facial expressions as well as your slides. This will allow you to develop a personal connection with them even when you aren't in the room.

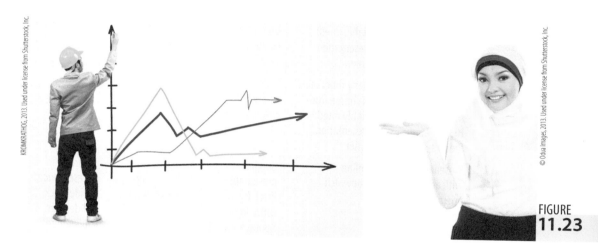

FIGURE
11.23

AVOID TELEPROMPTER APPS

A **teleprompter** is a prompting device that displays electronic visual text for a speaker to see and read from during their speech. There are a number of iTunes and Android teleprompter apps that seem like they might save you time and energy. However, these apps will most often create a giant chasm between you and your audience. You will be far more focused on reading the words than conveying your message.

Governor Bobby Jindal learned how difficult teleprompters are to work with in 2009. Jindal, whose performances on the campaign trail and in press conferences command respect and whose intellect and competence is usually unmistakable, gave a very different performance when he was asked to deliver the Republican response to President Obama's first State of the Union Address. Governor Jindal had not been trained in the use of a teleprompter and he lost much of his hard-earned reputation that night. Juan Williams of Fox News said, "Even the tempo in which he spoke seemed sing-song, and he was telling stories that seemed very simplistic, and almost childish" (Feb. 24, 2009).

FIGURE
11.24

President Obama has also been critiqued for his use of the teleprompter. While some attribute his allegiance to the teleprompter to "message discipline," others say that his constant use of the teleprompter distances him from the American people and makes him seem robotic.

FREE SOFTWARE OPTIONS

FREE presentation software for all of your devices (do a web search to find each of these)

Your device	Remotes	Timers	Face-to-face presentation	Real-time, online presentation	Asynchronous presentation
	Many remote apps to choose from Highly rated: Presenter	Many timer apps to choose from Highly rated: Presentation Timer	Thinkfree mobile, Google drive presentation. Highly rated: Deck Slideshow	Mighty meeting Join.me Highly rated: Google+ Hangouts	YouTube Slideshare
	Many remote apps to choose from Highly rated: Presenter	Many timer apps to choose from Highly rated: Presentation Timer	Haiku Deck, Google drive presentation	Fuze for iPad	Vcasmo
	Presenter works with any operating system and your smart phone	Online stopwatch	Google drive presentation, Prezi, Open Office Impress, Adobe Acrobat Presentations, Zoho Show	Any Meeting, Open Meetings, Zoho Meetings, Yugma, Vyew Many more . . . Search "online meetings free"	Voice w/ presentation: Slidesnack, Slideshare, A bit more creative: Go! Animate, Empressr. weVideo You and the slides: Present.me, Vcasmo, Zentation

FIGURE
11.25

FIGURE
11.26

BACKUP PLANS

Are you ready for your technology to fail???

Technology usually doesn't fail but when your technology fails you still need to speak.

Former President Bill Clinton had a somewhat legendary ability to "wing-it" when his teleprompter failed. In 1993 a white house aide had put the wrong speech in the teleprompter for Clinton's State of the Union address. For seven minutes Clinton gave a coherent and moving speech without any notes, and the press, who had been provided advance copies of the correct speech, afterward, fawned over Clinton's obvious abilities. Their estimation of his intellect soared.

Technology Failure	Backup
Remote control breaks _Q 18_	Deputize an audience member to click the forward arrow key when you nod (this will free you to walk and connect fully with the audience instead of being stuck behind the computer).
Loss of Internet connection _Q 17_	Bring a copy as a PDF on a flash drive so you can load it quickly and still give your presentation.
No presentation screen _Q20_	Use your PDF of your presentation on your tablet, phone, or monitor as your notes. Make sure to use vivid language and imagery to compensate for the lack of visual aids.
Giving your speech at a retreat where no technology is allowed (It could happen!) _Q 21_	Before you go, print a copy of the PDF of your presentation. Use the PDF as your speaking notes. Make sure to use vivid language and imagery to compensate for the lack of visual aids.

FIGURE
11.27

No matter what presentation technology you plan to use, MAKE A PDF of your completed presentation. Load it on your phone, tablet, laptop and on a flash drive to ensure that you always have a backup plan.

© Arcady, 2013. Used under license from Shutterstock, Inc.

FIGURE
11.28

© Ienetstan, 2013. Used under license from Shutterstock, Inc.

DELIVERY TIPS

...FOR PRESENTERS USING TECHNOLOGY

Practice out loud, ALONE until you get comfortable with the flow of the presentation.

© OPOLJA, 2013. Used under license from Shutterstock, Inc.

- Practice source citations until they flow comfortably and don't seem faster or slower than the rest of the speech.
- Practice without notes to ensure that you've provided yourself enough information to present comfortably without notes.

Practice with an audience. Ask:

© michaeljung, 2013. Used under license from Shutterstock, Inc.

- Which images are the most effective.
- Which images are confusing (replace confusing images).

Give your presentation to your audience NOT the screen.

- If the entire audience is looking at the screen we feel a deep, almost unstoppable, urge to look where they are looking. Don't look!
- Focus on incorporating audience reactions to the images throughout your delivery (Example: When an audience member gasps at a surprising chart: "I know! I found that hard to believe, too!").

Practice with the remote to unlearn the lifelong habit of pointing at the screen.

- Most presentation remote sensors work within thirty to fifty feet of the remote and are omnidirectional. No pointing is necessary.
- If presenting from a phone app the satellite or Wi-Fi connection isn't enhanced by pointing at the screen.
- Pointing at the screen turns us away from our audience.

Focus on CONNECTION rather than PERFECTION.

- Perfection is overrated. Your graphics, word choices, and delivery don't have to be perfect to be effective. Focusing on perfection puts your focus on YOU rather than your audience.
- Connection is the goal. Make choices regarding graphics, language, and delivery that are emotionally and intellectually evocative for your audience that help your audience connect with you and your message. Focusing on connection puts your focus on your audience rather than on you.

SUMMARY

Presentation technologies are merely tools that, when used well, can improve the success of your presentations. Good slides are: image-rich, use emotion-provoking images, include only titles or phrases, multisensory, simple, and iconic. Rather than waste time preparing a presentation that you won't be able to use in the room where you'll present, it is vital to talk with the venue ahead of time and find out exactly what technologies will be available to you as a speaker. Only after assessing the situation should you choose which technologies to use. Give yourself plenty of time to prepare, especially if you are using a technology you've rarely used in the past. Whether you are giving the presentation face-to-face or giving a mediated presentation, you have a wide variety of technologies to choose from. Regardless of what technology you choose you always need to have a backup plan. Once you've prepared the presentation, you need to practice with the technology and with an audience to ensure that you can focus on creating a human connection.

Review Questions

① Briefly explain five principles of good design.

② Explain three design failures when making technological presentation materials.

③ Which of the PowerPoint "don'ts" annoys you the most and what should be done instead?

④ Fire up a computer and try a cloud-based presentation app.

⑤ Which of the apps mentioned in the text have you tried?

Glossary

Asynchronous: One of the two types of mediated communication, in which the transmission of information is conducted without both participants participating at the same time. For example, an assignment on the online website is considered asynchronous communication.

Evocative images: Images that evoke an emotional response.

Mediated presentations: Use computer based technologies in order to present to an audience.

Synchronous: One of two types of mediated communication, in which all participants are online and communicating at the same time. For example, you and your friend using FaceTime on your Iphones is synchronous communication.

Teleprompter: A prompting device that displays electronic visual text for a speaker to see and read from during their speech.

References

Medina, J. (2008). *Brain Rules*. Seattle: Pear Press.

Pass, F., Renkl, A., & Sweller, J. (2003). Cognitive load theory and instructional design: Recent developments. *Educational Psychologist*, 1–4.

OTHER GREAT BOOKS ON PRESENTATION TECHNOLOGIES

Duarte, N. (2010). *Resonate: Present Visual Stories the Transform Audiences*. Hoboken: John Wiley & Sons, Inc.

Reynolds, G. (2010). *Presentation Zen Design: Simple Design Principles and Techniques to Enhance your Presentations*. Berkeley: New Riders.

Reynolds, G. (2012). *Presentation Zen: Simple Ideas on Presentation Design and Delivery*. Berkeley: New Riders.

CRITIQUING AND LISTENING TO SPEECHES

Neeley Hatridge and Vaun Thygerson

Learning Objectives

CHAPTER 12

① Differentiate between hearing and listening.

② Overcome common barriers and bad habits impeding effective listening.

③ Apply the listening process in everyday life.

④ Evaluate and critique speeches attentively and skillfully.

⑤ Learn to receive criticism of your speeches productively.

"Courage is what it takes to stand up and speak; courage is also what it takes to sit down and listen."—Winston Churchill

Likely, when you woke up this morning, it was from your cell phone alarm. You may have checked your missed texts and emails before you even stepped one foot onto the floor: this reflects the technological world in which we now live. Your teachers, coworkers, and friends are sending and receiving a plethora of electronic communication via emails, texts, and social media sites like Facebook and Twitter. With the use of technology in almost everything we do, listening may seem less and less like a necessary skill. Why try to listen and remember what someone told you when you could read it in a text message stream or email? Why ask someone about their day when you can look it up on Facebook? Although this is true for many things, the expectation to listen is still extremely high and the usefulness of this particular skill is invaluable in your educational pursuits and your future career goals. In the workplace, those with well-developed listening skills will be your leaders and those in charge (Johnson & Bechlar, 1998). In the classroom, the student who listens most effectively will have a greater likelihood of success. Effective leaders are good listeners. In the classroom, the student who listens most effectively will have a greater likelihood of success. Effective listening skills are valuable because they are a part of a commonly used process in our lives: communication.

Communication is not just an art of talking, but the better communicator knows that communication also requires active listening skills. An effective dyadic conversation begins with a foundation of active listening. When you take the listening process for granted, by assuming it just happens, you miss out on an opportunity to fully communicate. Communication professionals understand that listening is a complex process that requires practice and cultivation. You may have heard the well-known saying from the famous Greek philosopher, Zeno of Citium, "We have two ears and one mouth, so we should listen more than we say."

From the time your alarm clock, cell phone or otherwise, signals you from your sleep, you spend almost half of your day listening to friends' stories, a boss's instructions, teachers' examples, a child's worries. Nearly half of our daily communication time consists of listening. According to the International Listening Association, approximately 45 percent of our daily communication time consists of listening, compared to 30 percent speaking, 15 percent reading, and only 10 percent writing (Fujishin, 2012). Even though we spend more time listening, most people give little attention to the role this activity plays in our lives. How often do you complain or hear others complain about how no one listens?

Nearly half of our daily communication time consists of listening.

FIGURE 12.1

HEARING VS. LISTENING

"Wisdom is the reward you get for a lifetime of listening when you'd rather have been talking."—Aristotle

Ask yourself: Are you hard of listening or hard of hearing? Most people are "hard of listening" rather than "hard of hearing." What's the difference? **Hearing** is the physical process of perceiving audible stimuli without focusing on the stimuli. However, listening is not just hearing: it involves paying attention to the stimuli and assigning meaning to it. We can hear many different sounds at the same time, but not be listening to any of them. This is because **listening** is a transactional process of selecting, attending, understanding, evaluating, recalling, and responding to what we hear (Seiler & Beall, 2003). Listening helps you gain knowledge and learn from others. Knowing the stages of listening is valuable, not only for improving your listening skills, but also, to understand the perspective of your audience. As you learn the stages of the listening process, think about how you will account for them when you are an audience member or when you are the speaker and practicing your next speech.

THE LISTENING PROCESS

"The most basic and powerful way to connect to another person is to listen.
Just listen. Perhaps the most important thing we ever give each other is our attention."
—Rachel Naomi Remen (Ford-Brown, 2012)

On a daily basis, you are bombarded with messages from friends, family, teachers, coworkers, and marketers, along with all the environmental sounds in the background. All of these sounds and messages (stimuli) compete for your attention. When you are listening to a speech, it is no different; there are bound to be noises in the background. How do you filter through this noisy clutter? For example, when you are sitting in class and some students are whispering to each other at the same time the instructor is talking. What determines that you will listen to the instructor or the students? You listen based on the six steps in the listening process. Each stage is distinguishable and important in a communication exchange.

FIGURE
12.2 The listening process.

SELECTING

How do you decide which messages break through the clutter? Because you are constantly presented with message after message and noise after noise, your mind cannot possibly listen to everything that you hear. Your brain simply can only decipher one message at a time, thus the first stage in the listening process is selecting. **Selecting** is where a person chooses to hear a specific message. When you select what you are going to listen to, you are making a choice as to which stimuli you will give your attention and which you will ignore. Each situation will vary; however, you will likely choose to listen to communication that affects you directly and matters most to you. This is an important thing to consider when you are trying to get the attention of your audience. In Chapter 3, you learned about audience analysis and the importance of tailoring your speech to appeal to them. For example, if you are speaking to a crowd of college students who may be full-time students or work two jobs just to pay for tuition, and you have chosen to speak to them about how to join the local country club, your audience may easily become distracted and not select your message.

ATTENDING

After you have selected what you are going to listen to, you must also attend to it. **Attending** is the second stage in the listening process, where you use the mental process of focusing or concentrating on a specific message for a period of time. This activity requires acute mental concentration, where you focus in on one specific stimulus at a time, while downplaying or ignoring others around you. The more environmental sounds you hear in the background, the less likely you will be able to effectively listen to one, single message. Although selecting and attending seem to be very similar, they do differ in that selecting has to do with the initial choice of listening to a specific stimuli or message, and attending is the choice to *continue* listening with concentration and focus. What specific things could you do in your speech to encourage their attendance to your message? To encourage your audience members to attend to your speech, you need to provide compelling information in a creative way and use voice inflection and enthusiasm. This type of delivery style will make them want to listen more than a boring, monotone speech. Following the requirements for speech writing and delivery, described in this book, will prepare you for success.

The more environmental noise present in the background, the less likely you will effectively listen.

FIGURE 12.3

UNDERSTANDING

The third stage in the process of listening is **understanding**. After hearing, selecting, and attending to the stimuli, you now assign meaning to the communication. Based on previous experiences and knowledge, you can relate more to information you've heard in the past. You gain knowledge line upon line. For example, you can only understand the concepts taught in an advanced biology class after first learning the terms used in an entry-level biology class. If you don't understand the terms, you will not be able to make sense of the message. In effect, you will not understand. As you write your speeches, think about how you may use your knowledge of the audience and their experiences when you make choices on what content and examples to include. Getting to know and analyzing your audience, as described in Chapter 3, and considering their interests and background, should influence your message; thereby, influencing how well your audience understands that message. The level of understanding given to a message is the main distinction between listening and hearing. The best speakers are good listeners because they take the time to really find out what truly interests their audience and how to reach them.

EVALUATING

Once you understand the stimuli, you must evaluate it. **Evaluating** is where the receiver analyzes, judges, and assesses the message, often to determine the intent, effectiveness, and accuracy of the speaker's statements. This part of the listening process includes critical listening where you judge the validity of the speaker's words. In order to evaluate messages, you analyze evidence and determine facts from opinions, which are two different variables. A fact is a verifiable statement that can be proven. An inference draws conclusions from facts and circumstantial evidence, not from direct observations. Specifically, as an audience member, you must evaluate the message given by a speaker. Also, as a speech writer, you must be sure that the message you are sharing, holds up to the same kind of scrutiny. Additional items and the process of evaluating will be discussed in more detail later in this chapter.

RECALLING

After hearing, selecting, attending, understanding, and evaluating the stimuli, you commit it to either your short-term or long-term memory. In your short-term memory, you simply make sense of it at the time of hearing. In your long-term memory, you make a broader understanding of it and recall it later. Researchers have found that about a quarter of what most people listen to can be recalled. Of that 25 percent, 80 percent is distorted or not received accurately: this leaves only 5 percent of the total message accurately received (Benoit & Lee, 1988). Additionally, the majority of that is distorted or not received accurately. **Recalling** then is where you can remember and/or apply the information for future encounters. Some messages stored in your long-term memory could actually affect your life and change your attitudes, values, or beliefs; however, researchers aren't sure why we remember certain things while forgetting others. This doesn't mean that you as a listener can't use techniques and strategies to increase your understanding and recall.

One such technique used to increase this potential and remember information from what you hear is through a mnemonic device. Many mnemonics take the form of acronyms as a way to assist information retention. One example is an algebraic mnemonic that explains the order of operation: PEMDAS (Parentheses, Exponents, Multiply, Divide, Add, Subtract). Many organizations are aware of the power of acronyms when choosing the name that is used to identify them, such as: PETA (People for the Ethical Treatment of Animals), and MADD (Mothers Against Drunk Driving). Additionally, keep this in mind as you prepare speeches, especially ones that may contain a lot of important details.

RESPONDING

The final stage in the listening process is responding. **Responding** happens when the listener acknowledges verbally or nonverbally to the speaker whether or not the message has or has not been received. Giving feedback and interpreting feedback becomes an important part of being an effective listener and presenter. During a communication exchange, feedback gives you an opportunity to state your opinion, agree or disagree, or make judgments. Verbal communication responses for feedback include: paraphrasing, asking questions, or seeking clarification. Nonverbal communication responses can include: eye contact, smiling, nodding, frowning, or maintaining silence. These verbal and nonverbal responses can encourage or stymie communication during an interpersonal (one-on-one) exchange, but also in public presentations. Imagine as a speaker if your audience was looking everywhere else, but not at you. This would lead you to conclude that they lacked interest in your presentation. Watch for both nonverbal and verbal cues from your audience while speaking. Also, consider how you may look to a presenter when you're in the audience.

WHY DO WE LISTEN?

To answer why people listen to some messages while ignoring others, is not a simple task because it will greatly depend on many variables: the speaker, the intended audience, the environment and how conducive the setting favors a communication exchange, time restrictions, the self-interest of the listener, and the list could continue. There are, however, some common reasons to listen. Knowing these common reasons can help you to identify why you choose to listen to particular messages and it will also help to serve as a guide for developing the purpose of your speeches.

LISTENING FOR INFORMATION AND COMPREHENSION

One of the main reasons you listen to stimuli is for information. You listen to a teacher for directions on an upcoming assignment or a boss about instructions on a time-sensitive project. This type of listening requires concentration to comprehend and to remember details. Listening for **comprehension** has a strong focus on the understanding and recall of the messages, not necessarily how you feel about them or if they were effective. For example, when your instructor begins to tell the class about terms to study for the next quiz, your goal is to listen with the purpose of understanding where to focus your study efforts, not to judge whether the teacher chose concepts that create a well-rounded exam. Participatory activity like note-taking can often help with comprehending the material (Einstein, Morris & Smith, 1985).

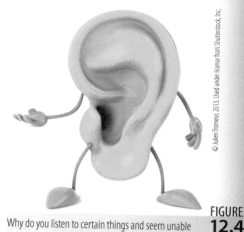

Why do you listen to certain things and seem unable to "listen" to others?

FIGURE 12.4

EMPATHIC LISTENING

Another reason why you listen is to provide comfort to people in your life. You listen to your friend who recently broke up with his girlfriend, a child who is being bullied at school, and a coworker who didn't receive the promotion he or she had been wanting. Providing emotional support by listening to your friends helps them feel better about themselves and their behaviors. Providing empathic listening differs from sympathetic listening. Sympathy means feeling sorry for someone, whereas **empathy** requires a comprehension of another person's feelings, thoughts, beliefs, and actions. Empathic listening requires listeners to imagine things from the perspective of the speaker. Often times, our responses to these encounters help to demonstrate whether we were engaging in sympathetic or empathic listening. For example, if someone tells you that their family dog just died, a sympathetic listener may reply "That's terrible, I'm so sorry." However, an empathic response would sound more like, "Pets can really become like family. You and your family must be really feeling the loss." The first response came from the perspective of the listener, whereas the second response made the attempt to show understanding from the perspective of the initial speaker, the one who's dog had died.

CRITICAL AND EVALUATIVE LISTENING

Critical listening is a chance to evaluate a message and determine the truthfulness of the content. You listen to an automotive repair technician explaining why your car leaks gas, a salesperson explaining the differences between competing brand names, and a presidential candidate during a debate with his or her opponent. The main goal with critical listening is to gather information to judge it for several reasons. Should we trust this person? Should we trust their message? Are their claims reasonable and supported? Was he or she effective? Critical or **evaluative listening** is listening with the purpose of judging the value or worth of the message. Essentially, as presenters and as audience members, we should know how to evaluate and critique other oral presentations. Evaluators identify both—areas that the presenter achieved success, as well as areas that need improvement. Meaning, when you evaluate others or when another person evaluates your presentation, it is not with the intent of finding fault, but done so with a desire to help improve.

APPRECIATIVE LISTENING

One of the most common reasons you listen is for recreation or enjoyment. You listen to your favorite actor reading a bestselling book on iTunes, a poetry reading at your favorite coffee shop, and the details of your best friend's trip to the Bahamas. With appreciative listening, you receive this stimulus for entertainment purposes.

LISTENING FOR CULTURAL UNDERSTANDING

In the global world where we now live, we meet people who have lived very different lives than our own, so how do you learn about your best friend's culture when it is different from yours? You may listen to her when she talks about the traditions and food from her native country. Listening for cultural understanding helps us learn more about others' culture so that we can understand them and break down stereotypes. Remember to have an open mind when listening for cultural understanding.

TYPES OF LISTENERS

Each of us learns to listen to others differently. Becoming familiar with the types of listeners can help you adjust your message to the audience. It is also essential to know what type of listener you are because it can help you when evaluating messages. We should always strive to be as objective as possible, which can be difficult at times. By knowing what type of listener you are, you can prepare yourself to listen for things you may not typically notice. Also, you can evaluate your findings and assess if they were at all influenced by your own personal listening type and preferences. Your preferred approach to listening can fall into one of the following categories that make up the mnemonic PACT (Watson, Barker, & Weaver, 1995).

© Ron and Joe, 2013. Used under license from Shutterstock, Inc.

FIGURE 12.5
PACT was crafted by Watson, Barker, and Weaver in 1995.

People-Centered Listeners—a listening style associated with concern for other people's feelings or emotions. This person will likely be a more empathic listener. They make the attempt to understand the listener from their perspective. They want the other person to feel like they were heard.

Action-Centered Listeners—this type of listener wants messages to be highly organized, concise, and error-free. This person is interested in both comprehensive and evaluative listening. However, they would prefer to have to do less work evaluating and prefer, instead, for a message to be explicit and transparent.

Content-Centered Listeners—associated with listeners who focus on the facts and details of the message. This person also often listens for comprehension and information. For them, the "devil is in the details."

Time-Centered Listeners—this type of listener wants messages to be presented succinctly. This person values their time and may be busy. Similar to action-centered listeners, they want messages to be concise, but more with the purpose of reducing time demands.

TIPS FOR USING YOUR LISTENING STYLE TO YOUR ADVANTAGE

1. Identify your style: Pay close attention to the recent conversations you have had. What do you remember about them? Were they long conversations, did you learn a lot about the person you were talking to, etc.? Knowing your style will help you improve where you may struggle.
2. What do other's think: Consider close friend's and family's comments about the way you listen. Would they consider you a good or effective listener? Why or why not? Looking at things from the perspective of others can help achieve two things, you can become more objective about yourself and you can learn to become more empathic.
3. Use your findings: Make an effort to learn and incorporate a new style. This isn't to say that you will be successful in making a complete switch, but it offers you more tools as a listener. For example, if you have discovered that you are typically a Content-Centered listener, then you can make a special effort to improve your People-Centered skills. This will offer you the advantage of considering multiple aspects of any given message.

BARRIERS TO LISTENING

"Any man who can drive safely while kissing a pretty girl
is simply not giving the kiss the attention it deserves."—Albert Einstein

As described earlier, you are frequently exposed to messages, you use the listening process to filter through them to find which stimuli to respond to and, as you decode the speaker's message, there will be many unwanted barriers. **Listening barriers** are anything that interferes with the listening process that does not allow the speaker's message to be understood properly by the receiver. Barriers can be both caused by either internal and/or external noise, which keep you from listening effectively. This can make it difficult to evaluate a speech because the audience is unable to hear or understand what is being said. Some major contributors of this noise have been broken down into four types: physical, physiological, psychological, and semantic.

TYPES OF NOISE: PHYSICAL, PHYSIOLOGICAL, PSYCHOLOGICAL, AND SEMANTIC

Physical noise happens when environmental sounds interrupt your message where the listener cannot literally hear your words. It may break the concentration of the speaker and the listener,

Sometimes what someone is saying is altered in our minds by various types of noise.

FIGURE 12.6

causing you to focus on the sound rather than the communication. Some examples of physical noise include traffic, people walking in and out of the room, construction machinery, a loud ceiling fan, or a classmate tapping their pencil. As a speaker, one way to reduce the likelihood of this during a speech is to try to maintain some control over the environment. This is accomplished by visiting the room beforehand. Scan the room for potentially noisy distractions. Plan on closing a window to muffle the outside noise, practice with a microphone if the audience won't be able to hear you, ask people not to enter or exit during the speech. Not all physical barriers can be successfully accounted for, but preparation will increase your chances for success.

HOW TO REDUCE PHYSICAL NOISE

1. Try to maintain some control over the environment.
2. Visit the room beforehand to scan for potentially noisy distractions.
3. Plan on closing a window to muffle the outside noise, etc.
4. Practice with a microphone if the audience won't be able to hear you.
5. Ask people not to enter or exit during the speech.

FIGURE 12.7 Physiological noise deals with bodily conditions that break our concentration and keeps us from listening effectively.

Physiological noise deals with bodily conditions that break your concentration and keep you from listening to the stimuli. For example, if you have a headache or a stomachache, you will not listen as closely to the message as you are more likely to focus on your discomfort. As an audience member, an obvious answer is to take medication or not engage in activities that are likely to cause distracting physiological reactions. A less obvious factor to consider is how to account for these as a speaker. When it is within your power, take all aspects of your audiences' environment into consideration. Are their seats comfortable? Is it approaching lunchtime? Is the room too hot or cold? Are there any special accommodations that could be made to increase comfort? Being considerate of your audiences' comfort goes a long way.

Psychological noise is characterized by the interference in the listening process due to internal, emotional conditions. With this type of interference, you focus on internal factors such as biases, stereotypes, fears, or intellectual distractions, where you are thinking about anything but the message being given. If you walk into class after getting a call from a bill collector, it is likely going to be difficult for you to stay focused on the class discussion. One common example of psychological noise is receiver apprehension.

Receiver apprehension occurs when the listener is fearful of not understanding or interpreting the message correctly. A student afraid of missing the date for a paper deadline or an employee fearful of not understanding the boss's instructions are examples of receiver apprehension. Additionally, if you have already decided that you don't like the speaker, it will make it challenging to listen as well. Some helpful tips about effective listening will follow shortly, but as a speaker, it is important for you to realize the effects of this type of noise on your audience. One way to combat this is by engaging in immediate practices.

Immediate behaviors are verbal and nonverbal communicative behaviors that create a sense of "psychological closeness" with others, increasing the effect for the speaker (Anderson, Norton, & Nussbaum, 1981). Some immediate behaviors include: positivity, friendliness, enthusiasm, verbal expressiveness, smiling, a relaxed body position, eye contact, closer proximity [meaning, don't stand behind a podium if you can help it], socially appropriate touch, and appropriate dress (Allen, Witt, & Wheeless, 2006; Comstock, Rowell, & Bowers, 1995). Essentially, you are trying to have them focus more on the presentation rather than the thoughts going on inside their own heads.

Semantic noise can interfere with the listening process when the sender and/or receiver do not understand the verbal and/or nonverbal messages in a communication exchange. Verbal examples of this noise include technical jargon or slang that is unfamiliar or misunderstood by the listener. Information overload can occur as result of semantic noise.

FIGURE **12.8**

Semantic noise can hinder the listening process. Remember to consider your audience before using jargon or slang that may be confusing to your audience.

Information overload occurs when too much new information (stimuli) is provided to us in a short period of time. When we are not familiar with a concept or terms, we will likely stop listening when we are no longer able to process all of the new information. Be aware of this when organizing your main points. Use presently known ideas, which can be a starting point for newer information. Earlier, the importance of repetition in speeches was discussed and repetition can help lessen the effects of listener overload. Nonverbal communication can also serve as a contributor of this type of noise when gestures or other nonverbal stimuli are unknown to the listener. This is likely to occur when there is a lack of knowledge or understanding of another culture and its accepted communication practices and, as a speaker, you must know your audience.

FIGURE **12.9**

When we are bombarded with too much information we often stop listening altogether.

POOR LISTENING HABITS

In addition to physical, physiological, psychological, and semantic noise that can interfere with the decoding of a message, poor listening habits can influence the retention of oral messages. When you listen poorly to messages, you will not be able to use them or recall them later. Most misunderstandings that occur can be attributed to poor listening skills. When you don't listen, you can create serious problems personally, professionally, and financially. Some poor listening habits include selective listening, message overload, talkaholism, fake listening, gap filling, defensive listening, and ambushing.

Selective listening happens when you only process the messages that appeal to your self-interests. Selective listening happens when you, as the listener, decide if this communication exchange has a "pay off" worthy of your time. You ask yourself, "What's in it for me?" Some examples of selective listening: When you listen to a teacher about an assignment because you want to get an A, listening to a radio station to win tickets to an upcoming screening, or listening to a friend only to find out how you can benefit from the information.

Talkaholics won't let you get a word in edgewise. During a conversation, he or she talks more than you, to the point of excluding others in the exchange. This person may have to dominate the conversation, directing the topics that he or she wishes to discuss without giving you or others the opportunity to share; this can also be characterized by individuals that try to "one-up" you. Meaning, anything you say, they have a similar, but more dramatic or significant circumstance that is said in a way to make your situation seem not as valuable.

© iConcept, 2013. Used under license from Shutterstock, Inc.

FIGURE 12.10 Parents and children are often said to be excellent at selective listening. Selective listening is a process of paying attention to specific information, while ignoring other information.

© Petr Vaclavek, 2013. Used under license from Shutterstock, Inc.

FIGURE 12.11 Talkaholics are often viewed as disrespectful, self-centered, and poorly educated. Talkaholism often ends up insulting others and should be avoided.

Fake listening or **pseudolistening** happens when we pretend to listen and use verbal and nonverbal response to continue the charade. Sadly, fake listening can resemble real listening to the speaker. People versed in pseudolistening have mastered the art of "faking it" and the speaker truly believes they are hanging on their every word. That is because the psuedolisteners often make eye contact with the speaker; they may lean forward and nod from time to time, and even provide verbal agreements to support the topic, appearing as if they are paying attention.

Gap filling is a result of the listening gap. You can speak one-hundred-fifty to two hundred words per minute, but you can understand up to eight hundred words per minute, which gives your mind time to fill in the gaps and assume what the speaker intends

© Evgenia Bolyukh, 2013. Used under license from Shutterstock, Inc.

FIGURE 12.12 Fake listeners often inspire hurt feelings in others. It's often perceived as passive aggressive and reflects disrespect.

© Oma Ytiur, 2013. Used under license from Shutterstock, Inc.

FIGURE 12.13

to say before he or she finishes her sentences. This results in interrupting and finishing people's sentences.

Defensive listeners misconstrue all innocent comments as personal attacks or reasons to be upset with the speaker. This bad listening habit has the listener looking for hidden meanings and innuendos in the spoken words and nonverbal gestures. The listener will most likely ask the speaker: "What did you mean by that?" "Are you being rude?" "Why would you say that to me?" This kind of exchange usually happens between people with a complicated history, where one person has hurt the other, in the past. The context of the relationship can determine the amount of defensive listening that happens.

Ambushing happens when you listen to the message with an ulterior motive to find information you can use to hurt the speaker. Oftentimes, particularly when communicating in close relationships, you listen for unflattering information to use against other people. When your boss confides in you and tells you about her struggles with binge drinking, you can use this information to manipulate your work environment to benefit you. Ambushing is a destructive type of listening that people use often to get ahead at work or direct relationships.

FIGURE 12.14

Ambushing is often used by people who like to manipulate others. It is a listening tactic that can be very powerful and hurtful.

FIGURE 12.15

LISTEN MORE EFFECTIVELY
ACTIVE LISTENING

In order to improve your communication proficiency, you can learn how to practice effective listening skills through active listening. People who practice active listening actually desire to listen. They listen the way they want to be listened to—it's the Golden Rule of listening (Fujishin, 2012). When listening to public speeches, you can use this technique while providing feedback, evaluation, and comprehension during the note-taking process. This type of active listening also works well for both the speaker and the audience during a question and answer session or interactive lecture series. This type of listening technique involves **paraphrasing** or restating in your own words the message sent by the speaker to accurately decode the stimuli.

Paraphrasing works particularly well when the communication exchange has high stakes with a crucial conversation. Many customer service representatives work for companies that provide services where people call in with emotional stories. When being trained, the representatives are taught to practice the art of paraphrasing. For example, when a representative from an insurance company receives a claim from someone who has suffered a major loss, they will restate the story for clarity making sure they understand the situation to the fullest. At this point, the client responds negatively or positively and can reiterate or clarify what the representative paraphrased. Then, this cycle repeats itself until both parties are satisfied that their needs are being met. This type of communication tool helps the listener and speaker truly understand the needs and perception of the other party.

WITH A SIMPLE FOUR-STEP PROCESS, YOU CAN BECOME AN ACTIVE LISTENER

1. The speaker makes a statement.
2. Then, the listener paraphrases in his or her own words, their understanding of the message.
3. The speaker decides if he or she agrees or disagrees with the listener's paraphrase.
4. If the speaker disagrees, the speaker restates the statement for clarity and the process continues. If the speaker agrees, the activity is complete (Adler & Proctor II, 2008).

L = Look at the speaker.
A = Ask questions.
D = Don't interrupt.
D = Don't change the subject.
E = Check your emotions.
R = Provide responses.

(Maxwell, 1993)

FIGURE 12.16 LADDER is an acronym used to discuss effective listening as outlined by John C. Maxwell in 1993.

LISTENING LADDER

In John C. Maxwell's curriculum, *"Developing the Leader Within You,"* he suggests an acronym to help people remember to practice active listening skills. His LADDER is an easy way to remember the necessary tools needed to make you a more effective listener (see Figure 12.16).

Look at the speaker: You should maintain eye contact with the speaker to avoid becoming distracted. Good eye contact makes the speaker believe that you are really listening to him or her.

ASK questions: Be interested and ask questions. One of the best ways to fully understand the topic is to ask questions to confirm what you know and clarify any confusing points.

Don't interrupt: Let the speaker finish his or her complete thought before stating your opinion or asking your question. Basic etiquette states that you take turns in the dyadic dialogue process: you let someone finish her or his sentence before you speak.

Don't change the subject: When you try to change the subject, you are in fact, telling the speaker that what he or she has to say is not as important as what you have to say. This is rude. If the speaker wants to talk about a certain subject, even if you don't find it interesting to you, let him or her finish before you talk about something else.

Emotions: During this step of the LADDER process, you must keep your emotions in check, even if you want to laugh, cry, or scream. Once you react emotionally, especially negatively, in a situation where it is inappropriate, you risk starting an argument or a complete shutdown of ideas from the speaker.

Respond: One of the best ways to practice responsive listening is by actually listening to the speaker. This ensures you will know the appropriate response to provide, showing the speaker you are really listening. Provide both nonverbal and verbal responses to the speaker so she or he knows you are listening to the message.

EVALUATING YOUR LISTENING SKILLS

Now that you know what skills you need to be an effective listener, you are asking yourself, "How can I become a better listener?" Then, you need to decide what type of listener you want to become and what to what level. You also need to define your goals for listening. Why do you want to listen?

The first step to becoming an active listener is to take a serious look at your current skills and realistically evaluate them. Ask yourself: What are some of the current situations that keep you from becoming the type of listener you want to be? Once you've identified these weaknesses, you need to come up with a plan to overcome them. For example, if you are a selective listener and only listen to the information that pertains to your self-interest, make it a priority to actively listen to all information that matters to both the speaker and the listener. You don't have to listen to every word, noise, and utterance that is spoken, but you can filter the important ones that have meaning to those people in your lives.

NONJUDGMENTAL FEEDBACK

Another way you can become a more effective listener is to become a nonjudgmental listener. In other words, don't prejudge what others are going to say before they say it. Listen with an open mind and be considerate of others' ideas and cultural beliefs. The more you listen with a world-view, the more you will learn.

DIALOGUE ENHANCERS

Another way to promote effective listening is to provide verbal feedback to let the listener know you are interested and engaged in the conversation. In order to regulate conversation and provide feedback to the speaker that his or her message is being heard, you can use dialogue enhancers. These brief verbal responses show that you are paying attention to the stimuli. These supportive statements like "I see," or "tell me more," or "yes, I hear you," encourage continued talking. Other ways we provide feedback include "really?," "that's so interesting!," "how fun!"

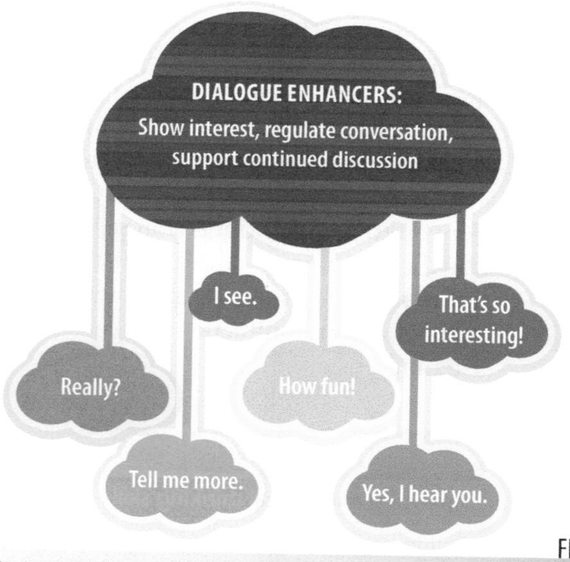

DIALOGUE ENHANCERS:
Show interest, regulate conversation, support continued discussion

I see.

That's so interesting!

Really?

How fun!

Tell me more.

Yes, I hear you.

© qushe, 2013. Used under license from Shutterstock, Inc.

Look at the dialogue enhancers above. Do you use these often? Not enough? Increase your use of dialogue enhancers today and see what happens!

FIGURE 12.17

HONOR SILENCE

Silence can be used to manipulate, but it can also be used to encourage listening. As a powerful communication tool, silence gives the speaker a chance to collect his or her thoughts and feelings. Silence also lets the speaker know that you are listening and taking the time to process the information thoughtfully.

PRACTICE LISTENING

One of the best ways to become a more effective speaker is to actually practice listening just like you would practice a sport or a musical arrangement. The old adage, "practice makes perfect," makes sense, even when listening. You have to practice this skill to improve it.

The speaker and listener share a symbiotic relationship as equal participants in the communication exchange. You have just read ways to improve your listening skills, which will help you as a receiver or an audience member as well as the speaker in your own presentations. Take the time to hone your listening skills to become not only a more effective listener, but a better communicator overall. These listening skills will also equip you to complete another valuable part of the oral presentation evaluation process.

IMPORTANCE OF EVALUATING ORAL PRESENTATION

If you grew up in a home where everyone fought to be heard and had to be loud to get noticed, you may react to messages differently than someone who was only allowed to speak when spoken to. We all come from different perspectives and thus different elements of a presentation will stand out to some of us, while being less obvious to others. The way we evaluate and critique others is heavily influenced by our culture, style of communicating, the expectations and rules for society, and specific situations, among other factors. Understanding and becoming familiar with the evaluation or critiquing process will help to build your critical thinking and public speaking skills. Forbes recently listed 10 skills that will get you hired, with critical thinking skills ranking #1 and active listening skills at #4 (Casserly, 2012). If you have had practice listening to messages and recognizing when they aren't using logic or that the source is unreliable, then it becomes easier for you to notice it in your daily life as well. Ultimately, becoming an effective and skilled evaluator will be a benefit to the person you are evaluating and to you.

We offer evaluations or critiques by utilizing some of the types of listening discussed earlier. For you to give a critique, you will need to use listening for comprehension to understand what it is they are saying, empathic listening to understand why the perspective of the speaker adds to the message or affects credibility and cultural to help you to assign meaning due to the impacts of cultural influence. However, the type of listening that will be used the most is critical listening.

Skills for Improvement	Corresponding Benefits
Analytical and critical thinking skills	In college, personal life, and in future employment
Reinforcement of speaking skills	Helps when writing your own speeches
Reflection and reflexivity skills	Allows an opportunity for you to evaluate and account for your own predisposition

FIGURE
12.18

Critical listening will provide you with the ability to read between the lines. This allows you to assess the reasoning, the reliability of the message and the speaker, and the overall worth and effectiveness of the message. Learning how to critique a presentation will not only assist you in giving more accurate feedback, but it will help you to see what others pay attention to while they are listening to you present. Critiquing oral messages will be invaluable, as you prepare and present future speeches, providing practice and equipping you with the desired analytical and critical thinking skills that were discussed earlier (see Figure 12.2).

ITEMS FOR EVALUATION: STRUCTURE, CONTENT, AND DELIVERY

In college presentations and future career-related presentations, you will likely be evaluated. Evaluations may be formal or informal, official or unofficial, but you may wonder exactly what will be considered when being evaluated or when you are required to give a critique of a presentation. You may also be wondering who gives evaluations; the answer is, everyone. For speeches given in your classrooms, your instructor will likely be evaluating you, but he or she may also require students to participate in this process as well. If students are required to give feedback, this is a good thing. This means that you will get information back from multiple sources and multiple perspectives. It also means that you will probably be required to provide feedback for your fellow classmates. You will then have practice at being a professional audience member and listener. Again, this will not only help you when you are writing your speech, but these critical listening skills will help you beyond the classroom. Numerous items are evaluated when listening critically to a speech, but there are three major areas of consideration: *structure, content,* and *delivery*.

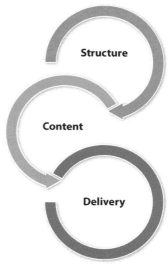

These are the primary areas evaluated when listening critically.

FIGURE **12.19**

STRUCTURE

In this area of evaluation, the evaluator will be looking at the format and organization of your presentation. Formats may change according to instructor or type of presentation, but the majority of speeches will follow the structure described in earlier chapters. For this reason, it is essential that you are familiar with the general structure of a speech as addressed earlier. Understanding this structural component to evaluation will not only make you a better evaluator, but a better speaker because you account for this when you are writing your speeches. When you are evaluating the structure, pay attention to the overall organization of the speech. Was there a clear introduction, body, and conclusion section in their speech or did it all seem to blend together? Was the organizational structure effective for the chosen topic or thesis? For example, did she or he give a speech on the history of the United States Civil War, but choose to organize the main points topically when chronologically may have been more effective? Were you able to distinguish between main points or ideas? Did the speaker jump from one point to the next without preparing the audience? Was it obvious that the speech was over or did the audience seem confused about when to clap? These types of questions, as well as ones that follow in the succeeding sections, are also items for you to consider when you are writing your speech. Although your structure may be apparent to you, think about how apparent it would be to the audience.

CONTENT

In this area of evaluation, the evaluator will be looking at the actual message and the value of the speaker's content. An evaluator should pay close attention to the logic and reasoning of arguments. Be sure that facts are not being misrepresented and that the speaker is making ethical choices. In Chapter 15, you will learn about *inductive* and *deductive* reasoning, along with some common fallacies. Evaluate whether the speaker is making arguments that don't mislead the audience with fallacious reasoning, which is unethical. Also, it is important to take note of the quality of evidence. A speaker has the responsibility of supporting the statements they make with evidence. There are different types of evidence and research as described in Chapter 5, but some include: examples, expert opinions, statistics, and visual evidence. Whatever choices are made about the type of evidence to include, the speaker should be sure to use credible sources and to cite them in their presentation. Along with reasoning and sources, was the speech effective?

The speaker could have used sound reasoning, made ethical choices, and used credible sources, but still not be effective. Perhaps, the reasoning or claims were sound, but weak or not very impactful. The examples used could have been great for explaining the content, but inappropriate for the audience. Also, the examples could have been relevant and appropriate, but they weren't explained well or were confusing. The content can fit all criteria, but still lack interest or impact. Take this into consideration when evaluating content, but also when you are writing your speech. Think about the audience when making your content choices.

DELIVERY

In this area of evaluation, you are evaluating the performance. Giving a speech can be a lot like theater because we often act or perform the role of a speaker. In Chapter 9, you will learn in greater detail about the essentials of effective speech delivery, but for now, we will focus on evaluating them. The way a speech is delivered will greatly influence the audience's perception of effectiveness. Even the most important, interesting, valid, and relevant messages can be lost if the delivery of them is poor. For this reason, be honest with the speaker about things you specifically observed during her or his speech. Keep in mind that it is the audience's *perception* of effectiveness that is important and you are a member of the audience, completely qualified to have an opinion on the performance.

When you were evaluating the structure and content of the speech, you were focusing on the "what" the person said, but when evaluating delivery, you will be focusing on "how" they said what they said. Body movements and vocal variations are the major contributing factors for performance. For body movements, you will be evaluating items such as: posture, hand gestures, facial expressions, how the speaker moves while speaking, if she or he fidgeted. For vocal variety, you will be evaluating items such as: volume, pace, if there was a change in tone, inflection, and/or pitch. Additional items to evaluate may include: confidence, credibility, enthusiasm, personal appearance, pronunciation, extemporaneous speaking, eye contact, use of notes, and use of visual aids. This list is not exhaustive, but each of the items that have been listed, all reflect criteria under the category of delivery.

PROCESS OF EVALUATING

The process of critiquing, or evaluating, is an internal and external process. To say that it is an internal process, means as an evaluator, you must listen, analyze, and judge internally. To say that it is an external process means that you must translate and articulate those evaluations in a form that is consumable by the presenter (person being evaluated)—this is accomplished with feedback. **Feedback** is the response to specific observations of oral messages and the constructive advice given by an evaluator, typically in written or oral form. The goal of the feedback is to tell the speaker what he or she should continue to do and what they should change for future presentations. Let's look at the internal process first.

THE INTERNAL PROCESS

1. Be Prepared: Do some minor investigation or inquiry as to the type of presentation to take place. This will help you to determine what to bring, what type of feedback to give, and what to consider during the evaluation.

2. Be Aware: As discussed earlier in this chapter, we each receive messages differently because of our own personal set of beliefs and expectations. Be aware of how these influence what you privilege or what you assign great value. We may have prejudice or bias toward the speaker or their message, which may affect how we evaluate them.

3. Ask yourself questions about their content (a few to consider): Was their topic appropriate for the audience and the occasion? Did the speaker get and maintain my attention? Were their main points and ideas supported? Were their sources credible and cited accurately? Did he or she achieve their general purpose of: informing, persuading, or entertaining? Was sound logic and reasoning used?

4. Ask yourself questions about their structure (a few to consider): Was their speech organized and easy to follow? Did the speaker include all the essential components of an introduction? Did the speaker include all of the essential components in the conclusion? Were tie-backs to the thesis or claim included? Did she or he follow instructions? Did the speaker use transitions in between their main points? Did their speech fit appropriately within the time restrictions?

5. Ask yourself questions about their delivery (a few to consider): Did the speaker commit to their performance? Did he or she show confidence in their message? Were their hand gestures and facial expressions effective for their speech? Was their volume level appropriate for the venue? Was the speaker monotone or did he or she manipulate their tone to create interest? Was the speech presented with the most suitable method of delivery (e.g., extemporaneous, manuscript, etc.)? Was it enjoyable as an audience member and why?

You may have the opportunity to write down a few of these questions before the presentation, so that you can answer them as you listen. Additionally, many instructors may require such an assignment and provide you with a list of questions. Understanding each of the above listed questions and what they are designed to evaluate can help you when it comes time to articulate those assessments, through the external process of evaluation and critiquing.

THE EXTERNAL PROCESS

Once a speaker has finished her or his presentation, the feedback will need to be given. Feedback may be provided in different forms—oral, written, or with a rubric, checklist, etc.—each with their own pros and cons, but it is essential to understand what must be used for all feedback.

ESSENTIALS IN EVALUATION

Ground your feedback with specific examples and remedies: Many of the answers to the above questions could be answered with a simple yes or no; however, explanation for each provides the speaker with grounded information to accept the critique. If you were to say that the presentation was "good," you haven't given him or her enough information to know what specifically was done well. Conversely, you should say "you really supported the claim you made. You backed it up with credible evidence and convinced me!"

Frame it in a positive way: Avoid criticisms that will sound like a personal attack. Be respectful in the tone of your feedback and use positive language. For example, instead of telling someone "stop looking down at the floor," rephrase it toward the positive, "look up at your audience." Essentially, be constructive. Also, avoid using "you" language; instead, use "I" or "me" language. This means, don't tell them, "*you* could have looked at the audience more." Instead, write, "I noticed that your eyes never landed on the audience. It made it difficult for *me* to connect with you as a speaker." Although the word "you" was used, it placed more of an emphasis on the perspective of the audience to reduce the impression of an attack on the presenter. One way to make criticisms more palatable, or easier to accept, is to offer positive feedback both before and immediately following the criticism.

Incorporate areas where they succeeded: In almost every speech, there was something done well. At the very least, it took courage to stand at the front of the class and speak. Be sure to point out what the speaker did well. You want to do this for three reasons. First, you want to make him or her feel like they did good and it gives him or her something from which to build more confidence. Second, by commenting on things done well, it makes it easier for the speaker to accept your constructive criticisms and points for improvements. Third, the speaker needs to know what was done well, so that it can be continued in future presentations.

The essentials of giving feedback apply to many types of feedback, all of which are important to understand for giving and receiving evaluations.

TYPES OF FEEDBACK

Oral feedback: This type of feedback is given verbally. It is typically much more informal, but still useful. It may be given in front of the class; for example, the instructor may offer a few points of feedback once you finish your speech. It could also be offered privately, such as your instructor asking you to see them after class. Whether or not there is an audience will slightly change the strategies used when giving oral feedback. Remember the essentials of evaluations we just discussed. When there is an audience, the feedback should be brief and focus more on the positives in the speech. It is important that the positive feedback be truthful and not exaggerated or others will notice and begin to doubt the sincerity of subsequent feedback. Although the focus is more on the things done well, do not ignore large mistakes that, if identified, could benefit the class in their presentations. The goal is to distance the criticism from the person. This is done with choice of words, but also with tone. All feedback, but especially oral feedback, should avoid sounding like a personal attack.

Written feedback: This type of feedback is given in a written format. It is much more formal and can be extremely useful. It may be handed back to the speaker immediately following the speech or days later, but the comments provided will be available for use in future speeches. Written feedback may follow different formats. Some evaluators may have a checklist or hand back extensive, written notes on a speech, whereas others may use a rubric. Rubrics are a type of written feedback that is similar to a checklist; however, they often have much more prewritten information and scores attached to them. It is typically found in a grid format with the list of **evaluative criteria**, or items that the evaluator will be assessing, running down the first column and the levels of scoring running across the top row. There is some debate about the effectiveness

Evaluative Criteria	No Attempt Made	Developing	Average or Satisfactory Accomplishment	Above Average	Excellent
Eye Contact	Looks anywhere but at the audience.	Occasionally looks at the audience, but only briefly.	Looks equally at the audience and other places.	Maintains frequent eye contact.	Maintains appropriate eye contact throughout.
Presentation Aids	Did not include any aids.	Aids do not meet the minimum requirements.	Meets minimum requirements.	Meets requirements and effective.	Exceeds requirements. Effective, well prepared and well executed.
Organization	No discernible organizational strategy or pattern is used.	Attempts are made, but it is still difficult to identify and follow the organization.	An identifiable organizational pattern is used.	Organizational pattern is appropriate and easy to identify and contributes to the audience attention.	Pattern is well executed, appropriate, and makes the speech effortless to follow.

A portion of a rubric used for feedback.

FIGURE 12.20

of rubrics, but when well thought-out, they can be very informative and easily utilized for feedback purposes.

The goal of this feedback is to provide the speaker with substantial information about the effectiveness of the speech and make comments grounded in specific observations so that the speaker will progress. It can be difficult for written feedback to be given in larger class sizes, especially for minor speaking assignments, but is generally the most useful to the students. The essentials of evaluation must be followed when giving written feedback as well. Below are two examples of written feedback from a checklist. Both include the same three criteria to be evalu-

Introduction	The introduction was easy to identify. You included all the required parts and each exceeded requirements. Your preview of your main points helped to prepare the audience for what came next and made your overall speech much more organized.
Facial Expressions	I appreciate that you chose to use your face as a way of expressing the seriousness of your topic, but there were a few that seemed insincere. When practicing your speech, look in the mirror or record yourself. This will help you to observe any awkward or overly exaggerated facial expressions.
Posture	For the most part, your posture conveyed confidence. At times, you leaned against the podium and crossed your feet. Try to avoid putting weight on the podium and evenly distribute your weight between both feet. This will help to avoid unnatural-looking body positions. The longer you were up speaking, the more natural and comfortable your posture became.

Sample evaluation areas.

FIGURE 12.21

Introduction	I liked your opening statement. You did a good job!
Facial Expressions	You made some funny looking faces. They kept it interesting, though.
Posture	Don't lean on the podium.

FIGURE
12.22 Examples of comments.

ated, but one shows a poor example of written feedback, whereas the other shows effective use of written feedback.

Clearly, Figure 12.20 was a more effective example. Each of the criteria included feedback that was grounded in observations from the speech; they were framed in a positive way and included comments on what was successful.

THE PSYCHOLOGY OF FEEDBACK

Receiving and/or giving feedback can be very difficult or very exciting for people. When feedback is given for ways to improve, some may find it very negative and difficult to cope. He or she may decide that the evaluator was being overly critical or unfair. It may discourage a person from trying in the future because it is easier to cope with failing as result of not trying than to try and still fail at the desired outcome. The goal of feedback is to help students progress and improve in speech presentations, but poorly constructed feedback can have the opposite effect, essentially, demotivating the student even further. Examining a couple of theories of motivation will help you understand why it is critical for you to learn how to give feedback the right way and also, what may be influencing your own motivation for giving speeches.

SELF-WORTH THEORY

One scholar wrote about students' having a "life-spanning struggle to establish and maintain a sense of worth and belonging in a society that values competency and doing well" (Covington, 2000, p. 182). Self-worth theory then, assumes that students highly value their own worth and that their worth is largely influenced by how well they do in school. Consequently, students may protect their self-worth through defensive strategies. The first is **withholding effort**. One instructional textbook wrote about self-worth theory, "Effort is a key feature of self-worth theory. Failure-avoidant students link effort with ability" (Powell, R. & Powell, D., 2010, p. 36). Therefore, students may consciously or subconsciously tell themselves, "It is better to not try and fail, then to try really hard and fail." This results in students who believe in their inevitable failure, not trying because they fear the failure of not succeeding more than not even attempting it. They don't want to feel incompetent or that they will be judged poorly by their peers. The second is **self-handicapping**. Students may procrastinate or spend too much time engaging in recreational activities, which gives them justification for not having done well. The third, **maintaining a defensive pessimism toward the task,** is where a student labels the assignment or instructor as "stupid" or "pointless." Understanding students' desire to maintain self-worth and what they may do to protect it is essential for you to understand as an evaluator and as the one being evaluated.

As an evaluator, keep in mind the recommendations provided earlier. Specifically, don't evaluate the person, evaluate his or her speech. By focusing on the speech, you can increase the acceptability of you evaluation. As the one being evaluated, the grade you receive on an assignment does not equate to your worth as a person, nor does it describe your capabilities. By following the advice and information in this textbook (including practice), you will see improvement in your presentations and this should motivate you to continue down the positive road of progress. Much of this theory deals with the perceptions students have about their abilities, but also how they want to protect their sense of self-worth. Similarly, another theory of motivation examines the personal perception of abilities.

SELF-EFFICACY

Self-efficacy describes an individual's willingness to attempt a task based on the perception they hold of their own ability to achieve the expected or desired outcome. Essentially, people that are confident, or highly efficacious, believe they are capable of producing the outcome that is desired. Simply, people are more likely to try something if they think they will succeed at it. This can determine whether or not the task is even attempted. When individuals have lower levels of self-efficacy, they may believe things are more difficult than they are. Also, efficacy is context specific. This means that someone who is highly efficacious in one area of their life may not be in other areas. For example, a soccer player may have a lot of motivation to try other sports, knowing that she is an athletic person, but she may not be motivated to speak in public.

LEVELS OF EFFICACY ARE INFLUENCED BY FOUR FACTORS

1. A person's previous experience in the particular or similar task.
2. If they have seen someone model the task and be successful.
3. Encouragement by others to attempt the task.
4. Physiological factors (nerves, physical limitations, etc.).

Self-efficacy theory is important to understand in public speaking and evaluation because students are often intimidated by speaking in public and receiving judgment or criticism for not doing well (not completing the desired outcome). By choosing your words carefully when evaluating, you have the opportunity to frame the speaker's experience as a success, instead of a failure. This will then help increase their levels of efficacy for the next speaking assignment.

WHEN YOU ARE EVALUATED

As described earlier, you will be evaluated. After your speech is completed, you may just want to sit down so that the audience's attention is no longer on you, you may feel very excited about your performance or you may want to gauge how the instructor graded you. Whatever your immediate feelings following your speech, there will be some form of evaluation. Your instructor may choose to make a few comments in front of the class (oral feedback). If this is the case, then it will be an excellent opportunity for you to engage in the listening process. You may be still feeling the effects of adrenaline and some jitters, so it will be important to actively *select* and then *attend* to your instructor's message. When she or he is offering feedback, avoid prejudging the information as criticism and focus on *understanding* what the instructor is trying to say and its value. In your *evaluation* of the feedback, try to identify how this information will be useful to you in the future. When the time comes to write and practice a future speech, *recall* the feedback your instructor gave you. It may even be useful to write it down on paper, once you have returned to your seat. Following your instructor's oral feedback, you may choose to *respond* initially, in class by smiling, and/or you may choose to respond by taking the information gathered from the feedback into consideration for future speaking assignments. Similar advice works for *written feedback*.

WHEN YOU RECEIVE WRITTEN FEEDBACK OR FEEDBACK FROM A RUBRIC, YOU SHOULD FOLLOW SOME HELPFUL TIPS:

1. Understand the comments by the evaluator. If they are confusing to you, then they won't be helpful. Ask for clarification or specific examples.
2. Don't internalize the feedback. All speakers have something to improve. Having specific areas of weakness pointed out or getting a bad grade, does not make you a bad person or a bad student for that matter. It just means that you have some more work to do.
3. Look at feedback as a positive thing. We cannot read minds, but feedback is a little like being able to look inside the mind of the audience. By reading feedback, you gain the opportunity to see exactly what you did well and what you need to improve. This gives you the tools to progress and become more effective.
4. Use the information. So often students get instructions to an assignment and then read them once. Teachers may even provide a rubric or a list of items, on which the student will be graded, but many students don't pay enough attention to these when writing and practicing their speeches. You will likely get feedback about the structure, content, and the delivery of your speech. Reread this feedback and take it into consideration, along with instructions and rubrics, in your speech writing and practicing processes. This will help to ensure that you have included ALL of the speech requirements.

SELF-FEEDBACK

At the conclusion of your speech it is typical to still feel the nerves and excitement that you had during the speech. Before, during and after a speech, speakers have the opportunity to use themselves as an evaluator. Chapter 2 discussed in great detail how you should prepare yourself for giving a speech and manage *public speaking anxiety*. Included in those recommendations was to keep the messages you tell yourself positive.

THE ESSENTIALS OF EVALUATION APPLY TO THE EVALUATIONS YOU GIVE TO YOURSELF AS WELL. FOLLOW THESE RECOMMENDATIONS:

1. Don't be a harsh critic of your own performance.
2. Recognize the value of the learning experience and that there is always room for improvement.
3. Remind yourself of the areas you were successful.
4. Identify what you need to improve and create a plan for making progress.

SUMMARY

Listening, like writing and giving speeches, is a skill. The more you understand about any skill and the more you practice it, the better you will get. Likely, while you were reading this chapter, you were able to think of moments in your own life where you were engaged in a poor listening habit or you identified a barrier that has made it difficult to listen to something important. Now you have the information on how to prevent and prepare for such issues. This will be helpful as you listen to messages and as you give your speeches.

Communication is not just an art of talking, but the better communicator knows that communication also requires active listening skills. There is a difference between hearing and listening. Hearing is the physical process of perceiving audible stimuli without focusing on the stimuli. However, listening is not just hearing, it is paying attention to the stimuli and assigning meaning to it. The listening process contains six steps: selecting, attending, understanding, evaluating, recalling, and responding.

You listen to conversations and information for a myriad of reasons including comprehension, empathy, evaluative, appreciative, and cultural understanding. Just as you listen for various reasons, each of us has a different type of listening style. Different types of listeners can be summed up using the acronym PACT, which stands for *p*eople-centered listeners, *a*ction-centered listeners, *c*ontent-centered listeners, and *t*ime-centered listeners.

Oftentimes you don't listen to the message being sent because of barriers that occur during the listening process. These barriers can be caused by both internal and/or external noise. There are four different types of noise: physical, physiological, psychological, and semantic. Some reasons we don't listen are information overload and receiver apprehension.

Along with listening barriers, you might not listen to the message because of poor listening habits. These types of negative behaviors include selective listening, being a talkaholic, pseudolistening, gap filling, defensive listening, and ambushing. You can learn to become a more effective listener by getting rid of these behaviors and practicing more active listening communication techniques.

Active listening happens when you paraphrase, or restate in your own words, the message sent by the speaker to accurately decode the message. This involves a four-step process: 1) The speaker makes a statement; 2) The listener paraphrases in his or her own words, the understanding of the message; 3) The speaker agrees or disagrees with the listener's paraphrase; and 4) If the speaker disagrees, the speaker restates the statement for clarity and the process repeats. If the speaker agrees, the process is complete.

Another way to become a more effective listener is to use the listening LADDER, an acronym describing listening tools. LADDER stands for the following: *l*ook at the speaker, *a*sk questions, *d*on't interrupt, *d*on't change the subject, check your *e*motions, and provide *r*esponses.

Once you understand the necessary ways to become an effective listener, you can take the time to assess your current skills. Ask yourself: What are some of the current situations that keep you from becoming the type of listener you want to be? Then, make a plan to overcome them. Some ways that you can do this is by providing nonjudgmental feedback, dialogue enhancers, and honoring silence. Just like with anything, practice makes perfect. If you practice active listening, you will become a more seasoned listener with excellent communication skills and also improve your evaluative skills.

The way we evaluate and critique others is heavily influenced by our culture, style of communicating, the expectations and rules for society, and specific situations, among other factors. Understanding and becoming familiar with the evaluation or critiquing process will help to build your critical thinking skills, speaking skills, and reflection skills. In evaluation, you will be looking at *structure, content,* and *delivery. Structure* is where the evaluator will be looking at the format and organization of your presentation. For *content,* the evaluator will be looking at the actual message and the value of your content. For *delivery,* the evaluator examines the performance.

The process of critiquing, or evaluating, is an internal and external process and must be conducted in a way that will be accepted by the presenter (person being evaluated)—this can be accomplished with feedback. *Feedback* is the response to specific observations of oral messages and the constructive advice given by an evaluator, typically in written or oral form. *Internal process* means you should be prepared, be aware, ask yourself questions about their content, ask yourself questions about their structure, ask yourself questions about their delivery. *External process* includes the essentials of evaluations and types of feedback. *Essentials of evaluation* include grounding your feedback with specific examples and remedies, framing it in a positive way, and incorporating areas where they succeeded.

The two types of feedback include oral and written. Oral feedback is given verbally and is informal. Focus more on the positives in the speech and be truthful. Written feedback is given in a written format. It is much more formal and can be extremely useful. Make comments grounded in specific observations so that the speaker will progress, this can be in a checklist, rubric or other form.

Receiving and/or giving feedback can be very difficult or very exciting for people. Theories of motivation will help you understand why it is critical for you to learn how to give feedback the right way. People highly value their own worth and how well people do in school affects their self-worth. They may use defensive strategies: withholding effort, self-handicapping, or maintaining a defensive pessimism toward the task. *Self-efficacy theory* describes an individual's willingness to attempt a task based on the perception they hold of their own ability to achieve the expected outcome. This can determine whether or not the task is even attempted. Levels of efficacy are influenced by four factors: a person's previous experience in the particular or similar task, if they have seen someone model the task and be successful, encouragement by others to attempt the task, and physiological factors (nerves, physical limitations, etc.).

By choosing your words carefully when evaluating, you have the opportunity to frame the speaker's experience as a success, instead of a failure. *When you are evaluated,* understand the comments by the evaluator, don't internalize the feedback, look at feedback as a positive thing, and use the information. With your *self-feedback,* don't be a harsh critic of your own performance, recognize the value of the learning experience and that there is always room for improvement, remind yourself of the areas you were successful, identify what you need to improve, and create a plan for making progress.

Most of us are familiar with the term constructive criticism, but the instructions given in this chapter go far beyond that. Having learned why feedback is critical for the speaker and for you, the different types of feedback, and how you can respond to feedback will better prepare you for the future. These critical listening and analytical skills will transcend your college and interpersonal experiences and go to work for you as you enter the workforce.

Review Questions

① Briefly explain the six stages of the listening process.

② Briefly distinguish between five different reasons people listen.

③ What is your worst bad listening habit and how will you overcome it?

④ Distinguish between structure, content, and delivery in evaluating a speech.

⑤ What key pieces of advice were given about receiving feedback for your speeches?

Glossary

Action-centered listening: Listeners who want messages to be highly organized, concise, and error-free.

Active listening: A communication technique where the listener restates a speaker's message for clarification and understanding.

Ambushing: Happens when you listen to the message with an ulterior motive to find information you can use to hurt the speaker.

Appreciative listening: Listening to stimulus for purely entertainment purposes.

Attending: The second stage in the listening process where you use the mental process of focusing or concentrating on specific message for a period of time.

Comprehension listening: Listening to understand and recall of the messages, not necessarily how you feel about them or if they were effective.

Content-centered listening: Listeners who focus on the facts and details of the message.

Critical listening: Listening that assess the reasoning and reliability of the message and the speaker, as well as the overall worth and effectiveness of the message.

Defensive listeners: Misconstrue all innocent comments as personal attacks or reasons to be upset with the speaker.

Dialogue enhancers: These brief verbal responses indicate that you are paying attention to the stimuli.

Empathic listening: Listening to provide comfort to people in your life.

Evaluating: The fourth stage in the listening process where the receiver analyzes, judges, and assesses the message, often to determine the intent and accuracy of the speaker's statements.

Evaluative criteria: These are items of the presentation that the evaluator will be assessing.

Evaluative listening: (See Critical listening.)

Fake listening: (See Pseudolistening.)

Feedback: The response to specific observations of oral messages and the constructive advice given by an evaluator, typically in written or oral form.

Gap filling: Results from the listening gap when we assume what the speaker intends to say before he or she finishes her sentences.

Hearing: The physical process of perceiving audible stimuli without focusing on the stimuli.

Immediate behaviors: Verbal and nonverbal communicative behaviors that create a sense of "psychological closeness" with others, increasing the effect for the speaker.

Information overload: Occurs when too much new information (stimuli) is thrown at us in too short of a time period.

Listening barriers: Anything that interferes with the listening process that does not allow the speaker's message to be understood properly by the receiver.

Listening: A transactional process of hearing, selecting, attending, understanding, evaluating, recalling, and responding to what we hear.

Maintaining a defensive pessimism toward the task: A defensive strategy used in self-worth theory where people may label the assignment or instructor as "stupid" or "pointless."

Nonjudgmental feedback: Providing feedback given with an open mind and consideration for others' ideas and cultural beliefs.

Oral feedback: Feedback that is given verbally, often more informal.

Paraphrasing: Restating in your own words the message sent by the speaker to accurately decode the stimuli.

People-centered listening: A listening style associated with concern for the other people's feelings or emotions.

Physical noise: Environmental sounds that interrupt your message where the listener cannot literally hear your words.

Physiological noise: Bodily conditions that break your concentration and keep you from listening to the stimuli.

Pseudolistening: Happens when we pretend to listen and use verbal and nonverbal response to continue the charade.

Psychological noise: Interference in the listening process due to internal, emotional conditions.

Recalling: The fifth stage in the listening process where you can remember and/or apply the information for future encounters.

Receiver apprehension: Occurs when the listener is afraid that he or she will not understand or interpret the message correctly.

Responding: The sixth stage in the listening process happens when the listener acknowledges verbally or nonverbally to the speaker whether or not the message has or has not been received.

Selecting: The first stage in the listening process when a person chooses to hear a specific message.

Selective listening: Happens when you only process the messages that appeal to your self-interests.

Self-efficacy: An individual's willingness to attempt a task based on the perception they hold of their own ability to achieve the expected or desired outcome

Self-feedback: Positive and constructive feedback you give to yourself following your presentation.

Self-handicapping: A defensive strategy used in self-worth theory where people may procrastinate or spend too much time engaging in recreational activities, which gives them justification for not having done well.

Self-worth theory: When people highly value their own worth and that their worth is largely influenced by how successful they are at achieving things like "As" in school or a promotion at work.

Semantic noise: Anything that interferes with the listening process when the sender and/or receiver do not understand the verbal and/or nonverbal messages in a communication exchange.

Talkaholics: People who monopolize the conversation to the point of excluding the others in the exchange.

Time-centered listening: Listeners who want messages to be presented succinctly.

Understanding: The third stage in the listening process when you assign meaning to the message.

Withholding effort: A defensive strategy used in self-worth theory where people who believe in their inevitable failure will not try because they fear the failure of not succeeding more than not even attempting it.

Written feedback: This type of feedback is given in a written format, often more formal.

References

Adler, R. B., & Proctor II, R. F. (2008). *Looking out, looking in* (2nd ed). Ohio: Cengage Learning.

Allen, M., Witt, P. L., & Wheeless, L. R. (2006). The role of teacher immediacy as a motivational factor in student learning: Using meta-analysis to test a causal model. *Communication Education, 55*(1), 21–31.

Anderson, J. F., Norton, R. W., & Nussbaum, J. F. (1981). Three investigations exploring relationships between perceived teacher communication behaviors and student learning. *Communication Education, 30,* 377–394.

Aristotle. (n.d.). Retrieved from http://www.bookbrowse.com/quotes/index.cfm?start_id=151

Bandura, A. (1977). Self-efficacy: Toward a unifying theory of behavioral change. *Psychological Review, 84,* 191–215.

Bandura, A. (2001). Social cognitive theory: An agentic perspective. *Annual Review of Psychology, 52,* 1–26.

Benoit & Lee. (1988). Listening: It can be taught! *Journal of Education of Business, 63*(5), 229–232.

Casserly, Megan. (2012). The 10 skills that will get you hired in 2013. Forbes. Retrieved from http://www.forbes.com/sites/meghancasserly/2012/12/10/the-10-skills-that-will-get-you-a-job-in-2013/

Churchill, W. (n.d.). Retrieved from http://www.quotationspage.com/quote/39728.html

Comstock, J., Rowell, E., & Bowers, J. W. (1995). Food for thought: Teacher nonverbal immediacy, student learning and curvilinearity. *Communication Education, 46,* 251–266.

Covington, M. V. (2000). Goal theory, motivation, and school achievement: An integrative review. *Annual Review of Psychology, 51,* 171–200.

Einstein, A. (n.d.). Retrieved from www.einstein-quotes.com/Love.html

Einstein, G. O., Morris, J., & Smith, S. (1985). Note-taking, individual differences, and memory for lecture information. *Journal of Educational Psychology, 77*(5), 522–532.

Fitch-Hauser, Barker, & Hughes. (1988).

Ford-Brown, L. A. (2012). *DK guide to public speaking: Researching, creating, outlining, organizing, supporting, presenting, listening, evaluating.* Boston, MA: Allyn & Bacon.

Fujishin, R. (2012). *Natural bridges: A guide to interpersonal communication.* Boston, MA: Pearson.

Johnson, S. D., & Bechlar, C. (1998). Examining the relationship between listening effectiveness and leadership emergence: Perceptions, behaviors and recall. *Small Group Communication Research, 29*(4), 452–471.

Maxwell, J. C. (1993). *Developing the leader within you: Workbook.* Nashville, TN: Thomas Nelson, Inc.

Powell, R. G., & Powell, D. (2010). *Classroom communication and diversity: Enhancing instructional practice* (2nd ed). New York, NY: Routledge.

Seiler, W. J., & Beall, M. L. (2003). *Communication: Making connections* (5th ed). Boston, MA: Pearson.

Watson, K. W., Barker L. L., & Weaver III, B. (1995). The listening styles profile (LSP 16): Development and validation of an instrument to assess four listening styles. *The International Journal of Listening, 9*(1), 1–13.

Zeno of Citium. (n.d.). Retrieved from http://en.wikiquote.org/wiki/Zeno_of_Citium

USING LANGUAGE EFFECTIVELY

Andrea D. Thorson-Hevle

Learning Objectives

CHAPTER 13

① Facilitate an understanding of the relationship between language and meaning.

② Investigate the language tools you can use in your speech including meaningful, vivid, simple, and styled language.

③ Learn the importance of considering the audience's culture as relevant to norms, expectations, beliefs, preferences, and oppressions.

④ Stimulate critical thinking about the power of language specific to oppressed and marginalized groups.

⑤ Consider the ways in which communication style can enhance your speech.

In order to be a great speaker you must have great tools; effective language is an essential one. The words we choose to use in our speeches can make lasting impressions. They can create long-term consequences and benefits and, as such, should be chosen very carefully. Language has the power to reinforce ideas and it has the power to dispel them. Language can paint a vivid picture in the mind of your audience or it can erase an image that had been in the mind for years. It has been used for some of the most memorable and wonderful moments in history, as well as the most devastating and horrific.

In order to discuss language we need to first clarify what language is. **Language** is any system of expression that uses words, gestures, motions, pronunciation, enunciation, and articulation to create a meaning. Language is often referred to as symbol making. Sometimes we use symbols to communicate an idea or feeling. Language is not just the spoken or written word, but many cultures rely on gestures to add meaning to their words and even the culture of sign language uses movement to communicate their language. Language is also symbolic because words and gestures represent meanings; they are symbols for more concrete things and abstract ideas as well.

For instance, when I say, "I saw a man," the word "man" conjures up a series of images that the listener associates with "man." Consider the term "accomplishment." When you define accomplishment what does it mean? Is that the same as the way your best friend, parents, siblings, teachers, or people much older than you would define it? Of course not. Understanding that there is no answer key to language is important—what one word or concept means to one person can have totally different meanings to someone else. This chapter helps you navigate the more complicated terrain of language choices as it pertains to your topic, ethos, and pathos, as well as how your language choices affect others. Specifically, this chapter discusses language and meaning, language tools to use during a speech and when constructing it, and the power of language.

The word "accomplishment" means different things for different people.

Image © Angela Waye, 2014. Used under license from Shutterstock, Inc.

Image © bikeriderlondon, 2014. Used under license from Shutterstock, Inc.

Image © bikeriderlondon, 2014. Used under license from Shutterstock, Inc.

Image © Blend Images, 2014. Used under license from Shutterstock, Inc.

Image © Tyler Olson, 2014. Used under license from Shutterstock, Inc.

FIGURE 13.1

If I asked you to picture, right now, in your mind a girl. Could you? Okay, please do. Picture a girl in your mind right now. What did you see? Did you picture a a human with long hair? Did this human wear a dress or colors such as red, pink, and purple? Many readers did picture a human with long hair, wearing a pinkish dress unfortunately. I say unfortunately, because of the sexism and stereotyping it suggests, but we will get to that latter on. What is interesting however, is that other people did not see that image at all. What did others see? Do we all have the same image of girls? No, we do not. If people from certain parts of the world pictured a girl they would see a short human with very short hair wearing only a bottom. So who is right? Which image of a girl is correct? We can't answer this question without investigating a few topics, so lets discuss a few areas of language and see what you can discern for yourself.

LANGUAGE AND MEANING

The history of language is built in categories and ways of thinking. Language is fundamentally a learned and accepted process. There are detonative and connotative meanings to language; each of these types adds a dimension of power to a word. <u>Denotative</u> meaning reflects the dictionary definition of the term or concept. <u>Connotative</u> meaning reflects the attached meaning and commonly associated emotional intent of the word. For instance, the denotative meaning of childish is "childlike." The connotative meaning can be anything from immature, selfish, etc. If you are trying to communicate that someone is immature or selfish, then childish is a good language choice. If, however, you were trying to point out someone is free, young at heart, and happy, the term "youthful" would be better because it has less negative connotations.

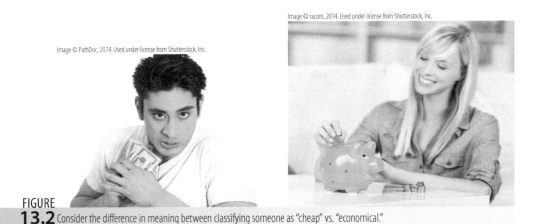

Image © PathDoc, 2014. Used under license from Shutterstock, Inc.

Image © racorn, 2014. Used under license from Shutterstock, Inc.

FIGURE 13.2 Consider the difference in meaning between classifying someone as "cheap" vs. "economical."

From person-to-person or culture-to-culture there are various degrees of and understandings for connotation. For instance, consider the popular phrase "hot mess." In recent years certain generations have taken on that phrase and used it to evaluate people. For some, when they say "Becka was a hot mess," they mean that Becka was a bit unorganized but still really attractive and pretty. Other cultures will interpret that to mean "the girl was disgusting, and sloppy and disorganized." The "hot" part of the word actually just adds to the degree of repelling quality, whereas in the first example the term "hot" actually referred to the fact that the girl was very attractive and perhaps part of her disorganization was what made her attractive. And yet, some cultures, perhaps the older generations who hadn't heard this before, end up picturing a steamy pile of stinky, messy, nasty food. No one is right or wrong, we are each able to have our associations. But when you are a public speaker you have an obligation to choose language that resonates with your audience and that your audience will understand (see Chapter 5 for more audience-centered ideas). On an important side note, I don't think there are many occasions in which using language like "hot mess" in your speech would be appropriate. It was used as an example that would keep your attention and be something you could relate to as my reader. I was not encouraging that language in speeches.

In 1923 a model was created to communicate these same ideas; it is called the Semantic Triangle of Meaning (Ogden and Richards). The **Semantic Triangle of Meaning** helps demonstrate how language choices can be understood.

Consider the connotation of "confident" vs. "arrogant."

FIGURE
13.3

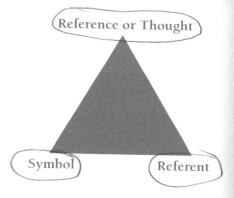

The triangle begins in the lower left corner with *symbol*. In this case, symbol refers to the specific term, word, or phrase that a speaker uses. The next part of the triangle is the lower right *referent*. Referent refers to the denotative meaning of the word—what the symbol (word) represents. The final area is the *reference* or thought. Reference refers to the connotative meaning of the word or phrase and/or its historical representation. The reference can hold emotional and physiological responses as well.

Let's say we use the phrase "an act of terror." In America before September 11, the phrase, "an act of terror" didn't hold much value to us beyond the denotative meaning. Now, after September 11, when Americans hear the phrase, "an act of terror," there is a great emotional and physiological response. Some people will have a flashback to that day, others will feel anger and fear, and still other people will equate that phrase to a particular group of people. The triangle demonstrates how although we may all understand the denotative meaning of the word we may not have the same connotative understandings. We may also have different emotional and thought-based reactions to hearing the terms based on our own personal and historical connections to a word or phrase. Consider using the semantic triangle when you encounter a term you are questioning using. Try to determine what possible reference the audience may have for that term before using it blindly.

LANGUAGE TOOLS

Once you have determined the proper terms to use when referencing groups of people you can move onto the language strategies that can advance your position, color your speech, and heighten your audience's interest. There are four primary language tools you can incorporate into

SPEAKING IS DIFFERENT FROM WRITING

Rules are not as explicitly followed

For instance, it is okay in public speaking to have a fragment or a phrase. We are expected to follow the basic rules of the language, but the expectations are flexible and moveable.

Mistakes can be quickly forgiven and forgotten

In speech-making when you make a mistake such as calling someone by the wrong name, you have the opportunity to correct it, apologize, and move on. You might even make a small joke about it and be able to connect with the audience over the mistake. In written form, when you use the wrong name, it significantly hurts your credibility. There is no opportunity to correct it later and make a joke. The words are printed and the books are in hands, your audience will judge your credibility on such mistakes and not likely forgive the error.

You can be funny more often, in more ways, and have it understood

In speech we can make a joke or use sarcasm and have an immediate understanding of how our audience is taking the joke. In some cases, you may need to apologize, reformulate, or even add more. I, for example, am a highly sarcastic and humor driven speaker, but while I'm writing this textbook I have had to dull that side of myself. If I don't, I run the risk of my readers not understanding my intention, or offending or irritating my readers. In a speech I can be funny and sarcastic and adjust according to my audience's needs and responses.

You need to repeat

In writing you are able to make your case and move on. If a reader doesn't fully grasp the idea they can go back and read the passage in question as many times as they need. They also have the ability to look back and forward to get an idea of where they have been and where they are going. In the spoken form, we are required to repeat key ideas several times and consistently remind the audience what we have discussed and what we will be discussing. We also need to watch the audience for any indicators that they are lost or may need further clarification.

your speech: meaningful language, vivid language, simple language, and styled language. The following section investigates these various tools and provides you with some ideas for crafting your speech.

MEANINGFUL LANGUAGE

"I am not unmindful that some of you have come here out of great trials and tribulations. Some of you have come fresh from narrow jail cells. And some of you have come from areas where your quest—quest for freedom left you battered by the storms of persecution and staggered by the winds of police brutality. You have been the veterans of creative suffering. Continue to work with the faith that unearned suffering is redemptive. Go back to Mississippi, go back to Alabama, go back to South Carolina, go back to Georgia, go back to Louisiana, go back to the slums and ghettos of our northern cities, knowing that somehow this situation can and will be changed."—I Have a Dream
by Martin Luther King, Jr., August 28, 1964

Martin Luther King, Jr.'s words drip in meaningful language. Each word was picked like a perfectly ripe fruit at just the right moment. There are five components to speaking with meaningful language—Marin Luther King, Jr. captured all of them in his speech—let's review what they can do for yours.

1. *Speak with passion.* This means the audience should feel as though you mean what you say. You should display acts of passion in your word choice. A speaker who clearly deeply cares what they are saying will be more likely to motivate, inspire, and persuade their audience. Keep in mind a helpful question that will inspire you to show your passion: If the audience doesn't think you passionately care about this topic, why should they?

2. *Avoid manipulation.* Public address should always have the best interest of the listeners at heart. It is not about putting on a show. If your audience suspects you are doing this, your ethos will be negatively affected. Do not speak unethically. In public speaking the speech to persuade must benefit the audience, not just the speaker's interests.

Image © Everett Collection, 2014. Used under license from Shutterstock, Inc.

When Angelina Jolie spoke at the press conference for the Third Annual Clinton Global Initiative Summit, Manhattan, New York, NY, September 26, 2007, she was captivating and moving. Her speeches are always impactful because her audience never questions her passion. The emotion she feels can be felt by everyone around her.

FIGURE **13.4**

3. *Be honest and authentic.* The appeal to the audience's emotions needs to begin with your own emotional connection. Pathos should be you sharing your emotion with others and thereby evoking an emotional response from them. If your audience feels you are being honest, and true to yourself, they are more likely to be affected by emotional appeals.

4. *Use personal pronouns.* This is not often seen in written work. You are usually told to refrain from using "I" in written work. In public speaking, however, it is not discouraged and can actually have a positive effect on the audience. You may notice several of us in this textbook have chosen to go against the norm and use our own voice of "I." This is widely in part due to the fact that we are all public speakers who recognize the value of the individual voice and a personal connection with our audience.

5. *Use emotion-evoking words.* Words can be emotionally charged or emotionally neutral. In a speech you want to have both, but it is important you have emotionally charged words when you are trying to affect the audience's emotional state. An easy reference to this type of emotional wording is found in everyday politics. Depending on the side and depending on the motive, political parties will describe the same events very differently and usually for the purpose of inspiring an emotional reaction from its listeners.

In recent years, the term **"terrorist"** has been used frequently by politicians and news anchors, and for a very specific reason.

The term "terrorist" has been shown to inspire emotions of anger or pride, and a sense of justice, revenge, and protection. Consider, if those speakers used, instead of "terrorist," the term "fighter" or "fanatic"?

It doesn't have the same effect does it? Of course, keep in mind ethics when choosing your emotionally charged terms; we never want to blur the line into lying or hate speech.

VIVID LANGUAGE

Vivid language is language that is colorful, concrete, and appeals to the senses. Vivid language choices help paint a picture in the mind of the audience. As the artist (speaker) your brushes and color palette are the tools with which you construct your argument, imagery, and purpose. The audience should be able to feel and see what the speaker is saying and vivid language choices are a great way to accomplish that task. There are very distinctly vivid language choices you can make as a speaker: simile, metaphor, analogy, and personification are among them.

FIGURE 13.5 Colorful, expressive, and vivid language can make our ideas come alive.

Simile is a device that depicts images through the use of concrete and distinct comparison of two or more unlike things. The easiest way to remember the simile is that it uses words "like" or "as." For example, "Justin grew *like* a weed," or "Justin was smart *as* a whip."

Metaphor is a simple device that depicts images through the use of an implied comparison of two or more unlike things. If your mother asked you how your recent presentation in your speech class went and you replied "nothing but net." You would be comparing how you did on your speech to landing a basketball in the center of the basketball hoop so perfectly that it didn't hit any metal, just net.

Analogy is a device that compares two similar cases and infers that what is true in one case is true in another. It is similar to a metaphor but more complex.

Personification is a device that gives human qualities to an object or animal. For example, "the wind whistled and screamed." The wind cannot actually scream or whistle, the sentence gave the wind human characteristics.

PERSONIFICATION EXAMPLES

The stars danced in the sky.
The sun wrapped its warm arms around me.
My hair cried for attention.

SIMPLE LANGUAGE

Public speaking in general calls for simpler language. The audience doesn't have the pleasure of being able to read a sentence or page over and over. If the speaker confuses the audience and doesn't clarify later on, the audience will be lost indefinitely. In order to obtain simplicity consider the following:

1. *Use familiar words.* Using words your audience is unfamiliar with will result in them feeling isolated or thinking about the word instead of what you are actually trying to say. Unfamiliar words are distracting.

2. _Make sure your sentences can be easily understood._ When you write a complex sentence you have the ability to choose from commas, semi-colons, colons, periods, etc. And all these options allow your sentence to read in a certain way. In speech-making we have no such tools, so we need to make sure our delivery is impeccable (see the delivery chapter) and that we are communicating in a way that is easily understood.

3. _Use concrete instead of vague words._ Concrete words are simple, to the point, and they tend to have less chance to have connotation issues. **Concrete** language references a specific object. **Vague** language (often termed abstract) is ambiguous language that is less clear in what it is referring to. In public speaking it is generally expected that you use more concrete terms to avoid misunderstandings or unintended interpretation.

Vague/Abstract		Clear/Concrete
Winter	Cold outside	Snowing and a fast wind
Very large	Bigger than me	6'6" tall and 325 lbs.
There are a lot of side effects.	There are about four side effects.	The side effects are nausea, tiredness, dizziness, and increased appetite.

4. _Being consistent is key._ Consistency in the word choice is especially important. For instance, while writing this chapter, I have to type the word "public speaking" frequently, but sometimes I write "public address" instead. I try to catch myself and amend the mistake. It's important in writing as well, but speaking even more so because the speech exists only in that moment and can't be amended.

5. _Use fewer words_ to communicate your point so the audience stays on track.

6. _Use contractions_ frequently. **Contractions** are words that put two words together to form one word. The term "contract" means to make smaller and that is the idea behind using contractions in public speaking; when we can make something more concise without losing meaning it is often a good choice. We use contractions frequently in oral communication, but not frequently in written communication.

CONTRACTIONS

Remember to put the apostrophe where the deleted letter had been.
"you are" = "you're"

The apostrophe is essential. Consider the sentence "She'll have a red nose." If you omit the apostrophe it reads, "Shell have a red nose."

Examples:
shouldn't   that's   they'd   wasn't   you'd   I'm   he'd   where's   he's   I've   I'd   they've   he's   she's   she'd   who's
Use contractions to create shortcuts in time and length of your speech.

7. _Avoid idioms._ Idioms can make members of the audience feel forgotten, unimportant, or oppressed. Idioms are a composition of words that create an idea that only certain people will be able to discern its meaning. Idioms do not make sense if you apply the denotative meaning of the words. For instance, "kick the bucket" means someone died, but those three words denotative meanings and even their connotative meanings don't tell the hearer what is meant. The only way an audience will understand this is if they belong to a culture in which it has been stated before.

8. _Use connectives._ Words that connect one idea to another and especially transitions from one point to the next are excellent ways to establish simplicity. Connectives can combine two sentences together and accomplish a cleaner sound. A lack of connectives can communicate the speaker may not have mastered the language they are speaking.

CONNECTIVES

We are late. Sebastian took a three-hour nap.
We are late _because_ **Sebastian took a three-hour nap.**

Montgomery lives in China. He doesn't speak Chinese.
Although **Montgomery lives in China, he doesn't speak Chinese.**

James was full of energy. We let him play on the trampoline.
Since **James was full of energy, we let him play on the trampoline.**

---

9. _Rephrase unnecessary jargon._ **Jargon** is language that is used by a specific group of people in a given occupation or culture that other cultures may not be able to understand. For instance, when doctors talk about heart attacks they call them cardiac arrest. When dentists are refereeing to the top portion of a tooth they call it the occlusal surface. This is jargon. When the jargon is specific to the field of work your audience belongs to then jargon is fine. Otherwise, jargon may confuse, insult, or irritate an audience.

10. _Avoid complex or unnecessarily large words._ For example, the word "patriarchy" is a great word, but if your audience doesn't know what it means then it's a poor choice. The exception to this is if your style calls for these kinds of words. Please see the next section for a discussion on style.

STYLISTIC LANGUAGE

When you begin crafting your speech you should do some self-analysis. You should consider what kind of speech and style you naturally have and what kind of style you would like to have for a particular speech. Style is practical, yet is an artful way to communicate a perspective.

All figures of speech are considered stylistic in nature. **Style** in public speaking refers to the ways in which something is said, expressed, done, or performed. There are three types of styles: grand, plain, and moderate. The particular types of stylistic devices and the degree to which you use them will help you determine which style you belong to. The first is the grand style. This is also called _high style_.

GRAND STYLE

Grand style is born out of a classical rhetoric, or at least that is as far back as we can find evidence of it. The **grand style** is characterized by heightened emotional attributes that can be seen in the speaker's performance, tone, diction, and figures of speech; it is a writing and speech style that is significant and empowered, impassioned and opulent. Cicero asserted, "the grand orator was fiery, impetuous; his eloquence 'rushes along with the roar of a mighty stream."

Speakers use a grand style for many reasons, but most come down to four things:

1. To move the audience
2. To persuade the audience
3. To inspire the audience
4. To motivate the audience

The beauty of the grand style is it has the ability to not merely present information in an interesting way, but perform the argument in a manner that demands the audience take notice, change their perceptions, and alter their behaviors. Masters of the grand style will consistently have speeches with metaphors, similes, amplifications, the most moving figures of speech, vivid words, and sentences constructed with rhythm in mind. Shakespeare consistently used the grand style in his writing and especially in the monologues of his most impassioned characters. If you choose to use the grand style you will want to choose many different "figures of speech" from the list that is provided.

These are some of the more commonly used, but not the only ones available to you	Commonly Used Figures of Speech
Antithesis	Contrasting ideas in balanced phrases *"One small step for man, one giant step for mankind."*
Irony	A series of words used to express a meaning opposite of their literal meaning. *Judgmental people are all alike.* *I only have impatience for those who are impatient.*
Hyperbole	A wild exaggeration used to magnify the effect. *"I'm so hungry I could eat a horse."*
Alliteration	Similar sounding internal vowels used in words close to each other. *My wig is like a pig without a bid for life.*
Onomatopoeia	Words that mimic the sounds associated with certain objects or actions to which they are referring. *It creaked and cracked and even popped as I walked along.*
Metonymy	Substitution of what something is to what is meant . The terms "gray hair" can be substituted for "getting old" or "old," for instance. *He is tired and gray.* *The pen is mightier than the sword.*
Anaphora	Is the same word or series of words used over and over. *I have a dream . . . I have a dream . . . I have a dream*
Pun	The use of a word in two of more meanings. Puns are intended to add humor and wit. In the example below "lies" has two different meanings. *A politician is someone who lies down his best ideas for the good of the people.*
Alliteration consonance	The repetition of the same consonance to increase effect. *Kate catches kittens.* *James joked with joy.*

PLAIN STYLE

Plain style is also known as low style and is characterized as a brief and clear form of speaking. Plain style is not concerned with figurative language, tonal passions, or other things associated with the grand style. The common use of this style is for the delivery of information without the intent to persuade. Speakers who employ this style usually do so for three reasons:

1. To be clear
2. To be concise
3. To communicate simple instructions or technical information

Plain styled speakers will have significantly less ability to influence the audience's beliefs, attitudes, values, or behaviors.

MODERATE STYLE

Moderate style is the style that incorporates some attributes from both the high and low styles. The goal of moderate style is achieve some emotional impact but also remain simple and clear. Often called the pleasing style, moderate style is known for amplification, effective word choice, and vivid language. Aristotle was most fond of this style.

Other Figures of Speech

Anagnorisis
This is a statement designed to keep your audience from doing something. It is often used in conjunction with hyperbole and cause and effect language strategies.
If you don't wear your helmet, someday your brains will be spread all over the asphalt.

Conduplicatio
The repetition of words or phrases at the start of successive phrases.
"I could list the problems that lead to obesity in America, problems like lazy lifestyles and lack of exercise and problems in diet and nutrition.

Climax
This is a figure that builds intensity in the speech by repeating words or phrases while increasing their power or significance.
Human rights matter, human rights are important, human rights are the foundation of our humanity, and the only rights that can in one moment reduce us to mere animals!

Epistrophe
This is the repetition of the same word or series of words in a sentence, clause, or phrase.
The time for justice has come. The time for thinking for ourselves has come. The time for doing instead of talking has come. Your time, our time, has come.

LANGUAGE AS POWER

Language should be the bridge that brings cultures together, it should not be used to divide or dehumanize. <u>Dehumanize</u> refers to the degradation of another, the oppression of and diminishment of a particular person or culture. In order to avoid dehumanizing and harmful language we must recognize we are limited by our own experiences, which means we need to consistently understand that our words have consequences. One example of this is the use of ethnocentric language. <u>Ethnocentric</u> means someone who thinks their culture is superior to other cultures. This chapter focuses on the role of effective language in public speaking. Specifically, we discuss how to create concise language, discuss how our language is reflective of our culture, understand how it affects other cultures, and finally examine strategies that can be used in public speaking.

Words have consequences. Language we may view as harmless may cause others great pain.

FIGURE 13.6

"It is obvious that sexist and non-inclusive language hurts women. It hurts their status in society, it hurts them physically, and it hurts them psychologically. Think about it— women are ignored, and deprecated everyday in general conversations as well as important discourse. How could this not have an effect on their status and mental states?"—(The Language We Use, 2014) http://thelanguageweuse.wordpress.com/2012/05/03/the-effects-of-sexist-language/

APPROACH LANGUAGE WITH CULTURE IN MIND

When you are a speaker you need to adhere to making appropriate language choices for the given audience and recognize that your words reflect who you are to the audience. The first amendment of the constitution protects speech, but it does not protect hate language, slander, or defamatory language. As a public speaker it is your obligation to understand what words and phrases are not protected and are hurtful to certain individuals or cultures. This section of the chapter helps you understand why some terms should be avoided and why others are preferred. We specifically examine sexist language, language surrounding sexual orientation and gender, ethnic language, and language regarding the disabled community.

Language that respects individuality and diversity respects persons.

FIGURE 13.7

Often people will say, "that is not what I meant," right after they said something insensitive. The use of insensitive language can be purposeful or it can simply mean that they were not considering who the audience was when they said it. Usually this happens because of ignorance or a general lack of education regarding particular words and cultures. It is important that we choose our words wisely and with sensitivity to other cultures in mind.

Idiom
A distinct expression used by a specific culture that other cultures might not understand because the denotative meaning of the words does not accurately describe the meaning. Avoid these in your speech because others may be confused or even offended by them.
"Get off my back."
"You totally missed the bus."
"He is not the brightest star in the sky."
"Don't let the flies out."
"The weight of the world is on your shoulders."
"They had me in stitches."

Image © Skylines, 2014. Used under license from Shutterstock, Inc.

FIGURE 13.8 The lenses of culture allow us to see what we otherwise might not.

In order to do this, we must first accept that we are biased in some way. We are biased and limited because we see and understand the world based on our culture and our limited experiences. Since we can't possibly know all cultures and experiences, we are all limited, but we don't have to be completely. In order to speak effectively, ethically, and justly, we must consider other culture's language, norms, and expectations. In a way, we are each looking through a pair of glasses that focus and blur certain things based on the cultures we belong to and the experiences we have had. Each culture we belong to (age, sex, gender, sexual orientation, ethnicity, race, nationality, occupation, hobbies, etc.) creates a lens that we use to see the world with. And, thus, a lens with which we judge the world and speak to the world. The more we can learn about other cultures and understand the power of language choices, the more we can change our language to have positive intents and outcomes. With each conscious attempt to consider other cultures we can adjust our sight to see a bit more clearly.

Ask Yourself . . .
Is this language offensive to some people?
Is there a term I could use that means the same thing but isn't offensive to anyone?
Have I evaluated my own bias and examined my word choice with that in mind?
Do I know the connotative meanings for the words?

FIGURE 13.9 Individual audience members will understand your words individually.

Chapter 3 discusses taking your audience into consideration when crafting a speech. This is the first step you need to make in order to use language effectively. Ask yourself who is in my audience? And also ask yourself which of your own cultures are affecting how you speak. Then cross-reference those results with the cultures of your audience. Try to adopt the stance of the audience and evaluate your language choices from their perspective.

Ask yourself, do you have the same effect as you intended or are there differences? Remember your language can also establish or harm your credibility, so pay careful attention to what your audience views as appropriate language choices for that given speaking event. Please refer to Chapter 3 for more ideas on audience analysis.

It may be common to use double negatives, slang, or generally poor grammar in your culture, but when you're engaging in a formal speech, you need to polish your language choices. Do not encourage hate language or insensitive word choices. For instance, language can age a speaker. There are certain terms and language that are used by different generations that are not used by other generations. Another age group will not necessarily understand slang language and colloquialisms that are used commonly in one age group.

Same Word, Different Meaning

Weiner = hot dog
Tennies = sneakers or running shoes, or tennis shoes
Hot mess = disaster, chaotic, not put together or sexy cool
Sick = cool, awesome, great
Shut-up! = no way, oh my gosh, oh wow, interesting, tell me more

Colloqualisms—Did You Know These?
"To bamboozle" = to deceive or manipulate
"A bunch of numpties" = a group of idiots
"Maggot bag" = a meat pie

Language can also communicate where someone is from culturally and regionally. For instance, if someone were to speak with a southern accent and said, "ya'll" in their speech, the audience would interpret that to mean this person was from a certain area of the country and even start a series of assumptions about the speaker. If a speaker uses improper English, it can be interpreted as symbolic of their background and include how credible the audience perceives the speaker to be. Knowing this, informal language choices such as slang should generally be avoided.

A LANGUAGE AND CULTURE EXPERIENCE

I was born and raised in a small town in Montana. When I was sixteen my family moved to California. For the first few weeks of school I could hardly communicate with students my age because of the differences in language. We all spoke English, but the word choices within the language of English were very different. To me, their words were strung together and lacked clear distinction; I couldn't discern one single word from a sentence most days. This was in part because the pronunciation and enunciation were different, but also because the California teen culture at the time used slang language that I was not familiar with. Eventually, I would learn that most my peers had initially thought I was "stuck up" because I spoke so precisely.

At my new high school in California a common greeting was, "Yo what's up fool?" Now, if you're a young Californian this makes sense to you. I was from a culture where I had never heard language like that and it became very stressful for me to be told something frequently that I really didn't understand.

For starters, I didn't know what the words actually were. To me that sentence sounded like, "yowadupfo"—one single word. When I finally made a friend and asked her to tell me what people were saying to me as they passed by. She explained people were asking, "What was up fool." I immediately became irritated and bewildered. Why would anyone ask what is up? What does that mean? And, more importantly, why were they trying to pick a fight with me by calling me a "fool"? What had I done to make so many people dislike me and call me names? I was shocked and then I became mad. In my culture when someone insults you in this way, and in front of others, it is often settled immediately and physically. I quickly took off after the last boy who said that to me. My girlfriend quickly stopped me and insisted I listen to her explanation.

Do you see how language choices can result in a problem? The above example demonstrates how words carry different meanings for different cultures. Although this example takes place in everyday life, the lesson is still relevant to public speaking. It is important to consider the culture of your audience or what you intend to say may quickly become what you did not intend to say.

In some countries flipping up your pinky finger is the same as showing the middle finger in the United States. Different cultures have different understandings of words and symbols of words. Learning about different cultures and their norms is important in real life and public speaking is no exception.

OPPRESSIVE LANGUAGE TO AVOID

When you read the header "oppressive language to avoid" you might have rolled your eyes and thought to yourself "I know not to use oppressive language, I'm not like that." But is that true? It has been found that more than half of Americans use oppressive language every day and do not recognize it. It's very important that as a speaker you understand what is considered oppressive language and learn strategies to diminish your use of it. Oppressive language is any word or series of words that uses an identifier of a person or a certain group as a negative or undesirable characteristic (class, race, sex, gender, sexual orientation, ability, etc.). It is usually used to suppress and belittle whether intentional or unintentional. It is considered a form of verbal violence.

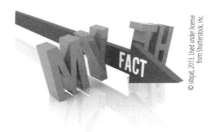

Cultural myths and stereotypes usually don't match the facts.

FIGURE
13.10

Oppressive language begins with some form of bias. Bias is communicating or treating someone differently because of their connection to a given culture. This includes such cultures as: age, ethnicity, sex, gender, disability, race, political affiliation, hobby-based groups, social affiliation, marital status, occupation, religion, and sexual orientation. Bias usually stems from one or more five reasons:

1. A lack of information or correct information about a culture
2. A fear of a culture
3. Hate of a culture
4. Stereotypes and prejudices about a culture
5. Ethnocentrism—a belief that your culture is superior to others

FIGURE
13.11

Bias is the breeding ground for hate crimes and should be avoided at all costs. Using any oppressive terms in a speech furthers the acceptability of the term, desensitizes others from the word, incites negative emotion, and reinforces stereotypes. In order to avoid biased language you need to first recognize the ways in which you are currently biased and your own use of oppressive language. This is not a fun process. It means you have to admit you hold negative and typically untrue ideas about different cultures of people based on totally irrelevant, inaccurate, or unimportant information. Furthermore, you must recognize that those beliefs have the power to physically and emotionally harm others. Once you have accomplished your self-reflection it is time to assess your language and make adjustments.

If you hear certain cultures refer to themselves in a certain way when talking to each other, this does not give you permission to use the same language. It is not important why or the fairness of this. What is important is that as a speaker you use language effectively and with empathy.

Take for example World War II when Hitler led Nazi Germany. Hitler gave a great number of speeches aimed at convincing his audience that a certain culture or cultures were bad and should be eradicated. Think about that for a minute. How powerful must language be to get you to decide that not only should a certain culture be eradicated, but also convince you to take part in the process? Hitler never called Jewish people just "Jewish." When he referenced Jewish people he added certain language in an attempt to incite and create a connotative meaning in the mind of his listeners. He would say "vermin" and refer to them as a "disease" that was infecting the country. We know that language is learned and that connotative meaning is very powerful. If you hear something often enough and that is the common way it is expressed, soon you will begin to accept it as truth. This is exactly what Hitler accomplished with his language choices and what ultimately lead to the Holocaust where millions of Jewish people were killed.

You can also reference the history of the United States. When settlers came to the United States, they invaded a country of what are now called American Indians. The language strategies that were used referred to native people as "savages." *Savage* has an entirely different connotative value to it than *native*. *Savage* implies a brutal, violent, and dangerous meaning. This could easily incite feelings of protectiveness and defensiveness. *Native* implies they were the first to inhabit and thus may be the rightful owners. It is far easier to kill a person or take something from someone who you think of as an intruder or dangerous than to take something from someone who is defending their home from you.

It is important to be aware of how a term has been historically used against various cultures so that you can choose an alternative word. Today the phrase "that is so gay," is commonly used. Those who use this phrase often say they are not intending to hurt any culture or even talk about gay people. So why is it a problem? Because intentions are irrelevant; the outcome is relevant. The outcome is that phrases like "that's so gay" are used every day to dehumanize gay and lesbian people. This phrase is also one of the most common forms of hate speech used in America today and has been linked to a significant number of hate crimes. That phrase has been noted for its consistent role in instigating hate crime in the United States. The bottom line is that phrase is not being used to applaud or support the gay and lesbian community it is used to suppress them, and as such, it is a phrase that has no place in speechmaking.

> ## AVOID THE COMMON WAYS SPEAKERS COMMUNICATE BIAS
>
> Assumptions
> Jokes
> Pronouns
> Stereotypical examples
> Fashion trends

Other common oppressive terms include "Oriental" or "Hispanic." There are no such "oriental" people. If you are referring to people who are Japanese, Chinese, Korean, Mong, and so on, you must call each culture by those specific names not an overarching name like "Asian." Oriental is considered highly offensive and racist. Hispanic is problematic because it technically attempts to classify Spanish, Cuban, or Mexican people in the same group. These are wildly different cultures, with very different norms, lives, values, etc.—to lump them together is unacceptable and insulting to some. If someone wants to be identified as "Hispanic" then you can use that term, otherwise refrain

© iQoncept, 2013. Used under license from Shutterstock, Inc.

FIGURE 13.12 Don't let bias ruin your speech. Be reflective and critical of yourself. You can only improve if you are honest about your shortcomings and start fixing them.

Avoid	Use	
Asian cultures	The specific culture you are addressing	
Hispanic	The specific culture you are addressing	
Oriental	The specific culture you are addressing	This is a term that should NOT be used
Native American	The specific tribe you are addressing	It is okay to use if you are referring all the tribes only

from using the term. The general rule is to call a person or a culture by its specific name, do not lump cultures together—doing so diminishes the independence and uniqueness of their cultures and can be insulting.

Common ways speakers communicate their bias to the audience comes in the form of assumptions, jokes, or offensive or stereotypical examples. The table of language options is here for you to consider. The list is not comprehensive, if you encounter a word you want to use in your speech, but think it may be problematic, do not use it. Consult an expert or research it and then make an educated decision.

There are many different types of language-based oppressions, ways in which people are put down by societies through the use of symbols. It is important to understand that just because you have a system of values and beliefs doesn't mean you practice a similar set of behaviors and language choices. You must be critical of not only what you believe and value, but of what you say. For instance, do you participate in the oppression category known as sexism? You might say "no" because you value men and women equally. But, if I asked if you often refer to a group of men and women as "guys" then you do participate in the oppression of women through your language choices at times. Let's do a quick run down of five of the many general oppression categories:

1. Sexism—some of the most devastating results of sexist language is that it tends to demonstrate that women either do not exist as members (as is the case in the "you guys" example) or diminishes their importance and value. Research sadly shows a strong correlation between people who use sexist language on a regular basis and violence against women generally. It is hypothesized that the language that reflects a devaluing of women makes it easier to hurt women, makes it more excusable to the attacker. Many people who participate in slip up's like "you guys" have no intention of harming women and cringe at the idea. If that is you, then remember this information and make a conscious choice to avoid those words in the future.

2. Heterosexism—Heterosexism is a subcategory of sexism and assumes that people desire to have sexual relationships only with people of the opposite sex. Those who do not fit this subscription are often judged, ridiculed, abused, tormented to suicide, and even murdered. Oppressive language is usually where all these tragic ends begin. Hate language, which I feel compelled not to write down in ink, is responsible for inspiring some of the most tragic and horrible crimes on gay and lesbian children, teens, and adults. Words that you may think are harmless, but refer to this culture in any derogatory way, is not okay to use.

3. Classism—Classism is a social pattern in which those with money and privilege associate with each other and use language to put down cultures with less money and privilege. This often occurs in language choices of people who come from money and don't

realize they are saying hurtful things. Common examples of classism include treating people poorly, or speaking badly, about people with certain kinds of jobs or the way they dress that indicate they don't make a lot of money or have certain opportunities.

4. Racism—Racism is a systematic categorization and oppression of a people because of one specific "racial" group to which they are perceived to belong. People who say "racism doesn't exist anymore" usually don't belong to a group that is being oppressed, or is lucky enough to be in an area where it is not as common. For the most part, there are some very problematic racist threads left is the U.S.A. and language is at the core of the problems. Racist language is never okay in public address. While, America may be aware that racism exists, we certainly do not appreciate it and many of us will punish those racists in every way we can when they show their racist ways publicly. Everyone can recall the the 2014 Clippers owner Donald Sterling scandal. In a taped recording, Donald Sterling chastised his female friend for hanging out with "black people." This racist language resulted in Sterling being banned from the sport for life. Words have consequences.

5. Lookism—Lookism is a form of oppression that is based on the appearance of a persons face/body and the degree to which it fits society's ideals for what that type of person should look like. If you were giving a speech on the increasing weight of American children, you would not say, "American children are fatter today than every before." You might say, "Obesity is on the rise in America." But, you would only use the term "obesity" if that was the right word, because there is a medical difference between "overweight" and "obese." So, be sure to know medical definitions of terms before you use anything. Our culture has very specific ideas about what people of each sex and gender and age should look like and we have a lot of words we can use to hurt people's feelings, to put people down, to make jokes, to self-deprecate, and dehumanize. It is important that we consider the power of our words at all times.

OPPRESSIVE LANGUAGE HAS BEEN DIRECTLY LINKED TO:

Stigma: an undesirable mark of disgrace associated with a person or group of people, quality, or circumstance.

Stereotype: misjudgment of a person by assuming that they belong to a certain group or that belonging to that group means they have a specific set of characteristics.

Prejudice: preconceived judgment based on opinion.

Hate language: any speech, gesture, conduct, or writing that may incite violence or prejudice against an individual or group.

Hate crime: crime directed at an individual or group of people based on their affiliation with certain groups or characteristics including race, religion, ethnicity, or sexual orientation.

SEXIST LANGUAGE

Sexist and gendered language is the most common type of oppressive language. Speakers who fail to use gender neutral and inclusive language run a great risk of being seen as uneducated and lacking empathy and credibility. One of the most common examples of sexist language today is the use of "you guys" when referring to an audience of men and women. "Guys" is a term that recognizes the male sex; it does not include the female sex. In public speaking, if a speaker uses "you guys," they are ignoring or diminishing the presence of the women in the room. Consider using a word like "everyone" when addressing an audience.

Before I can continue this explanation we need to establish the difference between sex and gender. Sex refers to the biological sex of an individual such as male, female, or intersex (having both sex organs). Sex considers specific chromosomes, sex organs, and hormones as a means of identification.

Fairness and social justice ask that our words represent women and men equally.

FIGURE 13.13

Gender refers to the degree to which a person confirms, identifies with, and/or adopts specific social roles, specifically we can break gender up into expression, identity and roles. **Gender expression** for example, refers to the ways people tend to communication their gender externally. This may come in the form of clothing, jewelry, tattoos, hairstyles and color, and even the sounds of their voice. **Gender identity** on the other hand refers to how a person perceives themselves and how they prefer to refer to themselves. **Gender roles** refer to the various expectations, roles, and behaviors that have been assigned to men and women based on the idea that men should be masculine and women should be feminine.

Gender is understood as encompassing two main concepts: masculinity and femininity. It is important, however, to comprehend the scope of gender. There are not two categories; rather, gender can be mapped out on a continuum with femininity at one end and masculinity on the other. The space exactly between the two is called androgyny. Androgyny is a mixture of feminine and masculine traits. Research has shown that most people have developed their gender by the time they are about three years old.

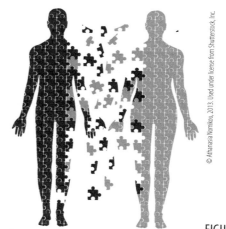

Gender is about social roles and norms. Most of us don't fit easy gender categories.

FIGURE 13.14

Masculinity is commonly associated with men and femininity with women, but this is not an entirely accurate assumption. Femininity is associated with certain characteristics and masculinity with certain characteristics. Between these two is androgyny, which is a blend of the two ends of the gender continuum, where a person can have some masculine traits and some feminine traits. Research has found that most people have a combination of masculine and feminine traits regardless of their sex.

In speech-making, the best speakers historically have had a mixture of both feminine and masculine traits. For example, Martin Luther King, Jr. displaced stereotypical masculine strengths of logic, loudness, and strength, but he also had the feminine traits of caring, passion, figurative language, and storytelling in his speeches.

When you refer to an audience of men, do not assume they relate to masculine traits, and when speaking to women, do not assume they respond to feminine appeals. Doing so can insult your audience and harm your ethos. For instance, I once was in an audience made up completely of women. The speaker noted that we were all females from the start and from that point on every example he gave was relevant to cheerleading, mothering, cooking, or shopping. More than half the women were irritated by the sexist assumption and several audience members left.

Over the decades we have tried to make right the biased language that fundamentally ignored the presence of women. At one time, it was commonly accepted to refer to anyone and anything

Poor Sentence	Change the Sentence by . . .	Good Sentence
"No man shall stand in our way."	Neutral words	"No **person** shall stand in our way."
"A student who takes their test will remain in **his** seat until everyone else is finished or until **he** is asked to leave."	Plural words	"**Students** taking the test will remain in **their** seats until everyone else is finished or until **they** are asked to leave."
"The group meeting summary is collected by the secretary each day and until **her** report is filed you cannot move onto the next step."	Definite article	"The group meeting summary is collected by the secretary each day and until the report is filed you cannot move onto the next step."
"Every student must pay all fees and holds before **he** can obtain **his** diploma."	"they" "them" "themselves" "their"	"Every student must pay all fees and holds before **they** can obtain **their** diploma."
"Any trainee who struggles with the fitness test must learn and train to finish it **herself**."		"Any trainee who struggles with the fitness test must learn and train to finish it **themselves**."
"If the parent of the child is satisfied with the level of accomplishment of **his/her** child then we are too."	Repeating the noun	"If the **parent** is satisfied with the level of accomplishment of the parents' child then we are too."
"If the officer finds there is reasonable suspicion then **he** should investigate further."		"If **the officer** finds there is reasonable suspicion then **the officer** should investigate further."
"The teacher may add a student after the deadline if **she** determines there circumstances that warrant **her** making the accommodation and if her class has enough seats available that it won't make **her** classroom too full."	Rewrite	"The teacher may add a student after the deadline if it is determined that circumstances warrant the accommodation, seats are available, and the class won't be overcrowded as a result."

that wasn't established to be a woman or girl explicitly as "he." For instance, if a person spoke about seeing a cute baby whose sex they did not know they would have said, "**he** is such a cute baby." Then society determined we should also allow women to be addressed and so it became proper to say, "**he or she** is such a cute baby." This is also where the "**his/hers**" and "**him/her**" became common. And although the "his/hers" method did finally allow women to exist in language, it was still problematic. Read the difference between those sentences again. The one where "he or she" is written is more distracting. By this I refer to the fact that some of the attention from the sentence is now focused on the sex language rather than the point of the sentence. It is also problematic for gendered reasons. By saying "his and hers" you are indicating there are only two choices of gender or sex which fundamentally ignores the presence of other groups of people.

Your language should always strive to be as inclusive as possible. So, today, in order to be inclusive it is recommended that we remove and distinguishing sex or gender terms and replace them with neutral terms. For instance, "that baby was so cute!" or "it was one of theirs," instead of "it was his or hers." As a general rule, you will want to limit the use of pronouns altogether.

Another distinction that you should be aware of is any language that brings attention to the rareness of something being done by a certain sex (this is often a perception of rareness not actual rareness). For instance, "the male nurse said I should take the pills twice a day." This sentence unnecessarily draws attention to the fact that the nurse was male and thereby reinforces the idea that men shouldn't be nurses or rarely are nurses, even though this is not the case. This is problematic because the more a culture reinforces ideas about what each sex should or can do or become, the younger generations buy into those beliefs. The same can be seen for female examples like, "the lady engineer will meet with us tomorrow." Again, the unnecessary word placement of a person's sex in front of a given occupation reinforces the ideas and stereotypes that are associated with it. In this case the idea is that women can't be engineers. If you say male or female terms as a qualifier to any given occupation you are engaging in sexist language that oppresses certain groups. The following table provides examples to guide you.

Say This!	Not This
Salesperson	Salesman
Mailperson	Mailman
Nurse	Male nurse
Doctor	Female doctor
Firefighter	Fireman
Supervisor	Foreman
Server	Waiter/waitress
Performer	Actor/actress
Fisher	Fisherman
Assistant	Male assistant
Humans or humankind	Mankind
Avoid	Man up
Chairperson	Chairman
Homemaker	Male homemaker

SIX PRINCIPLES TO AVOID SEXIST/GENDERED LANGUAGE

1. Use neutral words.
2. Use plural words.
3. Replace any possessive pronouns with a definite article.
4. When referring to singular indefinite nouns (his, he, hers, she) replace it with "they," "themselves," "them," or "their."
5. Repeat the noun.
6. If none of the above will result in a usable sentence you must reconstruct the sentence to eliminate the pronoun entirely.

SEXUALITY/GENDER

Sexist language is not the only kind of noninclusive language that can end up insulting, demeaning, or dehumanizing your audience. You also want to consider the effects of other oppressive language especially because it will have a direct effect on your ethos. Speakers who are not aware of the basic rules surrounding various cultures will find an audience that quickly labels them as incompetent, untrustworthy, or inconsiderate. This is in part because of the concept called linguistic relativity. Linguistic relativity asserts that language shapes the way we see the world and what a culture or person values. So, if a speaker delivers a speech with instances of sexist or culturally oppressive language, the audience will interpret that to mean the speaker doesn't value that culture.

Sexual orientation is often used inappropriately with relevance to sex and gender, and is a culture that is frequently oppressed with unintentionally oppressive language choices by various speakers. Sexual orientation is not something that is based on sex or gender; instead, it is based in two primary concepts: those who are attracted to the opposite sex, which is termed "straight," and those who are attracted to the same sex, which is termed "gay" or "lesbian." However, those are not the only categories and, in fact, there are not necessarily categories at all. Similarly to the gender continuum, there is a continuum of sexuality. The sexuality continuum is measured on a scale of seven—one being the most "straight" and seven being the most "gay/lesbian" on the scale.

In the twentieth century, Alfred Kinsey's research found that most people were not straight or gay/lesbian, and that they were somewhere in between. The research also showed that people who identify themselves as "straight" actually rate as a one to three on the sexual orientation scale when they answer a series of questions relevant to sexuality. Findings also discovered that most people who identified themselves as gay or lesbian were consistently ranking in the range of three to five.

What this research demonstrates is that in fact most people are a little bit in between straight and gay/lesbian. Terms for this middle area have changed over the years, but the most commonly used term in research is bisexuality. For speech-making it is important to know that you do not need to stereotype based on sexual orientation because most people are in between. It is also important to recognize that sexual orientation is irrelevant to sex and gender. Sex, gender, and sexual orientation are not related or dependent on each other at all. As a speaker you have a responsibility to use language that is accurate and doesn't perpetuate misinformation and the use of hate terms.

One of the more common mistakes happens with regard to the LGBTQ community. LGBTQ refers to several communities of nonexclusively heterosexual cultures: lesbian, gay, bisexual, transgendered, and queer individuals. Although I recognize that most people will say they know what those terms mean I am going to provide much needed clarification anyway. The term lesbian refers to women who are sexually attracted to other women and refer to themselves as lesbian in sexual orientation. The term gay refers to men who are sexually attracted to other men and identify themselves as a gay in sexual orientation. Bisexual is term used to identify people who are attracted to both sexes. The degree to which they are attracted to one over the other is not important.

Transgendered refers to individuals who exhibit behaviors and tendencies that reject the conventionally and socially taught gender roles of their sex. The label transgendered doesn't communicate a preference for sexual orientation. Queer refers to gender minorities that either don't directly identify as heterosexual or who are questioning their sexuality. Some LGBT members reject the Q and the "queer" term entirely whereas others embrace it. Those who reject it feel that because "queer" was a hate term that had been used to oppress gays and lesbians at one time, it should not be redefined today.

FIGURE
13.15 Sexual orientation is no more uniform than our fashion choices.

Those who embrace the term queer believe that the LGBT community should embrace all cultures that are not heterosexual regardless and they should be inclusive no matter what. Queer is a term that is not always included, but I have included it here in an effort to teach you the differences and reasons why you should consider your language choices for these communities.

Now that we know the exact meanings behind these terms, we can use them more correctly and cognitively. One common and insulting language choice made often in America is referring to lesbian women as "gay." For instance, a speaker might say, "in talking to the gay community, I learned that oppressive language has historically promoted inequality and prejudice." In this sentence the speaker is only referring to men who are gay, they are fundamentally ignoring the presence of the lesbian community. Now, if the speaker only spoke to gay men and was only referring to men, then using the term "gay" would be acceptable. If they are in any way including women in that statement, then the statement is problematic and considered oppressive language. The proper way to say that sentence in an inclusive way is to say, "in talking with the gay and lesbian community, I learned that oppressive language has historically promoted inequality and prejudice." Do you see the difference?

Do Not Say	Do Say
Homosexual	Gay or lesbian

Another common mistake is calling any member of the LGBTQ community "queer." As discussed before, queer refers to only those people in a state of question or in a non-heterosexual state. Equating that status to gays and lesbians, bisexuals, and transgendered people is insulting and ignores a significant part of their identity. Additionally, you may have noticed I did not use the term "homosexual" to define people who are lesbian or gay. For years it was deemed appropriate to call gay men and lesbian women homosexual. That is no longer the case. The gay and lesbian community largely rejects that term because when the term homosexual was first created it was considered a mental illness. Now we recognize it is not of course. Given its history and the fact that the community largely prefers it not be used, the term homosexual should be generally avoided. The LGBT acronym is preferable if you must refer to an entire community.

ETHNIC LANGUAGE

Ethnically proper language is language that considers the culture's preferred way of being addressed. In America there have been numerous transitions and rules about how to address certain co-cultures. There is a history of oppressive terms that people of certain ethnic groups have been called and there have been the more acceptable forms. For instance, in the last several years scholars and activists have pushed the term "people of color" when addressing non-white audiences. This has been widely preferred over the standard quantified "American" such as Asian-American, Mexican-American, African-American, etc. The problem that was addressed is that the terms characterize the culture first by being something other than American. The extra terms bring attention to a specific culture that may not accurately reflect that person. "People of color" is most commonly the more acceptable term to use. Martin Luther King Jr. used the term "citizens of color" and that is where the phrase originated.

"People of color" is meant to be a better option than "minority" as well. It is thought that "minority" has a connotation that implies someone one is less than another. In fact, in America, people of color are the ma-

© maxstockphoto, 2013. Used under license from Shutterstock, Inc.

FIGURE 13.16 Our common humanity begins from the simple fact that we all share the Earth.

jority, so much of the time it actually doesn't make sense to say "minority" unless you are referring to white (Caucasian) people. In general, "people of color" is preferred over terms like "minority" or "non-white." Yet this term is still not a perfect choice in all situations. It is important to understand some people have strong opinions on different labels and, if possible, it is best to use the language they prefer.

Some people feel that the label "people of color" focuses too greatly on color and labels them in a way they do not feel comfortable. In the end, as a public speaker, it is your responsibility to ensure your audience is not oppressed by your language choices. Usually there is no reason to refer to specific ethnic groups. However, if you must refer to a specific group of people select the specific group they represent not an overarching term that covers groups of diverse people.

It is usually not necessary to specifically point to a specific or broad ethnic culture in public speaking. Sometimes a quote of evidence will distinguish various ethnic cultures in its findings. If this is the case you should use the language the article used. Since you are quoting that source and their findings you should keep their language. The only exception is if hate terms are used, which should never be the case if your evidence is scholarly.

GENERAL RULES FOR ETHNIC LANGUAGE

1. Avoid it if you can. There shouldn't be many reasons to address particular ethnic groups in a speech. Even if a source specifically breaks down results by culture, do not repeat that unless it is important to your speech; instead, average all people together and address all people of our nation as one.

2. Use the specific culture not a general term for a great many cultures who are very different and prefer not to recognized as part of other cultures. For example, the term "Asian-American" is insulting to Pacific Islanders and any of the Asian cultures that wish to be recognized by their particular culture's name (Japanese, Filipino, North Korean, South Korean, Chinese, etc.).

3. If you are quoting a source use the language they used. The only exception is if they use offensive language—in which case you probably shouldn't be using that source to begin with (see the researching chapter).

DISABILITY LANGUAGE

Speakers must be aware of the connotative meanings of the words they use when talking about or talking to the disabled community. Language regarding the disabled community has changed many times. In recent years the terms have been the final and best choices for the community, but always be aware the terms for any community may change with time and it is your responsibility to ensure you are using the proper language.

There are three different types of disabilities that we need to understand the language for: physical, sensory, and intellectual. There is a long history of terms used to define intellectually disabled persons (ID) and there are certainly oppressive terms that are used to define a person with a physical or sensory disability as well. This section tackles those terms and provides you with more acceptable and culturally sensitive options.

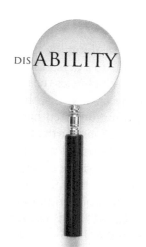

© antoniomas, 2013. Used under license from Shutterstock, Inc.

All of us have unique abilities and challenges.

FIGURE 13.17

FIGURE
13.18 The fastest runners in the world have all had to overcome personal challenges.

PHYSICAL DISABILITY

Physical disability refers to a person who has a disability that affects the body. It is important to always <u>address</u> the person first and the disability last when speaking of them, not vice versa. You want to be sure the disability does not define the person in total. "He is a disabled person." This is a sentence to avoid. Notice how the word "person" is after the "disability," thereby you are communicating that he is first and foremost defined by his disability.

There are several terms that have been used to address this community that are problematic to use in a formal speech and should always be avoided. Even if you hear members of that community using any of the problematic terms, it does not give you the permission to use them. As a speaker you set standards of what is acceptable, you also have the power to influence and create norms, so your responsibility is great. Terms to avoid are listed in the figure for you.

Terms to Avoid	Terms to Use
Cripple	Physically disabled
Wheelchair-bound	Person with a mobility disability
Lame	Person with a physical disability
Physically incapable	Physically disabled
Physically challenged	Physically disabled
Handicapped	Physically disabled

SENSORY DISABILITY

Sensory disability is a term appropriate to use when referring to a person who has one or more disabilities that affect the senses (hearing or sight, for example). As with many other areas, the way in which sensory disability is communicated has changed over the years. There are distinctions for those who were born without the ability to hear and/or see and those who subsequently "late in life" lost the ability to hear. For those who lost their ability to hear they prefer to be called "late-deafened." People born without the ability to hear often prefer to be called "Deaf" because they do not find identification with the "hard-of-hearing" label.

In recent years the capitalization of the word "Deaf" reflects pride in the deaf culture and less of a medical definition. Nowadays, you will find people associating with the term Deaf more and more, regardless of the classification of their medical deafness. Still some, for instance some older

Consider the materials you may need to accommodate people who may have sensory disabilities.

FIGURE
13.19

individuals who use hearing aids later in life, do prefer to be called hard-of-hearing. As a general rule, always keep to the language the person prefers. If you are giving a speech and are referring to the culture in general and don't know the classification, then I recommend suing both terms. For instance, "If there are any Deaf or hearing people who need my interpreter to move please let us know now."

If you are showing a film or a clip it must be closed-captioned for those who may be hearing impaired. Similarly, if you are making handouts consider printing them on non-white paper. People with albinism and other people with visual impairment can see much better on non-white backgrounds. Please glance at the presentation aid chapter for more hints on how to adjust for a sensory disability when you are delivering a speech.

SENSE OF SIGHT

Terms to Avoid	Terms to Use
Invalid	Visually impaired
Dumb	Visually impaired
She is blind	She is a person who is visually impaired

VERBAL

Terms to Avoid	Terms to Use
Speech disabled person	Person with a speech disability
Communication disabled person	Person with a communication disability

SENSE OF HEARING

Terms to Avoid	Terms to Use
Deaf-and-dumb	Hard-of-hearing
Deaf-mute	A person who is deaf

Avoid These Terms in Any Context
Mentally retarded
Mentally challenged
Crazy
Nuts (nutty)
Retard
Loony
Challenged

INTELLECTUAL DISABILITY

Intellectual disability (ID) refers to a person who has a disability of the mind. These individuals were once and are sometimes referred to with names I'm certain you are aware of. This terminology is unacceptable and should be avoided at all times. These terms are demeaning and oppressive in nature. In its conception the term "mentally retarded" referred to any person with an IQ below seventy and before the age of eighteen it was apparent they had a limited ability to adapt to surroundings. The term mentally challenged is now considered politically incorrect. Using this term will also insult, demean, and dehumanize your audience and subsequently negatively affect your ethos. These terms also result in the audience believing you think negatively about the disabled community.

It is important to note that there are other types of disabilities that often get lumped together but in fact are very separate and distinct. There are various emotional disturbances and behav-

Accessible Route

Accessible Lift

Assistance Dogs Allowed

Level access

Ramped access

Access for less mobile people

Accessible toilet

Accessible toilet

Telephone for wheelchair users

Facilities for the visually impaired

Facilities for hard of hearing

Loop facility

Accessible Restaurant

Accessible Parking

Accessible bus

Information

FIGURE 13.20 There are many ways to consider an audience with disabilities.

A History of Intellectual Disability Terms	When to Use	Defined As	Use Instead
Mentally retarded	Never use	Referred to any person with an IQ below seventy and before the age of eighteen displayed a limited ability to adapt to surroundings	**Intellectually disabled**
Mentally challenged	Never use	Insinuates these persons are a challenge and was a word used interchangeably with mentally retarded	**Intellectually disabled**
Intellectually disabled	Use if the person meets the criteria	Criteria to be ID: 1) Significantly subaverage intellectual function 2) Deficits in adaptive behavior that began between birth and age eighteen	

ioral disorders. It is generally expected that you use the specific type of disorder unless you are referring to multiple kinds then you can use the overarching terms of emotional disturbance or behavioral disturbance. For instance, instead of saying emotionally disabled you would specifically refer to bipolar disorder, anxiety disorder, or multiple-personality disorder.

Bottom line is, as a speaker, your words reflect your values, attitudes, and beliefs. Your words also perpetuate or discourage prejudice, oppressive, or hateful language that serves to harm others. Because of this, during any speech in which you address the intellectually disabled community, you will use the term intellectually disabled (ID) and for all others you will use the specific name of the condition (e.g., cerebral palsy, autism, Down syndrome, bipolar disorder, etc.). The only exception is if you are in fact referring to a broad range or you don't know the specific condition, in which case you will use the term emotional disturbance.

Avoid	Use
Emotionally disturbed	Emotionally disabled
Unstable	Person with an emotional disability
Schitzo	Emotionally disabled

SUMMARY

This chapter introduced you to language as it relates to public speaking. We discussed the meaning of language including denotative and connotative meanings as well as the semantic triangle and the differences between writing and speaking. Language tools were provided for you to consider when crafting your speech, specifically meaningful, vivid, simple, and styled language. We ended this chapter with an honest and reflective discussion on the power of language with regard to various cultures. Understanding the terms that are problematic and why is essential for a speaker. The purpose of this chapter was to inspire you to reflect upon your everyday language choices as well as influence how you craft your upcoming speech. Keep in mind, your language defines you as a speaker. The audience will make assumptions and judgments based on what you say and how you say it—so make it count.

Review
Questions

① What is the relationship between meaning and language?

② What are the language tools you can use to enhance your speech?

③ Why is it important to understand the historical meaning of words when constructing your speech?

④ How can language help or hinder oppressed groups of people?

⑤ What are the three communication styles and how are they different?

Glossary

Analogy: A device that compares two similar cases and infers that what is true in one case is true in another.

Bias: Communicating or treating someone differently because of their connection to a given culture.

Connectives: Words that connect one idea to another.

Connotative: Reflects the attached meaning and commonly associated emotional intent of the word.

Contractions: Words that put two words together to form one word.

Denotative: Reflects the dictionary definition of the term or concept.

Grand style: Characterized by heightened emotional attributes that can be seen in the speaker's performance, tone, diction, and figures of speech; it is a writing and speech style that is significant and empowered, impassioned, and opulent.

Hate language: Any speech, gesture, conduct, or writing that may incite violence or prejudice against an individual or group.

Hate crime: Crime directed at an individual or group of people based on their affiliation with certain groups or characteristics including race, religion, ethnicity, or sexual orientation.

Idiom: A distinct expression used by a specific culture that other cultures might not understand because the denotative meaning of the words does not accurately describe the meaning.

Jargon: Language that is used by a specific group of people in a given occupation or culture that other cultures may not be able to understand.

Language: Any system of expression that uses words, gestures, motions, pronunciation, enunciation, and articulation to create a meaning.

Metaphor: A simple device that depicts images through the use of an implied comparison of two or more unlike things.

Moderate style: Incorporates some attributes from both the high and low styles. The goal of moderate style is achieve some emotional impact but also remain simple and clear.

Oppressive language: Any word or series of words that uses an identifier of a person or a certain group as a negative or undesirable characteristic (class, race, sex, gender, sexual orientation, ability, etc.).

Personification: A device that gives human qualities to an object or animal.

Prejudice: Preconceived judgment based on opinion.

Plain style: Also known as low style and is characterized as a brief and clear form of speaking. Plain style is not concerned with figurative language are tonal passions. It is meant to be clear, concise, and simple.

Semantic triangle of meaning: Demonstrates how language choices can be understood.

Simile: A device that depicts images through the use of concrete and distinct comparison of two or more unlike things using words "like" or "as."

Stereotype: Misjudgment of a person by assuming that they belong to a certain group or that belonging to that group means they have a specific set of characteristics.

Stigma: An undesirable mark of disgrace associated with a person or group of people, quality, or circumstance.

Style: Refers to the ways in which something is said, expressed, done, or performed.

Vivid language: Language that is colorful, concrete, and appeals to the senses.

Reference

Ogden, C. K., & Richards, I. A. (1923). *The meaning of meaning: A study of the influence of language upon thought and of the science of symbolism.* New York: Harcourt, Brace.

REASONING

John Giertz

Learning Objectives

CHAPTER 14

① Construct compelling informal and formal arguments.

② Write exceptional arguments based on Toulmin's model.

③ Avoid using common logical fallacies in your reasoning.

④ Understand what deductive and inductive logic are.

College courses including philosophy, math, logic, English, argumentation, and many others introduce you to methods of critical thinking. However, public speaking is probably the only course in which you have one single opportunity to make your case. The audience will usually not be able to watch you speech several times, as they might re-read an essay, or examine math and logic assignments. So, how can you ensure that what you say is both understood, and reasonable?

In earlier chapters, you read about Aristotle's three-part approach to rhetoric, or persuasion—ethos, pathos, and **logos**. Ethos is the speaker's credibility or believability as assigned by the audience. Pathos is the speaker's appeals to appropriate emotional arguments, and logos is the speaker's use of logical appeals and speech organization. All three are interwoven. For example, solid logical appeals (logos) help to build a speaker's credibility (ethos) and a well-placed emotional appeal (pathos) can move an audience to action—thus, rhetoric. Some students find the formal study of logos appeals to be intimidating. However, just like ethos, and pathos, everyone uses logical appeals every day. This chap-

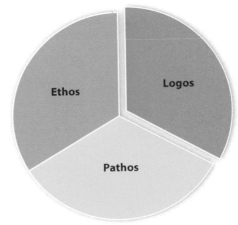

FIGURE 14.1

ter is simply an explanation of what you have been doing since you were old enough to scream for food and attention. (Hopefully, you have new arguments beyond screaming or crying.)

In general, lower division public speaking texts only provide a single chapter on logos or logic. This stand-alone approach is fine for a broad overview but not for an integrated analysis of how to apply logic into the speech assignments. This chapter attempts to bring in many unique examples of logic from public speaking assignments and speeches. (I hope you noticed that this chapter is also "stand alone" and therefore similar to the example given above—if so, you are already engaged in critical thinking. If not, give it time and you should be noticing the apparent contradiction by the end of this chapter.)

If you have taken a course in symbolic logic then you can understand just how difficult it is to open an in-depth discussion of formal logic. There are so many rules and forms to follow that it looks similar to math. The unique language of logic can make it seem only mildly relevant to a public speech. Of course, an audience tries to listen to the speaker's main arguments, but we seldom sit down to analyze thoroughly the full argument.

A more practical application of logos includes information to help you present solid and rational reasons for your audience. An audience will find you more credible if your points are easy to follow because an audience can assume that a disorganized presentation is the sign of an unprepared thought. Sometimes a disorganized presentation may even lead an audience to believe you have something to hide. It is much better to simply present one idea with sufficient supporting evidence than three or four scattered ideas, jumbled together with random thoughts and evidence.

Logical thinking and organization is required from informative speeches about flower arrangements, to convincing the audience they need to take part in the on-campus blood drive, or even trying to persuade them they should sign your petition to demand the restriction of gun purchases. In all cases, you must do your best to allow the audience to understand your position and to ensure that they are not swayed by poor or unethical messages. Although speeches about flower arrangements do not usually tread on the boundaries of ethics, the points must be arranged in a logical order the audience can understand.

KEY CONCEPTS

1. Logos
2. **Inductive** or informal logic
3. Toulmin's model of reasoning
4. **Deductive** or formal logic

Logos refers to organization and logic. However, most people naturally associate logos with basic or even symbolic, traditional logic—the two words seem similar enough. Indeed, *logos*[1] or logic is often taught as a stand-alone class with great emphasis on very formal rules. Understanding the basic rules of logic is important, but it is equally important to be able to use logical reasoning to present your position.

---

[1] As an interesting aside, *logos* as used in the New Testament Greek, references both "word" and "God." *Logos* was the beginning of the universe. In a sense, God spoke (used *logos*) to create everything. We are not simply studying some ancient set of long forgotten rules. We are, according to the ancient Greeks, and the New Testament writers, studying the very nature of creation. At least, that is one rhetorician's justification for the importance of *logos*.

ARISTOTLE'S RHETORICAL REASONING

1. To uphold truth and justice and play down their opposites
2. To teach in a way suitable to a popular audience
3. To analyze both sides of a question
4. To enable one to defend himself

FIGURE 14.2 Aristotle was one of the founders of Western civilization.

Aristotle's first reason for studying logic was to uphold truth and justice ("and the American Way"). Well, not the last part. The American justice system operates on the premise that anyone arrested is innocent until proven guilty.

Technically, the defense lawyer does not need to say anything. The prosecution must prove (through logic [logos], credibility [ethos], and emotion [pathos]) that the accused is guilty beyond a reasonable doubt. Logic and reasoning are crucial to proving a thesis or position. Just as in a court, anytime you give a speech you have to prove your thesis.

Aristotle's second reason is rooted in his concern for the audience. The better you understand what your audience knows and how they think, the better you will be able to teach and help your audience understand your point of view. For example, your audience will not appreciate or understand new rose bush varieties if they do not understand the basics of grafting. Knowing your audience's level of knowledge will help you to prepare the best type of outline and information. Aristotle's third reason for studying rhetoric is to be able to understand both sides of a question or issue.

Whether you are presenting an informative speech about interesting things to do in your city or a persuasive speech about the latest controversial topic, you will find different and possibly opposing views. You may be tempted to toss aside the different views, but studying them will help you present a much more rich and developed speech. You may have a chart about the different blood types and be unable to explain it because you did not read about blood types. Knowing more sides helps you to organize your thoughts and choose the best logical approach for your unique audience.

Understanding another perspective is difficult, but doing so helps you to defend your own view—Aristotle's fourth reason for studying logic. Your speech class may or may not require a few minutes of question time from your audience, but you will encounter these moments outside of class. Believing something is right or correct does not mean you can explain this view to others. Challenge yourself to learn another side and you will find yourself able to give detailed reasons and explanations for your views.

Logic, the focus of this chapter, provides a very specific method for becoming rhetorically prepared. There are two types of logic: inductive or informal logic, and deductive, or formal logic. In addition, the Toulmin model of logic provides a method for analyzing and applying logic to everyday human communication.

Inductive logic is most often associated with informal logic. Formal or deductive logic has explicit rules of validity or the actual structure of the argument. Informal logic has rules that attempt to determine the likelihood of truth. A court of law operates from rules that attempt to determine the likelihood of a defendant having committed a crime. At the end of the trial, a jury or judge is asked to determine the probability of the defendant being guilty.

Inductive logic is based on probability and the likelihood the audience will accept your reasoning. Inductive logic is never one-hundred-percent accurate and so must be rhetorical in nature to convince the audience to believe and even take action. For example, receiving the same grade on multiple quizzes is not absolute proof you will get the same grade on the next quiz. Here are three broad observations about the nature and structure of inductive logic.

INDUCTIVE LOGIC: THREE KEY POINTS

Inductive logic moves from specific to general. The argument begins with specific data or examples and ends with a broad conclusion. In order to move from specific data to conclusion we move to general rule two.

Inductive logic involves some type of "logical leap" or inference from data to conclusion, which leads to our final general rule.

Inductive logic is never one-hundred-percent reliable. There is always some room for error.

Scientists use inductive reasoning when they apply the scientific method. Someone may begin with some simple observations—most students drive onto campus ten minutes before the next class begins. This simple observation can lead to a hypothesis (or thesis) that the majority of students will always arrive to campus within minutes of their class. The hypothesis is tested and retested by various people and under many types of conditions, until a broad conclusion is made that "nearly all students at Cloverville College arrive within ten minutes of class." Traffic lights can now be reset to allow for maximum flow of cars into the parking lots with a minimum amount of cars leaving. The four most commonly discussed inductive arguments are **GENER-ALIZATION, CAUSE–EFFECT, SIGN, and ANALOGY.**

GENERALIZATION

Generalization arguments move from specific examples to a broad conclusion. If the audience believes the examples to be true and typical, then they may be more apt to accept the broad conclusion. Generalization arguments are excellent for discussing most any topic because all a speaker needs are reasonable examples that are typical and realistic for that particular audience. For example, if I were addressing an audience of college students, I would not need many examples of high price of textbooks for them to agree with my claim that "textbooks are very expensive." However, if my claim is that "the celibate life is best," that same audience of college students may need a lot more examples to consider it, whereas an order of Catholic nuns may be much more accepting. This is also a reminder of rule two that the audience may or may not accept your "logical leap" from your specific ideas to your broad claim.

The three key tests for a solid generalization.

© bigredlynx, 2013. Used under license from Shutterstock, Inc.

FIGURE 14.3

KEY TESTS FOR GENERALIZATION

1. **Are there enough examples?** Think again of the claim about expensive texts. A college audience already brings in many of their own personal examples and so this claim is simply reminding them of what they already experience and believe. A general guideline is: the more controversial your claim, the more examples you need.

2. **Are the examples typical of your claim?** There are always odd examples for any claim, but you are expected to use only those that are typical or expected. You might make a claim that "police in our town beat suspects" but, hopefully, your audience will not accept a few stories as being typical examples of all police officers. The speaker must give examples that are truly the most usual or typical of the claim. The speaker should not "cherry pick" the examples just to support their claim.

3. **Are there counter examples?** A counter example is the opposite of the claim. Examples about the typical beaches of Hawaii could include a couple of the most well-known locations. However, there are other beaches, including one in which trash is deposited every day due to unique tides. A counter example like this beach does not specifically disprove a claim, but it can weaken its strength.

You should try to provide answers to potential audience counter claims. If the counter example is well known, then the speaker may need to address this in order to let the audience understand why it does not truly disprove the claim. For example, making a claim that most Popes of the Catholic Church have been European is reasonable. But, now that there is a Pope from South America, the audience may think of him as a counter example. The speaker should say, "Although Pope Francis is from South America, generally Catholic Popes have been European."

CAUSE-EFFECT

Some event leads to or causes some other event. Rain causes the roads to be wet. Wet roads do not cause the rain. **Cause-effect** moves in the direction of the cause to the effect. A cause-effect argument can be thought of in a physical way. If you put the key in the ignition of your car and turn it correctly, then the car should start. This is reasonable, and we generally expect the car will turn on, but what are we to think if it the car does not start? Here is where critical thinking should begin. You may assume there is an engine problem or at least a battery problem. You probably do not immediately jump to the conclusion that you did not use the key correctly. After all, you have been driving for years, have put the key in the ignition, and turned it thousands of times.

The usual **cause-effect** relationship (using a key to start the car) had now changed to making sure I was using the correct key. I just assumed I was using the correct key. That questioning (or use of test) is how we can ensure a correct cause-effect relationship.

1. Is the cause capable of producing the effect?
2. Is the cause necessary?
3. Are there other causes which could produce the same effect?

FIGURE 14.4 The three key tests for a solid cause-effect relationship.

KEY TESTS FOR CAUSE-EFFECT

1. **Is the cause capable of producing the effect?** Can texting while driving a car cause a person to have an accident? Of course it can. This is almost the same as asking whether smoking can cause cancer. The degree of probability is very high between the cause and the effect and most audience members will readily accept the claim. However, whether anti-texting laws cause people to not text and drive is more difficult to prove. The degree of probability is not as high and the audience may not be as willing to accept this claim without more solid evidence.

2. **Is the cause necessary?** (The cause must be there). You will be more successful in getting you audience to sign a petition if you can convince them that their signature will make a difference. People who are not inclined to become involved question whether they personally make any difference. Such people may think: "I am only one person, what good can my signature, or vote, or hour of volunteering, or pint of blood, etc., really matter to helping solve this problem?" You would need to demonstrate that each person is necessary and without them the entire solution is weakened.

3. **Are there other causes that could produce the same effect?** A simple example should suffice. If you and friends are eating the same food at a restaurant and you become ill you could assume that the food made you ill. However, if none of the other people become ill, then the probability of your illness being food related decreases. At least some of them should be ill since you all ate the same food. However, if you learn that you were exposed to the flu a day before the dinner, then you might assume the flu made you ill. This can be verified if your friends become ill the day after you. The original cause (food) was not correct, but the counter cause (flu exposure) did make you sick.

SIGN

Sign argument is the opposite of cause-effect. Cause-effect begins with the cause and moves to the effect, but sign begins with the effect and moves backward to the cause. Often this argument is identified as effect-cause. Sign argument works by observing the effects and identifying the possible causes. Doctors use this approach in diagnosing sicknesses. A patient may have a high fever and a runny nose. These two effects are indications of various illnesses and not other ones. The doctor is moving through a list and removing some possibilities. The more effects the doctor can observe, the more likely the doctor can identify the main cause of the illness. Sign is also the weakest type of inductive argument because the same effects can be interpreted to mean several different causes.

Usually several thick steel bars in windows of downtown businesses indicate a high crime neighborhood. There is also the possibility it could indicate a low crime area. Successful business owners don't usually waste money. There may have been a time when there was a lot of crime, but the business owners installed window bars. Without other signs of crime, it could be reasonable to assume the bars are working and the criminal activity has lowered. Bars in win-

© Carsten Reisinger, 2013. Used under license from Shutterstock, Inc.

1. Is the reasoning cumulative?
2. Are the sign relations constant?
3. Are there counter signs?

The three key tests for solid sign reasoning.

FIGURE 14.5

dows indicate high crime, not the opposite, which demonstrates why sign argument is weaker than other arguments because it can be twisted into other conclusions.

KEY TESTS FOR SIGN

1. **Is the reasoning cumulative?** Do all the comparisons point to the same conclusion? New flowers, warmer temperatures, longer days, add up to indicate that spring is coming. Just one of these signs may not actually indicate spring. The more signs that indicate the same thing, the more likely the claim is acceptable. (Remember, inductive argument is based on probability, so the more signs you have, the higher the probability that your claim is true.)

2. **Are the sign relations constant?** Do the signs always mean the same thing? A speech about predicting earthquakes will not be effective if the various signs do not always mean the same thing. Many people believe that animals can feel the earthquake moments before people can. Noticing your pet suddenly get off the couch and run down the hall does not always mean there will be an earthquake. Animals do things we do not understand, and many times in random order. Your pet cat may have been bitten by a flea or suddenly decided it need to play.

3. **Are there counter signs?** Counter signs are similar to counter causes in that they provide an alternative explanation for the claim. "Next quarter will be great for the economy because unemployment is down." However, one counter sign is fewer unemployment claims, because fewer claims may indicate people have stopped looking for work. They are neither seeking unemployment nor seeking jobs.

ANALOGY

Analogy is a comparison between something or idea the audience understands to something or idea they do not fully understand. The circles below give a visual example of analogy argument. Assume that both circles represent two groups of things, for example, roses. Determine what the "?" mark is in Circle B.

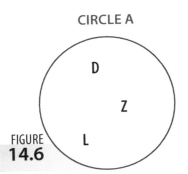

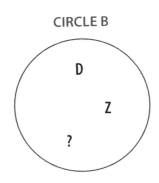

FIGURE **14.6**

Did you guess an "L"? You may have been making an analogy or not. Now look at the next two circles and try to determine what the "?" is in the second circle.

CIRCLE A

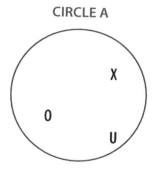

CIRCLE B

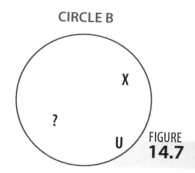

FIGURE
14.7

If you said "absolutely an 'L'" then you are not using analogical reasoning, because the contents in both circles are close enough to at least make you consider the "?" as being an "O." If you said maybe an "O" then you are using analogical reasoning because you are directly comparing the two circles. Reasoning by analogy, as with the other three inductive forms, is not one hundred percent, but it does give us a guideline.

One student speaker compared a still pool of water to the workings of a radar gun used by police to determine how fast a car is going. Imagine dropping a pebble into the very center of a still pool of water. Small circular waves will begin from the center of the pool, roll to the edge, and then roll back to the center. The time it takes for the waves to return can be calculated to the speed of the object, just like a person using the radar gun. The gun emits a radio wave, which will hit the car or moving object and then return. The analogy is not complete or perfect, but it does allow the audience to begin to understand the principles. The speech could have been more accurate, but far less effective, if the student had simply given us the math equations to calculate the speed of a moving object. Analogy works best when the audience understands one object very well and it is comparable to the object.

1. **Are the two objects of the same class?**
2. **Are there enough comparisons?**
3. **Are the similarities greater than the differences?**

The two key tests for a solid analogy.

FIGURE
14.8

There are two types of analogies: literal and figurative. Literal are those that make comparisons between two objects that are of the same category or class whereas figurative compares things that are not of the same.

Figurative analogies are often found in poetry or descriptive passages of writing. "The Kingdom of God is like a mustard seed," is figurative. It cannot be analyzed on a logical level because the two items are being compared on a more poetic or figurative level. Literal analogies can be analyzed logically and here are a few methods.

KEY TESTS FOR ANALOGY (remember, these tests only apply to literal analogies)

1. **Are the two objects of the same class?** You may be giving a speech on the need for gun control and find that Japan has strict gun control laws and much lower homicide rates than the United States. This is an analogy between the United States and Japan. However, the United States has a constitution, which guarantees legal gun ownership whereas Japan does not. The single difference is enough for several students to not accept you argument because your examples are not of the same class.
2. **Are there enough comparisons?** There is no formula for the precise amount of examples because it depends on the audience's predisposition to believe the claims. A doubting audience needs more examples than a trusting or believing audience. College students probably do not need many comparisons of college tuition to believe that most colleges are expensive. People who have not been in college for twenty years may need several comparisons to understand that tuition is expensive in most colleges.
3. **Are the relevant similarities more important than the relevant differences?** When drawing an analogy, it matters whether the two entities are similar enough to each other for the claim to make sense. But that is only one half of the comparison: if the items have relevant differences which are even more important than their similarities, the analogy would still be weak.

TOULMIN'S MODEL OF REASONING

Stephen Toulmin developed his "Data, Warrant, Claim" model as an antidote to the rising trend in viewing argumentation from the purely symbolic logical approach. (Symbolic logic is discussed specifically in the "Deduction" section of this chapter.) Toulmin believed that few arguments actually follow classical models of logic like the deductive syllogism, so he developed a model for analyzing the kind of argument you read and hear every day—in newspapers and on television, at work, in classrooms, and in conversation. Toulmin wanted a model that could explain logic and argument for all people to understand. He wished to return to a more aristotelian approach to human logic; which, therefore, involved the notion of ethos, pathos, as well as logos.

FIGURE
14.9 Basic Toulmin Model.

Toulmin's model focuses on identifying the basic parts of an argument. As a researcher and writer, you can use Toulmin's model two ways: 1) to identify and analyze the basic elements of your arguments, and subsequently 2) to test and analyze your own arguments.

Toulmin identifies the three essential parts of any argument as the **Data** or evidence that supports the claim, the **Claim** or concluding statement, and the **Warrant** which links or connects the data to the claim.

TERMS

Claim: A statement, usually supported with data or analysis advanced for other people to accept. This may be your thesis statement.

Warrant: The warrant is the logical assumption linking the data to the claim. The warrant explains why the data supports the claim.

Data: This is all the supporting information for the claim. Supporting material can include quotes, statistics, examples, testimony, photos, etc.

Here is an extended discussion of the Toulmin model for analyzing the claim: "California should legalize marijuana to raise tax revenue." The speaker needs to prove this claim and so begins with **Data**, or supporting information. The data might be a study about how much people are spending on marijuana right now and a how a simple ten-percent tax on that amount would raise "X" number of dollars. The speaker uses this data, along with the unstated **Warrant**, to move you to accept the claim that California should legalize marijuana. The **Warrant** or link between the data and claim, is that taxing marijuana is capable of generating "X" amount of money. Think of the warrant as answering the "why" question. Why or how will legalizing marijuana generate more tax money? The answer is in the warrant: "Many people in California use marijuana now, so once it is legal these same people will buy it from a store and pay the state tax." However, audience members may believe that people will continue to grow their own marijuana, or buy it from friends, so the tax amount will be much smaller. These doubts can be answered through qualifier and rebuttal statements.

Qualifier: The qualifier modifies the actual claim with words that limit the degree of certainty: "not likely," "possibly," "probably," etc. The qualifier is similar to the notion of probability in inductive logic. Qualifying statements are audience based, so the better you know what your audience will believe, the better you can construct your arguments to include the appropriate data and qualifiers.

Rebuttal: A potential refutation or answer to possible audience objections or doubt. Not all speeches need a rebuttal statement, but if you know you audience has doubts or reservations about your claim, then you should address these with some type of answers.

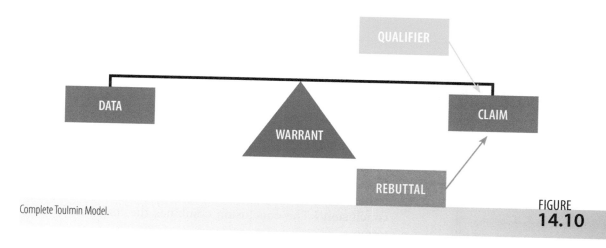

Complete Toulmin Model.

FIGURE
14.10

Here is a simple ad to analyze based on the Toulmin model: "Everyone wants whiter teeth. Therefore, for a cleaner, whiter smile, you should use our teeth whitening solution."

Data: The ad may include a testimonial or a before and after set of pictures to add proof and credibility.

Warrant: Our teeth whitening solution is capable of making teeth whiter. (Notice this is a standard cause-effect argument.)

Backing: This could include some explanation about how the teeth whitening solution works.

Claim: "For a cleaner, whiter smile, you should use our teeth whitening solution."

Qualifier: There may be some fine print that claims results in the testimonials are not typical for all users.

Rebuttal: The audience may not believe the claim because they heard this product is not easy to use. Therefore, the ad may claim that this product only works when used properly, and that the instruction are easy to follow.

The Toulmin model can explain inductive arguments. The warrant may be a cause effect or generalization link, such as legal marijuana is capable of increasing our tax base. The warrant can also be an appeal to credibility. For example, you may be claiming that students should get married while still in college because it provides stability, companionship, and many tax benefits. The audience may be more willing to believe your claim if they know that you just recently got married while being a student. The warrant is that your evidence and examples are credible because of your own experiences.

So far, you have studied informal logic. This type of reasoning is considered informal because it does not have specific, formal rules for evaluation. The next type, deductive logic, is also known as formal reasoning because it has formal, standardized rules.

DEDUCTIVE REASONING

Deductive reasoning moves from a broad statement to a specific conclusion. The standard format is: Major premise, minor premise and conclusion with the conclusion based entirely on the premises. Inductive reasoning requires a leap of logic but because deductive combines already known elements, the conclusion does not make this leap.

Categorical Syllogism: A syllogism is a three-sentence format in which the claim is based entirely on the opening premises or sentences.

Major Premise: All speech students must give speeches
Minor Premise: Tim is a speech student
Conclusion: Therefore, Tim must give a speech.

FIGURE 14.11 Committing fallacies can have undue consequences. Don't take these missteps.

The categorical syllogism has only three terms—major, minor, and the middle term—which may not occur in the conclusion. For example, in the above example, "*speeches*" is the major term, "*Tim*" is the minor term and "*speech student*" is the middle term. (The middle term occurs in both premises, but not the conclusion.) The conclusion combines the major and minor terms.

The next example seems very similar to the first, but is invalid simply because it does not follow the correct format. The order of the information makes the next example invalid.

All professors have at least a Master's degree
Tim has a Master's degree
Therefore, Tim is a professor.

The major term is "all professors," the minor term is "Tim," and the middle term is "Master's degree." The second example has the same basic terms, but you cannot logically assume that Tim is a professor. Not all people with Master's degrees are professors. Neither premise states that all people with Master's degrees are professors, only that all professors have Master's degrees. (A lot of people will readily accept the conclusion because it does seem truthful. However, the strength of deductive logic comes from the rigorous format, and not the appearance of what the audience may believe to be truth.) Of course, you want the audience to accept your conclusion, but deductive logic arrives at reasonable conclusions and not conclusions that appear truthful.

When using deductive logic you can only make a conclusion based on what the premises state, not on what you might assume. There are multiple rules about how to make "valid" or correct deductive arguments, but the bottom line is to listen, and think carefully and not to assume. Deduction may seem like something that you will never use because it is too rigid for speeches, but we use deductive reasoning all the time, and you can certainly use it in writing your speeches.

One way to build a speech using a deductive format is to use the thesis of your speech as the conclusion. Thesis: "People should not use cell phones while driving." Using this as the conclusion, answer the question of why. Why should people not use cell phones while driving? The answer can become the minor premise. The example below has the thesis as the conclusion and the minor premise is the answer to the "why" question. The major premise is a broad or universal claim that most of your audience will probably accept because it not too controversial.

Image © leonardo2011, 2014. Used under license from Shutterstock, Inc.
FIGURE **14.12**

Anything that makes people dangerous drivers should be avoided
Using cell phones while driving makes people dangerous drivers
Therefore, people should not use cell phones while driving.

You will need supporting material for the premises, but a well-designed deductive argument can make a very logical and compelling appeal. The above example works well for a simple claim, but sometimes you may initially need to use two or more deductive arguments to reach your conclusion. This is possible through chaining or stringing arguments together.

Here is another example, which begins with the thesis, "As Californians, we should legalize gambling casinos because we need more tax revenue." You might want to convince your audience that legalizing gambling is a good way to raise tax money. Here is the structure for combining these deductive arguments:

Major Premise: Anything which the public accepts as a legitimate means of raising taxes is good

Minor Premise: Gambling is accepted by the public as a legitimate means of raising taxes

Conclusion: Therefore, gambling is good.

You can now use the conclusion to help create your next deductive argument. The conclusion is the minor premise of the next argument.

Major Premise: Good things should be made legal

Minor Premise: Gambling is a good thing

Conclusion: Therefore, gambling should be made legal.

This is a long process for a possible eight- to ten-minute persuasive speech. You will probably narrow this down to the shorter, *enthymeme* form. The enthymeme is a deductive argument that does not state all the premises. It can be very effective because it allows the audience to fill in the missing pieces, thus keeping them very engaged.

Your actual argument may be something like this: Any legitimate means of raising taxes is good and should be legal. Therefore, gambling should be legal. (The missing premise is that gambling is a legitimate form of raising taxes.) If you believe your audience will easily accept this then you will not need to spend much time convincing them. Remember, deductive logic is only a form or a structure of an argument. It does not mean the audience will immediately be persuaded. You will need to provide proof: appropriate evidence, examples, stories, and other forms of supporting material. The more you know about your audience the better you can tailor your points.

Imagine you are doing a persuasive speech about the need to raise parking fees at your college; not a popular subject for anyone, yet it may be something that is necessary. How can you get your audience to listen to your entire position let alone even become favorable? Start with broad ideals or values that all students will accept like, *Education is important*. Most of your classmates may be attending a community college in part because of the cheaper cost.

Major Premise: We all agree the best solution to the parking problem is to fix it immediately

Minor Premise: The best way to fix the parking immediately is to raise parking fees

Therefore: The best solution to the parking problem is to raise parking fees.

Inductive is probably better for an audience that may not hold similar basic beliefs as you or if the audience does not understand much about the topic and so they need many examples to help them be persuaded or to understand. The syllogism is the best known for its classic three-sentence format, but the hypothetical and disjunctive are just as commonly used. The rules are based on the affirming or denying of the subject or predicate terms. In the following the antecedent or subject term, highlighted in yellow, is affirmed in the minor premise.

The Hypothetical Syllogism:

If I have an apple then I have a piece of fruit
I have an apple
Therefore, I have a piece of fruit.

1. You can affirm the antecedent or subject term
2. You can deny the consequent or predicate term

If I have an apple then I have a piece of fruit
I do not have a piece of fruit
Therefore, I do not have an apple.

The conclusion comes directly from the minor premise.

The disjunctive syllogism is composed of an either or structure and presents only two options.

Logic dictates only that we accept a minimum of one disjunct to be true. However, both could be true. **Therefore, the only way to reach a valid conclusion is to deny one disjunct in the minor premise.** The two valid forms of disjunctive syllogisms appear below:

1. Either A or B
   Not A
   Therefore B

2. Either A or B
   Not B
   Therefore A

Following is the classic disjunctive fallacy of affirming one of the choices.

Major Premise: Either you are in favor of candidate "X" or you are in favor of candidate "Y"
Minor Premise: You are in favor of candidate "X"
Conclusion: Therefore you are not in favor of candidate "Y."

This is fallacious because it is possible to be in favor of both candidates. This is why, logically, you can only make a conclusion by eliminating one of the choices.

This is not an in-depth discussion of the rules of deductive logic, but rather a quick overview to help you understand how to begin using and analyzing basic logic for your speeches.

FALLACIES OF LOGIC

A **fallacy** is an error in critical thinking. Fallacies are not necessarily a failure to persuade your audience, although a fallacy may keep your audience from being persuaded. Remember, people can be persuaded through unethical means, including the use of fallacies. Fallacies distort the audience's understanding, therefore, it is very important to learn the structure of common fallacies so you can write and speak clearly and can also identify poor, unclear thinking. Fallacies are easy to make, and easy to accept because they can appear to be reasonable. Why are fallacies so easy to commit? One reason is that our minds fill in missing gaps, or blanks, or try to make sense out of chaos. Read the following sentence: Aoccdrnig to rscheearch at Cmabrigde Uinervtisy, it deosn't mttaer what oredr the ltteers of a wrod are in; the olny iprmoetnt tihng is taht the frist and lsat ltteer be at the rghit pclae. The rset can be a total mses and you can sitll raed it wouthit a porbelm. Tihs is bcuseae the huamn mnid deos not raed ervey lteter by istlef, but the wrod as a wlohe.

The above example has been around for years and demonstrates how we tend to fix simple mistakes. The same is true of fallacies because people may say things that are reasonable, and we think we know what they mean, but their statements still can cause logical confusion.

FIGURE
14.13 The *ad populum* fallacy is concluding that something is true because many believe it.

FIGURE
14.14 The *ad verecundium* fallacy is concluding that something is true because an authority says so.

FIGURE
14.15 The *ad metum* fallacy is drawing a conclusion from an unwarranted fear of others or consequences.

FALLACIES

Fallacy of popularity, or *ad populum*, is also known as the bandwagon effect. "Everybody has the newest cell phone, therefore I need one too." While having the newest item may you feel popular, it does not prove the item is the best for you. Public opinion polls can also be fallacious: "four out of four dentists agree." This poll does not mean that a particular brand of toothpaste is actually the best; it only means it is the most popular according to the dentists that were actually polled.

Popularity of something does not prove that you need to "jump on the bandwagon." Although it can be difficult to resist following your friends, mentors, leaders, etc. popularity itself is never a rational reason to accept something.

Along with *ad populum,* there is the false appeal to authority.

Fallacy of false authority, or *ad verecundium*: A false authority is one that does not have credibility related to the specific claim. Brad Pitt is a popular actor, but we should not trust his statements he might make endorsing a particular item. Many actors make commercials for products they may not have even used. You are encouraged to use information and evidence to support your claims, but don't just use a source because the person is popular or well known for something. Make sure your sources are relevant to the information.

Fallacy of personal attack, or *argumentum ad hominem* is an abusive or personal attack on the person rather than the argument. "Joe is a horrible person who steals doughnuts from the school cafeteria, therefore why should we trust him as a math professor?" While stealing doughnuts is wrong, it does not prove whether he is qualified to teach math. It is appropriate to review and question the credentials of someone to make sure they are qualified to make claims. However, personal attacks are fallacious because they only serve to distort our understanding.

Appeal to fear or *ad metum* is drawing a conclusion from an unwarranted fear of others or consequences. Not all appeals to fear are irrational. For example, a police officer may use fear appeals to convince young drivers not to drink and drive by sharing stories and photos of teens who were killed because they were drinking and driving. This is not fallacious because the fear appeal is directly relevant to the claim of drinking and driving causing deaths. However, a fear appeal is fallacious if it is not relevant to the claim. Teachers telling students they may fail unless they do the homework is a fear appeal that is directly linked to making the student do their work. However, ads with pictures of abused and sick animals can be fallacious. Recent campaign ads about legislation for the rights of farm animals attempted to focus on chickens that were kept in small cages and how horrible that was. These emotional appeals can be considered as fallacious because the law itself may not directly make those chickens feel any better.

A **hasty generalization** is a fallacy in which examples are not logically linked to the conclusion. "All people of race "X" have "Y" qualities. Here are a couple of examples." You might immediately see this as a racist statement and it is because the person is basing his or her claim about all people on just a few examples. "All professional athletes are overpaid. Just look at the guy who just signed for $148 million for five years." The claim is that all athletes are overpaid, but this is based on just one example. Even if you can list several, it is still fallacious to make that claim that all are athletes are overpaid based on a small number of examples.

False cause fallacy is assuming a wrong or incorrect cause is responsible for the effect. Jim went jogging after dinner and caught the flu, therefore jogging caused him to get the flu. Jogging was not the cause, even if it happened just before he became sick. Think of a speech about recycling: "Our community landfills are overflowing with trash, and there is very little room for more landfills. If each of you would just recycle you bottles, cans and newspapers, we can make a huge difference." Although the sentiment is nice, a typical class of about thirty people recycling will not have a dramatic impact on a large city's waste facilities. The student should have claimed that if each student recycles, and they get their families to help, it is a starting point to making a difference. False cause arguments can seem legitimate, but be careful as a speaker and audience that you are accurately explaining and understanding the claims.

The false cause fallacy is concluding that something happened for the wrong reasons.

FIGURE
14.16

Band Wagon Effect: The argument of popular appeal or *ad populum* is best known by the old adage: "If everyone jumped off a cliff, would you join them?" This is so obviously flawed, unless you are a lemming, that we often ignore it. Consider the next statement though: "seventy-five percent of Americans are in favor of legalizing marijuana. If we are really a democratic country where the majority rules, shouldn't we legalize marijuana?" This may seem pretty reasonable since the majority of people want it. Now change the word "marijuana" to "increased tuition at American colleges," and the argument does not seem as reasonable. The band wagon fallacy can be persuasive because most people do not want to be left alone in their views, we like to think our opinions are supported by many others. An easy way to decide if a statement commits this fallacy is to ask how the argument directly support the thesis. How does the statement, "Vote for Bob. Nine out of ten residents of Urbana can't be wrong," support the thesis that "Bob

The band wagon fallacy is concluding that something is so because everyone believes it.

FIGURE
14.17

FIGURE
14.18 The straw man fallacy occurs when a speaker represents the opponents position in a weak way in order to make it easy to knock down.

is the best choice for city council?" Popular opinion simply proves popularity. By itself, it does not prove much of anything else.

The **straw man** fallacy is a fallacy that arguers use when they purposely misrepresent their opponents side in a weak way so it is easier to knock down (like a piece of straw). This fallacy is commonly seen in persuasive speeches and is highly unethical.

The fallacy of **affirming the consequent** occurs when a premise associates one particular instance to an entire consequent or result. Affirming the consequent can be represented this way:

If P then Q
Q
Therefore, P

If Oprah owns a castle she is rich
Oprah is rich
Therefore, Oprah owns a castle.

If Monty has an ear infection, then he has a fever
Monty has a fever
Therefore, Monty has an ear infection.

The fallacy of **denying the antecedent** happens when the minor premise asserts that the antecedent does not obtain. A statement that has the "If P then Q" form is called a conditional statement. P is the antecedent and Q is the consequent of the conditional statement. Arguments that deny the antecedent are invalid because their conclusions do not necessarily follow from the premises. Denying the antecedent can be understood this way:

If P then Q
Not P
So, not Q

If you smoke cigarettes you will get lung cancer
You don't smoke cigarettes
Therefore, you won't get lung cancer.

If they are not sweating, touching their mouths, and fighting they are telling the truth
They are sweating, touching their mouths, and fighting
So, they are not telling the truth.

The fallacy of **equivocation** occurs when the arguer uses a word that has two different meanings in their arguments. For instance, the word "bank" could mean the place you keep your money and get loans from. The word "bank" could also refer to the edge of a river.

The fraternity I want to rush has mostly kids that are rich
My teacher told me I am rich in all the ways that matter in life
I should rush and be admitted into that fraternity.

The **division** fallacy occurs when the major premise of a deductive argument is concerned with characteristics that apply to a group as a whole, and cannot be "divided" and applied to specific cases.

Small businesses are shutting down at a rapid pace
My mom owns a small business
My mom is shutting down at rapid pace.

The accident fallacy is an interesting one, because just the name itself seems to imply that it was unintentionally illogical, when this is most likely not the case. The **accident** fallacy occurs when an arguer claims that a rule is applied to something that it really doesn't apply to. In other words, A is understood by the rule of Z. But, A doesn't actually fall under the rule of Z.

Coach you can't go in the locker room, only athletes are allowed in the locker room.
You should not have shot that intruder, killing is bad.

Another common fallacy you see on TV, in your homes, and especially in political campaigns, is the false dichotomy or "either–or" fallacy. In the **false dichotomy** fallacy the arguer craftily misrepresents the number of options available to the audience. There are two options provided to an audience and usually one is clearly painted in a positive way and the alternative choice is awful, frightening, or completely unimaginable.

For example, you may have been told that, "If you don't vote Democrat, you vote Republican." This statement is not entirely true. There are more options out there, you could vote Libertarian, Independent, for the Peace and Freedom Party and many others. There are more options, but the arguer doesn't want you to think of them, they merely want you to think about how much you would never vote Republican.

Just think back to your childhood for a moment, you were sitting down to eat your meal and your father placed a large scoop of peas next to your potatoes and chicken. You refused to eat them, and so he said:

You either eat your peas, or spend the rest of the night in your room.

You see; either–or fallacies are everywhere!

Either we increase the punishments for drug use and distribution or we accept
defeat and legalize it.

SUMMARY

Logic does not have to be an intimidating affair revolving around multiple rules and strange words. Everyone engages in logical discussions every day and this chapter simply highlighted some of the ways we already think. The three general types of logic include **inductive** or informal logic, **Toulmin's model of reasoning**, and **deductive** or formal logic. Inductive logic is considered informal because of the lack of formalized rules, whereas deductive reasoning has many formally accepted rules. The Toulmin model is a means of examining typical human reasoning and is best known for the introduction of the **warrant**. The warrant is an often unstated link, made by the audience, between the data and the conclusion. Warrants may also help in identifying breakdowns in logic, or **fallacies**.

Fallacies are errors in logic and thinking and are generally based on the improper use of language, or the improper development of an argument. Although there are dozens of different fallacies, common ones include appeals to false authority, personal attacks, hasty generalization, and false cause. Logic may seem daunting, but with analysis, and preparation, you can deliver a well-reasoned speech that is easy to follow.

Review Questions

① Distinguish between formal and informal reasoning.

② Explain the four different inductive reasoning patterns discussed.

③ Show how the three basic parts and the three auxiliary parts of the Toulmin model work.

④ List and briefly explain five of the logical fallacies discussed in the text.

⑤ Argue why one of Aristotle's reasons to be logical isn't all that.

Glossary

Analogy: A type of inductive argument in which one thing that is well known is compared to something that is less known.
Argument: A statement or claim advanced for gaining the adherence of others.
Band wagon effect: A fallacy of argument that appeals to popular opinion rather than a logical connection between the data and the claim.
Categorical syllogism: One type of deductive logic based on a major premise, minor premise, and a conclusion.

Cause-effect: A form of inductive logic in which one thing is shown to cause or bring about a reaction.

Claim: The reasonable conclusion in the Toulmin model that follows from the data and is linked by the warrant.

Data: The support portion of the Toulmin model.

Deductive reasoning: Formal reasoning with specific formats and rules.

Fallacy: A breakdown in logic causing the data or support material to not link or prove the conclusion.

False cause: A fallacy in which a person associates an effect to an unrelated cause.

Generalization: A form of inductive logic that provides examples to prove a general claim.

Hasty generalization: A fallacy in which the examples are not linked to the conclusion.

Inductive reasoning: The use of informal logic, specifically with generalization, cause- effect, sign, and analogy.

Logic: The fundamental rules of inductive or informal reasoning, formal or deductive reasoning, and fallacies of reasoning.

Logos: Part of Aristotle's three-part model for rhetoric. Logos usually refers to logic and organization.

Sign: A type of inductive logic in which things or conditions are shown to be indications of a previous cause. Sign is also known as effect-cause argument.

Straw man fallacy: A weak argument that makes another point look strong by comparison.

Toulmin model: A model developed by Steven Toulmin for analyzing human logic with a less symbolic method than deductive logic.

Warrant: The link between the data and the conclusion.

SPEAKING TO INFORM

Debra D. Thorson

Learning
Objectives

CHAPTER 15

① Understand the purpose and goal of informative speaking.

② Present a well-structured and educational informative speech.

③ Apply the criteria for constructing an informative speech.

④ Organize an informative speech of your own.

⑤ Use supporting materials ethically.

© StudioSmart, 2013. Used under license from Shutterstock, Inc.

From the moment you started talking, you have been either seeking information or providing information. When you were first learning about the world and communicating with others, you were engaged in a primitive form of informative speaking. Your parents informed you about the alphabet, colors, shapes, parts of the body, and what to do and what not to do; even why or why not to do it. Once you understood the information, you would demonstrate your understanding through repetition and application. Their initial purpose was to create interest often through the use of exaggerated gestures and varied intonation. After they had your attention, they would repeat the information to help you understand the idea or concept. You, in return, would demonstrate your understanding by applying that information and repeating what they had said or demonstrated to show them that you now shared this knowledge.

You have been continuing this communication process by expressing and sharing knowledge throughout your life. Every time you have a conversation with your friends or family, respond to questions from teachers or peers, discuss

© Serhiy Kobyakov, 2013. Used under license from Shutterstock, Inc.

**FIGURE
15.1** When you were first learning about the world and communicating with others, you were engaged in informative speaking.

issues and concerns, you are engaging in informative speaking. Your access to information is constant. In school, the exchange of information is acquired from personal contacts, teachers, peers, friends, published material, textbooks, newspapers and magazines, and through technology, the Internet, social networks, and cell phones.

FIGURE 15.2

More information has been published in the past forty years than in the past five thousand years. The speed at which information is exchanged is ever increasing along with the amount available to us. With all that information at your fingertips, why are you wondering what topic to select for your informative speech? Pick something you are interested in, something you think your audience would like to know more about, and then start to research.

So, if you have been sharing information since you were a child, why is it when you are assigned an informative speech do you panic and feel sick? The answer rests with the audience. It is one thing to speak to our friends, our parents, even our teachers; it is quite another thing to speak to a group of people you don't know, may not have a lot in common with, or who may have little or no understanding of the concept that you want to explain, demonstrate, or describe to them. In a public speaking class, you have an advantage because you have something in common with everyone in your audience. You all will be giving a speech, and you all will be part of an audience.

INFORMATIVE SPEAKING: WHAT IT IS AND WHAT IT IS NOT

In Chapter 1 of this textbook, informative speaking was distinguished from persuasive speaking and speaking to entertain. The basic, initial distinctions we made were that an informative speech is designed to share knowledge or information, a persuasive speech is designed to motivate an audience to take action or to convince an audience to shift positions on a controversial issue, and a speech to entertain is designed to make an audience laugh or to provide pleasure to the audience through the creative use of language. Let us take a closer look at the purpose and form of an informative speech, and let us further explain and clarify how an informative speech is different from other types of speeches.

The basic purpose of any informative speech is to share knowledge. Sometimes you will be explaining how something works or how something operates, or even how *not* to do something. The point is, you are sharing information, information your audience should be able to understand, remember, and share with others. Your goal as an informative speaker is to help your audience leave the room with more information than they had before you spoke—information they can retain and apply.

In addition to a specific informative goal, an informative speech often also takes particular, well-recognized forms of informative discourse. Scholars recognize four primary text types: 1) description, 2) exposition, 3) argumentation, and 4) narration. Whereas the primary purpose of narration is to entertain and the primary purpose of argumentation is to persuade, the primary purpose of exposition and description is to inform. Therefore, an informative speech will often answer the same questions an expository news article would answer: Who? What? When? Where? and Why? An informative speech may also have well-developed, detailed descriptions of persons, places, or things.

Sometimes the dividing lines between a speech to inform, a speech to persuade, and a speech to entertain are not so clear. In one sense, all good speeches are persuasive, because they should have an underlying point or purpose to them. For example, a good speech to entertain will be enjoyable to listen to, but it will also have a deeper underlying message or moral. Similarly, a good informative speech will have an underlying point or persuasive purpose. As an informative speaker, you need to decide *why* your audience needs to be informed about a particular topic or subject, and you need to persuade your audience that your informative speech is worth hearing.

However, the primary purpose of your informative speech should still be to share knowledge, and not to persuade, change policy, alter opinion, or give a call to action. Sometimes sophisticated speakers present persuasive speeches *as if* they were merely informative speeches— the "ostensible" purpose of such a speech is to inform, whereas the real purpose is to persuade. Salespeople and advertisers, for example, often claim that they are merely "informing" you about a product or opportunity when they are most definitely trying to persuade you to buy this product or to take advantage of the opportunity that they are offering to you.

If you are supposed to give an informative speech in your public speaking class, your instructor probably will not be impressed if you decide to "inform" your classmates about a controversial topic like abortion or gun control. A speech about abortion or gun control, by the very nature of the topic, is really a persuasive speech, despite the speaker's claims that they are merely "informing" the audience members so they can make an intelligent decision. If you are asked to give an informative speech, stick to topics that will truly lead to a speech to inform rather than to a speech to persuade.

The dividing line between a speech to inform and a speech to entertain is also sometimes hard to clearly delineate. Good informative speakers will make their speeches entertaining. We have all had teachers to whose classes we looked forward. These teachers were interesting, entertaining, animated, and they possessed a wealth of knowledge. From the beginning to the end of the class, they had your attention and time just seemed to fly by. When you left their class, you felt energized, and you discussed the ideas, concepts, and lessons they taught you outside of their class. The information stuck with you. They taught, and you learned.

© Lisa F. Young, 2013. Used under license from Shutterstock, Inc.

FIGURE 15.3 Teachers are trained informative speakers.

Like any informative speaker, teachers who are boring, disorganized, unapproachable, condescending, or apathetic never form an effective relationship with their learning audience. Remember the teacher who gave boring, monotone, dry lectures? They may have had a wealth of knowledge, but their manner of dispersing it was counterproductive. If you want to be an informative speaker that shares knowledge successfully, you must gain your audience's attention and keep it. Informative speaking, like teaching, is an art that only improves with practice. As an informative speaker, you must have well-organized ideas, and you must present these ideas in an interesting and entertaining manner.

However, good informative speakers keep their primary informative goal in mind. They do not let the entertaining aspects of their speech outweigh or overshadow the information they are trying to share. Again, you may remember teachers you have had that got "off track" (or that you could easily get off track) when they began to relate stories or personal experiences. When the focus of their class became the entertaining stories that they were telling, the overarching points that they were supposed to be making sometimes got lost. Similarly, as a public speaker informing an audience, you need to make sure that your attention-getting and attention-sustaining devices and stories do not overshadow your informative goals and objectives.

SELECTING YOUR TOPIC

When choosing a topic keep in mind that if you have an interest in the topic, your audience is more likely to be interested too. Consider your personal interests, hobbies, and expertise. Think about what has recently made headlines in the news. Consider topics you want to know more about and are of interest to you. Your interest and excitement about the topic will add to your presentation. As you research and gather information, never forget your audience. Will your topic interest them? Can you do it justice in the time allotted? Is the topic appropriate for your audience and the situation? For example, let's say you are an avid stamp collector. You could give a speech on collecting stamps. You might explain what makes one stamp more valuable than another. You could explore the history of stamp collecting and famous printing accidents that have created rare and extremely valuable stamps. What you would not do is persuade your audience to collect stamps, as the intent of this speech is to inform, not to persuade.

© Curioso, 2013. Used under license from Shutterstock, Inc.

Choose a topic that you and your audience will be interested in.

FIGURE 15.4

Once you have decided on a topic and know what your goal is, you need to be ever vigilant in regard to telling the truth, being accurate, and providing current information to your audience. This is achieved through careful research on the topic, using credible sources, and verbally citing those sources in your speech. Doing so increases your credibility with your audience and helps create a trusting relationship. Nothing will turn an audience off quicker than outdated information or a presentation based solely on the speaker's opinion.

GOALS

The major goal of an informative speech is to share knowledge and ideas in a manner that your audience can easily understand. But, in order to do that effectively, you must meet specific goals: You must be objective, credible, timely, accurate, significant, and clear. No matter what type of informative speech you give—explanation, description, or demonstration—satisfying these specific goals is not optional.

FIGURE 15.5

OBJECTIVE

Would you like to listen to information that is biased or one sided? No, you wouldn't. When we take the time to listen to someone presenting information, we expect the speaker to tell the truth. Leaving out important information or presenting information from only one perspective is bias and deprives your audience of a balanced presentation, not to mention it tends to make your speech persuasive. In addition, knowingly leaving out information because it does not support your perspective is unethical. Audiences expect the knowledge a speaker shares with them to be accurate and not misleading. No one wants to hear half-truths.

So how can you create objectivity? My mother often told me, "Don't judge someone until you have walked in their shoes." Our judicial system works in this manner. When someone is arrested they give a statement. Other witnesses are questioned and give a statement. The police look at all the evidence and statements and decide what happened and who, if anyone, should be held responsible. Gathering as much information as possible and examining an issue from all perspectives reduces bias and adds to your credibility.

BE CREDIBLE, TIMELY, AND ACCURATE

Your credibility is dependent on the accuracy of your information and how timely that information is—meaning up to date and/or current. In order to present the truth to your audience, when researching a topic you want to use the most recent information. If you were giving a speech on the migrant population in the state of California you want information from the latest census and most recent evidence to back up your position. Using statistics from the 2000 census would be outdated and not reflect an accurate picture of that population.

If the source of your information isn't credible why would anyone want to listen to you? If you wanted information on the migrant population of California you would **not** use information from the *National Inquirer* or from your grandmother who lives in Kalispell, Montana. You would use information from the Federal Census Bureau, or your library's databases to get journal articles from scholarly periodicals.

Use the Internet with caution. Anyone can put information on the Internet and often those articles look professional, but don't be fooled. I once had a student do a speech on racial profiling whose main source was a paper written by an eighth grader. Always check out your source. Make sure that the author has the experience, education, and background to ensure that the information is valid and not just someone's opinion. Your sources' credentials are important and don't forget to verbally cite them when giving your speech. If you don't cite your source, you are telling your audience you are the expert and you did all the research and you are **plagiarizing**!

SIGNIFICANT

If you were to give a speech to the National Rifle Association on *The Evolution of Technology in the 21st Century* I doubt that you would hold the audience's attention for long. Your topic is not something of significance to that group. You are obligated as a credible speaker to meet the interests and needs of your audience. In order to satisfy the goal of significance, you must always consider your audience's reason for attending. An audience who attends on their own volition will be more receptive than one attending because attendance is mandatory.

CLARITY

There is nothing worse than trying to follow an unorganized speech. Truthfully, if you don't have in interesting introduction that clearly outlines what they are going to hear, on a significant topic to that specific audience, you might as well go home. A good informative speech is clear in purpose, concepts, and vocabulary. A well prepared speaker has done an audience analysis and has a good idea of the prior knowledge of the group. Possessing knowledge of your audiences' experiences and expertise on the subject helps the speaker organize and determine the appropriate vocabulary to use. Always assume your audience knows less on the subject rather than more. Don't be afraid to define terms and concepts. A common error made by speakers who know their topic well is that they inadvertently leave out important steps then wonder why they have lost their audience's attention. You want your informative speech to be memorable because it excited your audience, met their needs, incorporated personal histories, included engaging examples, and emotionally and physically got them involved.

NARROW YOUR TOPIC

Remember no matter what the topic, you must be able to explain, describe, or demonstrate it within the time limit. Picking too broad a topic is a common mistake of the novice speaker. Think about it. Let's say you love animals and have decided to give your speech on man's best friend, the dog. What are you going to tell us about dogs? There are over four hundred different breeds; they come in all sizes, miniature, toy, teacup, giant, long, short, smart, and rare dogs. There are working dogs, show dogs, service dogs, police dogs, and family dogs. There are short hair, long hair, and no hair dogs. You only have ten minutes! (See Chapter 4.)

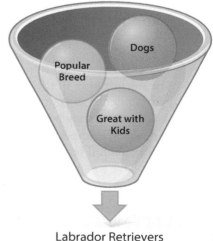

Labrador Retrievers

You must narrow your topic.

FIGURE 15.6

RESEARCH

Now that you have picked your topic you need to do some research. It is assumed that you chose something you are interested in and something you have some knowledge about, but to present a credible presentation your speech must consist of more than just your opinion. Your library is a wonderful place to start. Most libraries have databases (EBSCO, GALE, or ERIC, etc.) for you to access that have a plethora of creditable sources for you to choose from. Do not just do a Google search or use Wikipedia as a source. For example, you are going to inform your audience about "The Importance of Blood Donation." If you put in "blood donation" in EBSCO Health Source—Consumer Edition you will have multiple creditable

© Monkey Business Images, 2013. Used under license from Shutterstock, Inc.

Good informative speeches are often based on good research.

FIGURE 15.7

sources to cite from. There are reports, academic journal articles, pamphlets, books, and periodicals on the subject. Often, just by doing a Boolean search—searches that allow you to combine words and phrases to limit, or broaden your search—such as and, or, not, and near you can find what you are looking for. You not only have access to wonderful sources but discover how you want to narrow your topic. (See Chapter 5.)

INTRODUCTION

Once you have decided on a topic and narrowed it, you must organize your introduction so that you grab your audience's attention and keep it throughout your presentation. You need an introduction that includes an attention-getter, is relevant to your audience, and contains a thesis statement that lets your audience know what you are going to talk about, the order in which you are going to talk about it, and establishes your credibility. Think of it like a road map. You tell them where they are going and what roads you are going to take to get there and what they will find at the end of their destination.

BODY

The organization of the body of your speech should follow a pattern—which was presented to your audience in your thesis statement. (The thesis is found in the introduction.) The organizational pattern may be: topical, chronological, spatial, compare, contrast, geographical, classification, etc. The important thing is that whatever organization is used the purpose for choosing that pattern should be that it makes the topic easier for the audience to understand. Remember audiences have a short attention span, and if you don't get grab it from the start chances are you will never have it. If you do lose their attention it is difficult to get it back. So get their attention in the introduction and by choosing the right pattern for the body of your speech you will keep their attention.

Just as in an essay, a well-written speech needs good transitions and lots of showing statements. In other words you don't just want to tell your audience that "She is tall." What do you mean by tall? To some people anyone taller than they are is tall. Some people consider anyone over six feet tall as tall, male or female. So the statement, "she is tall," a telling statement, doesn't give the audience a vivid image of her height. Using showing statements gives the audience a better idea of what is meant by the statement.

To avoid bumping her head, she ducked as she opened the door and entered the room.

CONCLUSION

Contrary to popular opinion, "that's all folks" is not a proper conclusion. Your conclusion is the second most important part of your speech and your last chance to instill the knowledge you are trying to share. So take advantage of this time. Reiterate your important points. Review the map you shared with your audience in your introduction. Now that you and your audience have come to the end of your journey remind them how they got there and what they acquired along the way. Just as your introduction needs something to catch your audience's attention, your conclusion needs closure. (See Chapter 7.)

HOW WE LEARN

Sir Frances Bacon said, "knowledge is power." To gain knowledge requires the sharing of information, which cannot be done without gaining your audience's attention and keeping their attention so your message can be processed, retained and understood by your listeners. You learn by taking what you know and building on it. You learned how to crawl before you learned how to walk. You learned words before you formed sentences. You learned numbers before you learned how to add. You gain knowledge by building on information you already possess.

Because learning styles vary, when sharing knowledge you need to address more than just one modality. There are three basic learning styles: auditory, visual, and kinesthetic. Most people have a preferred learning

Different people learn differently.

FIGURE
15.8

style and learn best when knowledge is shared in that modality. But when addressing an audience you do not have that information nor are you speaking to only one person. You need to keep in mind when writing and delivering a speech that we all learn differently.

Because your audience consists of listeners with various learning styles, including supporting materials that address a range of learning styles will not only help gain your audience's attention, but keep it throughout your speech. Varying how the material is presented also helps to ensure that your message is not only accepted but retained. The most memorable speeches include supporting material presented not only verbally, but visually as well.

Supporting material may appeal to the senses. Some people prefer to learn by relating to experiences they have knowledge of or can relate to. Including examples of experiences you have had will give those learners concrete experiences to use as references; thereby, keeping their attention and piquing their interest. The related experiences don't have to be the speaker's. They could be experiences from people you know or have read about. The important thing is that those experiences will help your audience relate to your topic. For those listeners who prefer facts and statistics provide those examples. Doing so makes your topic relevant to those audience members whose learning style is best satisfied by a more practical approach. They need to see how to apply it. They need examples relevant to the topic in order to fully comprehend what you are saying. For those deep thinkers in your audience provide supporting material that includes some kind of analysis of the topic.

Let's not forget our visual learners—those who learn best by watching and seeing. These are your objective learners whose judgments require supporting material that reflects various perspectives and sources including but not limited to: books, government documents, magazines, professional journals, and academics. Visual aids most also be diverse and address different learning styles in order to appeal to all your listeners. A balanced speech uses supporting material that is objective and reflects a variety of perspectives.

Presenting material that addresses different learning styles is not a foreign concept. You have experience with this. When your parents were teaching you how to speak they would say the word and point to the object. By doing so they incorporated audio and visual modalities. When you learned how to jump rope the process was explained to you (audio), and then demonstrated to you (visual), and finally you jumped rope (kinesthetic). The process had a specific organization. It was that organization that made learning how to jump road understandable and doable. You then would perfect the skill by practicing and building upon that basic skill. Writing and delivering a good informative speech is based on the same principles.

ORGANIZATION MATTERS

There is no set strategy for organizing an informative speech. Your topic and type of informative speech will determine that. For example, if you were to describe the history of cancer research in the United States or the proper way to give an injection, chronological order would make sense. If you were going to explain how air quality impacts health care costs, causal strategy may be best. If you were going to compare wills versus living trusts you would do a comparative analysis. Depending on the topic and type of informative speech the organization could be topical, spatial, problem-solution, causal, chronological, comparative, or causal. But you must commit to that format from the beginning by determining your purpose and how you intend to share that knowledge with your audience. (See Chapter 7.)

GUIDELINES

No matter what type of speech you are presenting there are guidelines and principles that should be followed; this is especially important when presenting a speech that informs.

1. Is this topic relevant to my audience?
2. Is my speech organized in a clear logical manner?
3. Is my supporting material addressing different learning styles?

TYPES OF INFORMATIVE SPEECH
A SPEECH TO DESCRIBE

Descriptive speeches, a speech that describes, can be about an object, person, animal, place, event, or even a moment that made a difference in your life or in someone else's life. It verbally recreates the essential elements that made that object, person, animal, place or event impact a course of action, view or position, because of that experience. It describes the moment and the elements captured in time through the use of words that will help your audience visualize in vivid detail what you are describing. Your audience needs to relate personally, emotionally, and physically to what you are describing. Accomplishing this requires the use of figurative language and appealing to the senses of touch, taste, smell, sound, and sight. Using descriptive language eliminates confusion and creates a clear precise picture for your audience. In order to do this, you are going to have to expand your vocabulary, by using a variety of nouns and adjectives; in other words be descriptive!

He sauntered into my class with the confidence of a gladiator, yet this was in direct contrast to his physical appearance. At first I thought a third grader had lost his way and somehow had wandered into my Freshman English class. His skin was almost translucent. His hair was as white as an eighty-year-old man's and just as thin. There was just something about this seventy-five pound fourteen-year-old. He had that look in his eyes; you know that look a person has when they know something no one else does. I just knew this was a student with a story, a secret, and he was going to make a mark on my world.

If this were to be the opening of a descriptive speech on the effect HIV had on the pediatric hemophilia population during the 1990's, it would be a good attention catcher. Look at the first sentence: "He sauntered into my class with the confidence of a gladiator, yet this was in direct contrast to his physical appearance." Describing him so gives your audience a better picture in their mind's eye than if the speaker had said, "A small student walked into my classroom." Now let's take a closer look at the sentence. By using a metaphor and comparing this small student to a gladiator, you get the idea that despite his appearance he had confidence about him. He was not intimidated by his surroundings or his own physical limitations. Examine these sentences: "His skin was almost translucent. His hair was as white as an eighty-year-old man's and just as thin." The use of the simile, ". . . as white as an eighty-year-old man's and just as thin," now you have presented a better description of this young man, rather than just saying, "he was fragile." Through the use of figurative language, audiences better understand and connect with the subject. You hold their interest. They listen to what you are saying. Language and word choice are an important part of writing and delivering your speech.

Now let's look at an outline on this topic.

HEMOPHILIA, AIDS, AND MEDICAL ADVANCES
INTRODUCTION

I.   **Attention Catcher**: He sauntered into my class with the confidence of a gladiator, yet this was in direct contrast to his physical appearance. At first I thought a third grader had lost his way and somehow had wandered into my Freshman English class. His skin was almost translucent and his hair was as white as an eighty-year-old man's and just as thin. There was just something about this seventy-five pound fourteen-year-old. He had that look in his eyes; you know that look a person has when they know something no one else does. I just knew this was a student with a story, a secret, and he was going to make a mark on my world.

II. **Listener Relevance**: It was 1990, two months into my first year as a teacher. Todd took me aside and said, "Do you know what hemophilia is? I have it. When I was ten I was in an accident and given lots of blood and factor. I have AIDS along with every other hemophilic my age. All of us with pediatric hemophilia are going to die."

III. **Speaker Credibility**: At that time, I knew enough about AIDS to know it was a death sentence; but I knew little about pediatric hemophilia and AIDS. I knew I needed to help him, but before I could do that I needed to know more about hemophilia and AIDS.

IV. **Thesis Statement**: Today I am going to describe hemophilia, the impact AIDS has had on the pediatric hemophilic community, and medical advances that now protect this community from extermination.

V.   **Preview**: Do you know that there was a time in this country when blood products were not safe? Why would this be of special concern to the hemophilic community? First we need to understand what hemophilia is.

BODY

I. Hemophilia
   A. Description of hemophilia
   B. It's in the genes

Transition: Now that you know what hemophilia is, and how you get it, let's look at the impact AIDS has had on the pediatric hemophilic community.

II. Pediatric hemophilic and AIDS
   A. Post 1979
   B. 1979–1984
   C. 1985–present

Transition: Now that you know what Hemophilia is and its impact on the pediatric hemophilic community let's look at how the medical advances have improved their quality of life.

III. Medical treatments and advances
   A. Medical treatment before 1979
   B. Medical treatment 1979–2000
   C. Present day treatment

CONCLUSION

I. **Thesis Restatement:** Now you know what hemophilia is, how AIDS impacted children with this genetic disorder and the medical communities contribution to their present day quality of life.

II. **Summarize Main Points:** Hemophilia is a genetic disorder. Because the treatment from 1979–present requires blood product there is a ten year span where almost 90 percent of that community acquired AIDS. Children were impacted the most resulting in very few pediatric hemophilic survivors due to contaminated blood products. Because of medical advances in the treatment of AIDs, members of the hemophilic community, adults and children, quality of life has greatly improved. AIDS is no longer a death sentence.

III. **Clincher:** If only Todd were born ten years later he would be alive today. He told me he had three goals before he died: to get his driver's license, to be a state forensic champion, and to graduate from high school. He reached two out of three of his goals. Todd died on Mother's Day his junior year.

REFERENCES

Doyle, E. (2007). *Paediatric anaesthesia*. Oxford: Oxford University Press.

Flieger, K. (1993). Outlook brighter for youngsters with hemophilia. *FDA Consumer, 27*(6), 19. Retrieved from http://search.ebscohost.com/login.aspx?direct=true&db+ulh&AN=9308100 304&site=src-live

Jason, J. L. (1988). Human Immunodeficiency Virus infection in hemophilic children. *Pediatrics, 82*(4), 565.

The following is an actual example of a student's outline of an informative speech that describes.

THE SOCIAL IMPORTANCE OF TECHNOLOGY SKILLS
INTRODUCTION

I.   **Opening:** Raise your hand if you own a computer, laptop, or smartphone such as an android or iPhone. Raise your hand if you know how your device benefits you. For those who raised your hand to the previous questions, today you will hear the benefits that technology brings you. As a college student who has been required to incorporate computer usage and other technology to complete almost all educational tasks, I became interested in the useful benefits that technology can provide for our everyday life.

II. **Thesis Statement:** Today's technology offers various benefits that can be useful in the workplace and other aspects of life.

III. **Preview:** I hope that by the end of my presentation, you can understand how today's technological skills are more useful than the technology instruments that were used years ago.

BODY

I.   The typewriter
   A. A typewriter is machine used for typing mechanically in letters and characters like those produced by printers' types.
      1. Typewriters were slow, noisy, and unreliable because they often jammed and ran out of ribbon, a strip of inked material.
      2. Typewriters had limited usage because they could only be used for typing, nothing else.
   B. Comparing typewriters to computers can help identify the benefits technology has brought.
      1. Unlike typewriters, computers have multi-use tools like typing programs, and Internet, also known as the World Wide Web.
      2. Workplaces obtain more usage of computers than typewrites due to accessibility of information, interaction, and communication.
      3. Computers make it easier to maintain a social life through social networking, email, instant messaging, etc.

Transition: New technology tools can help you at your job.

II. The computer
   A. Computer and Internet technology make work convenient.
      1. Using computers allows employees to access information quickly unlike going through recorded information on pieces of paper.
      2. Computers also help employees stay organized online or on built-in calendars to keep up with appointments, meetings, etc.
   B. Computers at work make communication flexible and accessible.
      1. Due to technology people can email each other and access email accounts through another computer or even cell phones at any time of the day.

    2. Technology also makes employees collaborate from anywhere—for example, video meetings across the country with other companies, etc.

Transition: Technology offers various social advantages.

III. Social media
    A. Technology skills can benefit your social life by allowing you to communicate several ways with people.
        1. Social networks keep you updated with local as well as out-of-state family and friends.
        2. Using webcams allow you to video call people from a computer to another, or even now do video calls via cell phones.
    B. Technology can benefit your social life through entertainment.
        1. Browsing the web can help you to access entertainment information such as best-rated restaurant, and movie times when you're looking for something to do with someone else.
        2. Technology can also help you stay organized by keeping track of dates of events, parties, etc.

CONCLUSION

I.   **Thesis Restatement:** Having technological skills can be beneficiary to your job and relationships with others in different ways.

II. **Review the Preview:** Technology is a complex thing to grasp knowledge and usage of but now you know the comparison of old versus new technology, how it benefits your work life, and social life.

III. **Closing:** The late great Carl Sagan wrote: "We live in a society exquisitely dependent on science and technology, in which hardly anyone knows anything about science and technology."

A SPEECH TO EXPLAIN

Why or how something works, or doesn't work, why something happened, or didn't happen, even evaluating why a process is done or no longer done can be the goal of an informative explanatory speech. Avoid trying to wow your audience with higher level vocabulary. If you need to use terms specific to the topic, define them. Don't assume they have background knowledge that will allow you to skip over information necessary for them to understand what you are explaining.

    Audiences are comprised of individuals with different experiences, education, and interests. In order to keep them all engaged and interested in what you are saying, you don't want to talk over them. Doing so will create frustration and lack of interest. You also need to be careful of talking down to them. No one likes that. If you get too technical it is boring. If you only give your opinion your credibility will be jeopardized. Interjecting a little humor is a good way breaking the tension and keeping your audience's attention, especially after they have been given a lot of statistics or new information. So what you say and how you say it is a balancing act between dispersing information, entertaining your audience, and satisfying your audience's expectations.

EXAMPLES OF SPEECH TO EXPLAIN TOPICS:

- HIV and the hemophiliac community
- The science behind aging
- Henrietta Lacks and her contribution to science
- Shakespeare's ladies

OUTLINE EXAMPLE OF A SPEECH TO EXPLAIN
OUR AIR QUALITY
INTRODUCTION

I. Attention Catcher:

How many of you suffer from a respiratory problem such as asthma, lung disease, or know someone who does? Each year air pollution claims upward of fifty thousand lives in the United States alone. Every day when we watch our local news, we hear our weather forecasters talk about the AQ (Air Quality) index and most of the time it is in the unhealthy range, limiting outdoor activities for people with sensitive respiratory problems (National Defense Council).

II. Listener Relevance:

Breathing is not an option; it is something we have to do in order to survive. The Air Resource Board (ARB) shows that over ninety percent of Californians breathe unhealthy levels of pollutants during some part of the year. This is important because it affects the quality of our lives.

III. Speaker Credibility:

I am one of those ninety percent of the individuals in California who breathes unhealthy air. I live in Bakersfield, CA, and the American Lung Association (ALA) has ranked Bakersfield as the number one city with fine particulate pollution in the air, and has ranked it number two as the nation's second smoggiest city over the past three years. I suffer from asthma. I have researched and read numerous articles on this topic to get a better understanding on what I face on daily basis (American Lung Association).

IV. Thesis Statement:

Bad air quality affects us, our families, and the future generations; we can fight to give them a chance to breathe cleaner air by changing one thing in our lifestyles—we can make a difference—by riding a bike, carpooling, recycling, or getting rid of our gross polluting vehicles.

V. Preview:

1. The Central Valley's air quality and how it affects our health.
2. What we can do to help improve the Valley's air quality.
3. The programs available from the state government.

BODY

I. Air quality and how it affects us.

A. The two biggest air pollution threats in the United States are ozone and particulate pollution, stated by American Lung Association (ALA). Others pollutants include carbon monoxide, lead, nitrogen dioxide, sulfur dioxide, and a variety of toxic substances (California Environmental Protection Agency).

    B. Short-term effects include asthma, coughing, wheezing, shortness of breath, emphysema, and chronic bronchitis, whereas the long-term effects can cause heart, lung, kidney, and liver disease to name a few. The California Air Resources Board (CARB) has tripled its estimates of premature deaths in California from particle pollution to eighteen thousand a year (American Lung Association).

II. What we can do help improve the air quality?
    A. We can reduce, reuse, and recycle; walk or bike to work and nearby destinations; we can conserve energy, turn off the lights when not in use, plant trees, maintain our vehicles, carpool, drive less by combining our errands together, reduce fire place use; and look for durability in products when you buy.
    B. We can participate in Rideshare Week. Rideshare Week is held the first week in October—**October 1 to 5**. This annual statewide campaign promotes carpooling, public transit, and other alternatives to driving alone as a means of easing traffic congestion and improving air quality. Here is how it works: It encourages commuters to take public transportation, walk, or bike to work, at least one day a week to help clean our air quality.

III. How state government can help?
    A. The state of California offers the vehicle repair or retirement program Consumer Assistance Program (CAP) to qualified individuals. The state provides repair assistance for up to $500 to repair the vehicle's emission control system. However, certain restrictions apply such as the vehicle's emission control system provided that it had not been tampered with, missing, or modified, and the vehicle is not undergoing its initial registration in the state of California (State of California-BAR).
    B. The state also has another program called the vehicle retirement program, where the state buys the most polluting vehicles from you and pays either $1,000 or $1,500, depending if the person meets the income eligibility requirements. In order to qualify one must be the registered owner of the vehicle and the vehicle has to be driven under its own power to the salvage yard (Vehicle Repair, Retirement, Replacement for Motorist).

CONCLUSION

I. Each year air pollution claims upward of fifty thousand lives in the United States alone and the cost of treatment and penalties not to meet the stringent air quality standards set by the federal Environment Protection Agency continues to rise and is in the billions.
II. Bad air quality affects us, our families, and the future generations; we can give them a chance to breathe cleaner air by changing one thing in our lifestyles—we can make a difference—by riding a bike, carpooling, or getting rid of our gross polluting vehicles just to name a few.
III. We can do our part to help reduce poor air quality where we live. The air quality affects so many of us on a daily basis. By doing our part we will help contribute toward cleaning our air and help people breathe better and can help reduce the number of people dying each year in the United States due to poor air quality.

REFERENCES

American Lung Association. (n.d.). Retrieved September 21, 2012, from How can air pollution hurt my health?: http://www.lbl.gov/Education/ELSI/Frames/pollution-health-effects-f.html
California Environmental Protection Agency. (n.d.). Retrieved September 21, 2012, from Ca.gov Air Resource Board: http://www.arb.ca.gov/research/health/healthres.htm

KernCog. (n.d.). Retrieved September 22, 2012, from Ride Share: http://www.kerncog.org/rideshare/

Natural Resources Defense Council. (n.d.). Retrieved September 21, 2012, from What's at Risk-Clean Air Act: http://www.nrdc.org/air/cleanairact/default.asp?gclid=CML_76vozLICFWXhQgodWhsA0A

State of California-BAR. (n.d.). Retrieved September 21, 2012, from Department of Consumer Affairs: http://www.bar.ca.gov/70_SiteWideInfo/index.html

Vehicle Repair, Retirement, Replacement for Motorist. (n.d.). Retrieved September 21, 2012, from Public Repair Program: http://www.vrrrm.org/ForConsumers/VRRRMRepairProgram.aspx

A SPEECH TO DEMONSTRATE

A speech that demonstrates shows the audience how and why something works. It shows what it is or who it is. It is the "how to" speech. It literally demonstrates a product, process, procedure, object, or person, by showing the audience not just explaining. Presenting a demonstration speech often incorporates visual aids. Remember aids should just aid the speech not be the speech. (See Chapter 9.)

EXAMPLES OF DEMONSTRATION SPEECH PURPOSES:

- To inform my audience how a bill becomes a law.
- To inform my audience how cotton becomes cloth.
- To inform my audience how getting a college education impacts your financial future.
- To inform my audience how to incorporate PowerPoint into a presentation.

EXAMPLE OF A DEMONSTRATION SPEECH

HOW TO MAKE CANNED TOMATOES FROM FRESH TOMATOES AT HOME

General Purpose: To demonstrate
Specific Purpose: Canning tomatoes is economical and easy.
Central Idea: Canning tomatoes is a family tradition worth learning and sharing.

INTRODUCTION

I. As a child one of my fondest memories was helping my mother skin tomatoes in preparation for canning them. Nothing was as satisfying as seeing the jars of red neatly stacked on the counter cooling.

II. **Transition:** Like many projects you start by gathering materials.

BODY

I. The first step is to gather the materials.
   A. There are several supplies that are essential to complete the project.
      1. Tomatoes
      2. Water bath cooker
      3. Canning jars and lids

       4. Large pot
       5. Jar grabber
       6. Large spoons, ladles, and butter knife
    B. Some supplies are optional.
       1. Towels
       2. Stickers to label the jars

Transition: Now that we've collected all the materials we can get started.

II. Selecting the tomatoes.
    A. Growing your own
    B. Store bought
    C. Pick-your-farm
    D. What not to use

Transition: Now that we have selected our tomatoes, we need to prepare the equipment.

III. Get the jars and lids sterilizing
    A. Dishwasher method only for jars
    B. Large pot method
       1. Lids
       2. Jars
       3. Rims

Transition: Now that the equipment is ready we need to get the tomatoes into the jars.

IV. Preparing the tomatoes to pack into the jars
    A. Scalding tomatoes
    B. Peeling tomatoes
    C. Placement in jars
    D. Getting rid of the air
    E. Placing rings and rims on jars

Transition: We now have the jars packed with tomatoes and are ready to process them.

V. Placement in the water bath canner
    A. Boil
    B. Time
    C. Cool

CONCLUSION

I. Canning tomatoes is something you can do as a family and brings enjoyment year around.
    A. The first step is gathering the materials
    B. The second step is selecting the best tomatoes
    C. The third step is sterilizing
    D. The fourth step is packing
    E. The final step is the water bath
II. I'd like to serve you some of my canned tomatoes. I hope this demonstration will encourage you to try canning your own tomatoes.

THE IMPORTANCE OF ETHICS IN AN INFORMATIVE SPEECH

Ethics as defined by Merriam-Webster's dictionary is, "the discipline dealing with what is good and bad and with moral duty and obligation . . . a set of moral principles: a theory or system of moral values . . . the principles of conduct governing an individual or group." When preparing and presenting a speech you must never forget your audience, why you are speaking, and why the audience is listening. It is your obligation to present the most up-to-date information in an honest and direct manner. To the best of your knowledge, tell the truth. Don't intentionally twist information or leave out information; doing so is dishonest and unethical. Be ever vigilant to avoid logical fallacies and presenting misleading, biased information. Respect your audience by appealing to their intellect before their emotions. Don't wait until the last minute to do your research or to write your speech. Good research takes time. Make the time to do your research and work at finding the most up-to-date information. Don't be lazy. Be accurate and be prepared.

Don't cut corners when putting together an informative speech.

FIGURE 15.9

© Christian Delbert, 2013. Used under license from Shutterstock, Inc.

Preparation includes practicing your speech to make sure your verbal and nonverbal communication is in sync. We have all heard that speaker who is the expert in their field but whose body language is yelling at us, "I am tired . . . please don't ask any more questions . . . why am I here?" Your body language and tone communicate more about your credibility and honesty than your words. Don't neglect them. Last but not least, don't forget to verbally cite. None of us are experts in everything. Not orally citing your sources is taking credit for work you didn't do. It is dishonest, unethical, and arrogant.

SUMMARY

After reading this chapter, you should now have a greater understanding of the purpose and goal of informative speaking. You should also be able to describe and present an informative speech. The chapter examined the criteria necessary for the formulation of a strong informative speech, how to organize an informative speech effectively and how to identify and use credible material ethically.

REVIEW
BASIC REQUIREMENTS FOR AN INFORMATIVE SPEECH

- Time limit (in class this is determined by your instructor)
- Based on credible sources
- Language is simple, logical, vivid, and appropriate for audience
- Nonverbal communication as important as spoken words (confidence, gestures, eye contact, posture, facial expression)

- Fluent memorized presentation is ideal, but note cards may be acceptable
- Visuals aids may be allowed but should be limited

THINGS TO CONSIDER

- Needs of audience
- Knowledge level of audience
- How to get their attention
- Cite sources
- Signposts (road map)
- How to relate to audience
- Do not persuade just inform

Review
Questions

1 Briefly explain the specific goals of a well-made informative speech.

2 Distinguish between description, exposition, and demonstration informative.

3 Explain why we should keep learning styles in mind when writing an informative speech.

4 Write a scratch outline for a demonstration speech.

5 Explain why choosing to leave important information out can be unethical.

Glossary

Demonstration speech: A speech that focuses on processes and explains how something is done or works.

Description speech: A speech that paints a clear and vivid understanding of an event, person, topic, or object.

Explanation speech: Concerned with abstract topics such as theories, principles, and attitudes, values, or beliefs.

Informative speaking: A goal to communicate information and ideas. Its goal is not to persuade.

SPEAKING TO PERSUADE

Helen Acosta

Learning
Objectives

CHAPTER 16

❶ Understand the differences between persuasion and manipulation
as influence.

❷ Unlock unwilling minds with neurological keys and avoid stepping
on neurological landmines.

❸ Distinguish between propositions of fact, value, and policy.

❹ Craft persuasive speeches using different organizational patterns

One evening in the summer of 2012, I was watching TV when a commercial began. I saw a line of people thirty and older waiting to get the new iPhone, talking about the cool, but minor, changes coming with the iPhone 5. Then, outside the line, two young men touched their phones together to share information with one another. One of the women in the line says, "can the iPhone 5 do that?" and she pantomimes the touching of the phones. The commercial ends with "the future is already here: The Samsung Galaxy S III."

I was hooked! I wanted that phone. Even though I'd been teaching public speaking for seventeen years and teaching persuasion for a decade I felt this visceral NEED for a Samsung Galaxy S3. I looked down at my nearly four-year-old iPhone 3GS and knew that everything had changed.

In this chapter, we discuss:

- What persuasion is
- Why we are persuadable
- Why the audience is central to the process of persuasion
- How to frame your ideas to maximize persuasive potential

PERSUASION DEFINED

Persuasion is often confused with both influence and manipulation. The reality is that persuasion, like manipulation, is a form of influence. Manipulation is the dark side of influence—persuasion is the light.

The difference: Motivation. When we seek to persuade others we are trying to change their hearts and/or minds to align with our own so that we can better help individuals, groups, or society as a whole.

When we manipulate we are trying to act as puppet masters with little concern for the well-being of the people we are compelling toward our own goals. When we manipulate we are focused on ourselves.

Persuasion is a form of social influence in which we seek to change people's hearts and/or minds to align with our own. Healthy persuasion pinpoints real needs of your audience and seeks to satisfy those needs for the mutual betterment of all involved.

THE PERSUASIVE IMPULSE

Humans are social animals. We need one another to survive. Our innate need to interconnect drives us to search for people whose views of the world are similar to ours. In his 2008 book, *Tribes*, Seth Godin explains: "A group only needs two things to be a tribe: A shared interest and a way to communicate" (Godin, 2008). Once we've found a shared interest we try to wedge all of our other interests into alignment as well. In that tension, we work to influence one another.

	INFLUENCE	
	← persuasion	manipulation →
Intention	Audience believes you are trying to help them	Audience believes you are trying to use them ← Q1 answer
Will	Good will: Audience believes you have their best interests at heart	Ill will: Audience believes you are focused on your own bottom line
Results Now	Audience may or may not do what you hoped but they trust you and are open to further appeals	Audience will likely do what you want this time but their trust is broken. They won't be open to further appeals
Future	Audience will consider the ideas you shared earlier. You can build on those ideas in the future. Persuasion is more likely to succeed with repeated attempts	Audience will discard the ideas you shared earlier (and build arguments against if you anger them enough). Further appeals will fall flat and the audience will ignore or fight you
Synonyms	advise ask caution consult encourage fall in love with help inspire motivate propose recommend share suggest warn	blackmail brainwash compel coerce extort force induce pressure seduce spellbind squeeze tempt threaten

Helen Acosta 2013

FIGURE 16.1

IT'S ALL IN OUR HEADS!

The people you hope to persuade are individuals with complex and busy lives. Each person in your audience has thoughts and ideas running through their heads constantly. Some of our thoughts and ideas are conscious: "What do I have in the fridge that hasn't gone bad?," "Did I study the right concepts for my midterm tomorrow?," "Huh . . . that's an interesting point . . . I wonder if . . . wait . . . what did she just say?"

Some of our thoughts are subconscious. Subconscious streams of thought are more like roaring rivers. These processes are hidden from us while connections are tried, tested, retried in new locations and tested again—all before we ever think a thought consciously!

Our **subconscious** *is made up of the functions operating in our minds beneath or beyond our awareness.*

FIGURE
16.2

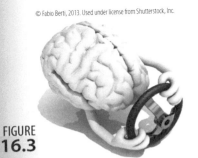

FIGURE
16.3

Think of a major street. Even the slower vehicles move so quickly that a pedestrian, up on the sidewalk, can't hear conversations in the vehicles and have little-to-no knowledge of what, if anything, is going on between the occupants. Pedestrians walk or jog along at a much slower pace than the vehicles. They are aware of the noises of the street and they process the information around them. They get to their destinations much more slowly than the vehicles speeding along on the highway. Think of your conscious mind as a pedestrian walking along on the sidewalk. Your subconscious mind is all those speeding cars, trucks, and motorcycles racing along toward places pedestrians have no notion of. Those vehicles will reach their destinations much more quickly than the pedestrian will.

In the November 15, 2012, edition of *Scientific American,* the results of a study conducted at Hebrew University in Jerusalem were published. The finding was that we can read short sentences and do simple math before we even have time to perceive the words and numbers in front of us. This is just the latest study to prove the power of our subconscious (Gannon, 2012). Those subconscious thought processes play a major role in persuasion.

NEUROLOGICAL LANDMINES THAT OBLITERATE PERSUASION

BIG TRUTHS

One odd interplay between our conscious and subconscious results in a strange irrationality that seems to be universal. After our subconscious has tested and wired and rewired a group of ideas into a pattern we seek out that pattern continuously. In his 1966 book, *Language as Symbolic Action,* Kenneth Burke called the resulting blind- ᵃʸ spots caused by our subconscious pattern-seeking tendency, "terministic screens" (Burke, 1966). To understand terministic screens think of the way a silk screen works: Once you imprint the pattern on the screen the pigment can only get through the screen where there are openings in the pattern. Now imagine thousands of imprinted screens stacked on top of one another. It's hard to imagine that anything could make it through to the bottom layer but, thanks to the swift work of our subconscious the screens are analyzed, stacked, and restacked hundreds of thousands of times to create patterns that are meaningful. All that stacking and restacking creates personal meaning for each of us. The personal meanings built in our subconscious over time become, in our own minds, our "Big Truths." These "Big Truths" are the ideas that, when we speak them aloud,

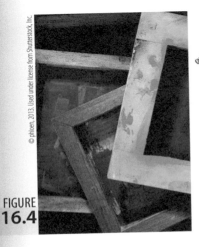

FIGURE
16.4

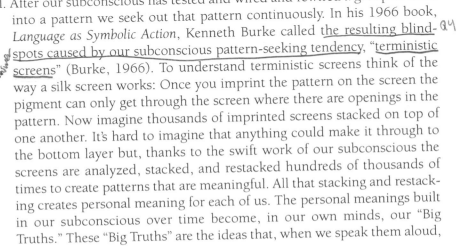

feel so true that we are sometimes overcome with the emotion of merely speaking them. We refer to our *big truths* as our beliefs, values and philosophies. <u>*Our big truths are the foundation*</u> Q3 <u>*of all of our assumptions about how the world works*</u>. These truths are so big in our minds that we cannot fathom that other people don't hold our same innate knowledge of the rightness of our truths. Our personal big truths blind us to the experiences of others and create enormous barriers to persuasion.

In order to effectively persuade when dealing with your own "big truth" issue you need to:

- Recognize that your big truth is not necessarily held by your audience.
- Consider the experiences and big truths your individual audience members might hold on this issue. Your audience may believe the opposite of your big truth, have some other big truth of their own that you haven't considered, or have no opinion at all on the issue.
- Think of ways to connect with audience members whose big truths might differ from yours.
- Look for other "big truths" that you may hold in common with your audience. These truths might help you connect through their terministic screens. If you can connect through a common truth it will be easier to get past your audience's blind spots on the issue and help them see the issue from your perspective.

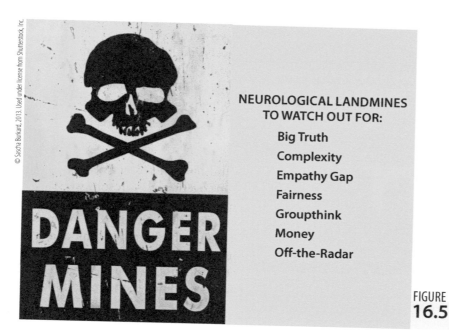

© Saicha Burkard, 2013. Used under license from Shutterstock, Inc.

NEUROLOGICAL LANDMINES
TO WATCH OUT FOR:

Big Truth

Complexity

Empathy Gap

Fairness

Groupthink

Money

Off-the-Radar

FIGURE
16.5

COMPLEXITY

While complex (involved, intricate, complicated) ideas can be dealt with effectively in persuasive speeches, when we don't break the ideas down into easy-to-understand components we confuse our audiences. If a speech is hard to follow or seems like too much work to process, the audience will just tune out.

EMPATHY GAP

We've all heard some variation of "never criticize a man until you've walked a mile in his moccasins." We are much better at "putting ourselves in someone else's shoes" when we've actually experienced the same thing that the speaker has. However, as time passes, or based on our current physical and emotional state, we lose our ability to empathize with other people's experiences.

George Loewenstein called this the empathy gap (Loewenstein, 1999). If you haven't eaten all day and someone gives a persuasive speech to convince you to take action to end hunger in America you are far more likely to empathize and want to take action than you would be if you experienced the speech on a full stomach. If a fellow student talks about how poorly they did on their test in another class because they were overwhelmed by too many responsibilities you are more likely to agree with them if you are exhausted when they talk to you. If, however, you are well-rested you are more likely to assume that they are slackers with poor time management skills.

As a speaker, you can see when your audience members are experiencing an empathy gap. If you tell an emotional story and they roll their eyes or zone out, they aren't empathizing.

FAIRNESS

Fairness, the perception that choices are free from favoritism or bias, can be an effective tool of persuasion but fairness is a two-edged sword. Fairness is always relative. What we believe to be fair is complex. We learn fairness from an early age and we learn to change our behaviors based on what other people see as fair or unfair. As a result, according to Ori and Rom Brafman in their book *Sway: The irresistible pull of irrational behavior,* we are often swayed not by what we think is fair but by what we perceive the people around us might think is fair (Brafman, 2008). Our analysis of what we think others would think is fair is often wrong. Which leads us to . . .

FIGURE
16.6

GROUPTHINK

People like to spend time with other people. We like to get along and have fun together. As a result, we self-monitor to avoid creating tensions within the group. We smooth over disagreements and avoid difficult subjects. We make huge assumptions about what others would think and we edit our words and actions to model what we think others would like us to be in order to maintain group cohesion. In 1982, Irving Janice of Yale University coined the term "groupthink."

MONEY . . . CHANGES EVERYTHING

Think of money as a neurological cluster bomb. Money is entirely abstract. We've all built our own big truths around the paper, coins, and electronic transactions that form these abstractions. When we bring money into persuasion a strange thing happens inside our brains. Money flips a neurological switch that completely shifts our focus. In one moment we might be thinking of protecting puppies and kittens from puppy mills but the moment a speaker mentions a monetary cost we are likely to switch off our empathy and altruistic impulses and switch on the parts of our mind that are most associated with risk taking and gambling (Brafman, 2008). Our cold, calculating brain centers start working. This leads to the neurological cluster bomb: All of our big truths about money and gambling come into play along with all the complexities that have been sewn into the fabric of these big truths. This can lead to a Grand Canyon–sized empathy gap. All of our big truth notions of monetary fairness rip us away from one another. BOOM!

FIGURE
16.7

OFF-THE-RADAR

My grandma was known to say, "Well, that can't be true! I've never heard of such a thing!" My grandma wasn't unique. We all experience these complete blind spot moments in which we dismiss something someone has told us and never think of it again. This mental dismissal happens as a natural part of the sorting that our subconscious does in the sense-making process. Incoming information is sorted into different piles: useful (reinforces what we already believe), worth thinking about, and the discard pile. Those discarded bits of information are never considered or stored in our long-term memories. While it seems impossible to move an idea from off-the-radar to on-the-radar it can be done, even with people whose awareness of an issue is nonexistent. First, we have to accept the idea that there are members of the audience who not only don't care about issues that we care about but for whom the issue doesn't even exist.

NEUROLOGICAL KEYS THAT OPEN MINDS

Although there are a number of neurological landmines that can limit the success of persuasion, there are also a number of persuasive strategies we can use that are based on the basic wiring pathways that are most common in our brains.

ALTRUISM

<u>Altruism is the impulse to help others without the expectation that you will get anything back.</u> Until recently it was thought that appeals to altruism were a weak form of persuasion. However, recent research has revealed that our altruistic impulses release neurochemicals that make us feel good about ourselves and enhance our coping abilities overall (Akhtar, 2009). Since we like to feel good about ourselves we gravitate toward appeals to altruism.

To appeal to altruism in your audience be aware of the following:

1. Appeals to altruism only work when you are connecting with your audience through their big truths. We only support altruistic efforts that align with our beliefs and values. We don't want to get burned when we try to help others.

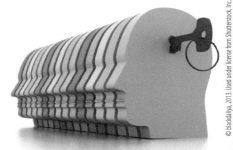

NEUROLOGICAL KEYS
TO OPEN MINDS:

1 Altruism
2 Dissent
3 Do-ability
4 Priming the Gap
5 Simplicity Principle
6 Top-of-mind Awareness

FIGURE
16.8

2. Nonmonetary appeals to altruism are most effective with audiences that have time but little money. Monetary appeals to altruism are most effective with audiences that have money but little time. Monetary appeals must be accompanied by more supports (based in ethos, pathos, and logos) than nonmonetary appeals. We undervalue our time and overvalue our money.

3. Appeals to altruism work differently for males than for females. Women respond more positively to appeals in which they are asked to help others and men respond more positively to appeals in which you can help people help themselves (Brunel and Nelson, 2000).

Appeals to altruism help you avoid the neurological landmines associated with the empathy gap, money, fairness, and off-the-radar issues.

DISSENT

Turn on the TV news any day and you'll hear the same political talking points that you've read on your Internet newsfeed and your friends have posted and reposted on your favorite social network. While we have more access to information today than at any other time in human history, the arguments we hear on a regular basis have narrowed. New arguments that appeal to our curiosity and connect with our big truths are fast-tracked to storage in our subconscious (Medina, 2008).

Dissent is powerful because it forces the subconscious to sort new information rather than merely agreeing or discarding. Dissent creates new mental connections that will often lead to later persuasion. *qb answer*

To appeal to dissent:

1. Use unique arguments that you've never heard anyone use before.
2. Appeal to big truths that you know most of your audience shares.
3. Don't disregard arguments that members of your audience may agree with. Instead, think of your ideas as a "third way."

Dissenting helps you avoid the neurological landmines associated with big truths, groupthink, and off-the-radar issues.

DO-ABILITY

If you are asking your audience to do something, make it easy for them to do. We take actions that we can see ourselves taking. Help us to see ourselves doing what you ask and we are more likely to do it!

To make ideas seem do-able:

1. Help the audience take the first step right there in the room. Bring a petition or sign-up sheet, give them pledge cards to sign and return to you. Make the first step easy and instantaneous.
2. Bring items that will remind the audience to take action. After your speech hand out cards that provide simple instructions and/or reminders, provide necessary contact information, or sample letters.

3. Help the audience see themselves doing what you are asking of them. Paint a mental picture in which they can see themselves in the lead role. Mahatma Gandhi said, "Be the change you want to see in the world." Help your audience see the change so that they will want to be the change.

When you make your ideas do-able you can avoid the neurological landmines of complexity, groupthink, and off-the-radar issues.

FAIRNESS

The other edge of the sword of fairness is the side that helps you persuade your audience. Since we tend to learn fairness from an early age and we learn to change our behaviors based on what other people see as fair or unfair, we can appeal to our audience's sense of fairness in order to persuade.

To appeal to fairness:

1. Use concepts of fairness that we learned in childhood. These concepts of sharing, 50/50 splits, and "one cuts, the other chooses" are simple and easy for people to agree with.

2. Use the "yes/yes" technique: present two to four statements you know most of your audience will agree with (either by nodding their heads or saying "yes" audibly). This will create a sense of groupness in your audience that will make them more vigilant of what others would think is fair.

3. Leave money out of the equation. The moment there is money on the table people lose interest in fairness and start gambling.

When you appeal to fairness you can avoid the neurological landmines of empathy gap, fairness, money, and off-the-radar issues.

PRIME THE GAP

When we prime the gap we create curiosity and interest where none existed before. We create a gap in understanding that leaves the audience craving more information. Teasers for news programs prime the gap: "Is your mouthwash killing you? News at 11" (Heath, 2007).

To prime the gap:

1. Surprise us. When we get the "surprise brow" (eyebrows lifted, eyes wide open as in Figure 16.9) we are more open to new information.

2. Prove that a problem exists. Show us how bad a situation has gotten. Make us crave a solution.

3. Tell us a story about a person who is struggling or overcoming. As people we are drawn to the human drama and, once we care about someone affected by the issue you present, we want to take action to support any change that would solve the problem you've presented.

© tommaso lizzul, 2013. Used under license from Shutterstock, Inc.

FIGURE 16.9

When you prime the gap you can avoid all of the neurological landmines. Priming the gap is powerful!

SIMPLICITY PRINCIPLE

On his hugely popular, Changingminds.org website, psychologist David Straker, discusses the "simplicity principle." Straker breaks the simplicity principle into five strategies.

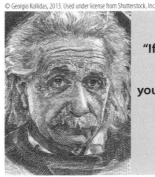

"If you can't explain it simply, you don't understand it well enough."

Albert Einstein

FIGURE **16.10**

1. **Language:** Use words that are familiar and comfortable for your audience. Field-specific terms (also known as "jargon") should be rephrased for clarity. All language should be targeted for clarity and vivid understanding. Use metaphors and analogies to help the audience grasp difficult concepts. Use short sentences to keep the path simple for your audience to follow.

2. **Reduce:** "Simplification can be achieved simply by showing or doing *less*. Talk less. Show them fewer alternatives. Make the idea more stand-alone with less associations. Reduce time, space, actions and people to make plan more straightforward" (Straker, 2006).

3. **Rearrange:** Take the time to try different arrangements of processes, arguments, and patterns. You may find that your ideas make more sense when arranged differently. Visit the organizational strategies section of this chapter to try on different strategies until you find one that clarifies your meanings most clearly. A helpful hint: The organizational strategies discussed later in this chapter work for organizing ideas as well as whole speeches! In one main point you could use a "minor repair" strategy to explain a single concept while the larger design of the speech may follow Monroe's motivated sequence.

4. **Replace:** If a concept is difficult to explain ask yourself if it is really the best concept to use. Is there a concept that is easier to explain that you could substitute? I find that visiting thesaurus.com and trying different search terms helps me find replacements when I get stuck on a difficult concept.

5. **KISS:** Keep it short and simple.

The simplicity principle helps you avoid the following neurological landmines: complexity and off-the-radar.

TOP-OF-MIND AWARENESS

In late 2003 I was at a party with some very liberal friends, several of whom were lawyers. As a member of the LGBTQ community I had already become aware of the issue of marriage equality (at the time this was widely referred to as "same sex marriage"). I wanted the lawyers' opinions of the possibility that same sex marriage would become legal in the United States. Even though two of the lawyers lived in San Francisco all of the lawyers thought that there was no way same sex marriage would become legal nationwide in our lifetimes. I asked about the 14th amendment (the equal protection clause) and wondered aloud if the courts would resolve the issue sooner rather than later. At the time, everyone at the party dismissed my thoughts and even I thought I was wearing rose-colored glasses.

Just before the 2012 Presidential election I was at an event with nearly the same group of people, many of whom were now deeply committed to marriage equality and talking about how the Supreme Court would absolutely overturn the Defense of Marriage Act and California's Proposition 8. This time, when I asked if same sex marriage would be legal nationwide in our lifetimes, I got an entirely different answer. In our lifetimes? Of course! It'll happen within the year!

What changed? Initially, when I mentioned marriage equality it wasn't even on-the-radar. As a result, my friends dismissed it as outside the realm of possibility. But, a lot has changed in just a few years. There has been an ongoing national dialogue on TV, on our newsfeeds, on our social networks, and in our homes about same sex marriage. We have seen more representations of people in same sex relationships than ever before in U.S. history. As a result, when we talk about same sex marriage today, we have immediate connections sparked all over our brains. We see and feel the many stories that people have shared in the media and with us personally. Marriage equality has achieved top of mind awareness.

Generally, it is easier to persuade about an issue that is part of a current national dialogue. When everyone is talking about an issue, our subconscious's stacking and restacking of ideas becomes nimble and we tend to be much more open to suggestions that help us resolve the issue in our minds.

To persuade through top-of-mind awareness:

1. Choose an issue that has sparked a current national dialogue.
2. Share unique stories that show how this issue is affecting regular people just trying to live their lives.
3. Surprise us. Show us how people just like us are suffering in unexpected ways as a result of this issue.
4. Keep it fresh: Avoid those talking points! Use fresh new arguments that your audience hasn't heard before.

Employing top-of-mind awareness helps you avoid the following neurological landmines: big truth, empathy gap, fairness, groupthink, and off-the-radar issues.

FOCUS ON WHO YOU HOPE TO PERSUADE

To break through the conscious and subconscious clutter, connect with your audience on a more personalized level.

When you are going to give a persuasive speech knowing your audience is far more important than in any other type of presentation. Most importantly, knowing how your audience feels about you and the issue you plan to discuss is necessary to your success in persuading them.

Vital Questions from Chapter Three:

What are the NEEDS of my audience?

What is the SPEECH SETTING?

What DEMOGRAPHICS and PSYCHOGRAPHICS will create connections or barriers between us?

What CULTURAL FACTORS will create connections or barriers between us?

How can I bridge the DIFFERENCES?

FIGURE
16.11

FIGURE
16.12

FOUR TYPES OF AUDIENCES
THE SYMPATHETIC AUDIENCE

A sympathetic audience is a person or group of people who already like you and agree with you on the issues and/or big truth you may be addressing in your presentation.

To persuade a sympathetic audience you can usually speak your own big truths and you have more leeway than with any other audience.

The goal: Get this audience to stop nodding blindly and motivate them to get up and do something to spread the ideas or changes you are talking about.

© Creativa, 2013. Used under license from Shutterstock, Inc.

FIGURE
16.13

THE UNINFORMED AUDIENCE

An uninformed audience is a person or group of people who have no previous interest in the issues and/or big truths you may be addressing in your presentation.

To persuade an uninformed audience you need to teach about your subject while also finding ways to connect your subject to your audience's big truths and shared experiences.

When you approach an uninformed audience it is good to have modest goals: Raise awareness, gain appreciation, provoke thought. You want the uninformed audience to leave as an informed audience who are open to further persuasion on the issue.

THE CRITICAL AUDIENCE

A critical audience is a person or group of people who are already aware of your issue, have formulated opinions about the issue, and are prepared to argue the issue. While this sounds like an uncomfortable situation, a critical audience is sometimes the most persuadable. Critical audiences tend to be informed and interested in action. However, they may already have negative biases against your position.

© auremar, 2013. Used under license from Shutterstock, Inc.

FIGURE
16.14

To persuade a critical audience, focus on the big truths you know you have in common. Show how your position on the issue reflects their big truths. Use unique arguments that create novel juxtapositions in their minds. A creative approach that makes critical audience members question their previous assumptions can be remarkably effective.

With a critical audience you may have a number of goals: Shift their stance on the issue, open them to later persuasion on the issue, or promote further internal dialogue to reconcile new ideas.

THE HOSTILE AUDIENCE

A hostile audience is a person or group of people who show open contempt for you and/or your stance on an issue. This audience will display their feelings openly and may even talk over you while you speak. If you prepare ahead of time, even the hostile audience can be persuaded.

To persuade a hostile audience it is important to focus on your common human-ness. Before you speak take time to get to know the individuals in your audience. Talk with them one-on-one about their own big truths. Learn about the experiences they have had that have led to the big truths that have created such hostility toward your position. LISTEN. Arguing with a hostile audience is counterproductive. NEVER repeat a "talking point" from a political TV show in front of a hostile audience. If you do, they aren't likely to listen to you on any topic in the future.

FIGURE
16.15

Instead, make your approach entirely unique and deeply personal. Use humor that speaks to the commonalities between yourself and your audience. This will break down the barriers and help this audience connect with you not as "the opposition" but as another human being. Use your own stories as well as published true stories from identifiable and reputable sources. Use surprising statistics and eyebrow-raising facts. Work to connect on a personal level with this audience and they will listen rather than arguing with you.

With a hostile audience you may have more modest goals: Open them to later persuasion on the issue, promote further internal dialogue to reconcile new ideas, or just get them to smile at you instead of scowling.

IN BRIEF: GIVE THEM ALL SOMETHING TO TALK ABOUT

- Current: A topic that is currently in the news or all over social networks
- Uncommon: A unique or surprising take on the issue
- Customized: Use what you know about the people in your audience to appeal to what they care about.

Neurological Landmines

Audiences	Big Truth	Complexity	Empathy Gap	Fairness	Groupthink	Money	Off-the-Radar
Hostile	X	X	X	X	X	X	
Critical	X	X	X	X	X	X	
Uninformed	X	X	X	X	X	X	X
Sympathetic		X					

FIGURE
16.16

Neurological Keys

Audiences	Altruism	Dissent	Do-ability	Fairness	Priming the Gap	Simplifying Complexities	Top-of-mind-awareness
Hostile	X	X		X	X	X	
Critical	X	X	X	X	X	X	
Uninformed	X		X	X	X	X	X
Sympathetic	X	X	X	X	X	X	X

FIGURE
16.17

FRAME YOUR ISSUE

Propositions	Goal	Types of Questions	Sample Topics
Fact	Convince your audience that your position on the issue is true.	What was?	The United States lost the War of 1812.
			The housing bubble didn't cause the recession.
			The refs won their negotiations with the NFL because of a bad call on Green Bay.
		What is?	Telecommuting reduces traffic jams.
			Corporate lobbyists have taken over our legislature.
			Global warming isn't real.
		What will be?	We are headed for another global economic meltdown.
			Nations that teach their children to be adaptive learners will emerge as the leaders of the 21st century.
			The slowing of the Gulf Stream will create a mini-ice age in Northern Europe.
Value	Convince your audience that your position is:	Right or wrong?	The use of torture by the U.S. government is wrong.
			Drone surveillance of U.S. citizens is unconstitutional.
			Breast feeding in public is natural.
		Good or bad?	The penny is bad for our economy.
			Casinos hurt the communities they are in.
			Lowering the voting age would be good for our country.
		Better or worse?	Name brand prescription drugs are better than generics.
			Diet sodas are worse for you than regular sodas.
			Two parent families are better for children than single parent families.
Policy	Convince your audience to take action on an issue.	Should I make a change in my life?	Stop negative thoughts from stopping you.
			Sleep for success.
			Clean up your social network profiles to get the job!
		Should I help create change in the lives of other people?	Volunteer at the Literacy Center.
			Help build a Habitat home.
			Practice random acts of kindness.
		Should I help create a big change that will change everyone's lives?	We should replace our broken foster care system with a system of regulated orphanages staffed by highly-trained and qualified social workers.
			Legalizing prostitution would decrease sexual assault in the United States.
			Public safety is not improved by breed-specific ordinances or bans on particular dog breeds. Taxpayer money would be better spent on spay/neuter programs.

ORGANIZE YOUR SPEECH FOR MAXIMUM IMPACT

Speeches have followed the same basic and effective structure for over two thousand years. Along the way, people have tried hundreds of strategies that work within the structure. Below, you'll find some of the most successful, time tested patterns. To choose which will work best for your speech try different strategies with your topic until you find the best fit.

COMPARATIVE ADVANTAGES

Introduction
I.   Discuss a few possible solutions to an established problem
II.   Share the positives about each of the solutions
III. Narrow to one solution that clearly outweighs the rest
Conclusion

Example: Stop smoking the easy way

   Introduction
   I   Possible solutions to the problem: list the most successful ways to stop smoking
   II.   Positives of each solution: discuss the benefits of each method
   III. Best solution: focus on the e-cig as the best and most effective method to stop smoking
   Conclusion

CRITERIA-SATISFACTION AKA VALUE-SATISFACTION

Introduction
I.   Establish a criterion that most of your audience would agree on (goal: get heads nodding)
II.   Show how your topic does or does not meet the criteria
Conclusion

Example: The Galaxy S3 commercial addressed at the beginning of this chapter

   Introduction
   I.   Criteria: The newest technologies are the best
   II.   Satisfaction: Galaxy S3 customers already have the newest technologies (you've been left behind)
   Conclusion

ILL-BLAME-CURE

Based on Aristotle's topoi, ill-blame-cure is an ancient organizational strategy that still works today.

Introduction
I.   Ill: Prove that a problem exists.
II.   Blame: Explain who is responsible for causing the problem and allowing it to persist.
III. Cure: Explain the change that will solve the problem, why it will solve the problem, and how we can help solve it.
Conclusion: Include a call to action as part of the conclusion

Example: Senator Elizabeth Warren (D-MA) most often uses the ill-blame-cure strategy.
I. Normal Americans are suffering while Wall Street prospers
II. Corporations now see lobbying as a successful investment strategy. This has left Main Street footing the bill for Wall Street's excesses.
III. Reform Congress, reform Wall Street, protect Main Street from Wall Street excesses.

MINOR REPAIR

The Minor Repair strategy is effective when a policy that is already in place is popular but one aspect of the legislation has made the policy ineffective. Many policies are passed without appropriate enforcement mechanisms (most commonly laws aren't funded properly and there is no money to enforce the law) or there has been a surprising unintended consequence that can be remedied through a simple structural repair.

Introduction
I. Benefits of a popular policy
II. Unintended consequence or missing mechanism of a popular policy
III. How to resolve the unintended consequence or fix the missing mechanism
Conclusion with call to action

- In personal motivational speeches a minor repair strategy might be:
  I. So, you're dieting to lose weight.
  II. Diet soda is popular but ineffective in aiding weight loss (use studies to prove diet soda actually makes you crave calories).
  III. Cut out the soda and you'll meet your weight loss goals more quickly.

- Policy example: March 22, 2013, Chana Joffe-Walt, a correspondent for NPR's Planet Money, used the minor repair strategy to explore the rise in disability claims since the 1990s.
  I. Benefits of a popular policy: Welfare to work did decrease unemployment in the United States.
  II. Unintended Consequence: States, now burdened with more of the cost of welfare, began hiring companies to help move qualified or qualifiable people from welfare to disability (as disability is a wholly funded federal program), these companies exploit a system set up to support disabled people when they appeal denials. It is a simplified court appeal process with a judge and the claimant, with or without legal representation. As a result, these companies send in a lawyer and, in a setting not built for argument, make undeniable cases. This change has resulted in a record fourteen million Americans who are currently receiving disability payments.
  III. Resolve the unintended consequence: Reform federal disability so that disabled people can still work and receive benefits and change the appeal process to assure that taxpayers are represented in a process that normally leads to $250,000 to $500,000 in payments over the lifetime of the claimant.

MONROE'S MOTIVATED SEQUENCE

In the 1930s Alan Monroe of Purdue University introduced a method of sequencing ideas that he organized based on the psychology of persuasion. The strategy has endured because it is effective. Below you'll see not only the sequence but also the neurological supports that are built-into the sequence:

- Attention: Go for the surprise brow here! (begin to "prime the gap")
- Problem: Prove that a serious problem exists (prime the gap, fairness)
- Solution: Lay out a simple solution to the problem (do-ability, simplicity principle, fill the gap you've primed)
- Visualization: Help the audience see a future where the problem has been solved or where they are now an active part of the solution (fill the gap, do-ability, altruism)
- Action: Ask the audience to take action to make the vision a reality (do-ability, altruism, simplicity principle)

Example: Feed the Need at the Renegade Pantry

See the sample outline and text of this speech to convince an uninformed audience starting on page 394.

Introduction. Attention: Story of a student who had to choose between feeding his kids or buying textbooks.
I. Problem: Statistics and examples to show that students at our school are too often unemployed, without money, and going without nutritious food.
II. Solution: Details about the programs of the renegade pantry with a focus on what the pantry does to alleviate hunger on our campus.
III. Visualization: As a student you may have a few hours to kill between classes. Visit the student activities office across from the cafeteria and volunteer. Also let your friends know about the program.
Conclusion. Action: You can help end hunger on our campus. Help the Renegade Pantry end hunger one student at a time.

PROBLEM-SOLUTION

Introduction
I. Prove that a problem exists
II. Share the solution that will best solve the problem
Conclusion

Example: Increase funding for unemployment benefits

Introduction
I. Unemployment is nearly eight percent, the recovery from the recession is stagnating
II. Increase funding for unemployment benefits. A study by Moody's Analytics recently found that every dollar spent by the government on benefits for the unemployed produces an overall return of $1.61 for the economy.
Conclusion

PRO-CON

Introduction
I.   Discuss the advantages
II. Discuss the disadvantages
Conclusion

Example: Attend a community college for the first two years

Introduction
I.   Advantages: Costs less, fewer giant lecture hall classes, greater focus on learning, courses will transfer to major universities
II. Disadvantages: Miss out on dorm life, less freedom, fewer campus activities
Conclusion

PROCESS OF ELIMINATION (THE FLIPSIDE OF COMPARATIVE ADVANTAGES)

Introduction
I.   Share several solutions to an established problem
II. Share the failings of the solutions presented
III. Discuss the best remaining solution in more depth.
Conclusion

Example: Exercise and nutritious food are the best path to health

Introduction
I.   Solutions: The most popular diets
II. Failings of the solutions: The failings of each of the most popular diets
III. Best remaining solution: Through it all, moderate exercise and healthy food choices are still the best method.
Conclusion

REFUTATION MODEL

Introduction
I.   Introduce and answer the most common argument against your position
II. Introduce and answer another common argument against your position
III. Introduce and answer a final common argument against your position
Conclusion

Example: Students who ride the bus are better off than students who drive

Introduction
I.   Folks think riding the bus takes too long. That's just time to do your homework.
II. Folks think the bus is too far from their homes. We live in a community with record levels of obesity and diabetes. The walk will save your life.
III. Folks think the bus is too expensive. Car payments, insurance, maintenance, and repairs cost an average of $800 a month. A bus pass costs $50.
Conclusion

STATEMENT OF REASONS

Introduction
I.   Share one reason that supports your opinion
II. Share a second reason that supports your opinion
III. Share a third reason that supports your opinion
Conclusion

Example: Sleep more for better grades

Introduction
I.   Sleep is essential to learning (explain the functions of sleep that support learning).
II. Sleep allows your subconscious to do much of the work for you (explain what the subconscious does while you are asleep that is can't do when you are awake).
III. Sleep allows for rehearsal of new behaviors and skills (explain how non-REM sleep works to allow for multiple practice sessions of new skills without all the anxiety that might normally accompany waking practice).
Conclusion

Questions of:		comparative advantages	criteria satisfaction	ill-blame-cure	minor repair	Monroe's motivated sequence	problem-solution	pro-con	process of elimination	refutation model	statement of reasons
FACT	what was		X						X		X
	what is		X						X	X	X
	what will be		X						X		X
VALUE	right or wrong		X					X	X	X	X
	good or bad		X					X	X	X	X
	better or worse		X					X	X	X	X
POLICY	change your life	X		X	X	X	X				
	personal action to change the lives of others	X		X	X	X	X				
	support a big change that will change all of our lives	X		X	X	X	X				

FIGURE
16.18

SPEECH TO CONVINCE AN UNINFORMED AUDIENCE (TEXT)

The audience: A public speaking class at Bakersfield College
Organizational strategy: Monroe's Motivated Sequence

FEED THE NEED AT THE RENEGADE PANTRY

Prepared October, 2013

Dominic Eskandor, a Bakersfield College student, was featured in an article by Jorge Barrrentos of the Bakersfield Californian on January, 28, 2010. Dominic, the single father of 3 children, talked about how, in the previous semester, he'd been forced to choose between buying his books and feeding his children. He did what anyone of us would do, he chose his children.

> ATTENTION—Sourced personal narrative. **Visual aid:** Photo of Eskandor.
>
> Connects with audience experience, "priming the gap" through human drama.

According to the National Center for Educational Statistics 2011 Bakersfield College Report, Dominic is just one of the 54% of BC students whose incomes are so low that they qualify for pell grants. 54%. That means over half of us in this room have likely had to choose between food and books or have had to choose between those extra hours our boss offered us and the study session necessary to pass a class.

> Credible source, surprising demographic statistic that connects with audience experience, builds interest.
>
> Connects statistic to shared audience experiences, personalizes the issue.

After the Northridge Earthquake I thought I would have to make that choice. I had just begun my fourth semester of Grad School. After the quake, the roads between North Hollywood and the Miracle Mile were closed for 3 weeks. There weren't even busses running that could take us to work. My husband and I both got laid off. I thought I was going to have to quit school. Thankfully, the Jewish food bank about a mile from our apartment kept our bellies full while we put the pieces of our lives back together.

> Speaker shares personal connection with topic, shows why speaker is a credible advocate for this issue.
>
> Personal narrative "primes the gap" through human drama.

That's why the Renegade Pantry, our campus food bank, is so close to my heart. Today, I'd like to talk to you about BC's starving students, what the Renegade Pantry does to feed the need and finally, what you can do to help satisfy the hunger that is so common on our campus.

> Transition to preview.
>
> Thesis: Overview of topic and main points.

While it may be hard for some to believe, students at BC really are starving for relief. The California economy over the last 3 decades has left students hungry for change. I looked back through the BC catalogs from 1987 to today. I found that the fees you pay have risen far faster than most students' earning power while in school. At the beginning of 1987, community colleges were still tuition-free in California. In the Fall of 1987, when I began college, tuition was collected for the first time. The price: $5/unit, up to $50. Everything above $50 was still free. A student enrolling at BC in 1988 could pay for 12 units with just about 15 hours of minimum wage work. Since then, there have been several tuition increases that led to the 2013 increase. Current cost: $46 dollars a unit. This means that today a student at BC who wants to take 12 units must work nearly 80 hours in a minimum wage job in order to cover their tuition alone . . . that doesn't include the $100–$200 for books that we all know is fairly standard for each class you take at BC.

> First main point claim: NEED.
>
> A. Subpoint claim.
>
> Credible source to establish statistical appeal, "dissent" appeal to shared big truth.
>
> Personal connection to topic.
>
> **Visual aid:** Graph of fee increases. Statistical trend analysis, appeal to fairness, "priming the gap."

The last recession made matters worse for students. Shawn Newsome, the first Renegade Pantry coordinator, was interviewed for the 2010 ReneGADE. He said that the leadership of the Student Government decided to start the Pantry because the majority of our students had lost their jobs in the recession, many had lost their homes to foreclosure and far too often, at the end of the day, they were greeted with empty cupboards.

> B. Subpoint claim.
>
> Expert opinion from source listeners relate to.
>
> Appeal to altruism that connects through shared big truth.

Our student leaders understood the hunger our students faced and, within months, the Renegade Pantry was born.

> Transition from 1st main point to 2nd main point.

The pantry began to feed the all-too-real hunger that had been growling in classrooms all over campus. According to a staff editorial in the Renegade Rip published March 14, 2012, the Renegade Pantry quickly became the most effective program offered by the Student Government Association. The staff of the Rip stated that in the Fall of 2011 the Pantry gave boxes of food to over 6,000 students.

> 2nd main point claim: SATISFACTION. **Visual aid:** Photo of the pantry with a line of students being served.
>
> A. Subpoint claim.
>
> Statistic from a source.

Those 6,000 students got boxes of food similar to the foods offered today. In an April, 2013 flyer from the Renegade Pantry the 3 options for food boxes are listed.

| B. Subpoint claim. |
| Fact from a source. |

Option A: Rice, Beans, Pasta, Pasta sauce, soup, tuna and fresh produce when available.

Option B: The kid-friendly box. In addition to the box I already described, parents are provided kid-friendly foods like Mac & Cheese, graham crackers, canned fruit and kid-friendly soups.

Visual aid (3): Foods provided in each option. Surprising fact (Option C), primes the gap.

Option C was added to better serve the increasing numbers of our students who are homeless. This option is all canned, ready-to-eat foods for students who don't have kitchens in which to prepare their meals.

The pantry is open to all students, regardless of need.

C. Subpoint claim.

BC Student, Jonathan Riccardi, was interviewed by KGET March 13, 2013. He said that before he knew about the Pantry there were times when he went hungry. He said that his hunger had affected his concentration and his grades. He learned about the program while sitting in this room, when I gave a speech very much like this one.

Sourced personal narrative. **Visual aid:** Photo of Riccardi.

Priming the gap.

Speaker's personal connection to the topic builds credibility.

Clearly, the Renegade Pantry is feeding a deep need on our campus. Now, let's see what you can do to help satisfy the hunger.

Transition from 2nd main point to 3rd main point.

The Renegade Pantry gets plenty of donations but there is one kind of support that you, as BC students, are in the best position to provide.

3rd main point claim: VISUALIZATION.

You probably set-up your schedule this semester with a few gaps in the middle of the day so that you can study between classes. However, if you are like most people, a few weeks into the semester you found those well-intentioned gaps filled up with friends who have similar schedules, or those gaps were filled with facebook and tumblr in the commons. Don't feel bad. Our brains need relief that studying doesn't provide between classes.

Top of mind awareness, do-ability.

Here's something you can do a couple times a month to feel good about the gaps you built into your schedule: Help out at the Renegade Pantry. The 2nd and 4th weeks of each month the Pantry needs volunteers to help prepare the boxes for food distribution. Next time you are walking through Campus Center stop by the Student Government Office in CC4 where they took your picture for your student ID card. Sign-up and help pack boxes during one of the gaps in your schedule.

A. Subpoint claim.

Simplicity, top of mind awareness, do-ability.
Visual aid: Photo, Student Government office, CC4.

You can also help by spreading the word. When you are in class and someone's stomach growls, tell them about the Renegade Pantry, when someone is scrounging through their backpack for change for the cafeteria, tell them about the Renegade Pantry. When someone posts on facebook, twitter or tumblr that all they have left to eat for the rest of the month is ramen, tell them about the Renegade Pantry. Basically, if a fellow student is hungry, tell them about the Renegade Pantry.

B. Subpoint claim.

Altruism, simplicity, top of mind awareness, do-ability.

You can tell them that they can sign-up for a box of food the Monday, Tuesday or Wednesday of the 2nd or 4th week of the month, then they can pick up their box of food on the following Thursday.

If you meet a student who is desperate, it isn't a distribution date and they have no money or access to food for a few days, they can also stop by the Student Government Office in CC4 for an emergency food box. Any student can get an emergency box once a semester and that box should last until the next scheduled distribution.

The Bakersfield College Renegade Pantry is the first of its kind in California. January 17, 2011, Jorge Barrentos of the Bakersfield Californian reported that UC Davis and UCLA have followed in our footsteps, launching their own Pantry projects. Our Renegade Pantry understands our starving students, they feed the hunger that gnaws at too many guts on this campus. You know what to do: The next time your

Surprising fact, transition to Conclusion.

Review of main points and ACTION step. Simplicity, top of mind awareness, do-ability.

procrastination meter goes into overdrive, opt for positive procrastination. Be a food renegade, fill some boxes and spread the word.

Together, we can help the Pantry fulfill its mission.
Together, we can: "eliminate hunger one student at a time."

> Closing. Sourced motto.
> **Visual aid:** Logo and motto.

SPEECH TO CONVINCE AN UNINFORMED AUDIENCE—FULL SENTENCE OUTLINE

The audience: A public speaking class at Bakersfield College
Organizational strategy: Monroe's Motivated Sequence

FEED THE NEED AT THE RENEGADE PANTRY

Prepared October, 2013

ATTENTION

Go for the surprise brow here! (begin to "prime the gap")

In this speech:

An emotion-provoking sourced story is used coupled with a surprising statistic and the speaker's personal connection to the topic.

Introduction
I. Attention Getter
Dominic Eskandor, a Bakersfield College student, was featured in an article by Jorge Barrrentos of the Bakersfield Californian on January, 28, 2010. Dominic, the single father of 3 children, talked about how, in the previous semester, he'd been forced to choose between buying his books and feeding his children. He did what anyone of us would do, he chose his children.

II. Creating Connections
A. According to the National Center for Educational Statistics 2011 Bakersfield College Report, Dominic is just one of the 54% of BC students whose incomes are so low that they qualify for pell grants. 54%. That means over half of us in this room have likely had to choose between food and books or have had to choose between those extra hours our boss offered us and the study session necessary to pass a class.
B. After the Northridge Earthquake I thought I would have to make that choice. I had just begun my fourth semester of Grad School. After the quake, the roads between North Hollywood and the Miracle Mile were closed for 3 weeks. There weren't even busses running that could take us to work. My husband and I both got laid off. I thought I was going to have to quit school. Thankfully, the Jewish food bank about a mile from our apartment kept our bellies full while we put the pieces of our lives back together.

III. Preview
    A.   Thesis: The Renegade Pantry changes lives one box of food at a time.
    B.   Today, I'd like to talk to you about BC's starving students, what the Renegade Pantry does to feed the need and finally, what you can do to help satisfy the hunger that is so common on our campus.

Body

I. While it may be hard for some to believe, students at BC really are starving for relief. The California economy over the last 3 decades has left students hungry for change.
    A.   I looked back through the BC catalogs from 1987 to today. I found that the fees you pay have risen far faster than most students' earning power while in school. At the beginning of 1987, community colleges were still tuition-free in California. In the Fall of 1987, when I began college, tuition was collected for the first time. The price: $5/unit, up to $50. Everything above $50 was still free. A student enrolling at BC in 1988 could pay for 12 units with just about 15 hours of minimum wage work. Since then, there have been several tuition increases that led to the 2013 increase. Current cost: $46 dollars a unit. This means that today a student at BC who wants to take 12 units must work nearly 80 hours in a minimum wage job in order to cover their tuition alone . . . that doesn't include the $100-$200 for books that we all know is fairly standard for each class you take at BC.
    B.   The last recession made matters worse for students. Shawn Newsome, the first Renegade Pantry coordinator, was interviewed for the 2010 ReneGADE. He said that the leadership of the Student Government decided to start the Pantry because the majority of our students had lost their jobs in the recession, many had lost their homes to foreclosure and far too often, at the end of the day, they were greeted with empty cupboards.

Transition: Our student leaders understood the hunger our students faced and, within months, the Renegade Pantry was born.

NEED aka PROBLEM

Prove that a serious problem exists (prime the gap, fairness)

In this speech:

The speaker uses statistical trend to validate audience feeling that there really is a problem, background from a credible source to show the historical need and emotion-provoking imagery to solidify the seriousness of the problem in audience minds.

SOLUTION

Lay out a simple solution to the problem (do-ability, simplicity principle, fill the gap you've primed)

In this speech:

The speaker shows the Pantry's success through reputation, number of students served, offerings and a personal story of a life changed by the program.

II. The pantry began to feed the all-too-real hunger that had been growling in classrooms all over campus.

   A. According to a staff editorial in the Renegade Rip published March 14, 2012, the Renegade Pantry quickly became the most effective program offered by the Student Government Association. The staff of the Rip stated that in the Fall of 2011 the Pantry gave boxes of food to over 6,000 students.

   B. Those 6,000 students got boxes of food similar to the foods offered today. In an April, 2013 flyer from the Renegade Pantry the 3 options for food boxes are listed.

      i. Option A: Rice, Beans, Pasta, Pasta sauce, soup, tuna and fresh produce when available.

      ii. Option B: The kid-friendly box. In addition to the box I already described, parents are provided kid-friendly foods like Mac & Cheese, graham crackers, canned fruit and kid-friendly soups.

      iii. Option C was added to better serve the increasing numbers of our students who are homeless. This option is all canned, ready-to-eat foods for students who don't have kitchens in which to prepare their meals.

   C. The pantry is open to all students, regardless of need. BC Student, Jonathan Riccardi, was interviewed by KGET March 13, 2013. He said that before he knew about the Pantry there were times when he went hungry. He said that his hunger had affected his concentration and his grades. He learned about the program while sitting in this room, when I gave a speech very much like this one.

Transition: Clearly, the Renegade Pantry is feeding a deep need on our campus. Now, let's see what you can do to help satisfy the hunger.

VISUALIZATION

Help the audience see a future where the problem has been solved or where they are now an active part of the solution (fill the gap, do-ability, altruism)

In this speech:

The speaker shows audience that they are needed, provides multiple specific images to help audience see themselves taking action.

III. The Renegade Pantry gets plenty of donations but there is one kind of support that you, as BC students, are in the best position to provide.

A. Here's something you can do a couple times a month between classes: Help out at the Renegade Pantry. The 2nd and 4th weeks of each month the Pantry needs volunteers to help prepare the boxes for food distribution. Next time you are walking through Campus Center stop by the Student Government Office in CC4 where they took your picture for your student ID card. Sign-up and help pack boxes during one of the gaps in your schedule.

B. You can also help by spreading the word. When you are in class and someone's stomach growls, tell them about the Renegade Pantry, when someone is scrounging through their backpack for change for the cafeteria, tell them about the Renegade Pantry. When someone posts on facebook, twitter or tumblr that all they have left to eat for the rest of the month is ramen, tell them about the Renegade Pantry. Basically, if a fellow student is hungry, tell them about the Renegade Pantry. You can tell them that they can sign-up for a box of food the Monday, Tuesday or Wednesday of the 2nd or 4th week of the month, then they can pick up their box of food on the following Thursday.

C. If you meet a student who is desperate, it isn't a distribution date and they have no money or access to food for a few days, they can also stop by the Student Government Office in CC4 for an emergency food box. Any student can get an emergency box once a semester and that box should last until the next scheduled distribution.

Transition: The Bakersfield College Renegade Pantry is the first of its kind in California. January 17, 2011, Jorge Barrentos of the Bakersfield Californian reported that UC Davis and UCLA have followed in our footsteps, launching their own Pantry projects.

ACTION

Ask the audience to take action to make the vision a reality (do-ability, altruism, simplicity principle)

In this speech:

The speaker uses vivid imagery to reiterate the actions suggested in the visualization step.

Conclusion

I. Review

Our Renegade Pantry understands our starving students, they feed the hunger that gnaws at too many guts on this campus. You can help by filling some boxes in your spare time.

II. Action

You know what to do: The next time your procrastination meter goes into overdrive, opt for positive procrastination. Be a food renegade, fill some boxes and spread the word.

III. Clincher

Together, we can help the Pantry fulfill its mission. Together, we can: "eliminate hunger one student at a time."

SUMMARY

As social animals we feel compelled to persuade others to help us change the world to match our personal vision of what is most beneficial for all. Persuasion happens in the tension between maintaining harmony with others and seeking our own best version of the world we live in.

When we forget to bring the audience's beliefs, values, ideas, and shared experiences to the forefront of our planning for our presentations we set off neurological landmines in our audience members' brains that make it difficult to persuade them. However, when we focus on the audience members' beliefs, values, ideas, and shared experiences we are far more likely to successfully utilize the keys that will open our audience members' minds to our ideas.

While there are a wide variety of organizational strategies we can use when we construct persuasive messages, it is important to choose the right strategy for our audience or our attempts at persuasion will fail.

Review
Questions

❶ Explain three different neurological landmines and how they function to undermine persuasive attempts.

❷ Explain three different neurological keys and how they can be used to persuade your audience.

❸ Give an example of a proposition of fact, of value, and of policy.

❹ Distinguish between the four types of audiences discussed.

❺ Explain what the main points in the body of a speech are using comparative advantages and problem-solution order of main points.

Glossary

Altruism: The impulse to help others without the expectation that you will get anything back in return.

Big truths: The foundation of all of our assumptions about how the world works.

Complexity: Involved or intricate, complicated.

Critical audience: An audience that has a deep awareness of you or your issues and has formed distinct opinions that conflict with your own on either or both.

Dissent: The refusal to conform to a particular doctrine or set of talking points regarding an issue.

Do-ability: Simplifying and illustrating a process so an audience can see themselves taking part in the process.

Empathy gap: Based on our current physical and emotional state, we lose our ability to empathize with other people's experiences.

Fairness: The perception that choices are free of favoritism or bias.

Groupthink: Self-monitoring and self-censoring to avoid creating tensions in a group.

Hostile audience: An audience that not only shows open contempt for you and/or your issue but is likely to voice their opinion loudly in the middle of your speech.

Money: An entirely abstract concept that, as an ever-present part of our lives, is intertwined with all of our big truths.

Off- the-radar: A complete mental dismissal of an issue that leads to an utter disbelief that the issue even exists.

Persuasion: A form of social influence in which we seek to change people's hearts and/or minds to align with our own.

Prime the gap: The process of creating curiosity and interest by creating a gap in understanding.

Question of fact: The first of the three types of questions people persuade audiences about; questions of fact ask speakers to prove that their position on an issue is true.

Question of policy: The third of the three types of questions people persuade audiences about; questions of policy ask speakers to convince their audience to take action on a particular issue.

Question of value: The second of the three types of questions people persuade audiences about; questions of value ask speakers to prove that their position on an issue is good or bad, right or wrong, better or worse.

Simplicity principle: A series of five rules developed by David Straker that we can follow to assure that our ideas are easy to follow.

Subconscious: Made up of the functions operating in our minds beneath or beyond our awareness.

Sympathetic audience: An audience that is predisposed to support you and your position.

Top-of-mind awareness: Choosing issues that are part of a current national dialogue that you know your audience has been following and discussing.

Uninformed audience: An audience that has no preconceived notions about your issue.

References

Akhtar, S. (2009). *Good feelings: Psychoanalytic reflections on positive emotions and attitudes.* London: Karnac Books.

Brafman, O., & Brafman, R. (2008). *Sway: The irresistible pull of irrational behavior.* New York: Doubleday.

Brunel, F., & Nelson, M. R. (2000). Explaining gendered responses to "help-self" and "help-others" charity ad appeals: The mediating role of world-views. *Journal of Advertising,* 15–28.

Burke, K. (1966). *Language as symbolic action: Essays on life, literature and method.* Berkeley, Los Angeles, London: University of California Press.

Gannon, M. (2012, November 15). The unconscious brain can do math. *Scientific American,* Retrieved July 1, 2013, from http://www.scientificamerican.com/article.cfm?id=the-unconscious-brain-can-do-math

Godin, S. (2008). *Tribes: We need you to lead us.* London: Penguin Books.

Lowenstein, G. (1999). "A visceral account of addiction." In J. Elster, ed. *Getting hooked: Rationality and addiction* (pp. 235–264). London: Cambridge University Press.

Medina, J. (2008). *Brain rules.* Seattle, WA: Pear Press.

Straker, D. (2006). Simplicity Principle. Retrieved May 15, 2011, from http://changingminds.org/principles/simplicity.htm

SPEAKING FOR SPECIAL OCCASIONS

Michael M. Korcok

Learning
Objectives

CHAPTER 17

❶ Master the moments that matter most with inspiring speeches.

❷ Craft speeches that rise to the celebrations and ceremonies of life.

❸ Honor, introduce, commemorate, and give respect to others.

❹ Lift the mood of an event or gathering with wit and humor.

Mark will be the best man in his brother Joe's wedding. As part of his best man duties, Mark has to organize a bachelor party and give a toast at the wedding reception. Mark is worried about giving a toast that is memorable. He thinks he should be able to share some funny stories from the bachelor party at the reception but his mom objects, worried that Mark will embarrass the family.

Andrea has just learned that she will be the valedictorian of her college class. While proud of her accomplishment, she is mortified to learn that she is expected to give a commencement address in front of an audience that will include her entire class, her family, and most of her instructors. Andrea has always kept her nose in a book and has never given a speech before. She walks out of her advisor's office wondering how she can speak in front of so many.

INTRODUCTION

The challenges faced by Mark and Andrea are common. By the time you take a public speaking course, you will have likely witnessed many special occasion speeches. Special occasions such as team banquets, funerals, weddings, retirement parties, and school graduations include speeches and toasts as part of their normal course.

In some cases, such as a wedding, tradition assigns the duty of giving a speech to particular members of the bridal party, like the maid of honor and the best man. In other cases, such as a retirement party, all of the guests may feel some pressure to formally congratulate the retiree in a toast or brief sendoff speech. Each special occasion dictates particular expectations and guidelines upon the content and structure of an offered speech. The incredible diversity of special event circumstances generates a very wide collection of special event speeches that vary according to their length, content, tone, and purpose.

The purpose of this chapter is to present strategies for the development and refinement of your special occasion speech. Upon the completion of this chapter, you will possess a strong understanding of the definition, purpose, and structure of the most common types of special occasion speeches: the speech of introduction, the speech of welcome, the speech of farewell, the speech of presentation, the speech of acceptance, the speech of dedication, the commencement speech, the speech of tribute, the eulogy, the toast, the after-dinner presentation, literary interpretations, and the impromptu speech.

You will also be aware of the common mistakes made in the crafting and delivery of special occasion speeches. The recognition of the particular considerations made in the crafting of each of these special occasion speeches will help you to distinguish special occasion speeches from informative and persuasive speeches.

The chapter concludes with a discussion of the role of humor within special occasion speeches. You will gain familiarity with the common uses of humor within special occasion speeches and factors to consider when planning to use humor in your speech. Sometimes a special occasion speech will call for the use of humor. Humor is particularly common within after dinner speeches. In other cases, humor may be deemed inappropriate or in bad taste. Effective humor serves a purpose within the speech. It promotes goodwill between the speaker and the audience, and it makes the speech and the associated special occasion more memorable. However, humor is far more difficult to deliver than it appears. Preparation and practice will help the speaker avoid inappropriate humor.

SPECIAL OCCASION SPEAKING

The previous two chapters discussed two of the three basic types of speech: the informative speech and the persuasive speech. In the informative speech, the general purpose is to inform the audience about a particular subject. In the persuasive speech, the general purpose is to convince the audience to adopt a particular perspective, to reinforce a particular belief, or to engage in a specific action. The final type of speech is the special occasion speech. As its name implies, a **special occasion speech** is a presentation delivered for a celebratory, congratulatory, or ceremonial event. The general purpose of a special occasion speech is to entertain or inspire the audience.

While the special occasion speech is distinct from an informative speech or a persuasive speech, it often incorporates elements of both.

Special occasions are some of the most important moments of our lives.

FIGURE
17.1

When speaking at a special event, you will share information with the audience about your subject. Your subject may be an individual person, an organization, an object or an event. However, your speech will also contain persuasive elements. You will share your enthusiasm about your topic with your listeners and invite them to come to agreement with you.

The term special occasion speech is an umbrella term. It applies to many different speeches whose length, content, structure, and specific purpose varies considerably according to the needs and requirements of their associated special occasion. A eulogy offered at a wake is very different from a congratulatory toast offered at a wedding or an acceptance speech offered at an award banquet—yet all three are examples of special occasion speeches. In fact, it is almost impossible to discuss the content of a special occasion speech without referencing the surrounding special event. Therefore, the majority of this chapter focuses on distinguishing particular types of special occasions and their associated speeches.

TYPES OF SPECIAL OCCASION SPEECHES

THE SPEECH OF INTRODUCTION

A **speech of introduction** is a short speech intended to introduce an individual to the audience. Often, the subject of the speech of introduction is another person. This type of speech sets the stage for a future speaker. If you are tasked with offering this type of an introductory speech, your job will be to prepare the audience for the upcoming speech and to encourage them to give their full attention to that speaker.

You may also be the subject of your speech of introduction. For example, when you are new to a workplace or starting a new class, you may be called on to introduce yourself to others. If you give this type of introduction speech, your goal is to offer a bit of information about yourself in order to help others get to know you.

DEVELOPMENT

The structure of the speech of introduction directed toward another person focuses upon creating a welcoming and receptive audience for the speaker to follow you. You can achieve this goal in a few ways. First, establish the credibility of the speaker by highlighting experience, education, and accomplishments. Second, pique the audience's interest in the subject to be discussed by the guest speaker. Third, express your personal gratitude for the speaker's attendance at the special event.

If you are introducing another person, you should ideally talk to that person prior to the special occasion. In a brief interview, you can determine any preferred topics to be mentioned. In addition, you can gain a better understanding of the content of the speech that will follow yours. However, if a personal interview is not possible, you must research the speaker. Develop a brief biography and highlight key events relevant to your subject's qualifications.

Speeches of introduction are generally short. After all, the person you are introducing is likely to be the star of the show, while you are playing a support role. The length of the speaker's speech can help you plan the length of your own speech. However, in general, you should expect to speak between two and four minutes. Therefore, you need to be efficient. Plan what you are going to say as you would for any speech and practice your delivery before the event.

CONSIDERATIONS

Watch the length of your speech and don't go over your allotted time. The speech of introduction isn't the main event—it's the precursor to the main event. While the speech of introduction fulfills an important role within the special occasion, it shouldn't eclipse the later speech and it certainly shouldn't run longer than the speech you are preparing the audience to hear.

Sincerity counts. The audience will take notice of your lack of attention to detail or a lack of interest in the speaker you are introducing. For example, if you have to look at your notes to remember the speaker's name, you are unlikely to appear sincere.

Preparation matters. Do your research so that you can adequately highlight key characteristics of the speaker. If a name appears odd to you, check the pronunciation before going up to speak. A mistake can be embarrassing and you do not want the speaker you are introducing to have to correct something you said.

Err on the side of moderation. You may initially feel pressured to praise the person you are introducing. While positive comments are not inappropriate, too much praise for the guest speaker may inflate the audience's expectations. If the speaker fails to live up to your glowing reputation, the audience's interest and enthusiasm will wane.

THE SPEECH OF WELCOME

The **speech of welcome** is a specialized form of introduction speech. It serves to introduce the subject of the speech to the audience and it also introduces the audience to the subject. For example, you may be called upon to welcome a new employee or a new student at a special event organized in their honor.

DEVELOPMENT

The speech of welcome combines elements of a speech of introduction and an informative speech. Like a speech of introduction, the speech of welcome presents an individual to the members of the audience. Therefore, you should research the subject of your speech so that you can present a brief but thorough biography that highlights the accomplishments most relevant to the occasion and audience.

In addition, the speech of welcome introduces the subject of your speech to the audience, organization, and surrounding environment. Therefore, the second part of your speech should give some information about the organization or place to which your subject is being welcomed. Explain to them why they should be happy to become a part of the new environment or community. For example, you can discuss the local weather, friendly population, or city accomplishments.

The closing of your speech of welcome should be proscriptive and positive. You can express your hope for a pleasant long-term experience if your subject is staying permanently, such as in the case of individuals moving to a new city or recently accepting a new position at your firm. Alternatively, you can express hope for a productive or profitable stay if your subject is only visiting for a fixed period of time.

CONSIDERATIONS

Overall, the tone of the speech of welcome should be positive. Avoid discussing topics that might make the subject or the audience feel uncomfortable. For example, when welcoming a new employee, you may consider mentioning the new person's previous employer but probably want to avoid explaining the reasons behind the move.

Again, sincerity is important for the successful delivery of a speech of welcome. Your enthusiasm about the subject and the location or organization should be clear and infectious. If possible, meet and converse with the person you will welcome prior to the speech. You do not need to overdue praise for either, however. Instead, mix praise and relevant information to create a welcome that is both pleasant and functional.

THE SPEECH OF FAREWELL

The **speech of farewell** is offered when leaving colleagues. The speech may be prompted by a decision to transfer within the organization, accept a position with another company, step down from an appointment with a fixed term, or retire. It is the opposite of a speech of introduction. Instead of speaking before unknown people, the speech of farewell involves speaking in front of a friendly and familiar audience.

DEVELOPMENT

The speech of farewell signals a transition. Its content may reflect upon the past and point toward the future. However, the past should be emphasized. Not everyone receives the formal opportunity to say good-bye. The opportunity to give a farewell speech is an honor conferred upon someone who has achieved distinction within the current position. Therefore, the speech content should be positive and convey gratitude toward those being left behind.

The first part of the speech can be used to reflect upon the position being vacated. For example, you may want to use the opportunity to talk about why you liked your time with the organization. The speech can also be used to identify and thank notable colleagues who contributed to making the experience enjoyable.

The speech of farewell should also reference the process of leaving. Everyone present understands that you are vacating your position. If appropriate, you may explain your reasons for leaving and plans after the transition. Conclude your speech by positively reflecting upon the future with some words of encouragement, an inspirational message, and well wishes for those you are leaving behind.

CONSIDERATIONS

The decision to leave a position or organization can often be difficult. The speech of farewell doesn't require an even or honest assessment of your time with the organization. Regardless of how you may feel about leaving, put any negative feelings aside for the duration of the speech.

THE SPEECH OF PRESENTATION

A **speech of presentation** makes a formal offering to a recipient. That offering may be a gift, an award, or a prize. The recipient may be an individual person, multiple people, or an organization.

DEVELOPMENT

The presentation speech has two goals. First of all, the presentation should explain the significance of the offering. For example, if an award is being offered, the history of the award, including a brief discussion of its requirements for consideration and past recipients, should be offered. This aspect of the speech will establish the importance of the award—why the audience cares.

The second goal of the presentation is to identify the recipient. The recipient's name and accomplishments should be detailed. Based upon this part of the speech, the audience should understand why the recipient deserved to be honored by the presentation. If a list of nominees is known, you should take time to acknowledge the accomplishments of those considered by not receiving the honor.

The basic structure of the presentation is composed of three parts. First, you should identify the nature of the award. Then, you should explain the criteria that are applied to select a recipient. Finally, you should identify the personal characteristics or accomplishments that led to the selection of the recipient.

CONSIDERATIONS

If part of your duties includes giving a physical item to the recipient, be prepared to interact with the recipient. You should hold the award in your left hand. This will enable you to offer your right hand in congratulations while passing the award to the recipient's left hand. Many recipients may not know what to do and your confidence can ensure a seamless transaction.

The content, structure, and length of the presentation will depend on the needs of the occasion. In some cases, the speech of presentation may be brief. The formal presentation may recognize the recipient's accomplishment and delivers the object being presented quickly. By keeping the presentation short, you enable more time to be devoted to the recipient's acceptance speech. However, some events will call for a more extended speech of presentation. Then, the presentation may be lengthened to include a long, formal tribute detailing the accomplishments of the recipient. If invited to offer a presentation, you will need to talk to the event's coordinator to determine your speaking duties.

THE ACCEPTANCE SPEECH 5

The presentation speech and speech of acceptance are closely connected. The **acceptance speech** offers the formal speech response to a presentation speech. The acceptance speech has two goals. First, it accepts the award offered within the preceding presentation speech. Second, the speech of acceptance expresses the recipient's gratitude for the honor conferred by the presentation.

Speeches of presentation and acceptance are the body of award ceremonies.

FIGURE 17.2

DEVELOPMENT

The acceptance speech is composed of two parts. In the first part, the speaker thanks the individual or organization responsible for selecting the recipient for the presentation. You should always take the time to thank those responsible for your selection first.

The second part of the speech thanks the recipient's supporters—those individuals who contributed to the recipient's success. This list of individuals is likely to include coworkers, collaborators, and family members. Within the second part of your speech, you may choose to include a brief motivational statement, such as a comment intended to encourage others to follow your example or pursue their own dreams. If you elect to include a motivational message, remember to conclude your speech with a final thanks, so that the lasting impression offered by the speech is one of appreciation.

CONSIDERATIONS

Acceptance speeches are often emotional. The reception of an honor can be a major accomplishment—one that recognizes your hard work and dedication. You may be surprised by the intense response you have to being honored. On the other hand, if you are in the running for an award and your name isn't called, you'll likely feel strong emotions as well. Prior to the event, try to prepare yourself for the emotions of the evening. Be ready for the potential ups and downs.

Ever watch the Academy Awards? If a tearful recipient spends too much on stage thanking anyone with a pulse, music will be played to drive the recipient off the stage. Don't be that recipient. If you are the potential subject of a presentation, prepare your response in advance and practice in order to ensure that you can offer thanks quickly and efficiently. Preparation will also help decrease the likelihood of an embarrassing comment or omission. You don't want your moment of triumph to be overshadowed by your failure to thank someone important.

THE DEDICATION SPEECH

The **dedication speech** is a formal, ceremonial speech given to highlight the importance of an event or object. Often, a speech of dedication commemorates the opening of a new building. For example, the president of a college may offer a speech of dedication upon the opening of a new science lab. A speech of dedication may also recognize the construction of a new landmark or the intent to protect an existing landmark through the process of formally recognizing its significance.

DEVELOPMENT

The structure of a speech of dedication should be guided by two goals. First of all, you should explain the significance of the dedication. Your explanation should identify the subject of your speech and the reasoning behind the dedication. Consider the interests of your audience and explain why the dedication is important to them, not just in general.

Second, you should recognize those responsible for the dedication. For example, if you are writing a speech of dedication about a new building, the speech should identify those who designed and funded the effort.

CONSIDERATIONS

A speech of dedication is often delivered by someone associated with the project. If you are personally connected to the subject of your speech, you can take a moment to explain your relationship and why the dedication is important to you.

THE COMMENCEMENT SPEECH 7

The **commencement speech**, also known as a commencement address, is an inspirational speech offered at a school's graduation ceremony. While traditionally associated with graduation from a college, a commencement speech may also be offered at a high school graduation. The individual offering the commencement speech is known as a commencement speaker. Distinguished guests, such as local political figures, business leaders, or scientists, are often invited to offer a commencement speech. However, students, such as the graduating class' valedictorian or salutatorian, and faculty members may also be called upon to give a commencement speech.

DEVELOPMENT

The commencement speech has two goals. The first is to congratulate the members of the graduating class for their academic achievement. You should begin your speech with praise directed toward the students.

The second goal is to inspire the graduates as they move forward to the next stage of their life. The speech commemorates an important transition. You can comment upon that transition and identify future goals for the new graduates. The speech should conclude by motivating, inspiring, and encouraging the graduates to work toward the successful attainment of goals identified.

CONSIDERATIONS

As a commencement speaker, you should aim to offer a message that all members of the class can enjoy. Keep in mind that graduation means different things for different people. For some students, the graduation ceremony will mark the end of their academic careers and the beginning of their professional experience. For others, one graduation ceremony will lead to the next stage of their academic careers. Your speech should not focus too much upon either group and instead offer a general message to motivate and inspire, regardless of the road ahead. Avoid political or other controversial statements that may divide your audience. Instead, utilize inclusive language, such as the pronoun "we," and offer a message that all of the graduating students can appreciate.

THE SPEECH OF TRIBUTE 8

The **speech of tribute** honors the subject. Its focus should be upon the accomplishments that make the subject noteworthy or special. While often about one person, the speech of tribute may also highlight the accomplishments of a group of people, a family, or an organization.

DEVELOPMENT

Like an introduction, the development of a speech of tribute requires considerable research. You should familiarize yourself with the subject of your speech, gathering relevant biographical and professional information, so that you may craft an effective speech.

CONSIDERATIONS

The speech of tribute should be focused. Choose to emphasize two or three points about your subject so that you do not overwhelm your audience with too much information. For example, if you are paying tribute to a person, discuss one or two defining personality characteristics and then one or two professional accomplishments to illustrate the subject's lasting impression upon others.

Focus upon the facts. It is very easy to overdo a speech of tribute by being too enthusiastic about your subject. However, you want to balance your praise with moderation. Too much praise can embarrass your subject, who is likely to be speaking after you. You don't do your subject any favors by making him or her uncomfortable. In addition, too much praise can make the audience skeptical of your claims.

THE EULOGY

The **eulogy** is a speech of tribute about a deceased person. Although accuracy is important, the point of the speech is to honor and respect while offering condolences to their family and friends.

DEVELOPMENT

The development of the eulogy mirrors the development of the speech of tribute. Pick a limited number of accomplishments to focus your speech. By being specific in your eulogy, you can illustrate your closeness and respect for the deceased. Specificity can also help you to develop broader themes to help describe the individual's life and achievements. By the end of your speech, you should offer the audience an explanation of how the deceased impacted their lives for the better.

FIGURE 17.3 Tributes and eulogies honor the deserving and offer respects to the deceased.

CONSIDERATIONS

Eulogies are commonly offered at funerals and wakes, or they are written to be published for a printed notice of death. When a loved one dies, emotions tend to be raw. The eulogy is not a speech for moderation. It is a speech for praise. You should focus upon the positive aspects of the deceased's life and character, omitting the negative. As a speaker, be aware of the feelings of the survivors and choose your words carefully to avoid offense.

You should also be aware of the influence of your own emotions. If you were close to the subject, you may experience strong emotions during the delivery of your speech. Practice prior to the event can help to prepare you for the emotional drain of offering an eulogy. If you are overcome by emotion when offering your speech, don't panic. Take some time to compose yourself before moving on.

Religious beliefs may vary between you and your subject. While you may not agree with that person's religious views, you should still be respectful of your subject's views during the eulogy. You don't have to pretend to be part of the same religion but you also don't have to air your disagreement with the audience. Therefore, your eulogy should be respectful toward the religious views of your subject. Interjecting a prayer or quotation consistent with your subject's views is appropriate.

EXAMPLE EULOGY:

My grandmother, Jessica Turnberry, was an exceptional person. She was adored by her husband Karl, her 3 children, and 8 grandkids. Nana Turnberry was born into a humble home, but that didn't stop her. Nana worked hard in school and showed her brains. She was one of the first women in the state to go to college: girls just didn't do that in the 1940s, but that didn't stop Nana. Jessica worked her way through college and when she graduated, she got a job as an assistant editor for the Beacon Press, the beginning of a long and distinguished career in publishing.

Grandmother Turnberry was born to James and Susan Turnberry in Pittsburgh, then a steel and coal city in October of 1930, a year after the Great Depression had started. Nana was the oldest of 4 children and told me that growing up was hard, partly because her father was always scrambling to find work and partly because back then, Pittsburgh's air was soot and ash, a gritty industrial city. Her youth got harder when her father James joined the Army to fight for his country in World War II. Her mother kept the family together, taking work in Pittsburgh's factories until James came home after the war. Her father got a steady job in a steel mill, and the family's prospects improved as the country began to build again.

During the tough years growing up, Nana escaped into her books. She was an excellent student, reading every book in her school's library. Nana showed me one of her 6th grade report cards a few years ago, all A's of course. Her love of books and learning would stay with her for the rest of her life. In her junior year of high school, Jessica Turnberry decided she would pursue her education into college. She applied to, and got accepted at, the University of Pittsburgh, one of the few women admitted at the time.

Nan met the love of her life and husband-to-be, Karl, at a spring social. Nan told me once that Grandpa's dance moves got her hooked almost immediately. It was love at first sight, they got married a few months later, and were together for 50 years before Grampa passed away a few years ago. Mom was the first of their 3 kids, born a year after Nana got her degree in English. My grandparents moved to Philadelphia a couple of years later, and Nana took a job as an assistant editor for the Beacon Press. This was unheard-of in the 50s, a woman who was juggling a career and children! Nana did what so many of us struggle with today.

Well, over the years, as their children grew up and my grandparents built their careers, they were always surrounded by family and friends. I still remember, sitting in my dad's lap after

Thanksgiving dinner at my grandparent's house, the music and laughter of a full house of their children and grandchildren and neighbors and friends enjoying good food and good company. I asked Nana's advice time and again as a teenager: she always seemed to know just what to say to make the tough stuff seem a bit less important and the good stuff a little better. When mom and dad just didn't get it, Nana seemed to understand me.

She took Karl's passing hard. The last 2 years have been rough on Grandma Turnberry and she was never quite the same after. We all tried to comfort her, but the laughter wasn't quite as frequent or as loud or as . . . joyful. I think the wind was taken out of her sails. Nana, we already miss you, your extraordinary life has and will serve as an inspiration to me and everyone who knew you.

TYPES OF ENTERTAINMENT SPEECHES

TOASTS

A **toast** is a very brief entertainment speech offered over a drink at a special occasion. Depending upon the event, the purpose of a toast may be to congratulate, offer a blessing, or commemorate the moment. It functions like a mini-tribute. A toast may be planned but they are often impromptu.

FIGURE **17.4** Toasts extend well wishes to the betrothed and an excuse to imbibe a bubbly beverage.

DEVELOPMENT

Unless you've already been introduced to the audience, a toast opens with an explanation of how the speaker is related to the subject of the speech. For example, if you are asked to give a speech at your sister's wedding, you can introduce yourself to the guests by name and refer to the bride as your sister. This explanation should be short and make up only a small percentage of the total speech, since the focus of the toast should not be on you.

CONSIDERATIONS

The majority of the toast should celebrate the individual or the occasion. When toasting an individual, you should avoid making inside jokes or references that only your subject will understand. Remember that the toast must be understood by all of the guests present, not just the person you are toasting.

Your last words should be inspirational and focused upon the future. Conclude the toast by raising your glass. This action will signal to the listeners that you are almost finished speaking and that they should drink with you.

Toasts should be brief. Others may also wish to give a toast. For example, weddings tend to include multiple toasts: the groom, the best man, the father of the bride, and the maid of honor may all speak—in addition to any guests who feel moved to offer a toast. At the time same, guests will want to return to enjoying the special event.

Furthermore, toasts are often accompanied by alcoholic beverages, which can impact the mood and attention spans of your audience members. Toasts may be offered just before, during, or immediately following a meal. Guests want to be entertained or inspired, not depressed or angered, by your toast.

The short time constraints placed upon a toast make preparation before the event particularly useful. Often, speakers will cheat by writing out their toast in advance. However, your speech will be more effective and sincere if you leave the notes in your pocket when you take your glass.

Humor works well within a toast. However, the direction of your humor should be determined by the special event. Be aware of the feelings of others. You may find a joke about a strip club involving the groom to be funny but his bride and his mother may not.

AFTER-DINNER PRESENTATIONS

Special occasions are often celebrated with meals, creating the opportunity for after-dinner presentations. An after-dinner presentation has many potential goals. Often, the after-dinner presentation celebrates the accomplishments of the group or organization hosting the dinner. Sometimes, this speech may also identify and discuss new efforts or goals to be pursued by the organization. However, the goals of an after-dinner presentation need not be so rigid. In many cases, the only goal of the **after-dinner presentation** is to punctuate the special occasion by entertaining the audience. The after-dinner presentation is distinguished by other speeches by its frequent reliance upon humor.

DEVELOPMENT

After-dinner speeches have a specific goal: to help the audience savor particular accomplishments, events, or positive feelings. That goal is best achieved through careful speech organization. Construct a thesis statement and main points to support that thesis before interjecting humor. Organize the speech into an introduction, a conclusion, and a body. Consider guiding or ending your speech with a message that is uplifting and inspirational.

CONSIDERATIONS

After-dinner presentations are often short and uncritical. After a meal, the audience is likely to feel content. Many will feel tired. Concentration is unlikely to be high. Avoid weighing down your speech with challenging or serious content.

When selecting a subject for your speech, consider the organization hosting and the purpose of the dinner. Then, avoid topics that are hostile or angry. This speech is not the time to criticize.

IMPROMPTU SPEECHES

Throughout this chapter, we've discussed the preparation of speeches for which you receive prior warning. However, this will not always be the case. At some point, you find yourself in a position to offer an impromptu speech—a speech delivered without any warning or time to prepare. For example, you may attend a business meeting and feel motivated to offer your opinion to your colleagues and boss. Alternatively, you may be asked by someone, such as a reporter, to offer a spur of the moment statement.

When delivering an impromptu speech, remember what you know about prepared speeches and apply that knowledge to the impromptu delivery. You should remain focused on three goals. First, have a thesis. An impromptu speech should have an overarching goal or point. Your thesis should be the reason you are going to speak. For example, you may attend a homeowner's association to hear the board discuss the option to ban holiday lighting. If you choose to speak, your thesis can be something as simple as, "I want the neighborhood to ban holiday lights," or, "I want the neighborhood to continue to allow homeowners to hang holiday lights as they wish." If you remain focused upon your thesis, you'll be able to stop yourself from wandering off topic.

Second, stay organized. Your impromptu speech should have an introduction, a body, and a conclusion. Your introduction can be as simple as explaining your thesis and previewing your points. If appropriate to the occasion, you can introduce yourself as well. The body of your impromptu will include the one to three arguments to support your thesis. While you won't have substantial time to gather evidence, you should still include relevant information, including personal details when appropriate, to support your thesis. Signposts and transitions can be simple, like "first of all" or "in addition." Their use will help keep you on track. Your conclusion will restate your thesis and summarize the reasons you support your thesis.

Finally, you should adapt to your situation. Time limits and audience interest will vary according to your situation. You may not have the time to present as many points as you would like or to discuss each subject in detail. Therefore, while speaking, you need to keep a mental log running to determine when you've said enough and when you need to move on. Also, consider highlighting points that you know will resonate with members of your audience. By adapting to them, you can find ways to capture and maintain your audience's interest during your impromptu speech.

Impromptu speaking can appear even more frightening than prepared speech. However, the best way to improve your impromptu speaking ability is to practice. Volunteering to speak or answer questions in class will increase your confidence and make you feel more comfortable when addressing an audience with little preparation. In addition, practice speaking even when you are alone. Take a minute or two to think about and say arguments that you would consider using later.

HUMOR

Humor is an important speaking tool that can serve many functions within a speech. When offered as part of an introduction, humor can establish goodwill between the speaker and the audience. Humor offered later in a speech can strengthen or sustain that positive relationship. The audience is more likely to respond positively to a speech if the speaker appears likeable and humor can create the perception of a rapport between the speaker and the audience.

Humor can also serve to put the audience and the speaker at ease. When a speaker introduces humor into a speech and the audience responds through laughter, the speaker receives a cue of the audience's enjoyment and attention. When integrated into a point or argument, humor can also help the audience to remember.

Humor can be placed within any speech. It is a defining characteristic of the after-dinner presentation. Even serious speeches, such as a eulogy or a persuasive speech about a proposed policy, can benefit from an interjection of humor.

The inclusion of jokes and humor into a speech may initially appear natural. However, humor is often very difficult to convey. A joke offered poorly can fail to illicit humor and create an awkward pause that is very difficult, if not impossible, to recover from. Humor may even offend members of the audience, squandering any goodwill previously developed by the speaker and creating a barrier between the speaker and the audience.

Therefore, humor should be approached cautiously. Whether you are using humor to establish good will with your audience, reinforce a point, or entertain, your humor should have a clear purpose. In addition, you should play to your strengths and try to interject humor in a manner consistent with who you are.

The effective use of humor requires comic timing. During the delivery of a humorous speech, interruptions by the audience should be expected. When the audience laughs at a joke, the speaker must remember to pause. A speaker who continues to speak while the audience is laughing will likely not be heard. However, too long a pause can also create problems. The speaker may lose momentum or even lose the position within the speech.

As with other elements of speech development, the effective delivery of humor requires preparation. Whether you write your own jokes or borrow jokes from someone else, consider practicing your jokes in front of others in order to test your timing and gauge the audience's response. If your test audience doesn't laugh at a joke, you can remove the joke or practice your delivery to make it funnier.

Keep in mind that humor is subjective. Cultural, personal tastes, and characteristics such as age and sex can lead individuals to disagree about what is funny. Some topics should be approached carefully or avoided entirely. As a general rule, you want to avoid jokes at the expense of others. Discriminatory humor that mocks a religion, a sex, or a race is unlikely to be appreciated and can very quickly create a hostile audience.

How do you create laughter? Sometimes you tell funny stories. Sometimes you tell jokes.

Let's look at five reasons why people laugh. There is actually a sixth reason, but that has to do with drugs and chemicals such as nitrous oxide (laughing gas), alcohol, marijuana, and such. By the way, the first two of the five reasons we will look at have very little to do with whether something is actually funny:

© Flashon Studio, 2013. Used under license from Shutterstock, Inc.

There are at least six reasons why human beings laugh.

FIGURE 17.5

1. **To be part of . . .** If you are the new person in a group of people who have known each other for some time, and someone says something that gets everyone else at the table laughing, the odds are that you will laugh too, even though you have no idea why it's funny. But you will still laugh to show that you are—or want to be—part of the group. Laughter signifies acceptance.

2. **Propinquity** . . . If people around you are laughing, the odds are that you will, too, even if the "people" are really just a recording on a TV show's laugh track. That is why TV shows use laugh tracks, and why emcees at comedy clubs like to get people to move in and sit closer to the stage and to other people. Laughter is contagious.

3. **Surprise** . . . Look at what happens when you surprise a baby. It will either laugh or be frightened, get angry, or cry. Those are ways to handle surprise. But if you are in the "mood" to laugh, you are more likely to find something that is surprising to be funny than you are to find it scary, or to let it make you angry. You are there to laugh and have a good time. You want to laugh, and will often look for any excuse to do so, even when the jokes aren't really that funny. And a joke is just a short story that takes an unexpected turn, a surprising turn.

4. **Exaggeration** . . . Now we get to actual comedy. Exaggerating something past the point of "logic" creates that "cognitive riddle" we mentioned earlier. Some examples:

Comedian Jack Benny started in vaudeville and went on to star in movies and have his own radio and TV shows:

> My wife Mary and I have been married for forty-seven years and not once have we had an argument serious enough to consider divorce; murder, yes, but divorce, never.

Comedian Phyllis Diller made herself the butt of most of her jokes:

> When I go to the beauty parlor, I always use the emergency entrance.
>
> Housework can't kill you, but why take a chance.
>
> You know you're old if your walker has an airbag.

The formula for an "exaggeration joke" is quite simple. Take something that everyone is familiar with, and then take one aspect of it and exaggerate it past the point of all common sense.

EXAGGERATION JOKE

Here is a simple way to start an exaggeration joke. Take a person, place, or object, and then think of the most ridiculous attribute or quality you can give to it. Once you have your "topic" make your "where to begin" list. The sample below is: "My car is so expensive that . . ."

The "where to begin" list could include things like: cost, size, color, mileage, add-ons, special features, wheels, tires, trunk, engine, etc.

I wrote ten punch lines. See how many you can add to it.

When you are writing jokes, always write at least ten. Sometimes it takes the first four or five jokes just to get your mind in gear.

Many comedy writers work in teams so they can bounce gags off one another and then combine and blend their ideas. When it comes to writing comedy, two heads often are better than one. So, find a friend with a similar sense of humor and see what you can come up with.

Have fun!

My car is so expensive that . . .

1. It doesn't have a stereo system because there wasn't room for that and an orchestra.
2. The hood and the trunk are in different zip codes.
3. The radiator is filled with *Perrier*.
4. The glove box seats six.
5. I let Bill Gates borrow it when he's trying to impress people.
6. Cops pull me over just so they can touch it.
7. It runs on gas from its own oil wells.
8. I keep a Lamborghini in the trunk in case of a breakdown.
9. Instead of a GPS I have my own Google Earth satellite.
10. My license plate has an unlisted number.

Comedy writers write a lot of jokes because not all of them work. The more you write, the more you have to choose from.

As with any other learnable skill—and it is a learnable skill—it takes time and practice.

Other setup lines to work with are:

1. My boss is so cheap . . .
2. My cooking is so bad that . . .
3. Parking at school is so bad that . . .
4. I got my grade back on my _____ exam, and I . . .
5. My speech teacher is so _____ that . . .

Try it!

5. **Silliness** . . . We learned how to laugh before we learned how to talk. Babies recognize silliness, and enjoy it. Is there anything sillier than peek-a-boo?

A vaudeville and Broadway star, Groucho Marx, one of the famous Marx brothers, also made numerous movies and had his own TV show, "You bet Your Life."

I once shot an elephant in my pajamas.
How it got into my pajamas I'll never know.

With exaggeration jokes you take something that the listener associated with the subject of the joke, and just stretch it beyond all recognition. With silliness jokes you go off in a brand new direction, adding things the audience does not expect.

Comedian, writer, and actor Steven Wright is known for both his deadpan delivery and the fact that you never know where one of his jokes will end up. Some examples:

I intend to live forever. So far, so good.

What's another word for Thesaurus?

A lot of people are afraid of heights. Not me, I'm afraid of widths.

Good speakers learn to look for the humor in their material, in their topic, and in themselves. Remember: the only person you can safely poke fun at—aside from politicians—is yourself.

The humor might not be in the subject of your speech, but in your own experiences in relation to the topic. What went right? What went wrong? What just went away?

Once you do have some lines that you think will work, try them out on your friends. Jokes are funny *only* if people laugh. And you don't have to have your audience rolling in the aisles and laughing so hard that their sides ache. If you can get some grins and smiles, you are doing well.

BEWARE THE JOKE-JOKE

The main problem with just telling jokes in the speech that do not tie into what you are talking about is that they do not tie into what you are talking about. Comedians will sometimes refer to a joke as a **joke-joke**. Yes, it can be funny. It can be very, very funny. But if it doesn't fit with the rest of their act, if it interferes with the flow of their stories, they drop it.

Speakers want you to remember what they are talking about. They want to persuade you, inspire you, motivate you, convince you to change the way you think or act, or take a specific action. They have a message, and everything they say has to fit into that message and help make it convincing and memorable. So throwing a joke-joke into the middle of a speech can interfere with the message they are trying to deliver. It can distract the audience. The problem is not making them laugh, but finding the material that will make them laugh, and keep them focused on your topic and the points you are trying to make.

When comedians perform, their entire job is to keep the audience laughing. The louder and longer the laughter, the more successful they are. Jokes are what it is all about. A public speaker's job is to keep the audience paying attention. The message you are delivering is what it's all about. The jokes are there to make the message go down a bit more smoothly.

And by the way, when they do laugh, let them. Stop what you are doing, smile and nod, and wait for the laughter to finish before you continue. The audience enjoys laughing almost as much as you will creating that laughter. I must warn you, however, that creating laughter and hearing an audience laugh can be addictive.

SUMMARY

The term "special occasion speeches" describes a wide range of diverse speeches that fall outside the standard definition of an informative or persuasive speech. The general purpose of a special occasion speech is to entertain or inspire the audience.

Common special occasion speeches include the speech of introduction, the speech of welcome, the speech of farewell, the speech of presentation, the speech of acceptance, the speech of dedication, the commencement speech, the speech of tribute, the eulogy, the toast, and the after-dinner presentation. Literary interpretations and impromptu speeches are two additional types of speeches that may be offered within a wide range of special events. All these speeches share some characteristics, such as the importance of sincerity and preparation in the development of an appropriate speech that will make the event more meaningful for all present. However, each type of special occasion speech is also shaped by the particular nature of the special event, the time limit, and the expectations of the audience.

Humor is an important communication tool. It is an integral component of the after-dinner presentation and may be included into other types of speeches as well. When used successfully, humor can establish a rapport between the speaker and audience, punctuate a point and entertain. However, poorly developed and delivered humor can tank a speech and turn a friendly audience hostile. Therefore, the use of humor should be approached cautiously. Preparation and practice will help to ensure that any planned jokes are functional and appropriate to the occasion.

Review Questions

❶ Describe and distinguish between three different special occasion speeches.

❷ Explain, in detail, a piece of advice given for a speech of introduction.

❸ Imagine an award you would like to receive and how you would accept it.

❹ Generate three different topics which might work for an after-dinner speech.

❺ Explain two mistakes to avoid when using humor in a special occasion speech.

Glossary

Acceptance speech: A speech to offer gratitude following a presentation speech.

After-dinner presentation: A celebratory speech offered after a meal which often incorporates humor to entertain the audience.

Commencement address: An inspirational speech offered at a school graduation ceremony.

Dedication speech: A formal, ceremonial speech given to highlight the importance of an event or object.

Eulogy: A speech of tribute about a deceased person.

Impromptu speech: A speech delivered without any warning or time to formally prepare.

Speech of farewell: A speech given by a speaker leaving a position or colleagues.

Speech of introduction: A short speech intended to introduce another person or yourself to the audience.

Speech of presentation: A speech that presents a gift, award, or prize to a designated recipient, group, or organization.

Speech of tribute: A speech that honors the accomplishments of the subject.

Speech of welcome: A specialized form of introduction speech that welcomes the subject by introducing the subject and the audience to each other.

Special occasion speech: A speech delivered for a celebratory, congratulatory, or ceremonial event characterized by the general purpose to entertain or inspire the audience.

Toast: A very brief entertainment speech offered over a drink at a special occasion.

ABOUT THE AUTHORS

ANDREA D. THORSON-HEVLE

Andrea Thorson-Hevle is a dedicated professor and author. With community college work from Bakersfield College, a BA from Bradley University, a MA from California State University, Long Beach, and some doctoral work from the University of California, Santa Barbara, Andrea has collected a variety of degrees. Her favorite areas of interest include: women's studies, interpersonal communication, disability, education, law, and language. She has published several books in the Communication discipline and enjoys giving invited lectures on issues of oppression, women, and education.

Andrea is currently teaching pubic speaking, small group, interpersonal, and rhetoric and argumentation courses at Bakersfield College in Bakersfield, CA. She thanks her parents James and Debra Thorson for their sacrifices and faith that lead her to a successful life, as well as her dear friend Sarah Crachiolo for her support and humor through the years. She is especially grateful to her loving husband Justin for his unwavering encouragement and for giving her the three greatest blessings of her life: Montgomery, Sebastian, and James.

"When you give a speech you are an artist. I want to see it. I want to feel it. Paint a picture that matters. Paint a picture that changes the world."

MARK L. STALLER

Mark Staller earned a BA in Liberal Arts from Saint Mary's College in Moraga, California, and an MA and PhD in Rhetoric from the University of California at Berkeley. He has taught a wide variety of college classes throughout the state of California, including classes in Communication, English, and Philosophy. He has taught oral communication courses at all three levels of the California state university system. He is currently a Professor of Communication at Bakersfield College, and he enjoys teaching classes in intercultural communication, interpersonal communication, small group communication, and public speaking. Mark lives in Tehachapi, California, with his wife Sylvia.

*"Public speaking is the most challenging and most rewarding course I have ever taught—
the most challenging because many students have high public speaking anxiety,
and the most rewarding because most of my students face their fear and become excellent
public speakers."*

MICHAEL KORCOK

By the time you're reading this, Michael is probably rich and famous and you have seen the videos and specials. In case we are not living in those possible worlds, a few words may be in order.

Michael was born in what used to be called Yugoslavia and his parents brought the family to the United States in the late 1960s. He grew up in the Midwest, joined the high school debate team, and competitive speaking transformed a shy bookish nerd into an outgoing, competitive, bookish nerd. For the next twenty-five years or so, he remained in intercollegiate policy debate as a competitor, coach, and program director.

Michael's education has been all over the map, but he earned a BS in communication from Southern Illinois University and an MA in Rhetoric from Kansas State University. He has been teaching at Bakersfield College for more than a decade and these have been the most rewarding years of his life. He has been teaching Public Speaking for nearly three decades and has evaluated at least seventeen thousand speeches by more than four thousand students. Michael Korcok has experienced ears.

Michael's life has been immeasurably enlivened by the love of his life and wife, Jessica. Their son John Edward is a minute-by-minute reminder of how amazing this world, among all possible worlds, is.

He is and always will be grateful to his mother Katerina and father Janko for a life filled with opportunity.

*"Realizing that we only ever observe those possible worlds in which we are
begins to answer the deep questions well."*

HELEN ACOSTA

Helen Acosta grew up playing in the halls of the Bakersfield College Fine Arts building while her dad, Norm Fricker, coached their award-winning forensics team from 1976 to 1985. Helen graduated from Cal State Northridge with an MA in Communication in 1994. A few months later she was hired at Bakersfield College and has been lucky enough to work with some of her favorite people for nearly two decades. Her husband, Enrique—a singer, musician, playwright, storyteller, and barista—embraced Helen's hometown as his own and they've lived in Bakersfield happily for the last eighteen years. Helen is a grassroots trainer, theatrical producer, visual artist, singer, actor, crafter, wife, aunt, dog mom, daughter, sister, and professor. In other words, she is a typical dyslexic whose life and loves all overlap and feed one another. She has reached a point in her life where her former students are becoming her colleagues and her high school and college friends are becoming grandparents. She is fascinated by innovation, design, and technology. She has an unfortunate addiction to Facebook and Pinterest and has found ways to maximize the use of both to also feed and grow her many passions.

"Connection NOT Perfection."

STEF DONEV

Stef Donev earned a BA in History from California State University, Bakersfield, in only thirty-five years of sporadic guerilla scholarship (starting when he was eighteen and spread out over five different colleges and universities). He graduated *summa cum surprised*. His MA in Mass Communications from California State University, Northridge, came in a record-breaking (for him) four years.

Over the years he has worked as a reporter, broadcaster, public speaker, editor, corporate communicator, disaster relief public affairs officer, soldier, speechwriter, author, and comedy writer, as well as a teacher, and has written two health books with doctors, hundreds of magazine articles, speeches for executives and politicians, and numerous short stories, Saturday morning cartoons, dinner theater, sketch comedy, jokes, puzzles, and more than twenty kids' books, as well as a master's thesis on how reporters covered the American Indian wars.

As a reporter, he worked for the Associated Press, the *Toronto Star*, and other news organizations in the United States and Canada. He has been adjunct faculty at Bakersfield College and other schools since 2002.

"I am a wordsmith. I work with words for a living. Actually, I just play with them.
I've found that when speakers play with their words and have fun with them, their listeners
usually do too. And since we're stuck with words, at least until someone comes up
with a mindreading app for a smart phone, we might as well make the best of them."

JOHN GIERTZ

John has taught public speaking, argumentation, persuasion, and forensics for over twenty-nine years, the last twenty-five at Bakersfield College. John has a BA and an MA in Speech Communication and a PhD in Rhetoric from Regent University. He has authored numerous papers for presentations and publications primarily in the areas of persuasion, political communication, and argumentation.

"Keep in mind that you are here to learn from others, to challenge others, and to engage others. Don't worry whether this course immediately fits your specific degree and career goals. Just relax and enjoy and you will find that a course in public speaking is time well spent."

NEELEY HATRIDGE

Neeley Hatridge is a life-long learner. She earned an AA in Communication at Bakersfield College, where she currently works as adjunct faculty and received both a BA and MA in Communication with the highest honors from California State University, Fresno. Her areas of academic interest are in instructional, interpersonal, small group, and intercultural communication. She has always said that she has enough interests to fill five lifetimes, with learning and mastering new skills to keep her busy. Along with teaching, Neeley also manages and assists in operating her family's local business. She credits her successes to her loyal and supportive family: her best friend and husband Niclaus; her sweet son, Nixon; father, Wiley Loveless; and mother, Dana Kates.

Neeley takes pleasure in teaching students from the community in which she was raised and now calls her former professors colleagues. She always tells her students:

"Life is one, big interview. Whatever you do, do it well and make good impressions along the way . . . you never know who's paying attention and what qualities they will recognize in you."

DEBRA D. THORSON

Debra's competitive speech experience started as a competitor in high school. Where she learned that you can never practice too much and that there is always something you could have done better. After graduating from the University of Montana, she taught public speaking at Bigfork High School in Bigfork, Montana. During her tenure at Bigfork High School she built a forensic program where a fourth of the student population competed on the team.

In 1997 she moved to Bakersfield, California. At Foothill High School she started a forensic program where she also built a state championship team. In summer of 2000, she started teaching public speaking as an adjunct professor at Bakersfield College. In 2006, after earning an MA in Administration. She went on to be Dean of Students at Highland High School in Bakersfield and presently is the Coordinator of Instructional Materials for Kern High School District. Regarding her accomplishments Debra asserts, "Without the support, encouragement, and love of my husband, Jim, for the past forty years, I would never been able to accomplish my goals. He is my hero." For over forty years she passed on this knowledge to her students:

"I know you are nervous and you wish you could die,
be assured I have never had a student die making a speech.
The cure for that feeling is practice, practice, practice, and more practice."

VAUN THYGERSON

Vaun Thygerson works as an adjunct faculty professor at Bakersfield College in the Department of Communication teaching both interpersonal communication and public speaking courses.

She also teaches writing, pop culture, communication, and sociology classes at the University of Phoenix.

As the mother of three children, she started writing for parenting publications with the birth of her first child, who is now fifteen.

She has worked at Central California Parent in Fresno, California, and currently writes for *Kern County Family Magazine* in Bakersfield, California.

Prior to writing family-related articles, she spent eight years in the radio industry as publisher services manager for *Duncan's American Radio*, a radio trade publication based in Indianapolis, Indiana.

Her volunteer activities include such organizations as the American Cancer Society, Kern County Family Week, American Elementary's Parent Teacher Club Association, and many others.

An Idaho native, Vaun received her bachelor's degree in Public Relations from Brigham Young University in Provo, Utah, and her master's degree in Integrated Marketing Communication from Roosevelt University in Chicago, Illinois.

She currently resides in Bakersfield with her husband Scott; three children, Bryce, Cade, and Zane; and their standard poodle, Max.

"The key to happiness is made up of three equal amounts of having a grateful heart,
taking time for yourself, and serving others."